Praise for *Search Engine Optimization:*
An Hour a Day

This is a fantastic resource for any busy person suddenly responsible for getting a website ranked in search engines. The book starts off with the very basics and builds quickly to a surprisingly deep level of sophistication. Tightly written and to the point, it gives you the knowledge you need to make a big difference in how your site appears in search engines. In addition to all the very specific recommendations on what to do, the authors give you the background to understand why their techniques work. I highly recommend it.

—RAFAEL BAPTISTA, SEO Specialist, Tripadvisor.com

Authors Gradiva Couzin and Jennifer Grappone give practical advice on SEO topics ranging from basic keyword research to more sophisticated technical SEO concepts, and lucky for the reader, they've added a nice dose of humor into what otherwise might be a dry topic!

The book is a terrific entrée into the Social and Mobile Web, framing the conversation in a way that is informative and helpful without being overwhelming. I have no hesitation recommending it to anyone new to the industry!

—ANDY BEAL, Coauthor of *Radically Transparent*; Founder and Editor of MarketingPilgrim.com

Gradiva and Jennifer stuff their new and improved 3rd edition with pearls of wisdom, practical advice, and rock-solid SEO knowledge. If you read even half of the book you'll be an SEO star. Imagine what will happen if you read the whole thing! Buy it now!

—AVINASH KAUSHIK, Author of *Web Analytics 2.0* and Google Analytics Evangelist

This book is a supremely well-organized tactical roadmap to help anyone tackle search engine optimization, step-by-step.

—REBECCA LIEB, Author of *The Truth About Search Engine Optimization*

SEO: An Hour a Day is an immediately actionable guerilla field guide for small businesses, corporate in-house marketers, and solo practitioners. I like the step-by-step, easy to understand approach. Gradiva and Jennifer have a terrific grip on what real SEO practitioners should undertake short, mid, and long term. This book literally teaches a daily SEO process, making search engine optimization a way of life, hour by hour.

—MARTY WEINTRAUB, President, aimClear

Your brand is what Google says it is! You exist only if your customers find you in search. Will you find the hour a day to help yourself be found or will you let your competitors have the advantage? This excellent book is full of practical advice and expert techniques that have been tested in the real world, and it will help you quickly develop a solid, actionable SEO strategy and framework.

—BRYAN EISENBERG, *Wall Street Journal* Bestselling Author of *Waiting for Your Cat to Bark?, Call to Action,* and *Always Be Testing*

Jennifer Grappone and Gradiva Couzin have taken their classic Search Engine Optimization: An Hour a Day *up quite a few notches. The third edition includes crucial updates and excellent new social media info that make it a must-read for all marketers.*

—DAVID SZETELA, Owner and CEO of Clix Marketing and Coauthor of *Pay-Per-Click Search Engine Marketing: An Hour a Day*

An hour a day: Is that all you really need for search engine success? If you faithfully follow the process outlined in this book, the answer is an emphatic yes, as you'll be far ahead of 95 percent of your competitors who either aren't spending any time or don't have a clue what it takes to make it to the top. This book contains distilled wisdom that's valuable for anyone wanting to achieve top rankings in search engines—beginners and experts alike.

—CHRIS SHERMAN, Executive Editor, SearchEngineLand.com

This book offers proven, helpful, easy-to-understand advice for beginners and even more advanced SEOs. This third edition now also explores the intersection of SEO and social media, shepherding readers through the mysteries of social marketing and providing down-to-earth guidance on creating a practical social marketing plan.

—JILL WHALEN, CEO, High Rankings

Written with a conversational, empowering, and engaging tone, Search Engine Optimization: An Hour a Day *is the only book that teaches SEO using a unique and successful approach. From strategy to implementation and optimization, this valuable resource gives you easily digestible, bite-sized nuggets containing proven, field-tested principles— it's SEO done right. What's more, this new edition provides you with great new content, especially around the intersection of search and social media. It's a must-read for anyone interested in the success of their business or organization.*

—AMMAN BADLANI, Manager, Online Marketing and Analytics, Planned Parenthood Federation of America

Search Engine Optimization

An Hour a Day

Third Edition

Jennifer Grappone

Gradiva Couzin

WILEY

Wiley Publishing, Inc.

Senior Acquisitions Editor: WILLEM KNIBBE
Development Editor: DICK MARGULIS
Technical Editor: ADAM AUDETTE
Production Editor: DASSI ZEIDEL
Copy Editor: LIZ WELCH
Editorial Manager: PETE GAUGHAN
Production Manager: TIM TATE
Vice President and Executive Group Publisher: RICHARD SWADLEY
Vice President and Publisher: NEIL EDDE
Book Designer: FRANZ BAUMHACKL
Compositor: MAUREEN FORYS, HAPPENSTANCE TYPE-O-RAMA
Proofreader: REBECCA RIDER
Indexer: TED LAUX
Project Coordinator, Cover: KATIE CROCKER
Cover Designer: RYAN SNEED
Cover Image: © TOM MERTON / OJO IMAGES / GETTY IMAGES

Illustrations used with permission by Gradiva Couzin. Copyright © Gradiva Couzin.

Copyright © 2011 by Wiley Publishing, Inc., Indianapolis, Indiana

Published simultaneously in Canada

ISBN: 978-0-470-90259-2

For general information on our other products and services or to obtain technical support, please contact our Customer Care Department within the U.S. at (877) 762-2974, outside the U.S. at (317) 572-3993 or fax (317) 572-4002.

Wiley also publishes its books in a variety of electronic formats. Some content that appears in print may not be available in electronic books.

LIBRARY OF CONGRESS CATALOGING-IN-PUBLICATION DATA

Grappone, Jennifer.
    Search engine optimization : an hour a day / Jennifer Grappone, Gradiva Couzin. — 3rd ed.
       p. cm.
    ISBN: 978-0-470-90259-2 (pbk.)
    ISBN: 978-1-118-02548-2 (ebk.)
    ISBN: 978-1-118-02550-5 (ebk.)
    ISBN: 978-1-118-02549-9 (ebk.)

    1. Internet searching—Handbooks, manuals, etc. 2. Web search engines—Handbooks, manuals, etc. 3. Computer network resources—Handbooks, manuals, etc. I. Couzin, Gradiva. II. Title.
    ZA4230.G73 2011
    025.04—dc22

                    2010047416

Dear Reader,

Thank you for choosing *Search Engine Optimization: An Hour a Day*. This book is part of a family of premium-quality Sybex books, all of which are written by outstanding authors who combine practical experience with a gift for teaching.

Sybex was founded in 1976. More than 30 years later, we're still committed to producing consistently exceptional books. With each of our titles, we're working hard to set a new standard for the industry. From the paper we print on, to the authors we work with, our goal is to bring you the best books available.

I hope you see all that reflected in these pages. I'd be very interested to hear your comments and get your feedback on how we're doing. Feel free to let me know what you think about this or any other Sybex book by sending me an email at nedde@wiley.com. If you think you've found a technical error in this book, please visit http://sybex.custhelp.com. Customer feedback is critical to our efforts at Sybex.

Best regards,

Neil Edde
Vice President and Publisher
Sybex, an imprint of Wiley

To Bennett and Enzo, my children, my heart. —jg

For Lowell, all full of funky fever. And to my beautiful friend, Margie. —gc

Acknowledgments

The authors wish to gratefully acknowledge our editors at Wiley: Willem Knibbe, whose dedication, wit, and companionship have helped make this journey a pleasure; Dick Margulis, who inspired us with his helpful insights and perspicacity; technical editor and SEO expert-on-demand Adam Audette; our talented copy editor, Elizabeth Welch; our production editor and schedule-keeper, Dassi Zeidel; our compositors at Happenstance Type-O-Rama; and the other hardworking members of the production team.

We are grateful that some of the best and brightest in the field of search marketing were also the kindest. Thanks to those who contributed directly to this book: Danny Sullivan, Jill Whalen, Barry Bowman, P.J. Fusco, Eric Ward, Andy Beal, Matt McGee, and Aaron Wall. Thanks also to those who have provided us with advice or education in other venues: Marty Weintraub, Greg Jarboe, Tim Ash, Avinash Kaushik, David Szetala, Rand Fishkin, Chris Sherman, Rebecca Lieb, Bryan Eisenberg, Matt Cutts, and Maile Ohye.

Thanks to the many good-natured members of the business community who shared their stories, successes, and challenges with us: Bryant Tutterow, Janet Sahni, Natasha Case, Dan Jones, Christine Moore, Gina Boros, Searah Deysach, Mark Armstrong, Sharon Couzin, Martie Steele, David Brennan, and Ann Meyer. We wish them all many targeted visitors and mad conversions!

We would like to thank all of the readers who have contacted us with questions and ideas, every one of which has made our purpose clearer and this task more rewarding. We are honored that you have shared your hopes and dreams with us! We are grateful to our clients, whose questions make us better SEOs and keep us happily challenged, and whose daily company is a genuine pleasure. Big ups and thanks to our employees, who bring fresh ideas and sparks of brilliance to Gravity Search Marketing.

We are fortunate to have family and friends with amazing talents. Thank you to Eric Fixler, Margaret Morris, Barbara Gold, and Karalyn Walker for your ideas, questions, and general enthusiasm. Special thanks to our beloved husbands, Lowell Robinson and Todd Grappone, for your love and support. And to our most beautiful and wonderful children, Jonah, Zehara, Bennett, and Enzo, who have spent many nights with the glow of the laptop for a night-light, whose sleeping breaths are the music to which we write, thank you for making this book a part of your lives, too.

About the Authors

Jennifer Grappone and Gradiva Couzin are the founding partners at Gravity Search Marketing, an SEO and social media consulting firm based in Los Angeles and San Francisco since 2006. Their thoughtful consulting and customized strategies have resulted in successful sites and happy clients in a wide range of industries, including media, entertainment, software, retail, and nonprofit. Jennifer and Gradiva have been working together in various settings since 1999.

Jennifer Grappone

After years of producing corporate videos and managing large-scale web development projects, Jennifer began working exclusively in search marketing in 2000. Jennifer advocates a holistic approach to SEO, one that combines elements of good writing, search-friendly site design, usability, and link building. Jennifer lives, works, and performs music in Los Angeles.

Gradiva Couzin

Gradiva has been working in search marketing since its early days in 1998. Her online marketing goal is to create win-win solutions by improving the match between searchers and websites. With a history as a civil engineer and experience in website and database development, Gradiva enjoys the technical side of SEO and social media marketing and loves to facilitate communication between techie and non-techie types. Gradiva lives in Berkeley, California, with her husband and two children.

Contents

Chapter 6 **Your One-Month Prep: Keywords, Priorities, and Goals** **111**

Part III   **Your SEO Plan**   169

Chapter 7 **Month One: Kick It into Gear**   **171**

Chapter 8   **Month Two: Establish the Habit**   **225**

Foreword

Some will say that search engine optimization (SEO) isn't "rocket science," that anyone can do SEO after just a little light reading. Some will even say that SEO isn't required at all. Just create good content, and success on Google and other search engines will come naturally.

They're right, and yet incredibly wrong at the same time. Simply create a website, and chances are you will start attracting traffic from Google naturally. Read a few easy-to-do tips, and you might improve upon that traffic. But for most websites, if you want to really be successful, you have to give SEO the attention it deserves.

SEO "deserves" your attention? Absolutely! There is no other marketing channel that matches the return on investment that SEO provides. Most of your investment will be time, rather than money. Your return will be a constant stream of people who are specifically seeking the goods and services you provide. They went to a search engine in "buy mode," ready to buy a solution from anyone they could find there. All you need to do is turn up in front of them.

SEO is well worth the time spent on it, and it should be more than an afterthought or a "fire and forget" activity. As the *Search Engine Optimization: An Hour a Day* authors Jennifer Grappone and Gradiva Couzin urge, SEO should be a habit, a daily routine of activities of all types. Get into that habit, get your SEO into shape, and as in real life, you'll develop some serious muscles—traffic driving muscles.

Few of us like to exercise or get into shape. Starting a diet, going to the gym, it can all seem like an impossible task. Where do you begin? How do you stay at it? The same is true with SEO. After the initial simple tips, it can suddenly seem overwhelming. What's your mobile SEO strategy? Are you tapping into video search? Why is your page description appearing in the way it does, with those little links below it? Tackling these and other aspects of SEO can feel as daunting as seeing all the equipment in a gym, designed to exercise different muscles, and not knowing where to start.

Relax. In this book, you have two fantastic personal trainers who will help you get into SEO shape slowly, in an incremental and sustainable manner. Bit by bit, they'll guide you through the SEO and social media basics and take you forward so that you have a regular exercise routine that gets your SEO into shape and keeps it that way.

DANNY SULLIVAN
Editor-in-Chief, SearchEngineLand.com

Introduction

How is your website doing on the search engines? Need a little help? Well, you're holding the right book in your hands. This book will walk you through the steps to achieve a targeted, compelling presence on the major search engines. There are no secrets or tricks here, just down-to-earth, real-world advice and a clear program to get you where you want to be. And, with luck, you'll even have a little fun along the way!

If you could think of the person whom you would most want visiting your website, who would that person be? Traditional advertisers might describe this person in terms of their demographics: 18 to 24 years old? Male or female? Wealthy or not so wealthy? But in the world of search, our focus is very different. This is how we think:

> **Pearl of Wisdom:** The person you most want to find your website is the person who is searching for what you offer!

Who could be a more perfect target audience than someone who is already looking for your company, your product or service, or just the sort of information you've got on your website? The trick, of course, is to figure out who those people are, develop an extremely targeted message for them, and put it where they will notice it.

Search engine optimization (SEO) encompasses a wide variety of tasks that improve a website's presence on search engines. Maybe you've heard a few SEO catchphrases—*meta tags*, *link bait*, or *PageRank*—but you don't know exactly how to tie them all together into a meaningful package. Maybe you've wondered how the Social Web fits into your online presence. That's where this book comes in!

Why SEO?

You already know that search engines are a primary channel for finding information on the Web, and that top-ranking websites bring in more visitors than sites that rank poorly. So let's talk about what a really good SEO campaign can do for you.

Think of search engine results pages as real estate. The primo locations are on the results pages for your top-priority keywords. Run a search for your favorite keyword and you'll probably see a page containing many of the following components:

- Organic web search results: the traditional "blue and black" text listings. Some of these listings are likely to be from review sites such as Yelp and Epinions.

- Featured listings containing news, local, shopping, video, or image search results.
- Real-time results showing recent posts from Twitter and elsewhere.
- Sponsored listings, a.k.a. advertisements.

Sure, planting your flag at the top organic web search result is great, but every one of these spots could also be an important place for your business to have a presence. So here's our goal for your SEO campaign:

 Pearl of Wisdom: For keywords that are important to you, we want you to *control or positively influence* as much of the real estate in the search engine results pages as you possibly can.

Anything that gets you more space anywhere in the search engine results is what we consider SEO. That means you may need to find your way into local search results. You may need to look into posting videos. You may need to create an XML feed to get your foot in the door of shopping search, or follow our suggestions to put efforts toward social media or online reviews. It's all part of the holistic SEO mindset you'll soon consider second nature.

The best thing about SEO is that when it's done correctly (follow the advice in this book, and you'll always be on the up-and-up), it benefits both you *and* your site visitors! The reason:

Pearl of Wisdom: Good SEO helps searchers get where they want to go.

How? By providing a clear path from need to fulfillment. By making sure your message is simple, accurate, up-to-date, and most important, put in front of the right people.

Why an Hour a Day?

Like water filling an ice-cube tray, SEO can fill up all the hours in the day you are willing to give it. So let's get this painful truth out of the way right now: Good SEO takes work—*lots* of work.

Now you're probably wondering, "How *little* time can I spend on SEO and get away with it?"

SEO is an amorphous, open-ended task. It includes a wide variety of activities, ranging from editing HTML to reading blogs. It would be overwhelming to try to learn every aspect of SEO at once, but jumping in without a game plan is not the most effective strategy either. You're busy, and SEO is not your only job. So for you, the best way to learn SEO is to roll up your sleeves and *do* something, an hour at a time. Complete one SEO task a day, and you'll see substantial results.

One of the benefits of breaking your SEO campaign into bite-size, one-hour morsels is that you'll have time to digest and learn. You can take care of your day's assignment in an hour and have plenty of time left in your day for thinking and reflecting.

How Long Until I See Results?

The SEO process includes a lot of waiting: waiting for search engines to visit your site, waiting for webmasters and bloggers to link to you, and oftentimes waiting for others within your organization to complete your requested HTML edits. Nobody likes to wait, and nobody really believes us when we tell them this:

Pearl of Wisdom: Believe it. SEO requires patience.

This book sets you up for a long-haul SEO process. We take you through a one-month prep period in which you'll bring together all the components you'll need to begin a successful SEO campaign—one that's just right for your unique situation. Then you'll launch into Your SEO Plan, a customizable hour-a-day routine designed to increase quality traffic and improve your site's presence on the search engines. Your SEO Plan is three months long, but you may start to see improvement in just days.

After three months of following the Plan, your website will have a solid foundation of results-minded optimization. Your SEO campaign will be moving along and becoming more and more specific to your needs and strategies. You will have smart analysis in place to determine which strategies are working and which aren't—and you'll drop the duds and focus your efforts in directions that are working for you.

Most importantly, after three months of following the Plan, you will be a full-fledged search marketer. You won't need day-by-day assignments anymore because you will be forging your own path. You will have great habits and tools for keeping your campaign buffed, and you'll be well on your way to teaching *us* a thing or two.

Who Should Use This Book

Truth be told, SEO is not hard. It's not rocket science, and it certainly doesn't require a degree in marketing, design, or anything else for that matter. While SEO is not hard, it can be tedious. It requires diligence and organization.

Our plan will work for just about anyone who is willing to make the hour-a-day commitment. We offer specific advice for

- Small organizations
- Large organizations
- One-person operations
- Business to business (B2B)
- Business to consumer (B2C)
- Web developers

- Nonprofits
- Bloggers
- Adult sites

You certainly don't need to be selling anything to need SEO! All you need is a website that would benefit from an increase in targeted traffic.

Even if you're considering outsourcing some or all of your SEO tasks, it's a good idea to become familiar with the SEO process before you pay someone to take it over. Obviously, we've got nothing against companies who hire SEO specialists—they're our bread and butter!—but nobody knows your own business like you do. You are, therefore, uniquely prepared for this task.

We don't like jargon, and we've tried to avoid it here (except, of course, when we teach it to you so you can impress others!). You'll learn concepts on a need-to-know basis and never waste your time on dead-end tasks. We don't bog you down with SEO history lessons, but we don't skimp on the important background knowledge either. Between the Eternal Truths and the Right Now of SEO that we've included in this book, we've got you covered. We know you're busy, and this book is written accordingly.

Does It Work?

"Significantly improved my Google rankings."

"Wonderful book. After I read it, I got on 1st and 2nd page results on Google for all of my keywords."

"I did spend many hours following the book's advice, and my website is now number 2."

"I didn't get it. But thanks, now I do."

This is a sampling of the feedback we've received from readers. And the positive feedback keeps coming, not only from people who are seeing results for their website, but also from people who are delighted to finally have a solid grasp on this slippery topic. Some people follow the three-month Plan from beginning to end, while others use the book as a trusty reference. As one reader put it, "I found that I could get what I needed by dipping in and out, skimming through." Does it work? Yes, it does. We know this because we use these techniques ourselves, and they have delivered high ranks and targeted traffic, and increased sales for our clients' websites.

What's Inside

The heart of this book is Your SEO Plan, a three-month, day-by-day program for improving your website's presence and increasing targeted traffic. We've divvied up the days into tasks that we estimate will take about an hour each. Depending on your circumstances, your familiarity with the subject matter, and the logistics of your website, it may take you more or less time to complete certain tasks.

The Plan is preceded by the preliminary planning and information you'll need to carry it out. That means you should read this book from the beginning and work through Your SEO Plan in order from start to finish.

Here's what you'll find inside.

Part I: Foundation

Chapter 1: "Clarify Your Goals" Helps you frame your thinking about your website and your goals in an SEO-friendly way.

Chapter 2: "Customize Your Approach" Provides guidance for adjusting your Plan to suit the special advantages and challenges faced by different types of organizations.

Chapter 3: "Eternal Truths of SEO" Gives an overview of the longstanding, or "eternal," factors in effective search engine optimization. Learn these truths to bring longevity to your SEO success.

Chapter 4: "How the Search Engines Work Right Now" Presents a current snapshot of the world of search and social media.

Part II: Strategy

Chapter 5: "Get Your Team on Board" Offers been-there-done-that advice for eliminating intra-organizational hang-ups that are common in SEO.

Chapter 6: "Your One-Month Prep: Keywords, Priorities, and Goals" Is all about preparation: researching, organizing, and setting the direction for Your SEO Plan, as well as choosing an all-important method of tracking and measuring your SEO success. Several worksheets and templates will help you along the way.

Part III: Your SEO Plan

Chapter 7: "Month One: Kick It into Gear" Launches Your SEO Plan with basic website optimization, site structure improvements, and a link-building method, including developing link-attractive content.

Chapter 8: "Month Two: Establish the Habit" Gets you started with a boot-camp approach to social media, then shows you how to set up a starter paid search advertising campaign. You'll also learn all about Local and Shopping search this month.

Chapter 9: "Month Three: It's a Way of Life" Takes your SEO campaign further with special opportunities in video and mobile search, and teaches you the best habits for keeping current with SEO news and trends. You'll take on in-depth troubleshooting, and finally you'll complete your first SEO status report.

Chapter 10: "Extra Credit and Guilt-Free Slacking" Gives you practical tips on reducing your SEO workload if your schedule is less than perfect, and helps you dig deeper in specific areas if you are especially enthusiastic.

What's New in This Edition

We've put a lot of thought into selecting only the new aspects of SEO that are worth your time and effort, so you can stay on the cutting edge of search while sidestepping fly-by-night fads and unproven techniques. This edition of *Search Engine Optimization: An Hour a Day* contains

- A kickstart guide to social media sites such as Facebook and Twitter
- Expanded and updated instructions on making the most of your site in local, shopping, and mobile search, which have grown in prominence and importance over the years
- Even more tales from the trenches: real stories from real businesses like yours

In keeping with our mantra of "no history lessons," we've dropped references to outdated strategies and we've skipped the walks down SEO memory lane. And naturally, we've updated all the information on search engine ranking algorithms and red flags.

This Book's Companion Website

In addition to the chapters you hold in your hand, you can find extra information and resources on our companion website, www.yourseoplan.com/book or, or www.sybex.com/go/seohour.

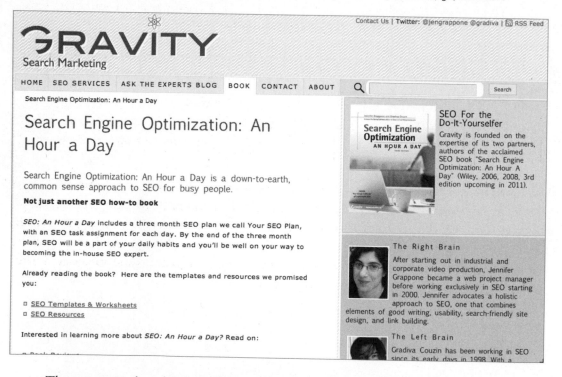

There, you can download all the worksheets and templates you need for the Plan and find plenty of useful SEO links and tips as well. When we're not saving the world one website at a time, we're posting topical articles and answering your "Ask the Experts" questions on the website. Lots of aspiring SEO experts just like you visit our site regularly and consider it one of their most useful bookmarks!

Conventions Used in This Book

We've been working together for so many years now that sometimes it seems our brains are fused. Gradiva tends toward the "left brain" side of our collective SEO brain, with enough logic, math proficiency, and analytical thinking for both of us. On the other hand, Jennifer is more of a "right brain" thinker, with a flair for writing and a preference for the creative aspects of SEO. One thing we agree on: Good SEO requires a little left brain *and* a little right brain! Throughout this book, you'll see the "left brain/right brain" icon wherever we think you need the view from both sides.

We love to learn from others' mistakes and successes, and you can, too! Look for the shovel icon accompanying stories from the real world: case studies, expert opinions, and even some tragic tales from the trenches. In some cases, we've changed the names to protect the privacy—and reputations—of the parties involved.

This pearl represents a special tip or tidbit of wisdom that you may find especially helpful.

The "Now" icon indicates an SEO task that's assigned to you. When you come across one of these, it's time to roll up your sleeves and get to work!

xtra cred

We wrote this book for the busy professional—that's why it's an hour-a-day plan. But sometimes, you might be inclined to take your campaign a little further. For you go-getters, we've provided the extra-credit icon.

slacker

And for those of you who spend most of your time wishing you had more time, here's the icon for you. Next to the slacker icon, you'll find options for trimming down your tasks without compromising results.

Finally, we've tried to make it easy for you to identify search queries and keywords in this book. When you encounter words formatted in brackets, for example, <baby clothes>, <crystallized ginger>, or <heavy duty truck liners> , you'll know that we're referring to words that can be typed into the search engines, or words that can be included on a website to match those queries.

If you're dying to do something *right now*, your enthusiasm is noted and appreciated. Fire up your computer, and we'll be waiting for you on page 1!

Foundation

So, you want to differentiate your website from the millions of others out there on the Internet? Great! Let's get started! Whether you're starting from scratch or just looking for a new approach, the hardest part of embarking on a search engine optimization (SEO) campaign is knowing where to begin. In Part I, we walk you through a little self-reflection and search engine basics to lay the groundwork for Your SEO Plan:

Clarify Your Goals

1

A good SEO campaign needs to be laser-focused on your business goals, so it has to start with a healthy dose of thought and reflection. In this chapter, we'll walk you through the key questions you'll want to consider before you get started.

Chapter Contents

What Is SEO?

OK, let's see a show of hands: How many of you are reading this book because you want a #1 rank in Google? Yeah, we thought so. As SEO consultants, we know how good it feels when your website makes it to the top of the heap. Listen, we sincerely hope you get your #1 Google rank, but it won't help you if it's bringing in the wrong audience or pointing them to a dead-end website. So don't think of SEO as just a way to improve your site's ranking.

The term *search engine optimization* describes a diverse set of activities that you can perform to increase the number of desirable visitors who come to your website via search engines (you may also have heard these activities called *search engine marketing* or *search marketing*). This includes things you do to your site itself, such as making changes to your text and HTML code. It also includes using specially formatted text or documents to communicate directly with the search engines, or pursuing other sources of traffic by creating listings or attracting links. Tracking, research, and competitive review are also part of the SEO package.

SEO is not advertising, although it may include an advertising component. It is not public relations (PR), although it includes monitoring your reputation and crafting your branding similar to PR. As a continually evolving area of online marketing, SEO may sound complicated, but it is very simple in its fundamental goal: gaining targeted visitors.

Do I Need to Perform SEO for My Website?

It may seem like a no-brainer, but actually, the answer is not necessarily yes. If any of the following examples apply to you, you may not be in need of an SEO campaign right now:

- You have a website that you really don't want strangers to find, such as a training tool for your employees or a classroom tool for your students.
- Your site is already ranking well, you're satisfied with your sales, and you don't want to rock the boat.
- You're in a big hurry—say, you'll go out of business without a major upswing in revenue in the next couple of months. This is not to say that SEO can't help you, but good SEO takes time. You may need to focus your energies elsewhere right now.

If this list doesn't apply to you, we think you're ready to begin your SEO adventure!

It is a rare site indeed that couldn't use a little improvement in the SEO department. Solid SEO is a prerequisite for a successful website these days, so if you don't need it today, it's a good bet you'll need to brush up your SEO smarts for tomorrow. So even if you don't think you need SEO right now, we recommend that you take the time to work through the questions in this chapter and make sure your goals aren't begging for a little help.

What Are the Overall Goals of My Business?

We get it: The fundamental goal of your business is to make money by selling a product or service. But let's take a moment to define your goals in a little more detail.

Perhaps yours is a large company with branding as an important long-term goal. Maybe your company wants to make money with certain products but is willing to take a loss in other areas. Maybe you are starting up with investor backing and don't need to turn a profit for years. Perhaps your company's branding and reputation is your top concern—you need to be perceived as high tech, or luxurious, or as the hippest in your competitive space. Or maybe you work for a nonprofit, with a goal to improve the world and inspire others to do the same. You may be working toward 2,000 small sales this year or be thrilled to get just 3 new clients. Whatever way you're leaning, your business goals will affect your SEO campaign strategy.

For instance, consider the fictional situation of Jason, a founding partner at Babyfuzzkin, a company selling unique, high-end baby clothes. This business makes its money directly through online sales. It's a small operation, so there is a limit to how many orders the business can handle. The Babyfuzzkin fantasy would be a steady flow of, say, 100 orders per month. But there is more to the story: The partners would love to get out of the direct fulfillment of orders and instead secure some contracts with big-name brick-and-mortar vendors.

In the case of Elizabeth, a marketing director at Elderpets, we have a different situation. Elderpets is a fictional nonprofit organization that provides meals, walks, and veterinary care assistance to animals belonging to elderly and infirm owners. The company relies on financial contributions and volunteers to fulfill its mission. At Elderpets, their fantasy is to decrease the time and effort spent on fundraising activities, such as silent auctions and community dog washes, and begin attracting more contributions online, which would in turn allow them to help more pets in need. In addition, they are constantly looking for more volunteers.

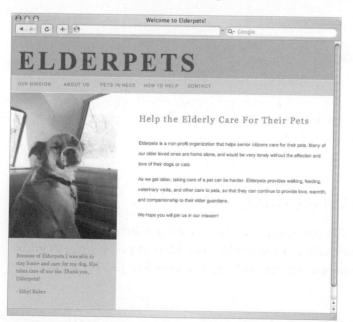

Though Babyfuzzkin and Elderpets have different goals, we have an exercise they can both perform to get the most out of their SEO plan. We've created a Goals Worksheet to guide clients like Jason and Elizabeth, and you can use it as you consider the questions in this chapter. You can download the Goals Worksheet at our companion website, www.yourseoplan.com. At key points throughout this chapter, we'll ask you to stop, reflect on your own business, and write down your own vital statistics. Once you've worked through the questions, you'll have a strong vision of the *why* of your SEO campaign—and you'll be ready to move on to the *what* and *how* in Parts II and III.

> **Now:** Download the Goals Worksheet from www.yourseoplan.com.

Now take a moment and look at "Business Goals" on your Goals Worksheet. Table 1.1 and Table 1.2 show how Jason at Babyfuzzkin and Elizabeth at Elderpets might fill out theirs, respectively.

▶ **Table 1.1** Summary of Business Goals for Babyfuzzkin

Goals	Description
Primary goal	Sell clothes directly to consumers online.
Additional goal	Attract brick-and-mortar stores to sell our clothes.

▶ **Table 1.2** Summary of Business Goals for Elderpets

Goals	Description
Primary goal	Help more animals in need.
Additional goal	Attract more donations.
Additional goal	Attract more volunteers.

> **Now:** Take a few minutes to write down your overall business goals in "Business Goals" on your Goals Worksheet. Don't be afraid to indulge in fantasy!

What Function Does My Website Serve?

It's not uncommon to hear that the reason a company built a website is "to have a website." While we all love a bit of circular logic before breakfast, if you're going to put a lot of time and money into promoting your website, it's important to have a good idea of what it's doing for you.

Most websites are built out of a combination of basic building blocks. Whether your site is an online store seeking sales; a personal blog seeking community connections; a political or religious outlet seeking to persuade, uplift, or inspire; a corporate brochure displaying branding identity and company information; or just about any other type of website you can imagine, it will likely include some or all of the following features or elements:

Corporate history, news, and press releases	Fun, games, or entertainment
Executive biographies	A strong brand identity
Product and service information	Art or craft portfolio
Online purchasing/donation	Educational materials
Support for existing customers, clients, and students	Information specifically for geographically local visitors
News and current events	Software or documents available for download
Articles, white papers	Media (pictures, audio, video) available for viewing/downloading
Religious, philosophical, or political content	Site map
Online lead generation forms	Site search function
Login for restricted information	Live help/live contact function
Instructions for making contact offline or via email	Ways for members of the community to connect with each other on the site (forums, bulletin boards, etc.)
Directions, hours of operation, etc., for brick-and-mortar location	Blog postings and reader comments
Links to other resources	Methods for your users to help promote your site (share on Facebook, Digg, etc.)
Customer testimonials or reviews	

Now, spend some time clicking around your website. You should be able to tell which of the features in the preceding list are included. How well is each component doing its job? For now, think in terms of presentation and functionality. (Is your product information up-to-date? Is your online store full of technical glitches? Are your forms asking the right questions?) Give each feature that you find a ranking of Excellent, Good, Fair, or Poor. Obviously, this isn't going to be a scientific process— just make your best estimate.

Now: On your Goals Worksheet, check off the boxes in "Website Features" that apply to your current site; be sure to note any features you hope to add in the future. Add your assessment in the rating column.

Jason's and Elizabeth's checklists might look something like Table 1.3 and Table 1.4, respectively.

▶ **Table 1.3** Ratings for Babyfuzzkin Features

Feature	Rating
Online purchasing/donation	Excellent
Product and service information	Good
A strong brand identity	Good
Instructions for making contact offline or via email	Good

▶ **Table 1.4** Ratings for Elderpets Features

Feature	Rating
Corporate history, news, and press releases	Excellent
Executive biographies	Excellent
Online purchasing/donation	Future Goal
Educational materials	Good
Online lead generation forms (volunteer signup)	Good

How Is My Website Connecting with the Goals of My Business?

Take a look at what you've written on your Goals Worksheet. Is there a disconnect between your business goals and your current website? Is your website focused on corporate info or, worse yet, executive bios instead of your business goals? Or does the website provide mostly content geared toward supporting existing clients when the primary business goal is to gain new clients?

> **Now:** Take a moment to write down any disconnects you've identified in "Connecting Goals" on your Goals Worksheet.

Jason at Babyfuzzkin is in good shape: The business goals and website features are in alignment, with an Excellent rating on the top business priority. Since the business goal includes not only sales but also a strong push toward future deals, the SEO campaign will need to support both.

On the other hand, Elizabeth at Elderpets may be in trouble. One of its primary goals is to get donations, but its website is currently focused on describing its mission and founders, and it doesn't even have online donation capability yet. This could pose a challenge throughout the SEO campaign.

Remember the big picture here:

The SEO You Have, Not the One You Want

In an ideal world, you could take your Goals Worksheet to your boss and say, "Hey! We've got a disconnect here. Let's fix it!" But let's just suppose that *ideal* is not the word you would use to describe your organization. The fact is, your SEO campaign may need to work with certain handicaps.

Over the years, we've worked with a lot of folks who have had to support their business goals with a less-than-perfect website. Here are the most common reasons we've seen for this:

- There is political opposition to change.
- There are scheduling bottlenecks: Everybody else's project comes before our own site.
- The current marketing team inherited an outdated or lousy website.
- Marketing the site isn't really anybody's responsibility.

Some Interim Solutions

It's your job as the in-house SEO expert to lobby for a website that will deliver for your company. But you may be wondering, "If my site is far less than perfect and—for whatever reason—I can't fix it right now, should I even bother with SEO?" Probably. Here are some ideas for approaching SEO while you're waiting for your site to come up to speed with your company's goals:

- Work on getting traffic, but lower your expectations for sales (or whatever action you want your visitors to perform) for the time being. When you assess your website's performance, you may notice an upswing in traffic, which you can use to motivate your people to make positive changes to the site.
- Ask for ownership of just one page, or just one section, and try to bring it up to snuff. Can't get a whole page? We've had customers who were given just one chunk of the home page to do with as they wished.
- Use your powers of competitive analysis. Take special care to note if your competitors' sites are doing things well in the areas in which your site is lacking (we'll give you a chance to do this in Chapter 6, "Your One-Month Prep: Keywords, Priorities, and Goals"). This may motivate those in power to give your recommended changes a higher priority.

- Focus on *off-page* SEO activities. While you're waiting to get your site spiffed up, you can always work on improving inbound links, attracting new Twitter followers, or posting news and specials on Facebook.

- As a last resort, if your current site is so hopeless that it's actually doing your business more harm than good, you might decide to take drastic measures and disinvite the search engines. We'll show you how in Chapter 7, "Month One: Kick It into Gear."

SEO Infighting at UpperCut and Jab

Here's a true story involving the Law Offices of UpperCut and Jab (the company name and some identifying details have been changed to prevent embarrassment), which specializes in medical malpractice suits. One of the firm's primary goals for its website is new-client acquisition.

In This Corner: A Legal Team Looking for Prospects Like many law firms, UpperCut and Jab relies on the searching public for a portion of its new clients, so every online inquiry is screened promptly by qualified staffers to determine if and how to follow up. They've customized the messaging on their site to speak to potential clients who are a good fit for their legal talents and courtroom experience.

In This Corner: A Hotshot Web Developer with a Vision She has serious database skills and has her heart set on creating *link bait*, website offerings that are designed to attract attention and links from other sites. She wants UpperCut and Jab's site to offer a huge directory of pharmaceutical companies, saying, "This directory will be the most comprehensive on the Web and will be a great reference for lawyers and potential clients!"

The Plan of Attack The website, which is already well targeted to potential clients, is outfitted with a massive, searchable, browsable, comprehensive database of big and small pharma companies.

So Who Wins? Unfortunately, no one. The link bait database was successful in driving a great deal of traffic to the site, and online form submittals increased dramatically. But a vast majority of forms were filled out by unqualified leads. ("Please remove my company from your database." "Do you know how I can participate in a drug trial?" "Are generics just as effective as name-brand medicines?") Looks like they forgot that having a unique offering on your site isn't the same as having a unique, *targeted* offering! In this case, building and maintaining the huge pharma database was a waste of time and money because it was not properly targeted to attract high-quality leads.

The Moral of the Story Bringing traffic to your site is not necessarily the same as meeting your company's goals!

Who Do I Want to Visit My Website?

In the introduction, we pointed out that the person who you *most* want to find your website is the person who is searching for your website! And, of course, this is true. But now let's dig a little deeper and describe your ideal audience so that you can help them make their way to you.

Who is the target audience for your website? Surely it will include potential clients or customers. But don't forget that it may also include members of the press, employees at your own company, current and past customers seeking support, and even potential investors nosing about for the inside scoop!

Using your Goals Worksheet, describe your target audience with as much detail as possible: professional status, technical vs. nontechnical (this will affect how they search or even which engines they use), age, workplace vs. home users, and geographic locality.

Knowing your target audiences will help you make important decisions—such as keyword choices and budget for paid listings—when you start your SEO campaign. It will also help you segment your site for each audience, which can improve your sales and other goals, as well as usability.

Jason at Babyfuzzkin says, "Our target audience is parents of infants and small children with a great sense of style and plenty of surplus income. They're probably fairly technically savvy, maybe a little short on time because of the kids—that's why they're shopping online. Also, a lot of our customers are grandparents, buying the clothes as gifts. Some parents don't want to spend a lot on clothes they know are just going to get covered in oatmeal and grass stains! And the grandparents, they're a lot less savvy with the Internet. They use it from home, maybe with a slow connection, and they're located nationwide."

Elizabeth at Elderpets describes her target audience as "Caregivers or relatives of the elderly or infirm—they're usually the ones who contact us about our services. Our volunteers range from high school students hoping to beef up their college applications to retirees who don't have much money but want to do something worthwhile with their time. And then there are our donors, who can be all over the map in terms of age and income and in their status as individual, family, or business. The one thing that ties them together is that they love animals."

Jason's and Elizabeth's goals and corresponding target audiences are shown in Table 1.5 and Table 1.6, respectively.

▶ **Table 1.5** Babyfuzzkin Goals and Corresponding Target Audiences

Goals		Target Audience	
Primary goal	Sell clothes directly to consumers online.	Primary audience	Parents of small children
		Secondary audience	Grandparents and friends
Additional goal	Contracts with brick-and-mortar stores.	Primary audience	Buyers working for retailers

► **Table 1.6** Elderpets Goals and Corresponding Target Audiences

Goals		Target Audience	
Primary goal	Help more animals in need.	Primary audience	Caregivers of the elderly or infirm
Additional goal	Attract more donations.	Primary audience	Pet lovers with surplus income
Additional goal	Attract more volunteers.	Primary audience	High school students, retirees

Now: Go to the "Conversions" table on your Goals Worksheet and fill out your target audiences under the appropriate column. Be as specific as you can!

What Do I Want Visitors to Do on My Website?

In SEO, the term *conversion* has come to mean your website users doing whatever it is you want them to do. So when we say "conversion," think of it as shorthand for "Score one for you—you're accomplishing your goals!"

Wondering what your site's conversion is? Here's one of the really fun facts about SEO:

Pearl of Wisdom: For your site, you can define a *conversion* however you want.

It's *your* party—you decide what you want your guests to do. Now that you have all your goals written down in black and white, defining a conversion should be easy. Here are a few likely examples: Users convert when they

- Purchase a product.
- Fill out a form.
- View a certain page on the site.
- Subscribe to a mailing list.
- Comment on a blog.
- "Like" you on Facebook.
- Follow you on Twitter.
- Register to join your community.
- Post a review.
- Phone your 1-800 sales number.
- Drive to your retail store.
- Contribute to your political campaign.

- Change their mind about something.
- Find the information they were looking for.

Now look at the "Conversions" table on your Goals Worksheet. You will need to have a conversion defined next to each goal. Some of the conversion definitions will be straightforward; others may seem vague or touchy-feely. There's no harm in writing them all—we'll help you sort them out later in your SEO campaign when you're measuring results.

Jason's and Elizabeth's worksheets are shown in Table 1.7 and Table 1.8, respectively.

▶ **Table 1.7** Babyfuzzkin Goals and Corresponding Conversions

Goals		Target Audience		Conversion
Primary goal	Sell clothes directly to consumers online.	Primary audience	Parents of small children	Purchase via online store.
		Secondary audience	Grandparents and friends	
Additional goal	Brick-and-mortar clothing store contracts.	Primary audience	Buyers working for retailers	Make inquiry via online form or offline contact.

▶ **Table 1.8** Elderpets Goals and Corresponding Conversions

Goals		Target Audience		Conversion
Primary goal	Help more animals in need.	Primary audience	Caregivers of the elderly or infirm	View our mission statement.
Additional goal	Attract more donations.	Primary audience	Pet lovers with surplus income	Donate via online form or call our toll-free number.
Additional goal	Attract more volunteers.	Primary audience	High school students, retirees	Make inquiry via online form or offline contact.

With your goals, audiences, and conversions spelled out, it's easy to connect the dots from goal to audience to desired conversion:

To achieve my **goal**, I need my **target audience** to **convert** on this **page**.

For example, Babyfuzzkin would say this:

- To achieve more **clothing sales**, I need **parents of infants** to **buy my products** on the **Clothes for Under $20 page**.
- To achieve more **clothing sales**, I need **grandparents and friends of parents** to **buy my products** on the **Gift Sets page**.
- To achieve **brick-and-mortar clothing store contracts**, I need **buyers working for retailers** to **make an inquiry** using the **Contact Us page**.

And Elderpets might say this:

- To achieve **more online donations**, I need **pet lovers with surplus income** to **make a donation** on the **Donate Now page**.
- To achieve a **higher number of volunteers**, I need **stay-at-home parents and retirees** to **contact us** using the **Become a Volunteer page**.
- To achieve a **higher number of volunteers**, I need **high school students** to **contact us** using the **Students Volunteer Program page**.
- To achieve **being found by those in need**, I need **caretakers of elderly and infirm pet owners** to **visit** the **Our Mission page**.

Now: Go back to the "Conversions" table on your Goals Worksheet and fill out your conversions under the appropriate column.

Which Pages Do I Most Want My Website Visitors to See?

Now it's time to start thinking about the top-priority pages for your SEO campaign. These are the pages you'll optimize when you get to your daily tasks in Part III. These are the pages that you most want people to get to from the search engines, and for best results, they should contain the most compelling content and the most useful information. Because your visitors land on these pages from the search engines, we call them *landing pages* (you might also hear them referred to as *entry pages*). The main functions of your landing pages are that they speak to your desired audience and contain a call to action for your desired conversion. Figure 1.1 illustrates possible paths through your website from entry to conversion.

Often, your landing page and your conversion page will be the same, as is the case with Babyfuzzkin's Gift Sets page. This is a great situation because your site visitor doesn't have to navigate within your site to complete a conversion. Other times, your conversion page will not be an appropriate entry page because your visitor will need to review other information first and then make the decision to continue. After all, the Web is a highly nonlinear space, and your visitors are free to ramble around your site in all sorts of ways.

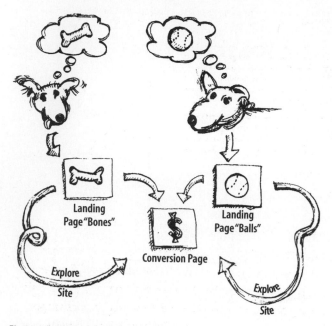

Figure 1.1 Possible paths to conversion

For the purposes of your SEO campaign, you need to ensure that for each type of conversion, there is at least one clear path between the search engine and the conversion outcome. We find it helpful to think backward: First consider where you want your visitor to end up, and then work backward to find a great page for them to enter your site.

For example, consider the Elderpets conversion:

To achieve **more online donations**, I need **pet lovers with surplus income** to **make a donation** on the **Donate Now page.**

Next, Elizabeth might work backward, starting from the Donate Now page and clicking through the website to find a possible landing page:

Donate Now page → How Can I Help page → Dogs in Need page

In this scenario, the Dogs in Need page is the chosen landing page. Why? Because it's a very convincing, compelling page for this specific audience.

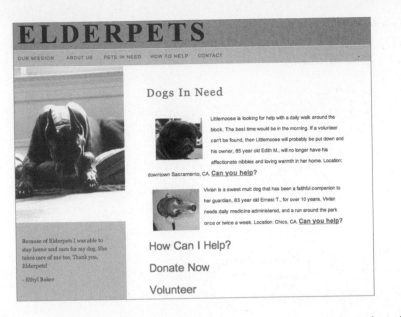

What makes a good landing page? One with just the right information that your target audience is looking for. It should reassure your visitors that they've come to the right place (for example, a tight focus on a specific product line, not just a link to "view products"), and make it easy for visitors to take the next step (for example, a prominent "sign up now" button, not just "learn more"). In Part III, we'll walk you through the specifics of how to choose your landing pages and how to make sure the right information is on those pages. For now, we want you to begin thinking about what pages might work. If you don't have any pages that fit the bill, don't despair! Get some landing pages built if you can, or think about ways you can add compelling content to existing pages to turn them into excellent landing pages. And just a heads-up: Once you start your SEO campaign, all of your top-priority pages will probably need to be revised at least a bit as part of the optimization process.

Notice that the landing page Elderpets chose for this conversion is *not* the home page. Many site owners don't think in terms of deeper pages and think that they just want their home page to be found on the search engines. But in truth, your home page is probably only good for achieving the most general of your goals. Your deeper pages are more likely to contain a wealth of *specific* information and *specific* calls to action that you'd be thrilled for a *specific audience* to find one click away from a search engine!

Now: Go back to the "Conversions" table on your Goals Worksheet and enter your landing pages in the appropriate column.

How Will I Measure the Success of This SEO Campaign?

Most companies understand the importance of measuring the performance of their websites, and lots of useful tools are available to help you do just that. Adoption of web analytics programs has grown enormously between 2005 and 2010, but in our experience, many companies—especially the small ones—aren't taking the best advantage of this data. A 2009 study found that 52 percent of those who use analytics tools "fail to effectively use more than half of all capabilities offered by their tools." Why are so many companies missing out? We think the cause is a combination of factors:

Lack of Definition When goals or conversions are never defined, there's no way to measure your accomplishments.

Lack of Communication Different departments or individuals with different goals may not be sharing information.

Math Anxiety Herding conversion data into a tidy, meaningful spreadsheet can be harder than it sounds, and busy business owners may not be in the mood to relearn high school math.

Technical Difficulty Even with the slickest web analytics tools at your disposal, some SEO metrics are difficult, or impossible, to track with out-of-the-box features.

Hitch up your high waters and get ready for another painful truth:

Pearl of Wisdom: You must track the accomplishments of your SEO campaign.

There are a few good reasons why. Let's discuss them next.

Tracking Lets You Drop the Duds

Have you ever heard this military strategy riddle? You are waging battles on two fronts. One front is winning decisively; the other is being severely trounced. You have 10,000 additional troops ready to deploy. Where do you send them? The answer: Send them to the winning front as reinforcements. Strange as it sounds, it makes more sense to reinforce a winning battle than to throw efforts into a losing one.

This strategy is also reflected in the maxim "Don't throw good money after bad." You need to know which of your efforts are bringing you good results so you can send in the reinforcements, and you need to know which efforts are not working so you can bail out on them. And the only way to know this is to *track results*.

Tracking Will Help You Keep Your Job

If you work for yourself, you're the president of your own company, or you're reading this book for a hobby site or your blog, feel free to skip this section. For just about everyone else, we suspect that someone, somewhere is *paying* you to do this work.

Eventually, that someone is going to wonder whether they have been spending their money wisely. Even if your boss ignores you every time you walk in the office with a report, even if your department head refuses to back you up when you try to get IT support for *conversion tracking*, even if Sales tells you there's absolutely no way you can track sales back to the website, trust us; someday, someone is going to want this information—preferably in a bar chart, with pretty colors, and summarized in five words or less. If you don't have the information, the measure of your accomplishments is going to default to this:

Are we #1 on Google?

And, if you're not, get ready for some repercussions!

Tracking Helps You Stay Up-to-Date

"Do it right the first time." It's a great motto and a great goal, but it's not a realistic plan for your SEO campaign. For one thing, you will need to continually re-prioritize your efforts as you drop the duds. But there's also another, unavoidable reason that your SEO campaign will need to constantly evolve: The search engines are changing, too! Don't worry; this book sets you up with best practices that should have a nice, long life span (in Internet years, that is!). But you will inevitably need to be prepared for some changes. What works best today will not be exactly the same as what works best three years down the road. And the only way to know what has changed is to track your campaign.

Now that you are convinced that tracking is important, take a look at your list of conversions. Some of them will be easy to track; some may be difficult or close to impossible. Later, we'll take some time to think through possible ways to track your successes (and failures). Here are the methods that Babyfuzzkin and Elderpets are considering for measuring their SEO campaign results:

Jason at Babyfuzzkin says, "We're using Google Analytics for tracking our web traffic, but we don't really understand what we're looking at in there. Since our primary goal is online sales, I'm going to figure out how to use some of the goal tracking features. Then, it will be easier to use Google Analytics to determine if SEO causes an increase in sales. Our secondary goal is attracting attention from vendors. We'll track those leads back to SEO by asking any vendors that contact us how they heard about us."

Elizabeth at Elderpets describes her tracking plans by saying, "Our primary goal is donations, so we'll be watching for an increase in the number of individual donations after we start our SEO campaign. As for volunteers, we'll add a 'How did you find us?' question to our volunteer applications."

Clearly Jason and Elizabeth are on the right path. They've examined their goals and their websites. They've identified their targeted audiences and target pages, and they're even thinking ahead to tracking. If you're stuck on any of these answers for your own company, take some time now to put your head together with others in your organization and hash it out. Understanding your own goals is a basic element of your upstart SEO campaign, and you'll do best if you have a firm grasp on them before you move on.

How Much Tracking Do I Need to Do?

Tracking can seem like a daunting task if you've never given any thought to it. Site owners like Jason and Elizabeth are wondering: Should tracking be approached with baby steps like the rest of SEO?

The Left Brain says, "Whoa there, Jason and Elizabeth: You're going to be collecting flawed data! Elizabeth, how can you be sure that a change in donations is tied to your SEO efforts and not to something else, like the start of the holiday season? And Jason, if those vendors contacted you via an online form, you can use your analytics program to find out specifics about how they found you, which is a lot more reliable than the information they'll give you themselves. And, forget the goal tracking feature in Google Analytics—there's something even more robust: e-commerce tracking! You'll finally be able to tell how much revenue is coming from each traffic source!"

The Right Brain says, "I admire your left-brained hunger for irrefutable facts. However, it can be tricky to set up advanced tracking features, and even if you have all the data in the world, most people are too busy to make numbers-watching their highest priority. I say we encourage any effort at all to track conversions, as long as it's based on some logic and is done consistently. Even a little bit of tracking can bring up some interesting findings. And these findings often get people interested in learning more, which may in turn motivate people to do more detailed tracking. Believe it or not, tracking can be a creative process!"

Wow! You've done a lot of thinking in this chapter. You now know that you probably need SEO for your website. You have a great grasp on your overall business goals. You know what your website is doing and whether these things are good or bad for your company. You know your target audience and your desired conversions. And, we trust, you are convinced that tracking is a necessity. Now, meet us in Chapter 2, "Customize Your Approach," for some light reading about your favorite subject: you!

Customize
Your Approach

Let's say you want a great car wash, one that gets up close and personal with your car's curves and addresses its individual problem areas. You wouldn't trust a gas station car wash—you'd do it yourself! Likewise, the SEO plan in this book presents a method that can be applied to a wide range of SEO efforts, but you have to customize it for your particular business and website. This chapter gives you a great head start.

Chapter Contents

It's *Your* SEO Plan
Business-to-Business
Business-to-Consumer
Large, Small, and Really Small Organizations
Brick-and-Mortar
Blog
Web Designer
Nonprofit

It's *Your* SEO Plan

When you heard about this book, you may have had one of two reactions. Maybe you thought, "Great! A quick and easy SEO plan that I can follow!" Or maybe you thought, "Uh-oh! An oversimplified approach to something complex." Both of these reactions are perfectly reasonable. A simple approach is important, but you should be wary of anything that promises a one-size-fits-all SEO solution.

So let's make one thing clear: There's nothing cookie cutter about *Your* SEO Plan. And because nobody knows your organization and website like you do, guess who's in charge of the fine-tuning? You!

Small and large companies, brick-and-mortars, bloggers, and nonprofits—each type has its own set of needs, advantages, and challenges. Your assignment is to identify which categories your company is in, read our tips and guidelines for those categories, and think about how you can apply the customization to your own SEO efforts.

This is a "check all that apply" chapter—your company may fall into multiple categories. For example, let's say you run an independent toy store in Des Moines, Iowa. You would want to read at least three of the categories in this chapter: brick-and-mortar, business-to-consumer (B2C), and small organization. If you're the world leader in granulators for the plastics industry, you'd want to read B2B and large organization. Read what applies to you, but also consider reading what may not seem to. After all, part of being an SEO expert is knowing the breadth of what the Web offers. You never know where you might find something interesting and useful for your own site!

Business-to-Business

Business-to-business (B2B) sites run the gamut from the small company selling restaurant-grade deli slicers to the huge corporation selling enterprise-level software and services. B2Bs of all stripes should be taking a serious look at SEO: In a 2009 Enquiro survey, 55 percent of B2B buyers reported that even if they knew the site they were going to, they would still use a search engine to get there. Here are some of the advantages and challenges of SEO for the B2B category:

Advantage: Niche Target Audience Because your business depends on it, you probably already know your customer well. Your customer fits into a particular niche: restaurant owner, plant manager, candlestick maker, and so on. Although your customers may not all hang out at the same bar after work, it's a good bet that they're frequenting some of the same websites or talking about the same topics on Twitter. And if you don't know where to find these online hangouts, it only takes a bit of time and creative thought to find them. If you already know what magazines your customers subscribe to, what trade shows they attend, and what organizations they belong to, you're well on your way to finding analogous sites on the Web that speak to them. If you know what your customers love to obsess or complain about, you can probably find them doing just that en masse on the Social Web.

Challenge: Difficulty Gaining Inlinks You may have heard that getting relevant, high-quality links to your website is an important SEO endeavor, because it can improve your ranks and traffic. This is going to be a challenge for you. You're not a big entertainment site or a fun blog with a cult following, and unless you're a giant in your industry, your activities are not automatically newsworthy. Although you may have the respect of your customers, building a self-sustaining buzz is not the kind of thing that comes easily to a B2B website. After all, your site probably isn't built for buzz; chances are you're offering straight-up product information, corporate bios, and white papers. You may have tried and failed to come up with a raison d'être for a Facebook page. You may be able to improve your site's *linkability* by offering useful noncommercial content or a corporate blog. Paying for carefully chosen directory listings might even be a good strategy for you.

Advantage: High-Value Conversions SEO is appealing to B2Bs, for a good reason. Because each new customer or lead is valuable to your business, your SEO campaign can make a quick and measurable difference to your bottom line by bringing in just a few conversions. Don't skimp on tracking—you'll want your SEO campaign to get credit for these high-value conversions.

Challenge: A Slow SEO Life Cycle You know why scientists love that little fruit fly called drosophila? The reason is that the drosophila has such a short life span that many generations of them can be studied in a relatively short amount of time. In a similar way, an SEO campaign can be studied and improved in a relatively short amount of time if you have lots of visitors coming through and converting (or not converting). For a B2B, however, this is probably not the case. You will have a smaller, more targeted audience and will likely have a longer conversion life cycle. That means less information, and a slower evolution, for your ongoing SEO campaign.

Advantage: Text-Heavy Content Got FAQs? How about product specifications and support documentation? As a B2B, you probably have lots of text on your site, which the search engines love. While some site owners will be scratching their heads looking for ways to fit text into their design, you will probably have tons of text on which to focus your optimization efforts. And if not, you may have marketing materials such as white papers and PDFs ready for quick and easy appropriation onto your site. Of course, all of the text-heavy items mentioned here have the potential to be about as exciting as a glass of warm milk, so make sure you're putting out text that people actually want to read!

Challenge: Difficult-to-Measure Conversion Values One of the joys of online marketing is how easy it can be to measure what you're getting back in return for your investment of money or time. Unfortunately, this return-on-investment (ROI) loop can be difficult for B2Bs to close. What is a visitor to your webinar really worth to you, in dollars? What is the lifetime value of a new registration for your email list? For best SEO results, you'll need to do some head scratching and get your best estimate of the dollar value of every one of your conversions.

B2B Guru on Telling the Right Story

Barry Bowman is VP of SEO Operations of Boulder, Colorado–based SmartSearch Marketing and is a contributing writer for the "Strictly Business" column at searchengineland.com.

When we asked him about the most common barriers to SEO for B2B sites, Barry was revved. "I've been preaching this for 10 years!" he says, and delivers some refreshing straight talk about everyday B2B SEO challenges.

According to Barry, the top priority for B2B sites is to "get inside your customer's head and tell the right story."

To tell the right story, you have to start by opening up to the keywords that your prospects care about, not just the ones that you use to describe your own company. B2B site owners can be "entrenched in their own philosophies" and completely miss the customer's point of view. Barry shares an example of a B2B client who suffers from this problem: "The CEO told me 50 keywords they wanted great ranks for—but they didn't want to put any of those 50 keywords on their website!" (A basic fact of SEO is that it's next to impossible to get good ranks for keywords that aren't present in visible text on the website.) Barry convinced another client to shake their attachment to the keyword "claims repricing software" and embrace "medical repricing software" instead. This seemingly small difference was a radical mindset shift for the client, but great SEO results ensued.

Bringing traffic to your site is only half the battle. The other half? "Your site has to convert," says Barry. Once someone arrives at your site, "you have about 8 seconds to capture their attention, and give them a reason to click through." One example of conversion-busting entrenched thinking is the ineffective messages that many B2Bs offer on their sites. "Most B2Bs have taken their marketing brochures and slapped them online," Barry groans, and "the bureaucracy and red tape to change content is phenomenal."

He encourages B2B owners to use their site to tell a story that focuses on the needs of the client. "It's easy to talk about 'us'—what we do, how great we are, how cool our location is. But it's difficult to turn the story around," says Barry. It's important to speak clearly to your prospects' issues and needs, and ultimately leave them clamoring for the contact button.

Business-to-Consumer

Business-to-consumer (B2C) is such a huge category that we hesitate to lump all B2C sites together. B2C ranges from big flower vendors making a killing on Mother's Day to one-person operations selling homemade soaps. You may have a local, national, or international customer base, and you may have anything from a phone number or a Yahoo! store to a complex, media-rich e-commerce experience. However, there are some key elements that B2Cs have in common when performing SEO.

Challenge: A Fickle Audience The people searching for your product or service are probably more interested in a trouble-free shopping experience than in buying a product from you specifically. And you can count on them to have a short attention span and a trigger-happy clicking finger. That means your precious searchers could easily be waylaid at any point along the searching process, for example, by a colorful local listing, or bargain-centric results from a shopping aggregator like PriceGrabber. If searchers do land on your site from a search listing, the landing page should be a great match to the keyword they searched for, or they'll gladly employ the Back button and seek easier solutions elsewhere.

And while you may have the benefit of marketing research and brand differentiation, your potential audience may be frustratingly unaware of your preferred labels for your own product or service. Are you selling "the finest micro-techno-fiber all-weather apparel"? That's great, but your general user base is probably searching for <blue raincoats>. In addition, they may be misspelling your product or—*the horror*—your brand name. Careful keyword research can help you tremendously.

Advantage: User-Generated Content Our own site visitors: We love them when they're helpful, and we hate them when they're spamful or spiteful. *User-generated content* (UGC)—things like product reviews, forum postings, and blog comments written by your visitors—is actually a yummy advantage and a prickly challenge all rolled into one. On the plus side, UGC bulks up your website, giving search engines lots of text information to chew on. It also helps engage your visitors, adds freshness to your site, and often helps your customers make the best choices. After all, according to a 2010 study by the e-tailing group PowerReviews, "63 percent of shoppers consistently read reviews prior to making a purchase decision." On the downside, if you don't have time to police every posting that makes it onto your site, you can be caught with some embarrassing search engine listings. Hey, it even happens to the big guys:

> The New **Facebook Sucks!** | Facebook ☆
> The New **Facebook Sucks!** is on FacebookSign up for Facebook to connect with The ... The
> New **Facebook Sucks!** Just for those who dont like the new facebook. ...
> www.facebook.com/group.php?gid=70149742528 - Cached - Similar

Challenge: Keeping Up on the Social Web These days, B2Cs may feel pressured to have an active and meaningful presence everywhere at once online. You don't want to miss out on those web surfers who may want to help you promote your company or product on Facebook, follow you on Twitter, or learn about your newest initiatives on your blog. You may be losing sleep knowing that people believe the reviews they read about you. And social shopping is becoming more and more prevalent, as numerous studies in 2009 and 2010 have shown users putting great trust in social networks and online word-of-mouth when making shopping decisions. Your Social Web presence is intertwined with your search engine presence, and you may need to invest significant time and resources into developing a solid social media strategy, which may include an *online reputation management* (ORM) component to monitor and address online communications that affect your brand. Consider hiring a professional writer to put your best face forward.

Challenge: Unexpected Search Competition As your audience is potentially large and diverse, so is your competition. We mean your *search* competition, of course. You may know exactly who your top five competitors are in the real world, but when you get down to identifying your top-priority keywords in Your SEO Plan, you may be surprised by the sites that are clogging up the top ranks. They might be competitors you've never heard of, or they might be individual consumers talking about how much they hate your products. Or, as we often see, they may not be related to your industry at all. Did you know there's a song called "Famous Blue Raincoat"? Well, there is, and the last time we checked, almost all of Google's top 10 results for the term <blue raincoats> were about songs, not shopping.

Advantage: Knowing the Value of Online Sales One of the primary struggles in SEO is knowing exactly how much a conversion is worth. We often play "Stump the B2B" by asking, "How much is that white paper download really worth, in dollars?" But if your B2C website deals in online sales, placing a value on your conversions is a piece of cake. With a little help from your web developer, you can track the dollar value of every sale along with your traffic data. One of the many benefits of doing this is that you'll actually know whether your paid search campaign is worth the money you're spending on it!

Challenge: Page View Conversions If, like many B2C websites, your measure of conversion is a page view—for example, if you're using traffic data to sell ad space on your site, or if your main goal is brand awareness—get ready for an exciting ride. Simply going by the traffic numbers can have you shouting from the top of the parking garage one day and weeping into your latte the next. This next bit of advice may be hard for a slick up-and-comer like you to swallow, but we're telling you because we like you: Accept that you have less control than you think you do. The Google gods are fickle. An algorithm change, or a search engine marriage or divorce, may be all it takes to sink your traffic.

Large Organization

If you're about to embark on SEO for your large organization, brace yourself—this is going to sting a little:

Pearl of Wisdom: You do not have dibs on the #1 spot in the rankings just because you're big.

    In fact, your SEO campaign is likely to be challenged by your bulk, both in terms of your website and your organizational structure.

Challenge: Internal Bureaucracy From an organizational perspective, your SEO challenges are often a result of *too much*. Too much in that your site is likely to be run by committee: designers, IT department, copywriters, and coders, not to mention the executives who, with a single comment, can have you all scrambling in different directions. We know how pressed you are for time, how many people in your organization are putting their dirty fingers in the pie that is your website, and we know what a struggle it can be to get any changes made on your site. Here are some common SEO tasks; see if you can get through this list without cringing about how many individuals you'll need to round up to complete them:

- Convert graphics to HTML text.
- Edit elements of the HTML code on every page of the site.
- Re-embed Flash files with alternate HTML text.
- Create a specialized text file called robots.txt and have it placed in the root directory of the site.
- Set up a server-side redirect.
- Rewrite page text to reflect more commonly searched terms.
- Change file-naming conventions.

The takeaway here is that you'll be putting a lot of extra time into internal communication and organization. You need to know your team and get them in your corner if you want to succeed at SEO. In other words, get your team on board. This topic is so important it has its own chapter in this book!

Why is this door always *so sticky*?

Challenge: Outdated Content Another *too much* challenge for you lies in the need to keep your brand current. You have probably already witnessed several major changes to your site, steered either by real market forces or by the perceptions of your marketing department. Maybe you have a redesign every six months, frequent new products or product updates, or new branding guidelines to implement. Structurally, you may also have multiple subdomains, more than one URL leading to your home page, and lots of fragmented bits of old versions of your site floating around out there. (Think you don't? Check again. We can honestly say we haven't met one large website that didn't have something old and out-of-date live and available on the search engines.)

Maybe you have all of the above, multiple times over, because you have different teams responsible for different portions of your website. Because of all these factors, the large organization has a special need to keep its calling cards on the Web consistent with the current state of its site. Making sure your search engine results portray your current products and services accurately should be one of your highest priorities.

Advantage: Budget and Existing Infrastructure Of course, *too much* works to your advantage, too. You may have a larger budget, which means that you can probably afford to buy some of the pricier tracking and competitive intelligence tools that are available, or you can hire a professional writer for your social media efforts. And your company probably has existing marketing data about your customers, their behaviors and habits, and their budgets, which your SEO campaign can tap into.

Challenge: Social Media Resistance The larger an organization becomes, the more likely it is to have significant obstacles to a successful social media campaign. Marketers often use the word *transparent* to describe the ideal social media presence—that is, an honest and open depiction of your company's goings-on, and a natural, personal voice. Social media feeds on transparency, yet transparency doesn't come naturally to a large organization. If you're in a company that shuns open dialogue with the public, you'll want to rethink whether your organization is benefiting from this careful message control. Social media activity has direct and indirect benefits that include—but go far beyond—potential improvements to search engine placement. If you're ready to dip a toe into a more open philosophy, take a look at the book *Radically Transparent: Monitoring and Managing Reputations Online* by Andy Beal and Judy Strauss (Sybex, 2008).

Advantage: Lots of Landing Pages Large sites often have a wealth of opportunities for landing pages. Go long—*long tail*, that is: Think beyond your home page and main section pages when determining which pages to optimize. This long tail approach—driving site visitors to a large number of unique pages on your site—can help you compensate for other challenges we've discussed.

Challenge: Paid Search Pitfalls *Sponsored search advertising* such as Google AdWords campaigns can help you accomplish your long tail goals, and a well-run paid search campaign can be cheaper on a per-conversion basis than other forms of advertising. But paid search campaigns for large organizations have the potential to be unwieldy. Even with the built-in management tools that make your paid search campaign a fairly user-friendly experience, the sheer magnitude of a thousands-plus keyword campaign can be time-consuming. Paid search campaigns are an unlikely mix of the creative (word choice, campaign strategy) and the tedious (daily budget caps, maximum click price). The danger for the large company is that it's easy to shift your attention away from important customer-facing details—such as clarity of message and appropriateness of landing page choice—and use average data alone to drive your campaign. No matter the size, every paid search campaign needs attention to detail as well as thoughtfully selected metrics to ensure advertising decisions are based on the *why*, not just the *what*.

Advantage: Making News Last but not least, being large might mean that just about everything you do is automatically newsworthy—which translates into incoming links on the Web. That's great news for your SEO potential!

Small Organization

Small businesses, we salute you as the most vibrant sector of today's Web! You are the equivalent of the corner store—the mom-and-pop sites—personalizing the Web and providing an antidote to the MegaCorp, Inc., mentality and design. Whatever you're selling, you're probably doing it on a careful budget, and you're probably doing everything with minimal staff.

Did you read the section about the large organizations and find yourself feeling a bit envious of all that money and manpower? Don't be. SEO can be the field leveler you need to compete with larger companies, whereas competition in offline advertising venues would be much too expensive for you. And, being smaller, your team and your site—and your SEO campaign—can benefit from a more centralized approach.

Advantage: Less Bureaucracy A busy small organization is often too tapped for resources to work on bettering its own marketing message or position—serving the customer always comes first. Your company doesn't have room for large teams of marketing writers and strategists. So you may be the one person who is the gatekeeper for all of these activities. Sure, it's more work for you, but on the positive side, it means you won't have to go through a huge bureaucracy every time you need to change your website. *You* have the power to make a real difference.

Challenge: Lack of Time If your business is doing well, your biggest SEO challenge is going to be a shortage of time. You might even be sweating out the notion of finding your hour a day for SEO tasks. The great news is, SEO gives back what you put into it.

Do what you can, and read Chapter 10, "Extra Credit and Guilt-Free Slacking," for ideas on how to devote your precious SEO moments to the tasks that are going to give you the best time-to-results ratios.

Advantage: Simpler Is Often Better With the wider adoption of advanced technology for the latest-and-greatest e-commerce and entertainment features, many high-budget sites need to engage in complex SEO tactics and highly technical fixes, just to ensure that the search engines can read their websites. You may be spared this headache: Budget websites are more likely to be built with simple and straightforward technology that does not pose a handicap to search engine visibility. In an effort to pinch pennies, you may have built your site using a template from a large hosting service, or you may have chosen popular and free blog software for your site. You're in luck! Sites built on popular platforms are often well supported with features that you can use to achieve basic site optimization.

Challenge: Small Budget Your time is tight, and your budget is modest. Probably the smartest investment you can make, in our opinion, is a paid search campaign. Surprised? It makes a lot of sense. If you manage it closely, your paid search advertising campaign gives you almost-instant feedback. Is your message compelling enough? Are you targeting viable keywords? Is your landing page doing its job? With paid search, you can tweak to your heart's content for pennies on the dollar compared to other advertising methods.

Advantage: Tools to Level the Playing Field Of course, you know your product or service inside and out, and your customers may seem like close, personal friends. But you might not be well versed in your customers' web habits and searching behavior. You may have little or no experience in marketing. Luckily, you don't need to be a pro—or a big business—to excel in SEO.

A 2009 report from Borrell Associates found that small and medium-sized businesses were responsible for $6.7 billion in locally generated, locally targeted interactive advertising in the United States in 2008—more than half the nation's total. You are big business for the search engines, and therefore, keyword research tools, local listings, traffic analysis software, and the like are all often free, or priced within the budget of the small business.

Even with a small budget, you can pick up an advantage by studying your competitors. Get ideas and insight from their websites and paid search campaigns, and use *their* resources to *your* best advantage! You may get as much out of the do-it-yourself competitive analysis later in the book as you would get from an expensive marketing study. If you've got the time and some natural curiosity, it doesn't cost you anything to look at the companies ranking in the top 10 for your desired keywords and figure out what they're doing right.

Advantage: Starting from Zero It may be that you have given no thought to SEO. Don't let that discourage you! Confession time:

 Pearl of Wisdom: SEO consultants love working for companies starting out at rock bottom because you have nowhere to go but up.

But think carefully about your plan of attack. With a small staff, it is possible to go from famine to feast more quickly than you may be comfortable with. So, if each conversion on your site creates work for you, you may want to take it slowly.

Challenge: Seductive Quick-and-Dirty SEO Schemes Don't be tempted, as some smaller businesses are, to put your money or energy into quickie link schemes or questionable practices such as *comment spam* (using blog comments to plaster the Web with links to your site), which are likely to backfire. (We'll talk more about practices to avoid in Chapter 3, "Eternal Truths of SEO.") Remember: The search engines aren't perfect, but they all attempt to provide more exposure to high-quality sites and less exposure to low-quality sites. Don't buy links from low-quality, irrelevant sites, and don't stuff your site with keywords or awkward text aimed at getting rankings. For best long-term results, keep your focus on maintaining a useful site with a high-quality, focused message.

Really Small Organization

Take everything we said about small organizations, reduce the head count to one or two people, and pile on several additional demands for your time. Sound like you? We've had the pleasure of working with a lot of really small businesses, and even solo operations, and we know how ludicrously tight that belt can get. But we also know how satisfying it can be to see a homegrown marketing effort turn into a big upswing in business.

Advantage: Slow Periods Everybody has slow times, but for really small businesses, when you're between projects or in the slow season, things can seem to grind to a complete halt. SEO gives you a way to fill the downtime, while giving structure to the things you should be doing anyway: snooping on your competitors, fine-tuning your goals, and ultimately working on growing your company.

Disadvantage: *Not* Slow Periods You're negotiating your own contracts. You're dusting your own office. You're filing your own taxes. In addition, you've got that not-so-small task of keeping your customers satisfied. How do you feel about hunkering down and learning all about search engines, basic HTML, and SEO industry trends? That desperate feeling in the pit of your stomach is exactly why there are so many low-low-priced SEO firms out there vying for your money. Problem is, in SEO you often get what you pay for. You might want to work less formally: Read through this book to get the big picture. Don't fill out the worksheets. Abandon the hour-a-day concept. Tackle the parts that you can, when you can. Whatever you accomplish, pat yourself on the back—your job is hard enough.

Advantage: Your Own Name In many cases, the name of the company is the same as the person behind the company. In other cases, your company may have its own name, but, being so small, your name and your company name are used interchangeably. Building up your personal reputation will benefit your business reputation as well, and luckily, the Web has some exciting nooks and crannies you can fit into that larger companies can't. Professional networking sites such as LinkedIn offer great opportunities to create a personal profile, and these can often translate to a lovely, professional search engine listing for your own name. Want your target audience to view you as the expert on corporate training or historical aviation models? Just be your witty, knowledgeable self in the right forums and blogs, and your name—and expertise—will be in front of the right people. If you have a lot of insight to share and you have a way with words, you can try to make a name for yourself with a professionally oriented, personally managed blog. (Just be sure to read the "Blog" section in this chapter, too.)

Little Flower Candy Co.: Know When to Hold 'Em!

Christine Moore is a former pastry chef who knows a great deal about making delectable hand-made desserts using high-quality ingredients. Now she's in business for herself. Working in her own kitchen, using her own hands, she has developed a formidable reputation for making some of the tastiest candies in Los Angeles. But she admits she knows almost nothing about marketing.

And she's never had to. Thanks to great connections in L.A.'s visible foodie scene, word of mouth, and some very complimentary press coverage, her business is doing extremely well. When we spoke with her, she was looking toward the upcoming holiday season with excitement—and a good deal of trepidation. Acknowledging that the appeal of her product relies on the small-batch, handmade approach, she says, "I could ruin my reputation in one fell swoop by being greedy."

Little Flower Candy Co.: Know When to Hold 'Em! *(Continued)*

We have no doubt that an SEO campaign could bring Christine lots of new customers. But if things heat up too quickly, she may have more work than she can handle. At her current pace, she has time to get on the phone and call a web customer to work out an ordering glitch and to be there for her family. Of course, she's open to SEO for her site, but, as Christine says, "It's hard to know whether to put the cart before the horse or the horse before the cart." Like any marketing strategy, SEO requires that careful consideration be given to the balance between a business's long-term goals and current capabilities.

Christine is in control of her company, and she is in a position to have control over its web presence. She has a good kind of problem. Her real-world buzz will be easy to translate into a web buzz, when the time is right!

Her site was built in a hurry, under pressure to get a store online in time for an article about her company that was about to go to press. The publication made it clear: no online store, no article. A friend quickly built her site, and Christine wrote the text just hours before it went live. Since the site was built for a ready-made audience of readers who had the URL in print, almost no thought was given to the search engines.

As SEO experts, here's what we noticed about her site: There were only two links pointing to it, and neither of them came from the large publications that have printed articles about her company. With such a rabid following and word-of-mouth marketing happening in the real world, she could easily get more links. Also, her site features the words *hand made* because she's not fond of the term *gourmet*. But what are her potential customers searching for? A little research would go a long way in determining if she's losing out on traffic by using the wrong terminology.

Brick-and-Mortar

If you had the chance to put one thing in front of your customers, you'd probably give them your street address, not your web address, and that's the way it should be. Your site plays second fiddle to your day-to-day business. After all, the best way to turn browsers into customers is to get them to walk through your door. You may not even be sure why you have a website, except that everyone else is doing it. So let's talk about how to make your site do its job of playing the supporting role.

Advantage: An Achievable Goal If you're not selling your product online, then the best use of your site is probably to help people find your physical location. Your SEO campaign begins with a simple goal: You want to be found when your company name is entered in the search engines. You'll focus your SEO campaign on variations of your business name and location. You're likely to get the results you are hoping for because you won't run up against too much competition for such tightly targeted keywords.

Advantage: Local Search   And speaking of location, welcome to one of the most useful areas of SEO for both searchers and website owners: local search. It picks up where the local Yellow Pages left off in the last century. See Figure 2.1 for an example.

We love local search. Who wants to waste time slogging through nationwide search results when you're looking for the sandwich shop around the corner? If you're a cafe owner in Evanston, Illinois, you can put yourself directly in front of someone searching for <cafe Evanston IL>. Talk about a targeted audience!

Like the targeting? You'll love the placement—local listings are often displayed right at the top of the search results page. But wait, there's more: Standard local search listings on the search engines are free, and even offer an easy way to bask in the glow of online reviews, which often accompany these listings. In Chapter 8, "Month Two: Establish the Habit," we'll show you how to take control of your local listings and keep an eye on shape-shifting results as local search evolves.

Advantage: Mobile Search   Even if they know your web address, it's often too taxing on the thumbs for your customers to type it into a mobile browser, so they are likely to use search as a shortcut. This means that you should pay attention to your mobile search listings, and your website as viewed through mobile devices—these can add up to an important web strategy for your site. As a brick-and-mortar company, it's helpful to think of your mobile searchers as customers who are in your neighborhood and at that critical decision point of choosing whether to walk through your door or keep walking. Imagine the information you want these people to find easily: contact information, hours of operation, address and directions, and, of course, positive reviews! Along with this exciting mobile search opportunity comes a bit of a burden: keeping up with evolving standards and best practices of the Mobile Web. You'll learn more about this in Chapter 9, "Month Three: It's a Way of Life."

Figure 2.1   A local search on Google

"It's Not Second Nature to Me"—Maplecroft Bed & Breakfast

"I didn't touch a computer until my mid-forties," says Dan Jones, innkeeper at Maplecroft Bed & Breakfast in Barre, Vermont. While his partner, Yasunari Ishii, entertained guests at the grand piano in their cozy Victorian inn, Dan spoke to us about how they are slowly but surely working through a mostly homegrown online marketing strategy despite not being digital natives.

Maplecroft Bed & Breakfast — Experience Vermont from its heart.

HOME ❖ ABOUT MAPLECROFT ❖ ACCOMMODATIONS ❖ ACTIVITIES & ATTRACTIONS ❖ DIRECTIONS

CENTRAL VERMONT COMES ALIVE

The warm weather of spring and summer has brought Vermont alive once again, and Barre-Montpelier and Maplecroft B&B are perfectly located in the heart of Vermont to take it all in. A drive in any direction takes you through lush green mountains and colorful meadows, by peaceful rivers and streams crossed with covered bridges, and through picturesque towns and villages with church steeples on village greens where you'll find antique and craft shops, galleries, cafes, gourmet restaurants and more.

Many small business owners don't know where to start, and neither did Dan and Yasunari. But they took their time and made the right first step: They found a good web developer who specialized in the bed-and-breakfast (B&B) industry. Dan advises, "If you're not an expert at something, get someone who knows what they're doing and pay them to do it right." This is harder than it sounds. While there are a lot of industry-specific developers specializing in everything from hospitality to law, medicine, or retail, it's not easy to find a good one with a solid SEO offering. The firm chosen to develop www.maplecroftvermont.com added a solid SEO foundation to the website: They populated the site with location-specific keywords and encouraged the inclusion of lots of text on the site to give the search engines more to love.

Dan and Yasunari also took the time to get to know their industry online. "We had the idea of doing a B&B years ago, so over the years, we paid attention to websites. What attracted us, what made us go into the site, the navigation, the visuals. We had an idea of what we thought was important." The result was a website that people often compliment. "They say it's very simple and easy to navigate."

With their new website in place, Dan and Yasunari chose to spend their online advertising dollars carefully, on just a few directories. For general traffic they bought a listing on bedandbreakfast.com, a directory that not only brings in traffic but also ranks well, giving Maplecroft's listing excellent search engine placement. For niche traffic they bought a listing on purpleroofs.com, a gay and lesbian travel site. Both of these listings paid off in customers. Next, they tested a six-month listing on a ski directory. This listing was not as successful—driving just a few customers, it barely paid for itself, so it was dropped.

There's also an online word-of-mouth effort in the works. Soon the rooms at Maplecroft will display reminders for guests to post reviews on www.tripadvisor.com. (Dan has heard from several guests that those five-star reviews helped convince them to choose Maplecroft.) And Dan has enlisted friends to help him understand how to use Facebook and start an e-newsletter.

Dan voiced something that we hear from a lot of small businesses, especially brick-and-mortar businesses: The website isn't his first priority, and SEO isn't the first thing on his mind. When we asked him about analytics, Dan recalled his first time looking at traffic data: "We had the interest, and then we saw it, and it looked complicated, and we stopped looking because we didn't have the time."

Of course we don't recommend ignoring your analytics data. But if you're going to do just a little bit of SEO at a time, do it like Maplecroft's innkeepers. Tune out unsolicited emails and phone calls yelling at you to buy directory listings or pay for SEO services you may not understand. Ask your customers lots of questions: "How did you find us?" "What do you think of our website?" "Did you see any reviews?" Take your time to get to know your online environment. And proceed with what you can, thoughtfully and carefully, until you are ready for the next challenge.

Blog

It's shockingly easy to publish web content when you have a blog, but putting out lots of content is not the same thing as building and maintaining a readership. To keep your site from joining the millions of blogs already collecting dust in forgotten corners of the Internet, you need high-quality content offerings to maintain your audience and an SEO strategy to increase your reach. Although search is only one of many potential sources of visitors for most blogs, it can be a key source of *new* visitors—and new visitors have the potential to turn into engaged, active, long-term readers and participants.

Advantage: A Naturally Social Site You won't have to leap over any conceptual hurdles to become a participant in the Social Web: You're already there. Blogs are social sites by definition and form the backbone of the Social Web. The *blogroll*, a list of links to favorite blogs, is a standard blog feature that reinforces a link-friendly culture. As a blog, your site automatically has a better chance of receiving links from other blogs than a traditional website does.

Even better, there are free means of promotion on the Social Web to help your blog succeed. You have Facebook, Twitter, Digg, and other social sites at your disposal to promote your newly published posts. If your blog provides valuable content, it may receive additional exposure from fans on these venues, which can be helpful in gaining targeted traffic.

Challenge: Real Participation There's no denying that a lot of blogs offer poor-quality, derivative content, or worse, spammy autogenerated dreck. But you will also find an overwhelming number of informative, intelligent, funny, insightful, and down-right fancy-ticklin' blogs in just about any niche you can think of. How will yours be noticed—both by potential readers and the search engines?

First, you need a solid big-picture understanding of your blog's purpose, target audience, differentiation, and value compared to other sites. With that as your foundation, get to know the social landscape of other blogs and Twitterers in your niche. These microcommunities have all the affinities, grudges, schisms, feuds, accusations, and drama of a family reunion, with not nearly as much barbecue sauce.

Getting links to your blog is your goal—and the best way to achieve it is through *real participation* on other sites in your niche. You'll focus not just on gaining links, but on building relationships, sharing your thoughts in venues beyond your own site… in short, making your best possible contribution to the community. Be interesting and topical, and throw in a dash of helpful, or funny, or whatever you do best.

Even if you usually cross to the other side of the street to avoid chatting with a neighbor in the real world, you need to force yourself to be a much more gregarious animal online. Time-consuming as it may be, reading and participating on other blogs is one of the best ways to connect yourself to a community and ultimately build links and visibility for your own blog.

Challenge: Optimizing Every Post Since your site probably doesn't have a traditional site map, with sections, subsections, and conversion pages, you won't have traditional landing pages to focus your SEO attentions on. Instead, you will have to put your time into making *every post* a better place for searchers to land. All of the SEO rules we lay out in this book for landing pages—rules like including keywords throughout body text and in URLs, using keywords in linking text, writing unique and keyword-rich titles, and linking internally to related content—should become part of your every post.

Advantage: SEO-Friendly Authoring Tools For small and large businesses alike, it's a great idea to use out-of-the-box blog authoring platforms such as WordPress, TypePad, and Movable Type. Fortunately, when you use these tools, there aren't many special technical tasks required of you to make sure that the major search engines can find your blog. Don't worry if you're feeling fuzzy about how to set good default HTML titles for your posts, whether you should include tags on every post, or the mysteries of *pretty URLs*; you'll find plug-in and blog optimization specifics in Chapter 8.

Are You Selling Out if You Optimize Your Blog?

The Right Brain says, "Wait a minute. I'm uncomfortable telling bloggers to optimize their postings with search-targeted keywords! Shouldn't a blog be a bastion of personal expression and entertaining writing? Shouldn't the blogosphere be free of the marketing mentality that pervades the rest of the Web? We've seen it time and again: Good writing can really take a beating when a marketing agenda is attached to it."

The Left Brain says, "Right, and bloggers are all out there working on their own personal time, with no need for the luxuries in life like food and shelter. Heck, no! Blogs have a legitimate need for SEO, just like any other business website. I would never counsel a blogger to dilute his or her message or change the blog's subject matter based on conversions—just as I don't give that sort of advice to any other website owner. But creating highly readable headlines that are compelling and clear—that's just common sense. And isn't 'search-targeted keywords' just another way of saying, 'Use the text that makes the most sense to your audience'? After all, what good is a message if nobody finds it?"

Advantage: A Shortcut to Real-time Search Does it go without saying that you are going to need to update your blog very, very frequently? We sure hope so. Google's real-time search results, introduced in 2009, are sometimes featured on the first page of search results, and Facebook and Twitter searching is on the rise. Although these features continue to evolve and mature, one thing will remain constant: You can be sure that freshness will be an advantage in real-time search. If you update it frequently, your blog will be a perfect candidate for a position in the real-time spotlight.

Challenge: Domain Considerations It's easy to create a blog that shows up within your website domain. But maybe you started your blog a few years ago, and it's currently living on a free hosting domain like biotech-now.blog-mega-service.com or your-company-blog.com, miles away from your company's primary domain. Ouch: As you may have heard, it's preferable to consolidate your online efforts onto a single domain, especially to achieve maximum link-building benefits. So you've got some thinking to do: Bite the bullet and move the blog now, or keep it as is and try to leverage it from where it stands? There's no simple answer: Moving domains is always disruptive to search presence.

Advantage: A Venue for Personal Touch Any salesperson will tell you that making a sale is about trust. If you are trying to sell something through your blog, you have a great opportunity to give your audience a chance to get to know and trust you. Aaron Wall of www.seobook.com is both a blogger and an expert search marketer. His blog is one way that potential customers find and purchase his e-book. But it's also a comprehensive, information-rich site that both helps others and bolsters his reputation in the industry. His advice to bloggers getting started and looking for SEO strategies: "Learn your community well, find and use your real voice, and link out early and often."

Adult Sites: Time to Get Passionate about SEO

If your website is of the adult variety, prepare yourself for a difficult SEO experience. Besides dealing with mind-boggling levels of competition for keywords, you are also faced with several other disadvantages: a website that is, shall we say, more visually oriented than text oriented; a plethora of *black-hat* (questionable or unethical) SEO competitors; an entry page, in some cases, to boot out the under-18 crowd; and search engines that may not allow your site to advertise.

We spoke with Searah Deysach, president of Early to Bed, a feminist sex toy store with a brick-and-mortar storefront in Chicago and an online store at www.early2bed.com. Like many small business owners, Searah wears many hats: "finances, payroll, advertising, buying, managing employees, light graphic design, cleaning the bathroom, and whatever else needs doing." With a volunteer managing the company website, SEO and online promotion falls to Searah as well.

So, what works for Early to Bed?

- An active social media presence: "We have jumped on the social networking bandwagon big time... it is exhausting but totally necessary." But watch out: Facebook can unpredictably ban adult-oriented pages. Walk that line with care and be sure any content you post on Facebook is also backed up elsewhere.

- Blogger outreach: "We have sent products out to bloggers to review, and we try to comment on others' blogs when we can." These posts often result in a link to the Early to Bed site, which helps ranks and directly brings traffic.

- Online word of mouth on review sites such as www.yelp.com: "I find that a lot of people find us on Yelp, where we have lots of really good reviews."

- Dropping efforts that don't pay off: "The Yellow Pages grouped us with all novelties... we only got calls from people looking for balloons or party rentals!"

You may have noticed that Searah's favorite tactics don't include working on getting top ranks in organic search: "When I search for us organically, I have to be pretty specific before we come up on the first page of Google, so I am guessing most customers come from somewhere else." When some time frees up between Searah's many full-time jobs, we'd recommend a selective SEO strategy. She's already using Google Analytics—can she find any landing pages that *are* receiving organic search traffic? Those pages could become her SEO focus. Or, could she brainstorm some two-to-three-word phrases that would speak to this store's niche audience? These will be less competitive than single words describing Early to Bed's products. SEO for an adult website will never be easy, but if you choose your tactics carefully, SEO can complement and enhance a well-rounded online marketing effort.

Web Designer

Web designers are natural partners in SEO. After all, shouldn't the person who designs and builds a website have a strong interest in knowing how to make it search friendly? SEO has become positively mainstream, and we guarantee that your clients and prospects have SEO on their minds. To be viable in today's business climate, SEO literacy is a must for any web developer, and offering SEO as a service or add-on is an advantage for client acquisition. Want to use SEO for a bigger slice of the proposal pie or to gain a longer list of prospects? Here are some of the challenges and advantages we expect you'll face:

Advantage: The Inside Track You're already on the job, providing web design services. Your client trusts you, and the site files are nestled safely on your hard drive. Lucky for you, it is often difficult for an outside SEO consultant to be inserted into the very early stages of web design. This is because much of the website is still theoretical early on, and theoretical SEO can only get you so far. Use your status to your advantage: As the designer, you can easily introduce SEO early in the conversation and be sure it is integrated into design decisions throughout the process.

Challenge: Hucksters Abound No, no, we're not talking about *you*. We're talking about those *other* web designers. You know, the ones who feature SEO as an add-on to their regular services, and then just stick HTML titles on some pages, with no keyword research or insight to back them up? They probably charge a couple hundred bucks for the add-on, spend 10 minutes on the work, and accomplish nothing for their clients. Unfortunately, you have to compete with these guys. To protect your reputation (and ours!):

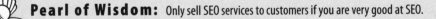 **Pearl of Wisdom:** Only sell SEO services to customers if you are very good at SEO.

A comprehensive SEO service includes three major components. First, there are the technical elements: creating a search-friendly site and page structure so that search engine robots can access and index all content on the site. Second, there are strategy and marketing elements: researching keywords, organizing content around searcher intent, crafting keyword-rich text, optimizing for different types of search results such as local and shopping search, and integrating SEO and social media strategies. Finally, there is measurement: ongoing monitoring of key metrics, analysis, and strategy adjustments. Real SEO results demand a generous helping of all three of these components! We've seen web developer/client relationships turn sour because the developer only provided the first one. If all you're offering in the way of SEO is a technically search-friendly site, that's great! But be sure the client knows it.

Challenge: A Short-Term Project SEO is a long-term effort. It requires months if not years of ongoing work. Most web development projects, however, are structured to last only through site launch and perhaps a short support period—not long enough for the type of holistic SEO approach we advocate in this book. Many SEO contracts have a term of 3–12 months, and if you're really confident about your SEO skill set, you'll want to push for an ongoing contract, too. Remember that the added value of your SEO services can't possibly be known until the website has been up for at least a few months.

Challenge: A Change of Perspective You're a web designer, which means you probably know a little something about graphic design, information architecture, usability, look and feel, and techie back-end development. This is great news because file-naming conventions, choice of site architecture, and scripting and page structure choices all play a part in the search engine friendliness of a site. However, your skill set may or may not include writing and marketing strategy, and your relationship with your client may not go there on a regular basis. If you're not a natural wordsmith or strategist, you'll need to update your tool belt or find a partner who can complement your skills.

Nonprofit

Those of you in nonprofit organizations are working with a different sort of bottom line for your websites. Rather than following the corporate mantra of "money, money, and more money," you fine people are out there trying to change the world, educate, and improve society! And as a thank-you from the world of web search, you have some big advantages in SEO.

Advantage: Linkability The culture of the Web generally adores noncommercial content—something that your website should be chockfull of. And, let's face it, giving you a link doesn't cost a thing. Any webmaster, blogger, or social media user who supports your cause—or at least has no major problem with it—will see adding a link as a cheap and easy way to help out. You will want to adjust Your SEO Plan accordingly, giving extra effort to link building and the Social Web.

Advantage: Less Paid Search Competition Many nonprofits think that there's no way that they can survive in the competitive world of paid listings. However, there are a few ways that you can, as a nonprofit, get your foot in the door. For one, it's possible that the keywords that matter most to you are not the same words that commercial organizations are vying for. After all, nobody's out there selling <AIDS in China>. Even better, Google offers a free advertising program for nonprofits, called Google Grants. Learn more at www.google.com/grants.

Challenge: Internal Issues Internal disorganization, an overworked and underpaid workforce, lack of funding, and lack of a clear bottom line could throw hurdles in the way of Your SEO Plan. If you are a small operation, you may not even have a marketing department to manage the website. And without a clearly measurable bottom line, it may be very hard for you to prove the value of your efforts. You will need to do some creative thinking to figure out a way to get that return on investment (ROI) measured.

Is there a specific event that you can promote? A campaign or drive that can be earmarked as an SEO testing ground? With any luck, your SEO campaign will be funding itself after a few months of effort. You may be surprised to find that it becomes one of the most important outreach venues your organization will use.

Mon Yough Community Services: SEO on a Shoestring

Mon Yough Community Services (MYCS) is a nonprofit organization near Pittsburgh, Pennsylvania. It embodies some of the common challenges of nonprofits: lack of funding, lack of resources, and an organization that embraces low tech. When we asked Gina Boros, formerly the organization's MIS manager, what kind of effort they put into SEO, she just laughed.

At first blush, it seems there's no reason to market MYCS on the Web. This is an organization whose target population is the homeless and mentally ill. Its most successful marketing efforts are in the form of bus stop advertisements, not the Internet. Pittsburgh's nonprofit service agencies are a tight-knit group, and the referrals that come are almost always word of mouth.

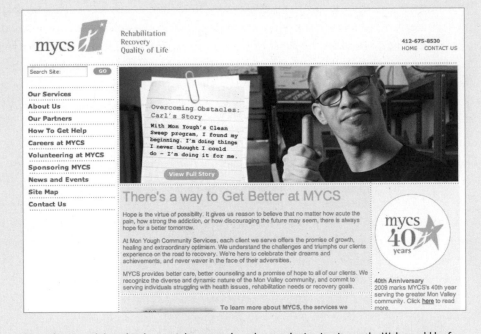

But, when you delve a bit deeper, it becomes clear that marketing its site on the Web would be far from pointless. MYCS constantly seeks new volunteers and interns to keep its therapy programs running smoothly, and website owners love linking to these kinds of opportunities. MYCS throws fundraising events: The more people that attend, the more funds are raised. If they're using flyers and newspaper ads to promote these, why not the website? And it turns out that there are some case managers in the region who haven't heard of MYCS. The search engines might give a little boost.

One final word of encouragement: We asked SEO luminary Jill Whalen (one of the most renowned names in the SEO industry) whether she thought do-it-yourselfers could do as good a job as professionals in SEO. Her response? "Absolutely!" You know your business—and all its nooks and crannies—better than anybody. After reading this chapter, you should have a long-view understanding of how you'll need to approach SEO so that you can make the most of your advantages and minimize your challenges. In the next chapter, we'll start talking details about the search engines. Get ready to be imbued with some Eternal Truths of SEO.

Eternal Truths of SEO

You've probably heard that SEO and the search engines change constantly, and it's true. But there are some things about SEO that haven't changed much and probably won't for a long time to come. These Eternal Truths include basic information that you will use starting in Part III and for the duration of your SEO campaign. You don't want to chisel this stuff in stone, but it calls for something a little more permanent than a dry-erase marker.

3

Robots Deliver

We're going to start with the basics of how the search engines work, and a major component of this is a *robot,* or *spider,* which is software that gathers information about your site and brings it back to be analyzed by a powerful central engine. This activity is referred to as *crawling* or *spidering.* There are lots of different metaphors for how robots work, but we think ants make the best one. Think of a search engine robot as an explorer ant, leaving the colony with one thought on its mind: *Find food.* In this case, the food is HTML text, preferably lots of it, and to find it, the ant needs to travel along easy, obstacle-free paths: HTML links. Following these paths, the ant (search engine robot), with insect-like single-mindedness, carries the food (text) back to its colony and stores it in its anthill (search engine database). Thousands and thousands of the little guys are exploring and gathering simultaneously all over the Internet (Figure 3.1). If a path is absent or blocked, the ant gives up and goes somewhere else. If there's no food, the ant brings nothing back.

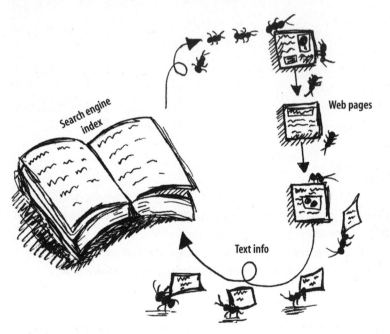

Figure 3.1 Search engine robots at work

So basically, when you think of a search engine, consider it a database that holds pieces of text that have been gathered from millions of sites all over the Web.

What sets that engine in motion? A search. When a web surfer enters the term <grape bubble gum> into the search engine, all of the sites that *might* be relevant for that term are brought to the forefront. The search engine sifts through its database for sites containing terms like <*grape* growers>, <stock market *bubble*>, and <*gum* disease>. It uses a secret formula—a.k.a. a search ranking *algorithm*—to sort the results, and in a fraction of a second, a list of relevant sites, many containing the exact phrase "grape bubble gum" (or with links from other sites containing this phrase), will be returned in the results page.

Lots of things factor into the way search engines determine the ranks for their search results. But just for a start, in order to be in the running for ranks, you need to provide HTML text to feed the search engines and HTML links as clear paths to the food. Keeping those robots well fed and happy is one of your biggest priorities.

SEO in 30 Seconds

We've said it before but it bears repeating: SEO is not rocket science. These two basic elements have formed the foundation of our SEO work for over a decade:

- Make sure that search engine robots can access and read text content on your site.
- Craft website content to feature keywords that your target audience is searching for.

As the search engines have evolved, the job of SEO has become more complicated, but these two fundamentals have never changed.

Search Results Are Blended

If you've spent much time searching, you have probably noticed that the search engines are not displaying a homogeneous set of results. Most search engines take the chef's salad approach, displaying a mix of simple text links; image, video, shopping, and local results; paid ads; and more. Knowing what each type of listing looks like and where they come from is the first step in being able to influence your own listings in a positive way.

Organic Listings

You just read about search engine robots gathering information from the Web. These nonpaid listings—called *organic* or *natural* search results—are the ones that are most prominent in the search engines, as seen in Figure 3.2 and Figure 3.3.

Organic listings are what the majority of this book is about because, let's be honest, these are the listings that *you* care about most. Not only do organic listings get the most clicks, they imbue top-ranked websites with credibility that no paid listing can provide.

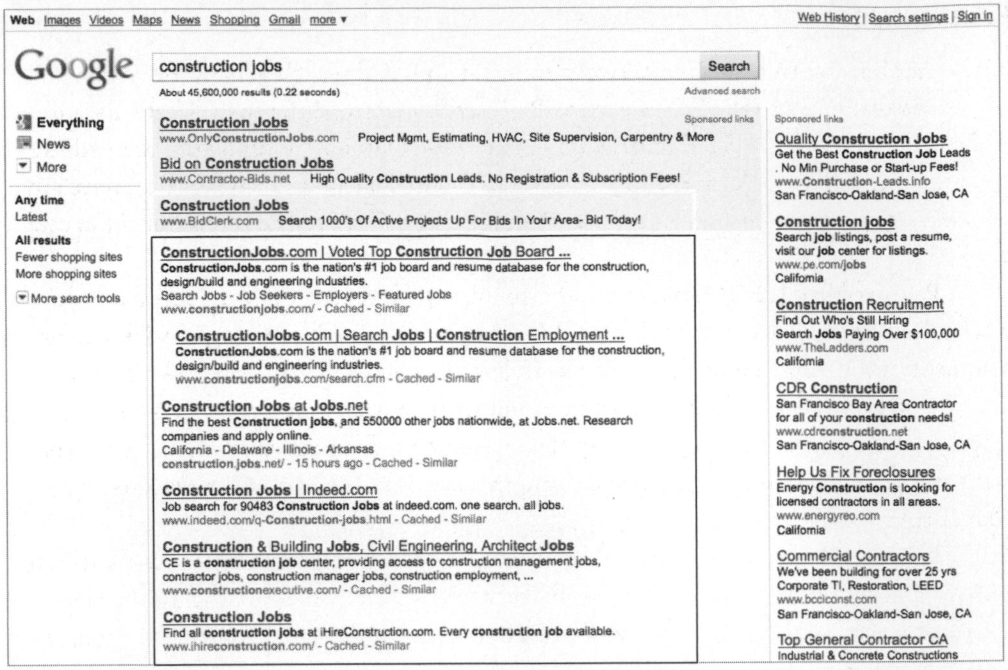

Figure 3.2 Organic results in Google

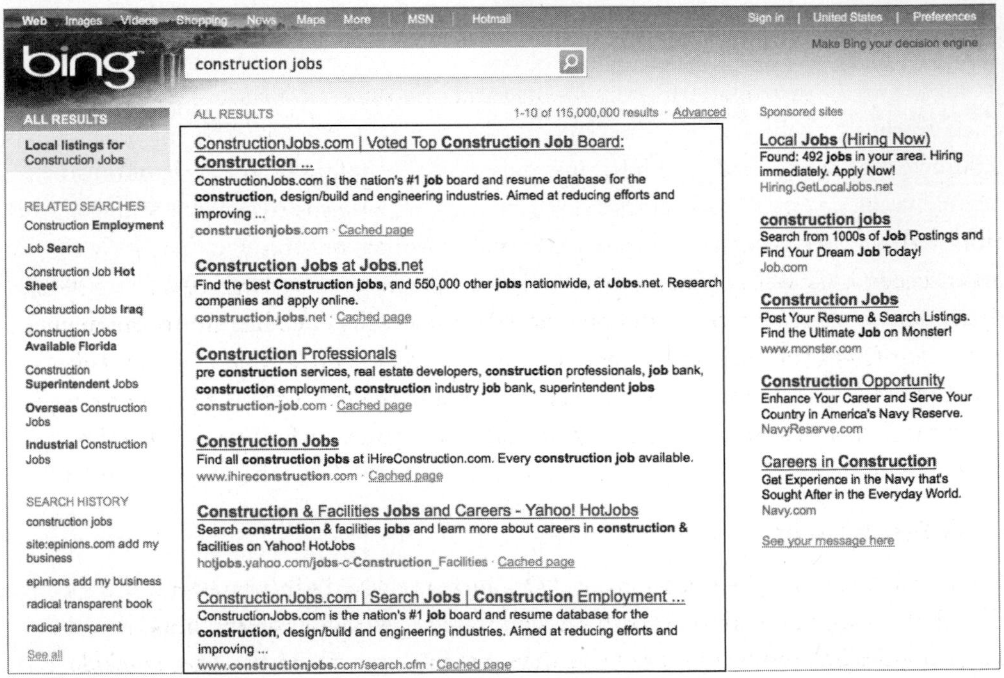

Figure 3.3 Organic results in Bing

Paid Search Ads

No matter how blurred the line between nonpaid and paid search gets in the search engine results, you, as the SEO expert, will always know the difference. That's because, while it's possible to get listed in organic search results without actually doing anything, you (or someone you delegate) will have to actively implement and carefully manage any paid advertising for your own site. And, of course, there's that little matter of the checkbook, too.

Pay-per-click (PPC) services are the simplest paid search option. Here's how it works: You open an account with a paid search provider, such as Google AdWords or Microsoft adCenter. You decide which search terms you want your site to be seen for, and you write your own listings to correspond with your chosen terms. Every time a searcher clicks on your listing, you pay the provider a fee. You control the amount you want to spend for each click (your *bid*), and this is a major factor in the placement of your listing.

Paid search is the SEO marketing venue over which you have the most control. It offers you a chance to micromanage your website marketing by giving you the ability to target specific messages to specific terms and even specific geographical locations. It gives you the opportunity to change your message on a whim, and it provides some of the most conclusive tracking around. Therefore, although paid search is by no means a requirement for good SEO, it's an Eternally Attractive Option to have available to you.

Site Feeds

Site feeds have been around for years in one form or another, but their methodology is still morphing. Available in various forms, they are Eternally Helpful, particularly for large or frequently updated sites. Just as you may use a feed reader to be notified of your favorite blog or news topic, the search engines use feeds to sit back and receive information from websites without sending spiders out to constantly gather, gather, gather. Feeds work well for regularly edited websites such as blogs and news sites (feeding the content of their articles and blog posts), online sellers (feeding up-to-the-minute shopping information such as product descriptions and prices), and media-rich websites. Generally, these types of listings get thrown into the mix with the main organic search results, or in search result categories called *verticals*, such as news, blog, or shopping search.

Vertical Search Results

"Connect people with their passions…" "Organize the world's information…" It's a tall order! To keep up with their own mission statements and searchers' appetites, the search engines add results that are more than just links to web pages. These include images, videos, news, local listings with maps and reviews, shopping results, real time results, and more. Figure 3.4 shows a variety of results.

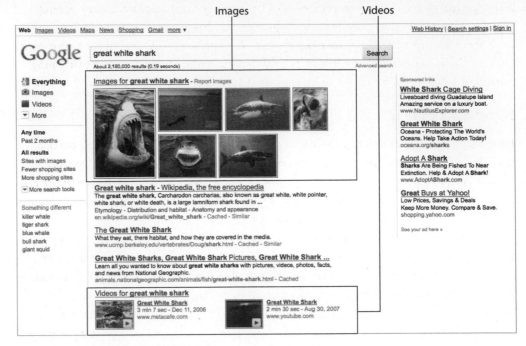

Figure 3.4 Google results for <great white shark>

In Google, these are called *universal search* results, but the more generic term is *vertical* or *blended search*. The search engines display these vertical results whenever something in your search query hints that this vertical might be what you're looking for. For example, Bing knows that people who search for the term <leonardo dicaprio pics> want to feast their eyes on Leo's mug, not just a bunch of blue and black text, so the search engine shows an array of images along with its standard web search results.

In contrast to the main web search results, the listings that search engines display in vertical search results are gathered using different methods and ranked according to different criteria. For example, the news search results in Google come from a relatively small group of news-only sources (including news agencies, newspapers, magazines, and major blogs), which are individually vetted by Google's staff. The news search algorithm uses its own criteria for ranks, which are different from the main web search algorithm. That means getting into vertical results can require a completely different process than getting into the main organic results! It takes a practiced eye to know whether the listing you're looking at is paid, free, lucky, or impossible to get without a couple mil in your pocket. This book should give you a fighting chance for the first three types, anyway.

Meta Search Engines and Search Aggregators

Some people are comparison shoppers, flitting from store to store to review all the merchandise before making a decision. For people who like to compare search results, meta search engines and search aggregators make it easy to review listings from different search engines in one screen—no flitting from site to site necessary. Simply put, these search engines compile and display results from several search engines and rank them according to their own algorithms. You can't use SEO to improve your presence on these engines directly; if a meta search engine like Dogpile.com is using Bing results, the way to do better on these engines is to do better on Bing.

Algorithms Change

Here's something that drives people crazy about SEO: You can't ever be 100 percent sure that what you're doing will be rewarded with the rank and the listing you want. This is because the search engines keep their internal ranking mechanism, even the criteria by which the ranking is determined, under wraps. Welcome to the secret formula of SEO: the Search Engine Ranking Algorithm.

The algorithm is the formula that a search engine uses to determine its ranks. It's a way of sifting through a multitude of factors, including keyword repetition and page titles, inbound links, and even the age and speed of the site. Some elements have more weight, meaning that they are considered to be more important in determining rank, and some have less. Each search engine uses its own algorithm to determine which results to show and in which order. And search engines change their algorithms constantly, without so much as a friendly warning. So the truth is this:

Pearl of Wisdom: You will never really know exactly how Google works.

(unless you work there, in which case, give us a call sometime!).

One of our favorite bits of SEO jargon is the term *permaflux*, which describes the way that search engines (Google, in particular) constantly tweak and evolve their ranking algorithms. Google is said to average one algorithm change *per day*! Imagine if other forms of marketing worked this way! What if you couldn't rely on alphabetical order in the Yellow Pages anymore? What if the TV networks chose to air only the parts of your ad that *they* felt were most important? What if your billboards were periodically relocated without your consent? We're so glad you've got a good head on your shoulders because, now that you're doing SEO, you will have to find a balance between keeping up with the algorithm and keeping your sanity.

Search engines guard their algorithms closely because, first and foremost, they value the searcher's experience. If Bing published a guide called "Instructions for Ranking #1 on Our Search Engine," you'd use it, of course. And so would everyone else. Then all of the results on Bing would become so manipulated by site owners that relevance would disappear—investment sites could rank high for <grape bubble gum> on purpose—and searchers would drop the engine like a big useless hot potato. Even without a manual, the little bits of algorithm that people figure out themselves often get so abused that the search engines eventually devalue them.

How do you find the balance between seeking the Eternally Unknowable Algorithm and making sure your SEO efforts are effective? Matt Cutts, the popular blogger and Google employee who sometimes indulges his SEO-obsessed readers with tantalizing bits of inside information on Google's algorithm, says, "Most of the right choices in SEO come from asking, What's the best thing for the user?" Bringing targeted users to your site is, of course, the point of SEO, and that's the reason we made you clarify your audience and site goals before we started talking about how the search engines work.

We asked Danny Sullivan, probably the best-known and most respected authority on search today, what he considers to be eternal about SEO. His answer: "Good HTML titles, good body copy, great content, ensuring that your site doesn't have roadblocks to crawling—these have worked for nearly a decade." Notice he didn't mention anything about chasing the algorithm.

Now, you won't hear us saying, "algorithm, shmalgorithm." One of the Eternal Truths we've learned over the years is this:

 Pearl of Wisdom: Often, factors that matter most in the search engine algorithms are good for both websites and their users.

It's fine to keep an eye on the latest and greatest rumors about *exactly* how Google works, but don't go nuts or you will lose focus on what really matters: your site visitors.

Humans Are Smart—Computers Aren't

Let's face it: The search engine's job is not easy. Take a look at your filing cabinet, multiply it by about a billion, and imagine someone throwing you a couple of words and then hovering impatiently behind you, tapping a toe, expecting you to find exactly the right document in the blink of an eye. Nobody could! We humans are wonderfully intelligent creatures, but we're just a tad on the slow side when compared to computers. Unfortunately, machines are still just that: machines. They struggle with ambiguity that even a kindergarten student could handle—not to mention misspellings, regional dialects, and punctuation. For search engines to bring back great results, they have to combine the best of both worlds: the speed of the machines and the intelligence of the human mind.

What's a search engine developer to do? Two things: First, combine results from several sources, as discussed earlier. This allows the search engines to intertwine the massiveness of the machine-driven system (robot results) with the finesse of the human touch (vertical and paid results). Second, structure the ranking algorithms to integrate votes from human beings. Putting the human touch into a ranking algorithm can be done in a variety of ways, and search engines continue to experiment with solutions. Counting inbound links from other websites, for example, is a way of measuring how many votes a site has from human—and presumably intelligent—webmasters and bloggers. Other ideas have included measuring how many search engine users click through to your site and how long they stay. *Personalized search,* in which your click behavior influences future ranks, and *social search,* in which search results are biased based on your contact list, are forms of artificial intelligence intended to improve the search experience.

But artificial intelligence still has a long way to go. In movies, you can say to a computer, "Computer, rotate and enhance!" and the computer will somehow manage to turn and unblur a grainy image from a security camera just the way you need it. In the real world, we just aren't there yet. Search engines remain literal creatures, unable to improvise very far beyond the exact words, even the exact syntax of the words they are given. Which leads us to our next Eternal Truth.

Text Matters

You probably *can* etch this one in stone:

Pearl of Wisdom: Text is Eternally Important in search.

The entire process of a web search is text based, even when the item being sought isn't text at all, like a picture or video file. The search engines care about how much text you have on your site, how it's formatted, and, of course, what it says. In Parts II and III, we will walk you through the process of keyword selection and placement. Here are some Eternal Truths of text.

Keyword Selection Is Key

Careful keyword selection is the heart of the SEO campaign. Site owners who are on top of their SEO game often have a list of top-priority keywords that they use on their site, with reasonable repetition, in strategic places. We never let a site go for six months without checking the keywords to make sure they're still appropriate. If a site's focus or positioning changes, new keywords are in order. If a company adds new products or services, new keywords are in order. If a new competitor comes on the scene, it's worth peeking into its site for new keyword ideas. Even if none of these changes takes place, regular keyword analysis is in order because search behavior and trends may change as well.

SEM: An Hour a Day?

When we were thinking about possible titles for this book, we had to take a bit of our own advice: Look into the minds of your users. Most of our potential readers would use the term search engine optimization (SEO) to describe what we do, so we stuck with it for our title. But our industry isn't crazy about the term SEO. Many in our industry prefer to give the service more all-inclusive labels such as search marketing, SEO/SEM, audience development, or even competitive webmastering.

What's wrong with calling it SEO? The term *optimization* only accounts for editing the code and content of your website, which is just one segment of the many tasks included in this book. Other components of search marketing, such as link building, paid advertising, and social media outreach, don't readily fall under the banner of optimization.

To add to the mix, many people use the terms SEO and organic SEO interchangeably to refer to all nonpaid efforts. This would include edits to your website, as well as work involved with increasing your inbound links and usability. The complement to organic search is paid search, commonly called SEM. Confused yet? We'll sum it up for you:

- The total package is usually called search marketing, SEO, or SEO/SEM.
- Nonpaid search is usually called organic or natural SEO, or just SEO.
- Paid search is usually called SEM.

Are there exceptions to the rule? Sure there are. Paying a onetime fee for a directory submittal would fall under organic SEO. As long as your listing is going to display in search results that are not labeled "Sponsored Listing," you can probably call the work organic.

With all this potential for confusion, we're keeping it simple. In this book, it's SEO for everything.

Your Site Has Many Keyword Placement Opportunities

The code that makes up your web page's text falls into two categories—visible and invisible—and they are both important for optimization. The *visible text* is made up of the words that you put on your page for the world to see, including obvious things like the paragraphs of carefully crafted content aimed at your target audience, but also less-obvious elements like your HTML page title, the text inside your links, and the navigational text that tells your visitors how to use your site, such as "Click the thumbnails for a full-size image." *Invisible text* refers to the words that do not display on the page but are added to your HTML code and gathered and analyzed by the search engine robots. This includes your *meta description tag* and your *image ALT tags*.

Your Site's Message

We can't say it enough: Your site's text needs to be compelling, clear, focused, and directed to your users. It also needs to be formatted so that the robots can read it. This means HTML text, not *graphical text*, which the search engines can't read. If a lot of the text on your site is displayed in graphics rather than HTML text, switching to robot-readable text is critical to getting the search engines to give your site the visibility you desire.

Take a look at this page full of text:

Unfortunately, almost all the text on the page is composed of GIF files, not HTML. So to the search engines, it looks like this:

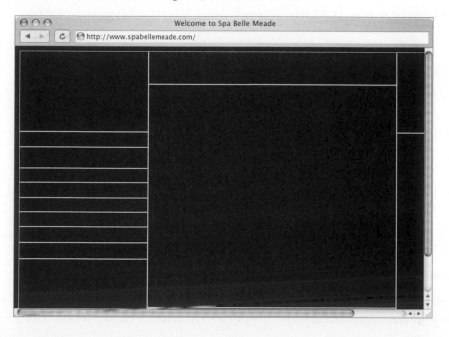

HTML Page Title

Most SEO pros agree that the HTML page title is the most important place on your page to include keywords. In the code, the HTML title looks like this:

```
<title>Dave's Custom Bikes, Santa Cruz, California - Electric Bikes</title>
```

On the page, it looks like this:

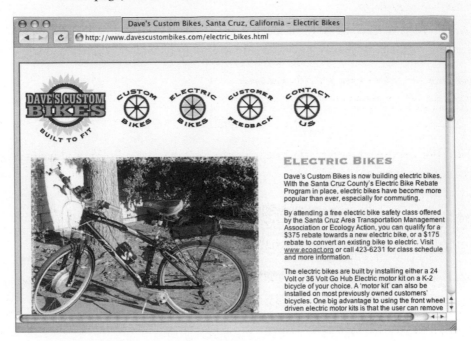

And in the search engines, it gets top billing, usually as the bolded first line of a search results page, like this:

The page title is Eternally Important because it gets maximum exposure in the search engine results pages and is an important part of the search ranking algorithm.

If you care about getting clicks to your site, this text should be succinct and compelling, and for your best chance at conversions, it should accurately summarize the page content. Keywords in the HTML title won't do you much good in rankings if they aren't also present in the text on the page, so be sure these two elements work as a team. We'll visit the specifics of writing great HTML page titles and meta descriptions in Part III.

Meta Description Tag

The meta description tag is an example of invisible text.

In the code, it looks like this:

```
<Meta name="description" content="Bobux baby shoes are the original soft soled shoes with the elastomatic ankle system that makes them easy to slip on and they stay on.">
```

And in the search engines, it can be displayed as the description under the page title. Notice how the searched-for keywords are bolded in the search engine results:

Bobux **Baby Shoes** Online **Baby Shoes** Soft Soled **Baby Shoes** Leather...
Bobux **baby shoes** are the original soft soled **shoes** with the elastomatic ankle system that makes them easy to slip on and they stay on.
⊗ | www.bobuxusa.com/ | Cached | Save

Much of the time, however, the meta description tag is passed over, and instead, a snippet of the page is displayed:

Bobux Baby Shoes Online Baby Shoes Soft Soled Baby Shoes **Leather...**
New Styles. Animals. Bows & **Mary Janes**. Flowers. Summer/Sandals. Classics ... Bobux® baby shoes are made from **Eco-leather**, a natural **leather**...
⊗ | www.bobuxusa.com/ | Cached | Save

You can't control when or where your meta description tag will display, but like your page title, it should be compelling, keyword rich, and unique for every page.

Meta Keywords Tag

The meta keywords tag, another invisible text element, is the place where site owners can list their keywords, including variations of keywords such as misspellings, that wouldn't be appropriate for the visible text elements.

In the code, it looks like this:

```
<meta name="keywords" content="movies, films, movie database, actors, actresses, directors, hollywood, stars, quotes">
```

We're shouting it from the mountaintop:

Pearl of Wisdom: The meta keyword tag carries little or no weight in search engine rankings.

When good SEOs talk about including keywords on your page, they're *not* talking about the meta keywords tag. Don't feel bad if this is news to you—if our reader mailbag and speaking engagements are any indication, lots of people are still holding onto the misconception that the meta keywords tag is important for SEO. It's not; now go out and tell someone you love.

You have plenty of work to do for your site, and organizing target keywords is one of the most important. But plopping keywords into your meta keywords tag—especially if the terms don't exist elsewhere on the page—is like putting lipstick on a pig. It won't make it any more kissable. Save your precious time for work that you *know* will help you gain search engine success.

How Other Sites Are Linking to Yours

As we discussed earlier, search engines need human help in their Eternal Quest for that perfect ranking algorithm. They look for links to your website, not only to follow those links and find your site, but also to determine more information about your site. Does someone else link to your website using the words *Click Here to Find Very Fancy Foxhounds*? That's giving the search engine a clue that your website just might have something to do with foxhounds. And the search engine may go even further, looking at other words surrounding the link for more clues. If the linking page also contains the words *fleas*, *fur*, and *Finding a Breeder*, it's reinforcing the notion that your website will be a good destination for that foxhound-seeking searcher.

It's Not Just about Rank

While your ranks are the easiest aspect of SEO to grasp, don't let them be the only thing you care about. We don't mean to be dismissive of people who really, truly live and die by their Google rank. We know that there are industries that are so cutthroat and specialized that this *is* the only thing that matters. But we have found this to be true:

 Pearl of Wisdom: The vast majority of businesses do best when they use a holistic approach to SEO, combining elements of organic and paid search with a healthy dose of good writing, usability, and social media outreach.

Remember, good ranks do not guarantee conversions or website success! As you learned in Chapter 1, "Clarify Your Goals," your business goals for your website may range from online sales to political persuasion—whatever it is you want your visitors to do. Your keywords must be chosen to directly match these goals. You could easily gain some high ranks for, say, the term *hydroplaning monkey*, because nobody else is optimizing for it. Of course, nobody's searching for it either. Likewise, if you make some iffy choices regarding your top-priority keywords, it's possible that you'll track top-10 ranks, month after month, and have no conversions to show for it.

Ranks Change

Let's say you are lucky enough to be getting good organic ranks for a coveted, competitive term. Congrats, but don't take these ranks for granted; any number of factors outside of your control could send your site on a nosedive:

Competitor Activity Sometimes, SEO success is achieved not by brilliant optimization, but rather as a result of the laziness of a site's competitors. If yours is the only site in your niche giving SEO any effort, you're going to come out on top. But you never know when your competitors are going to get their act together and start a successful SEO campaign.

Common SEO Misconceptions

If you're brand-new to SEO, you may have a couple of incorrect notions in your head. Let's get rid of those right now:

"Our site gets a ton of traffic! We're so popular, we're a shoo-in for top ranks!" Search engines don't have insider information about your overall web traffic, so they don't know exactly how popular your site is. But they can count up how many sites they find that link to your site, and this is one factor in how they judge your site's popularity.

"We've got to get more sites to link to us so that our ranks will improve!" If the only reason you set out to get more links is so that Google will rank you higher, you are missing the big picture. Inbound links are pathways that allow people to visit your site. They can be excellent, direct sources of targeted traffic!

"Our site is doing great! We ranked #1!" Ranked #1 for what? Starting now, erase "We ranked #1" from your vocabulary and replace it with "We ranked #1 for the term _____." Ranks are irrelevant unless they are tied to a meaningful target keyword.

"If we're not careful, we could get banned from search engines." It's unlikely that you'd get penalized for spamming the search engines if you're not doing it on purpose. (Follow the advice in this book, and that *definitely* won't happen.)

"We've filled in our meta keywords tag… we're good to go!" The meta keywords tag carries little to no influence with the search engines, and it's certainly not going to do anything for your ranks if the rest of your site isn't shipshape. Just like any element of SEO, the meta tags work best in the context of a holistic approach.

Your Server Performance The search engine robots visit your site on a reasonably frequent basis to make sure they've got the most up-to-date content to offer searchers. But what if a robot happens to visit your site while it's out of commission? Portions of your site may drop from the search results temporarily, until the robot comes back and rediscovers them.

We're talking billions of pieces of data from millions of sites. There's no way the search engines could keep it all in one database. This means that, at any given time, searchers are looking at one of a number of search engine databases, each giving out slightly different search results. Expect that your ranks are going to hop around a bit on a daily basis. Try not to sweat these little dips or put too much stock in the little jumps.

Algorithm Changes As we mentioned earlier, you never know when an existing search engine algorithm is going to morph into something different. A great many people chase the search engine updates and lose sleep over the next little tweak in Google's algorithm—so many, in fact, that a phrase was coined to describe them: *algoholics*. We urge you not to become one of them.

A Holistic Approach Helps

All of the rank-busters we just listed underscore the need to fill out your SEO campaign to tide you over with targeted traffic should your high ranks desert you. As the investment bankers will tell you: diversify, diversify, diversify. These aspects of the SEO campaign that you'll develop in Part III will help you weather ranking fluctuations:

Buzz Generation This means getting sites to link to you out of admiration (Donutopia makes great donuts!), commendation (Donutopia's Donut News wins "Bakery News Site of the Year."), or reciprocity (Please support our friend, Donutopia.).

Niche Directories The big search engines are not the only paths to your site. There are niche directories (also called verticals) for aficionados of everything from animal husbandry to Zen Buddhism. A small but fervently targeted audience is not to be ignored.

A Paid Search Campaign Sponsored listings can be a very effective way to get those targeted visitors to your site, especially if something is preventing you from breaking through the competition for organic rankings.

Good Writing and Usability Quality material on your site will always be there for you when the winds of algorithm fate shift again.

Social Strategies Write a killer blog, reach out on Twitter with the right message, participate in the conversation when your product or company is being discussed—make time to join in. A well-rounded online presence requires that you keep your image well-groomed on the Social Web.

Remember that Your SEO Plan should focus on conversions, not just search engine ranks! If you're doing well with the SEO elements listed here, you may discover that a dip in ranking won't affect your conversions in any disastrous way.

Search Engines Don't Like Tricks

The search engines are aware of the many sneaky ways that site owners try to achieve undeserved ranks (in SEO lingo, these underhanded activities are called *spamming*). If they discover that your site is spamming, even if you're not doing it on purpose, your site may be penalized: Your rank may be downgraded, or your page—or even your whole site—could be banned. Even if your site is never caught and punished, it's very likely, we dare say inevitable, that your tricky technique will eventually stop working. Here are some practices that have been on the search engines' no-no list for so long that they can safely be labeled as "Eternally Bad for Your Site":

Cloaking When a search engine robot visits your site, it expects to see the same content that any normal human visitor would see. *Cloaking* is a method of identifying robots when they visit your site and showing them pages that contain substantially different content from what human visitors see. This thwarts the search engines in their attempt to deliver the most accurate search results to their users. In the vast universe of website technology, there are sometimes valid reasons for showing different content to different entities. Tricking the search engines to give you higher ranks than you deserve is not one of them.

Duplicate Content Are you the kind of person who thinks, "If one aspirin works, why not take two?" If so, you might be thinking that if one paragraph of keyword-rich text will help your ranks, why not put it on every page in your site? Or worse, if one website brings you sales, why not make a bunch of identical websites with different names and get even more sales? The problem with this kind of thinking is that it ignores the headache it causes for searchers. If the search engines listed identical content multiple times, it would destroy the diversity of the search engine results, which would destroy their usefulness to the searcher. If search engines notice a lot of duplicate content on your site, they may remove a portion of your site's pages from their index, and they may not visit your site as frequently.

Machine-Generated Text We've all seen pages that vaguely resemble the English language but are actually a computer-generated cacophony that reads a bit like a surrealist's bad dream. And the reason we've seen these pages is because they sometimes rank in search engine results. But you can be sure that domains containing content like this don't stick around in the ranks for long. The search engines are constantly tracking them down and weeding them out. If you care at all about the long-term success of your website, steer clear of autogenerated text.

Keyword Stuffing Adding a keyword list to the visible text on your page is not exactly scintillating copy. We're not talking about overly optimized text, which may come off as pointless and dry. We're talking about repeating the same word or words over and over again so that your page looks like an industry-specific grocery list. At best, sites that do this cause eyestrain for their visitors. At worst, they're risking penalties from the search engines.

Invisible Text When we mentioned invisible text previously in this chapter, we meant specific elements that are included within specific parameters in your site's code and recognized by the search engines to be legitimate. We did *not* mean making a ton of keywords invisible by making them the same color as the background. The search engines caught on to this one a long time ago, and they're not likely to let you get away with it.

Participating in Link Schemes Have you been tempted to buy into a service that promises you a plethora of high-quality links for just a few hundred bucks? Don't! While you may not be avid readers of the search engines' quality guidelines or webmaster blogs, we are, and they've been saying it clearly for years: Participation in pay-for-links schemes will not help your site's ranks and may even be harmful to your ranks if detected by the search engines.

SEO Is Not Brain Surgery

So many people feel intimidated when approaching SEO. They think it's ultratechnical or it requires a huge budget. Many people think SEO requires some sort of degree or a lot of insider knowledge. But SEO doesn't take any of that.

The only thing that is necessary for SEO is the willingness to learn. So here is our most special gift to you, an SEO mantra that you can adopt as your own:

I wonder why *that's* happening.

SEO: Art or Science?

It's an oft-repeated cliché: SEO is one part art and one part science. The Left Brain and Right Brain delve a little deeper into two Eternal Truths:

The Left Brain says, "SEO is a Science! I originally learned SEO by using an experimental approach: trying different strategies and observing how successful they were. There's nothing fancy or difficult about science. It just means asking questions and seeking answers: Will adding keywords to my H1 tag help my rankings? Which of these two landing pages will bring more conversions?

"A paid search campaign provides a good opportunity for testing hypotheses because this kind of advertising gives you a great deal of control over your listings and your landing pages. And most important, paid search has a quick turnaround, so you won't have to wait months for the results of your experiments. So give it a try (we'll help you do this in Part III)! Compare results for two ads with slightly different phrasing. Or build a landing page just for testing purposes and see what happens when you link to it directly from your home page. Or make the "buy now" button bright orange. Science is fun—hey, don't look so surprised!"

The Right Brain says, "SEO is an Art! SEO can never truly be a science because you'll never be working in a vacuum. Your competition pulls a surprise move, the algorithm throws you a curveball... you can't control for these factors. Sure, your tests are fun, and they can even give you a lot of helpful insight. But anyone doing SEO needs to be comfortable working in an environment that is often more guesswork than empirical proof. Isn't it better to focus on the art of SEO—well-crafted text, a thoughtful, user-friendly site design, and personal connections? In its purest form, SEO is the art of persuasion!"

This is the approach that got us to where we are today; it helped us gain our SEO knowledge, and it keeps the clients coming. This is how we attacked almost every SEO question or problem before SEO was a big industry with hundreds of books, e-books, and websites devoted to it. And more often than not, this is how we still approach things. It can work for you, too!

It goes something like this: You say to yourself, "All of the pages on my site have the same HTML title, and I know that Google always displays an HTML title as the first line in a listing. So why are my Google listings displaying different titles?" Then you spend a few minutes searching for that text on your site. "*Aha*," you say, "Google is lifting linking text from my site and using that text as the first line in my search engine results!" Now you've learned two things: one, that Google can generate its own unique listing title if your page titles are not unique, and two, that you'd better get to work on writing your own unique HTML titles instead of leaving important decisions to a bot.

Or you say to yourself, "I wonder why my competitor has such good placement in that shopping directory." Then you click around until you find the "advertise with us" link on the shopping directory, figure out if that placement is a service they offer, and determine whether you want one, too.

Developing a healthy curiosity about how the search engines work, and an itch to solve interesting puzzles, is key to do-it-yourself SEO. It's a poor man's or woman's marketing study, and it's the best way to find your own path toward getting more targeted traffic.

Now that you understand the longer-lasting aspects of SEO, it should be a lot easier to make sense of the *right now* qualities, which are described in the next chapter.

How the Search Engines Work Right Now

What's the inside buzz among SEO experts? What do the search engines care about? What works? What doesn't? In this chapter, we present a current snapshot, including some of the more ephemeral facts of SEO: which search engines dominate the industry and how they work today.

Chapter Contents

In Pursuit of Right Now

We admit it: We were shaking in our stiletto heels just thinking about writing this chapter. The *Right Now* of search engines? Committed in ink, on old-fashioned paper? Give us a break. Everybody knows the Right Now of SEO changes every five minutes and you'd do much better finding this stuff on the Web.

Just kidding. We wear sensible shoes. Oh, and there are lots of reasons for you to hang onto every word of this chapter.

First off, researching SEO and social media on the Web is a difficult way to learn new concepts and get the basics. If you set out to discover the Right Now of SEO for yourself, you're likely to run into a mishmash of organic, paid, and social strategies spanning beginner and technically advanced concepts. You'll find conflicting advice, forums running rampant with rumors, and blogs that range from excellent to abysmal. And not all SEO advice on the Web is correctly date-stamped, so you may not know whether you're reading current advice or yesterday's news.

So, instead of trying to jump into your own frustrating pursuit of the Right Now, read our rundown of the current search landscape. Later, in Chapter 9, "Month Three: It's a Way of Life," you'll learn how to keep your knowledge up-to-date using our favorite trusted sources of information.

Now let's get down to the details.

Google Basics

Simply stated, Google is the standout leader in search today. It has the most traffic by far, and it's the only search engine with its own entry in the dictionary. Far removed from its previous existence as a search-only entity, Google now offers email, maps, feed readers, a calendar, online document sharing, web analytics, and webmaster tools, plus a diverse menu of vertical search options, including news, real-time updates, video, image, blog, product, and local. The Google app for smartphones offers Mobile Web search with location-aware enhancements. See Table 4.1 for handy Google facts for SEO.

▶ **Table 4.1** Google basics

URL	www.google.com
Percent of US desktop search usage	65.1% (Source: Nielson, Sept. 2010)
Percent of mobile search usage	98% (Source: StatCounter/Pingdom, July 2010)
Primary results	Robot crawler: standard and mobile
Major blended listing sources	Shopping results from Google Product feeds, Local results from Google Places (Google Maps), Google Images, Google Video, music from iLike and Lala
Ways to submit your site	XML Sitemap (free, good for large or dynamic sites), shopping and video feeds, or wait for the robot to find you

URL	www.google.com
Pay-per-click services	Google AdWords
In five words or less	Still the one to beat
Keep an eye on	Google Instant, Near Me Now (a Mobile Web enhancement)

Google has been an all-out trendsetter in the evolution of the search space. Link popularity? Google made it hugely important. Integration of vertical search results within standard results? Thank Google. For years, the world of search has been playing Follow the Leader, with Google at the head of the line. But if you listen to industry chatter, you'll sense that a change is in the air: With increasing traffic moving onto the Social Web and newly strengthened search competition, Google feels Facebook, Twitter, mobile apps, and Bing nipping at its heels.

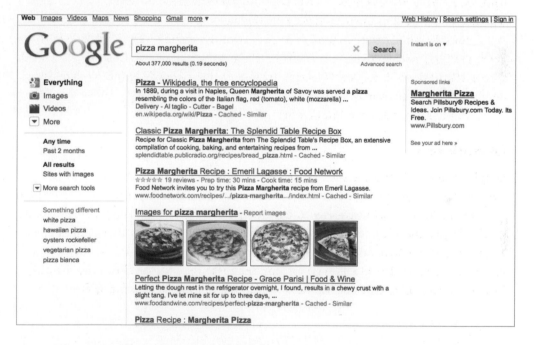

The current hot topics around Google are its adventures in speed: From Google Instant, a feature that causes search results to change as a query is typed (before a searcher hits the search button), to real-time search results, to voice-activated mobile search, the big G is in a hurry. Overcaffeinated, anyone? Staying on top of the long, and ever-lengthening, list of services Google offers can be overwhelming for a website owner. But you don't need to, as long as you focus on the search behaviors of your target audience. Most people are still using Google at its most basic level, typing a phrase in the search box and seeing what results come up.

Google's current relationship with SEO pros and webmasters has its points of light along with some black holes. SEO practitioners appreciate the monitoring and management options available through the webmaster tools service and outreach by corporate representatives via blogs, forums, and conferences, but many SEO experts kvetch about Google becoming too powerful. One topic that currently brings out the bristle is Google's seeming takeover of above-the-fold real estate in search results. Between paid advertising and OneBox features, which often link to more Google pages, the search engine doesn't leave as much space as it used to for non-Google properties in the standard organic results.

Speaking of Google properties, more searches are performed on Google-owned YouTube than on Yahoo! or Bing (source: ComScore, June 2010). Some point to this data and label YouTube as the second most popular search engine today.

PageRank, ShmageRank

Google's PageRank is a measurement of a page's worth based on the quantity and quality of both incoming and outgoing links. The concept behind PageRank is that each link to a page constitutes a vote, and Google has a sophisticated and automated way of tallying these votes, which includes looking at a vast universe of interlinking pages. Google awards PageRank on a scale of 0 to 10; a PageRank value of 10 is the most desirable and extremely rare. Like the Richter scale, the PageRank scale is not linear, so the difference between 4 and 5 is much greater than the difference between 3 and 4.

More often than not, pages with high PageRank have higher Google rankings than pages with low PageRank. And therein lies the link obsession. Throughout the SEO community, the scrambling for, trading, and even selling of links became such a focus over the past several years that Google modified its system and began to devalue certain kinds of links. It's widely accepted, for example, that links from content-deficient "link farm" websites do not improve a page's PageRank, and getting a link from a page with high PageRank but irrelevant content (say, a popular comic book site that links to a forklift specifications page) probably won't help your ranks much for terms you care about. Google now displays updated PageRank values at infrequent intervals to discourage constant monitoring.

Keep a holistic head on your shoulders and remember these points:

- Google's ranking algorithm is not based entirely on inbound links.
- A high PageRank does not guarantee a high Google rank.
- A PageRank value as viewed today in the Google toolbar or other browser plug-in may be months old.

PageRank is still a fairly good indication of how Google regards your website's pages, and you'll learn how to gather your own measurements in Your SEO Plan. But in the Right Now of SEO, think of PageRank as a hobby, not a religion.

Even as you gobble up the free tools, services, and advice from Google, remember that there's no such thing as a free lunch. Google is a for-profit company, and an incredibly powerful one at that. Google will look after Google and, in doing so, may make policy changes that can create seismic shifts in website owners' lives. It's always best to create your site for your *users*, not for what you think will cause Google to rank you higher this week.

Bing Basics

In case you didn't know, Bing is a property of a quaint little organization known as Microsoft Corporation. After many years of flailing around under the names MSN and Live Search, Bing launched amid great fanfare in 2009. Microsoft had been courting Yahoo! for years, and one massive alliance later, Bing's organic search results quietly replaced Yahoo!'s organic search results in mid-2010. Yahoo!'s paid search advertisers were transitioned to Microsoft's search advertising platform, called adCenter, in late 2010.

With its alliance with Yahoo!, Bing is estimated to have increased its share to approximately 30 percent of the search market. Few people are looking at Bing as a Google-killer, but there is no question that Bing now demands the attention of site owners and SEO pros. Even Google loyalists have to agree that Bing exceeds industry expectations. More traffic for Bing translates to more user data for Bing's engineers and product developers, which means that Bing is expected to make rapid improvements to its search offerings over the next few years. SEO pros are eagerly awaiting new organic and paid search opportunities. Check out the Bing facts in Table 4.2.

URL	www.bing.com
Percent of desktop search traffic	13.9% on its own, 27.0% including Yahoo! (Source: Nielson, September 2010)
Percent of mobile search usage	Less than 1% (Source: StatCounter/Pingdom, July 2010)
Primary results	Robot crawler: standard and mobile
Major blended listing sources	Bing local listing center, Bing shopping, music from Zune
Ways to submit your site	Submit URLs in webmaster tools, XML Sitemap, shopping and video feeds, or wait for the robot to find you
Pay-per-click services	Microsoft adCenter
In five words or less	Deep pockets, big dreams
Keep an eye on	Facebook integration, hyperlocal search

Bing has excelled in image and video search, and has succeeded in creating a more visually rich presentation than Google, without sacrificing usability. Its vertical search offerings were particularly strong in its first year, with Automotive, Shopping, Health, and Travel seeing double-digit growth in usage (source: Hitwise, September 2010).

"Hundreds of Search Engines?"

You may have received emails telling you about the "hundreds" of search engines to which some company will submit your site, or the "thousands" or search engines where your site needs a better rank. Most of these thousands of search engines are actually local variations (for example, Google .fr or Google.co.uk), or they are meta search engines that derive their results from major search engines (for example, Mamma.com and Dogpile). The number of independent search engines is much smaller, and the true independents have a tiny portion of the overall search market share. In this book, we'll focus on the major search engines that make up the vast majority—around 95 percent—of the search market share. If you know your target audience is using a smaller search engine such as Ask, Wolfram|Alpha, or ChaCha, we applaud you in putting more efforts toward it!

Yahoo! Basics

Yahoo! (yes, the exclamation point is part of its name—a bane to copy editors everywhere) is one of the oldest and still one of the best-known search engines. Already an established directory when Google was still in diapers, Yahoo! has now settled into the #2 spot (the #3 spot if you count Google-owned YouTube). Yahoo! is still a popular content provider and search engine, and it may be a significant referrer of visitors to your site. However, all of Yahoo!'s organic search results are powered by Bing, which makes it a low priority for SEO attention. Table 4.3 shows you handy Yahoo! facts for SEO.

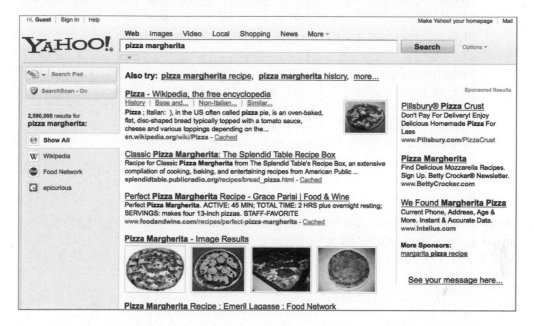

▶ **Table 4.3** Yahoo! basics

URL	www.yahoo.com
Percent of desktop search traffic	13.1% (Source: Nielson, September 2010)
Percent of mobile search usage	Less than 1% (Source: StatCounter/Pingdom, July 2010)
Primary results	Bing
Ways to submit your site	submittal to Bing (see Table 4.2)
Pay-per-click services	controlled by Microsoft adCenter
In five words or less	Powered by Bing
Keep an eye on	User interface innovations; a richer multimedia experience

Despite Bing's control of Yahoo's organic search results, there are some areas where Yahoo! continues to display independently sourced results as of this writing. Most notably, Yahoo! Local results are still derived from Yahoo!'s own index. It's impossible to know whether this will remain true in the future. You won't hear much more about Yahoo! in these pages, because the last thing we want is to make more work for you than necessary, but we will instruct you to think about Yahoo! when the occasional optimization opportunity presents itself.

SEO Is Dead

When we began working on the first edition of this book, we met for coffee and questioned whether SEO would be around in three years. Over the years this apocalyptic sentiment has been echoed among SEO pundits, many who cite the following reasons:

- As search engine algorithms have improved, ranks are becoming harder to manipulate, so there's no need for SEO.

- Barriers to robot crawling are starting to fall away. Once search engines can run JavaScript and index Flash, they'll be doing most of the SEO's job.

- The search engines are handing out Sitemap submittal tools and insider information that negates the need for SEO.

- Who needs a search engine? The Mobile Web will soon take over, and nobody will use search to navigate.

- Social media is becoming the dominant way that people discover websites, not search.

We agree with some elements of these arguments, but we don't think SEO is dead. And a close reading of most experts who say "SEO is dead" shows that they don't think so either (but it makes a catchy title!).

Here's why SEO isn't dead:

What the doomsayers call SEO is just rank-wrangling for standard organic web search results. What we call SEO is the methods laid out in this book: a holistic approach that starts with understanding your website goals, matches your site content and social outreach strategies to these goals, moves on to monitoring and improving your online performance through analytics and experimentation, and doesn't end until you retire your online presence. These aspects of online optimization—whether you call it SEO or give it a new name—will never die.

In the future, you can bet your Aunt Agatha that search engine robots will be able to leap tall buildings in a single bound, social search will be adopted by the masses, and the traditional search experience may even be abandoned entirely. But not yet. To be competitive, you still need to make sure that your website content is readable and reachable by search engines. And it's well documented that right now, the right SEO campaign will bring about substantial benefits for your site. As long as website owners have an interest in presenting the best possible site they can to the world, there will always be a need for SEO.

Organic Web Search Ranking Factors

You already know that search engines use complicated secret formulas, called ranking algorithms, to determine the order of their results. You even know from Chapter 3 that some of the most Eternally Important factors are your visible web page text and your HTML title tags. Now we're going to wrap what you already know into an organic optimization cheat sheet that you can peek at the next time someone asks you, "What do search engines care about, anyway?"

But first, a disclaimer: There are radically differing opinions within the SEO community about what works and what's important. The SEO profession is an upstart one, with no degrees to be earned or widely accepted canon of literature (and if there were, it'd change every five months anyway). So we're all trying to figure out this stuff on our own, using different test cases and chasing morphing search engines. We've distilled what we believe to be the best-of-the-best advice and present it here in a simplified form.

Here's the lowdown on the most important factors:

- Inbound links (quality and quantity)

- Inbound link anchor text

- Site authority

- HTML page title

- Visible HTML text on the page

- Age of domain

- Primacy (being the primary source/original publisher of content) and freshness (publishing new or updated content)

- Site speed

- Lesser factors

We'll get into how to optimize all of these factors in Part III. But for now, as you read through them, think about how much attention you've given to each of them on your own site. Maybe, like a lot of site owners, you've been focusing on the bottom of the list—the least important factors—more than the biggies at the top. As you think about what matters to the search engines, keep this in mind:

Pearl of Wisdom: Each page on your website is analyzed individually by the search engines.

That means each and every page is an opportunity to optimize for the following:

Inbound Links (Quality, Quantity, and Diversity) Coming in at the top in our list of search engine ranking factors is inbound links to your website. Why are inbound links so important in the search engine ranking algorithms? Because they can indicate a page's quality, popularity, or status on the Web and site owners have very little control over their own inbound links. (Being off-page factors, inbound links can be influenced only indirectly.) Links with the most rank-boosting power are links from a home page (as opposed to links from pages buried deep within the site), and links from *authority pages* in the *topical community*, meaning pages with their own collection of fabulous inbound links from other websites covering the same topic. The same quality factors hold true for links coming from within your site. Link diversity—having inbound links from a wide variety of sites—provides another signal to search engines that your site is genuinely worthy of high ranks.

Inbound Link Anchor Text We mentioned in Chapter 3 that the way other websites refer to your website provides clues that help search engines understand your content. *Anchor text*, also called linking text, is the text that is clickable when a web page links to another web page, and it is an important factor in search ranking algorithms. Anchor text that contains your page's targeted keywords can help boost your page's ranks. Combining this keyword-rich anchor text with relevant text surrounding the link can amplify this good effect.

Site Authority Site authority is a blanket term meaning "how important the search engines think your site is." Many SEO wonks speculate that individual pages belonging to websites with higher authority will gain higher ranks, even if the individual page does not have high ranking factors. It's as if the search engines are thinking, "This page is from a good family—let's give it the benefit of the doubt." Authority can be general (Wikipedia is an example of a site with general authority), but it's more illustrative to think about authority in terms of a single topic. For example, www.sony.com has very high authority on the topic of home electronics, but it has low authority for topics like <paper dolls> or <mountaineering>. Several sitewide factors are combined to measure a domain's overall level of authority on a particular topic. This may include inbound links, age of the domain, and any of the other factors we have listed in this chapter.

HTML Page Title The HTML page title is an Eternally Important factor in search engine ranking algorithms. Unlike most of the link-related factors, it's relatively easy to optimize HTML titles because you have control over the content on your own site. As a bonus, optimizing your HTML page titles is one of those activities that will quickly affect the way your listings look in the search engines.

Visible HTML Text on the Page It seems obvious, but you would be surprised at how many site owners miss this simple point: In order to rank well for a particular set of keywords, your site text should contain them. True, there are examples of pages that rank well for words not actually appearing on the page, but this is not something you want to leave to chance.

You may see SEO articles insisting that you need a certain number of words on a page, and that a certain percentage of those words must be your target keywords (SEO folks call that percentage *keyword density*).

However, we believe that keyword density is an outdated concept. As long as you have robot-readable text on your page (a great first step that many of your competitors, believe it or not, may have missed), you should use *as many keywords as you need to state your message clearly* and *as many opportunities to insert keywords as makes sense within the realm of quality writing.* Your marketing message is much too special to be put into a formula.

Primacy and Freshness of Content We know that Google News has methods of determining which news publisher is the primary source of a particular story (as a simple example, if www.nytimes.com publishes an article earlier than several similar articles, and those articles link back to the article on www.nytimes.com, Google News will probably deduce that www.nytimes.com is the primary source of that story). Some SEO pros believe that Google now applies this same consideration to pages in its organic index. Sites that republish other sites' content (including affiliate websites) may have a disadvantage compared to primary sources of the same information. Similarly, as Google makes continued advances into finding and displaying the freshest content on the Web, there is some agreement among folks in the SEO industry that new or frequently updated content is getting a bit more attention from the bot than static pages.

Site Speed No mysteries to unravel here: Google stated in its Webmaster Central blog that site performance is a factor in its ranking algorithm. In other words, the speed at which your site loads for an average user can affect your ranks. However, according to Google spokespeople, this factor is only at play in fewer than 1/100 of search queries, so (and we are quoting a distinguished Google engineer here) "Don't panic." If your site has everything else going for it but it loads significantly slower than the average site, you should look into improving site speed. If your site loads at an acceptable speed, you're probably safe focusing on other SEO factors.

Age of Domain Newer domains have a tougher time making their way up the ranks than older ones. The exact mechanism behind this may be the search engines' measuring the actual length of time that a website has been live, or it may be primarily indirect factors, such as the fact that inbound links tend to accumulate over time. On a positive note for folks with brand-new sites: We've seen plenty of examples of new sites that have performed well in search engines within a couple of months. Take this factor into consideration if you're purchasing a new domain or considering changing an old, established domain name (proceed with caution!). Otherwise, unless you're a spammer or a fly-by-night operation, this is a factor that you don't need to think about a whole lot.

Lesser Factors There are a large number of additional, lesser factors that can influence your rankings. Google, for example, probably includes hundreds of factors in its algorithm. Things like keywords in your page URL, image ALT tags, and meta tags all have some degree of influence, as do factors that may be harder for you to control, such as the click-through rate or bounce rate of a page (as measured by the search engine's own tallies) or how often it is updated. For a comprehensive list of ranking factors, including commentary from several knowledgeable SEO professionals, see this page: www.seomoz.org/articles/search-ranking-factors.php.

What's Most Important in SEO?

Starting in Chapter 6, "Your One-Month Prep: Keywords, Priorities, and Goals," this book will guide you through a soup-to-nuts SEO plan, covering the top organic ranking factors listed in this chapter and much more. Here, the Left Brain and Right Brain debate which single aspect of SEO is most important.

The Left Brain says, "Every site owner's top priority should be to have a site that the search engine robots can crawl, with no significant structural problems.

"Assuming crawling issues are squared away, I'd select inbound links as my top SEO priority. For years now, one of the most important ranking factors has been the number, diversity, and quality of links that point to your website. And it takes a lot of effort to do link building right! There are no shortcuts to making significant and long-lasting improvements to your site's inbound links. The best way to get those inbound links is to publish high-quality, unique, and engaging content, and help others find it."

The Right Brain says, "In today's search environment, you have to focus first on your conversion path, that is, making your site speak to your target audience and giving visitors a clear path to the sale. I've seen websites that focus on link building or adding keywords to the exclusion of all other activities, and, oh, the things they neglect! Things like poor website design that can destroy credibility and increase bounce rates. Things like confusing or nonexistent calls to action, or content that alienates site visitors by speaking to the wrong target audience. I wonder how many site owners are spending money on questionable link-building services or obsessing over text optimization, when they should be improving their sites' visitor experience instead? Especially considering all of the nonsearch options—mobile apps, for example—that can deliver traffic to a site, it's critically important to pay attention to usability, engagement, and targeted messaging that encourage visitors to convert."

Blended Search Ranking Factors

As you learned in Chapter 3, many search results are blended. Vertical search results such as local, shopping, image, video, real-time updates, and news have become increasingly prominent within standard search results.

Here's a slightly speculative rundown of top factors that may help your offerings to be indexed and ranked in several of the highest-priority verticals:

Local

- The business has a listing in the local index (Google Places, Yahoo! Local, or Bing Local Listings).

- The actual business address is in the location specified in the search query.

- The business has a local phone number for the searched location.

- The business website contains the local address and phone number in robot-readable format.

- The business has positive reviews on influential sites.

- The listing title contains keywords.

- The listing description contains keywords.

- Listing categories contain keywords.

- The business is listed in third-party data providers and Yellow Pages. (These listings are often referred to as *citations*.)

- Geo-tagged images on photo-upload services such as Panoramio are captioned or otherwise associated with the business name.

- The local listing has been claimed by the business owner and is filled out fully, including photos if applicable.

  For a nice rundown of local search ranking factors, see `davidmihm.com/local-search-ranking-factors.shtml`.

Shopping

- The website provides a shopping feed to the search engines.

- Product names, both in the feed and on the page, contain keywords.

- Product descriptions, both in the feed and on the page, contain keywords.

- The online store has good quality and quantity of merchant ratings on influential sites.

- The website has SEO authority by the same measures as the organic web search ranking factors we discussed previously.

Image

- Images are accessible to search engine robots.
- Image filenames contain keywords.
- Image captions and other text on the page contain keywords.
- The website has relatively strong SEO authority by the same measures as the organic web search ranking factors we discussed previously.

Video

- Videos are listed for search engines on an XML video Sitemap or MRSS feed.
- The video's title and description on the video Sitemap closely match the title and description on the page where the video resides.
- Separate videos are displayed on individual URLs.
- The page on which video is displayed is optimized for keywords.
- The website has relatively strong SEO authority by the same measures as the organic web search ranking factors we discussed previously.

Real Time

- Your content is published in the form of tweets, news, blog posts, or other social media posts.
- The post contains keywords.
- The post is recent.
- The post's author has a relatively large number of reputable followers.

News

- The website has been designated by the search engine as a news provider (this requires a formal submission and editorial review).
- The article is the primary source for a news story as measured by chronology and citations from other sources.
- The article is timely to current news events.
- The article originates from a publisher situated in the geographic location of a news story.
- Keywords are included in the title and text of the article.
- The website has relatively strong SEO authority by the same measures as the organic web search ranking factors we discussed previously.

You'll work through optimization for many of these search verticals in Chapter 8, "Month Two: Establish the Habit."

When the Pendulum Swings Too Far: From SEO to Spam

An unfortunate Eternal Truth of SEO is that right-now ranking factors become the subject of intense attention by SEO practitioners, and over time, these factors fall prey to manipulation and overuse. (The rise and fall of the keywords meta tag, influential once upon a time but now ignored in the ranking algorithm, illustrates this pattern perfectly.) SEO implementation ranges from solid strategies to naïve overuse to deliberate scamming. Nonsensical text, bait-and-switch search results, misleading links—these are some of the unpleasant outcomes when desperation for high rankings is combined with just a touch of SEO knowledge.

At SEO conferences, we've listened to Q&As with Matt Cutts, the head of Google's Webspam team, while all the SEO junkies in the room sat on the edge of their seats as he divulged small insights into Google's secret algorithm. Think about it: Here is a man whose primary job is to define *spam* as it relates to Google's algorithm, and he is so sought after that an announcement had to be made to allow him to use the bathroom in peace. What secrets is he guarding? The difference between overoptimization and spam. The difference between edging out your competitors in the ranks by using sharply hewn SEO tactics, and being penalized or dropped from the ranks for taking SEO too far.

Nobody enjoys having to chase a secret algorithm, but staying tight-lipped about many of the ranking factors and their relative importance is probably the best way for search engines to keep spam from getting out of hand.

Here are the current ways that SEO tactics are being turned into spam:

- Link spam is rampant, with unhelpful links being planted into nonsense copy, on sites that were built just for the purpose of housing these links. Some companies generate thousands of domains containing low-quality content and sell links from pages within these sites. Some companies generate barely respectable content networks for this purpose; other companies build jumbled nonsense blogs for link building.

- Sites are built on long domains with keywords separated by dashes (think www.best-toys-under-25-dollars-for-babies-toddlers-boys-and-girls.com) by merchants attempting to gain ranks with keyword placement instead of good content.

- In an effort to gain fresh, keyword-optimized text, some websites *scrape* (use a software program to find, copy, and republish) other people's copy, violating both copyright law and ethical guidelines.

Spam is not an effective long-term SEO solution. Whatever form the spam du jour takes, you can be sure that the search engines know about it (or will know about it soon) and will work to devalue the sites that are employing it. This is one reason top ranking factors continue to evolve to include characteristics—such as site speed and primacy of content—that can't be faked or manipulated, and that indicate high quality.

Paid Placement

Search ads make up a significant and effective venue for online advertisers, and they are the answer to the frequently asked question, "How does Google make money?" Most search ads in the United States are provided by the two major search advertising platforms, Google AdWords and Microsoft adCenter. In late 2010, search ads on Yahoo! were taken over by Microsoft adCenter.

The mobile search advertising market is growing rapidly, although it currently makes up less than 2 percent of the overall search advertising budget (source: RBC Capital Markets). Strong targeting capabilities and a higher response rate from mobile users than from those who view standard web search ads are in part fueling the growth of mobile search advertising. As you learned in Chapter 3, search advertising is generally an auction-based system, with advertisers jockeying for their listings' positions based on bid price. See Figure 4.1 for an example.

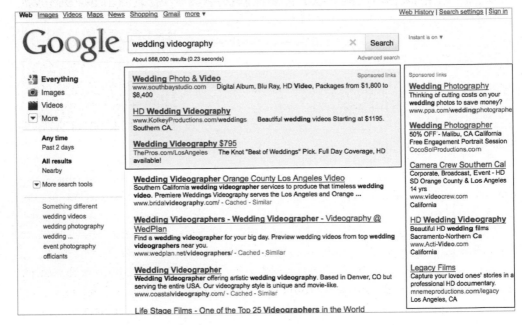

Figure 4.1 Pay-per-click advertising on Google

If you were looking to paid search as a way to skirt around the Eternally Hidden Algorithm, we're sorry to say there's one to puzzle over in paid search as well. In Google AdWords, for example, ranks are determined by a combination of advertiser bid price and an algorithmic measurement called a Quality Score. Google AdWords assigns rank based on several factors, including click-through rate, bid price, and relevance of the ad text to the landing page.

Google AdWords and Microsoft adCenter offer an opt-in feature that will display your listings on partner sites in addition to their own search engines. In this system, called *contextual advertising*, your listings are matched to the content of the page where they are displayed. See Figure 4.2 for an example. You can manage your contextual campaigns separately from your search-based ads.

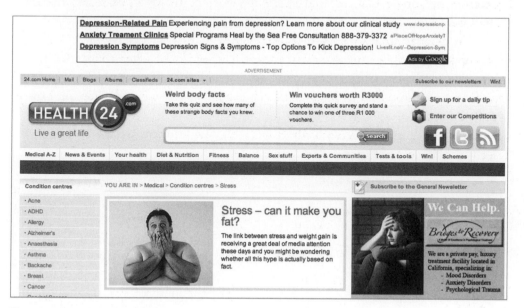

Figure 4.2 Contextual ads by Google

There are many variations on the theme of standard text ads. You can enhance your ads with location information and review stars. You can advertise using a cost-per-click or cost-per-thousand-impressions model. You can experiment with choosing sites for contextual ad placement or let the algorithm decide for you. And you can even select the time of day when your ads will run, down to 15-minute increments. In this book, we focus on standard pay-per-click text ads, because of their omnipresence in the search marketing industry, and because we think they are a reasonable place to jump in.

A quick rundown of the major paid search services appears in Table 4.4.

▶ **Table 4.4** Pay-per-click basics

	Google AdWords	Microsoft adCenter
URL	http://adwords.google.com	http://adcenter.microsoft.com
Name of pay-per-click product	AdWords	adCenter
Name of contextual placement product	AdSense	Content Ads

	Google AdWords	Microsoft adCenter
Major partnerships (sites where ads are shown)	`Google.com`, Gmail, Blogger, AOL `.com`, YouTube Mobile, and thousands of small sites. See `www.google.com/adwords/displaynetwork/find-your-audience/partner-sites.html` for a current list.	`yahoo.com`, `msn.com`, `CNBC.com`, `msnbc.com`, Verizon Wireless devices, and many more sites within Microsoft Advertising's Media Network. See `advertising.microsoft.com/learning-center/product-information/content-ads-network` for a current list.
Industry chatter	Google AdWords is allowing more granular control to advertisers in terms of targeting and display options. Google has announced reporting requirements for third-party AdWords managers: They must report account-level cost, clicks, and impressions to their clients.	At the dawn of its alliance with Yahoo!, which has significantly expanded adCenter's reach for advertisers, Microsoft is focusing on improvements to campaign management features. There's no consensus yet from the SEO industry as to whether an adCenter campaign is a must-have or just a nice add-on to a strategy with an existing Google AdWords campaign.

Paid search advertisers have a terrifically useful selection of tracking and reporting tools, as well as support available for free. With low minimum budget requirements and easy setup procedures, the barrier to entry for self-serve advertisers is low. A carefully managed paid search advertising campaign can bring in targeted traffic and conversions for just a few hundred dollars a month.

Paid search is unmatched in the power it gives you over your listing: what it says, who sees it, and when. We also love paid search as a tool for studying the searching public's response to your keyword choices. So in Chapter 8, with our guidance, you're going to set up a starter campaign and get to know the basics while you get yourself some targeted clicks.

Social and Mobile Web

If you want to be found on the Web, you'd better embrace this fact: The Social Web is redefining the way people find their online content. Apps, friend referrals, and Twitter hashtags are all popular alternatives to traditional search engine queries. There are roughly a billion social media users worldwide in 2010, and projected growth in mobile device usage is likely to add to social media's continued growth. We believe that SEO and social media marketing are sister activities, and to make sure you're doing due social diligence, we'll help you delve into your own social media strategy in Chapter 8.

Here are some ways that SEO, social media, and the Mobile Web intersect:

- YouTube, the popular video-sharing site, is owned by Google. YouTube videos often score primo placement in Google results. Besides the visibility in Google, YouTube is a large search engine in its own right: By the numbers, it's the #2 search engine, with 3.7 billion search queries per month—that's about a third as many as Google has (source: comScore, March 2010). Some people in the SEO and online video industries speculate that YouTube may one day begin indexing videos elsewhere on the Web. Search rankings within YouTube are determined using an entirely different set of criteria than those used by Google.

- With over 500 million members, Facebook regularly surpasses Google in its number of US daily users. Rather than the walled garden it once was, much of Facebook, notably Facebook Pages for businesses, is open to Google's crawler, and these pages can be prominently listed in Google. Web results for searches performed on Facebook are powered by Bing.

- Twitter statuses (*tweets*) are searchable on Google and display in Google's real-time search results. Twitter itself is estimated to handle nearly 20 billion searches per month. Granted, Twitter searches are mostly performed through automated programs and not consumer actions; nevertheless, that's a lot more monthly searches than Bing, and about one fifth as many as Google.

- Mobile search is currently estimated to account for approximately 10 percent of all Google queries.

- Use of location-aware applications such as Foursquare and Yelp is growing rapidly. Information about nearby businesses is incorporated into these applications as well as in search results on Google's and Bing's mobile search apps.

Today's online experiences are delightfully intermingled, taking place on the standard, Social, and Mobile Web. It's a wild ride, and after more than a decade in this industry, we can tell you with confidence: It isn't stopping any time soon. We suggest you enjoy the ride, because inside every new online experience may be a new opportunity for savvy online marketers like you.

SEO Trend Spotting

SEO trends move fast, so it's OK to jump in where you are! Use this primer to get clued in to some of the current jargon and trends in SEO.

Mobile Search With the widespread adoption of smartphones, mobile search is beginning to receive a lot of attention in the SEO community. Mobile usage is projected to increase in mind-boggling percentages, doubling in the four years from 2010 to 2014, with 2014 being the year it surpasses desktop usage. Google and Bing are working hard to place themselves in the middle of this growing search sector. Meanwhile, online marketers are feeling their way around this new medium, asking questions like: Will people stick with search apps on mobile devices, or will other methods of navigation take over? How is purchasing behavior different in mobile? What is the relevance of location-awareness to search?

Real-time Search Google sometimes displays recent posts from Twitter, Facebook, blogs, and news sources within its standard search results. The launch of these results, known as *real-time results* or *updates*, was a source of great excitement to the SEO industry, but the general population reacted with a collective shrug. Still, we've got our eyes on real-time results. A Google real-time homepage was launched at http://google.com/realtime in August 2010, offering new capabilities such as searching within a specific geographic location. And Bing has been integrating Twitter into its standard search results. Bing also offers a fantastically fun Twitter integration to see tweets on a local map—find it by clicking the small Map Apps icon on this page: http://bing.com/maps/explore.

HTML5 HTML5 is an improvement on the basic HTML code with which most web pages have been built for over a decade. The new code allows browsers to play video without Flash or any other video plug-in. HTML5 also improves the semantic markup that allows search engines to understand the meaning of the content on your page. For example, in HTML5 an element might be marked nav; search engines would understand that this indicates internal site navigation. Better markup means you have more opportunities to speak to search engines in a language they understand—something all SEO pros love to do!

Google Instant Launched in late 2010, Google Instant attempts to predict a search query as it is being typed and displays results to the user while he or she is typing. The effects on search behavior could be significant; for example, some in the SEO industry believe that Google Instant will reduce the number of searches for longer search queries. Google Instant results are based on the list of words contained in Google Suggest (the dropdown list of related words you see whenever you search), so one thing is certain: Site owners need to pay close attention to those Google Suggest terms because they are clues about the keywords that Google thinks are important, popular, or timely!

Twitter Search As we mentioned previously in this chapter, there are a large number of Twitter searches taking place each day. Twitter offers search capabilities within its native interface at http://twitter.com, and there are also myriad other ways to search Twitter, including tools such as TweetDeck, Seesmic, HootSuite, or Twhirl, search engines such as Twazzup and Topsy, and of course, real-time search on Google and Bing. Any website owner who is courting a Twitter-happy target audience would do well to get to know these tools. Start by searching your own company name and see what comes up.

Personalization, Geotargeting, and Hyperlocal Search Paid search advertisers have appreciated the beauties of geotargeting for years. After all, if you run a barber shop in Oshkosh, Wisconsin, there's no reason for you to run a paid search ad in Hoboken, New Jersey.

Recently, *personalized search* (which means search results that are biased based on a user's previous search behavior) and *localized search* (which means search results that are altered based on his or her geographic location) have made their way into major search engines. *Hyperlocal search* is the natural extension of this trend toward highly individualized search results. The concept of hyperlocal first made waves in the news industry, with news sources both large and small attempting to satisfy the public craving for neighborhood-level community updates. When it comes to hyperlocal search, Google and Bing are pedaling furiously to keep up on the Mobile Web with upstarts like Yelp, Foursquare, and AroundMe.

SEO and Social Media Slang

Just like any other topic with a big online following, SEO has its own colorful vocabulary. There are far too many terms to include here, but here's a sampling of what you might come across in your own SEO endeavors:

SERP Search engine results page, that is, the listings you see when you use a search engine.

Link Juice If you're one who likes to use the word "juice" to mean "power," then this is the expression for you. Link juice is a synonym for link equity or page authority, the accumulated measure of a web page's value in the eyes of the search engines based on the quality and quantity of its inbound links. As the expression implies, link juice is fluid and can flow between web pages via links.

Twitterati/Tweeps/Tweeple The Social Web is teeming with slang, Twitter probably most of all because its 140-character limit necessitates creative use of language. Twitterati, Tweeps, and Tweeple are names given to the vast collective of Twitter users.

Nofollow/Dofollow In standard HTML, the code that defines a link contains more than just the URL being linked to; it can also contain other attributes that describe the link. The nofollow attribute tells the search engines not to follow a link or grant any ranking benefits to the linked-to page. The nofollow attribute can be added to any link, but is most commonly seen on blog comments to prevent sleazy webmasters from gaining ranks via link comment spam. The SEO goal is to attain links without this tag, which are sometimes called dofollow links even though there is no such thing as a "dofollow" attribute.

Fail Whale The nickname for the adorable whale graphic that Twitter displays when its servers are overwhelmed.

Foursquare Mayor Did you ever want to be mayor of your corner store? Depending on your neighborhood, this might be more competitive than you think. "Mayor" is a term from Foursquare, a location-aware service used on mobile devices. Players get points for *checking in* at locations such as restaurants, airports, and schools, and the player with the most check-ins at a certain location becomes the mayor of that location.

Now that you've had your fill of background knowledge, join us in Part II, where you'll create an SEO strategy that will set you on the right track for Your SEO Plan.

Strategy

Before you can implement Your SEO Plan, you need to develop a workable strategy. In this part, you'll begin by getting your internal team on board and by identifying the various disciplines that are necessary for effective SEO. Next, you'll spend a month performing the brainstorming, research, and assessment to point you in the right direction for your ongoing campaign:

Get Your
Team on Board

5

*Search engine optimization is truly a team effort.
A great SEO campaign encompasses skills that
nearly always surpass those of any individual:
writing, marketing, research, programming, and,
yes, even a bit of math. In this chapter, we guide
you through the all-important task of getting your
team on board, from techies coding your website
edits to customer service reps tracking offline
sales.*

Chapter Contents

The Challenge of SEO Team Building

You're busy, and SEO isn't your only job, so we're pretty sure you won't be thrilled to hear this:

Pearl of Wisdom: SEO requires you to be proficient in several different areas.

Your SEO campaign will incorporate a wide variety of tasks: writing and editing, usability and site architecture, coding, ad copy creation, landing page optimization, research, web analytics, and interpersonal communication for link building and social media. If you're doing this all yourself, bravo! You're just the sort of multitasking do-it-yourselfer who thrives in SEO. If your entire company can't ride to lunch on the same motorcycle, we're putting you in charge of coordinating the SEO team. Either way, once you've read this book, you'll be the in-house SEO expert, so the responsibility for all these tasks ultimately falls on you.

Before you close this book forever and run for the antacid, let's clarify a bit. We're not saying that you have to be the one to code the website or set up the analytics software. We're saying you need to know enough to be able to speak intelligently to the people who do these tasks. And here's the hard part: you also need to convince them to spend some of their precious time working on Your SEO Plan.

Why is it, after all, that organizing an SEO team is so hard? We have observed four common reasons:

- SEO requires effort from multiple departments and a variety of skills, such as marketing, sales, IT, public relations (PR), and creative/editorial.
- SEO is a relatively new discipline and doesn't have established processes within the corporate system.
- Measuring return on investment (ROI) on SEO—especially the organic variety—is no cakewalk, and predicting ROI in advance is even harder.
- The SEO industry carries around a bit of a bad reputation—and some folks still think SEO is about tricking or spamming the search engines.

This chapter is here to guide you through the SEO crusade within your organization. There are some common patterns of resistance you might meet in each of the departments discussed here, and we'll share with you the most effective ways to counteract them.

As with any team-building effort, building your SEO team will be an exercise in communication:

Pearl of Wisdom: Educate your team about SEO, and you will be rewarded with their participation and enthusiasm.

But remember this: they're probably just as busy as you are, and that's why we advocate a pace-yourself approach. Don't overwhelm your team with information—just explain the SEO best practices that pertain to the task at hand.

"But I Don't Have One of Those!"

In this chapter, we discuss ways that you can approach various departments within your organization to get help on your SEO campaign. We are well aware that, due to size or focus, your organization may not include each of the separate departments described here. If this is the case with you, figure out what entity takes on these roles. Who closes the deals with customers? That's your sales department. Who manages your web hosting? That's the IT department. Who posts your social media updates? That's your PR department. Look to that entity—be it a small staff, an entire department, or a half-day intern—for the SEO help you need.

Even if you're planning to go it alone with your trusty hour-a-day book and a cup of coffee by your side, this chapter should offer some insight on approaching the work with the right hats on.

We have worked in many situations in which team participation was less than ideal for an SEO campaign, and we know how this can reduce the campaign's effectiveness. What happens when those carefully prepared page edits aren't implemented, keywords aren't incorporated into site rewrites, or a planned-for paid search budget never comes through?

Pearl of Wisdom: Without your team on board, SEO suffers.

Besides being frustrating for you, it can be a huge waste of time and money. What follows are some thoughts for keeping the enthusiasm going in all your departments.

Marketing, Sales, and Public Relations

Marketing, Sales, and Public Relations make up a corporate SEO trifecta. Get all three excited about your SEO campaign, and you'll have built your "brain trust" foundation for success. Here's some food for thought that should come in handy when you need to deal with these departments.

Marketing: VIPs of SEO

In most organizations, the marketing department serves as the hub of SEO operations. We're guessing you're a member of this department yourself. It's a natural progression: the marketing department may already be handling the website as well as *offline marketing*—such as print ads, television, radio, billboards—and *online marketing*—such as banner ads and direct emails.

The marketing team will likely be instrumental in SEO tasks like keyword brainstorming and research, writing text for descriptions and page titles, writing sponsored listings, managing paid search campaigns, and executing *linkbait* or *sharebait* campaigns.

The folks on the marketing team have, quite literally, the skills to pay the bills, and they probably don't need any convincing that SEO is a worthwhile effort. What they may need, however, is some organization and some focusing.

What does your marketing team know about the importance of robot-readable text, keyword placement, and paid search campaign management? Maybe a lot. Maybe nothing. Maybe they know something that was worthwhile a few years ago but is now outdated. Since you're in charge of the SEO team, it will help you to know what the general knowledge level is and then think of yourself as the onsite SEO educator.

We have found that marketing staffers are almost always open to a little education about how the search engines work, as long as the information is provided on a need-to-know basis. For example, whenever we brainstorm for keywords with a marketing manager, inevitably their list contains terms that are extremely vague ("quality") or so specific that nobody is searching for them ("geometric specifications of duckpin bowling balls"). When we trim down that list, we always explain the basic concept of *search popularity* vs. relevance. We deliver that message in a two-paragraph email—for you, it's an easy deskside chat.

But what if you're not working in such a receptive environment? Maybe you are the only one convinced of the positive powers of SEO. Perhaps, for reasons of budget or time, you don't have the buy-in you need to move forward. Perhaps other marketing programs are taking precedence, or the department can't seem to make the leap from offline to online marketing, or from online advertising to organic search efforts. If that's the case, it's time to convince the marketing manager of the importance of your SEO project!

Here's one way to approach it: focus on the needs of the marketing department. Go into therapy mode: "You seem a little stressed. How can SEO help?"

Here's how: SEO can provide the low-cost improvements that you might be craving when marketing budgets are tight. Or it may justify an overdue website revamp. It may provide an argument for dropping less-successful advertising venues. It can forge new alliances between Marketing and IT. On the warm and fuzzy side, it may provide an outlet for a creative soul who feels trapped in marketing-speak or a chatty digital native who would be delighted to spend a few minutes a day trolling Twitter for website mentions. And SEO can be telecommuting-friendly. Is there a new dad in the department who would love to spend a portion of his week working from home?

Once you've found some common ground and the enthusiasm is starting to grow, consider starting Your SEO Plan with a pilot project that you can focus your SEO efforts on together. Pick something close to the hearts of the marketing staff: a recent or upcoming launch, a section of your site devoted to a special event, a promotion, or a product line that's down in the dumps. Cherry-pick if you can! It's important that these early experiences be positive ones.

What If You're at the Bottom of the Pecking Order?

If you're on the bottom of the food chain in your organization, you may be either ignored or micromanaged by the people you answer to. Here are some tips that might work for you no matter what department you're dealing with:

- Create regular reports, even if nobody's looking at them. As consultants, we have often asked ourselves, What's the point of documenting everything if nobody reads our reports? But it always comes down to this: we need them for our own reference. After several months, stats begin to blur together—don't expect to keep this stuff in your head.

What If You're at the Bottom of the Pecking Order? *(Continued)*

- Don't report too often. We recommend waiting at least a month between reports, even if you are initially asked for more frequent data. There are rare exceptions to this rule, such as short-lived promotions or unusually volatile paid search campaigns. But for almost everything else, it is helpful to set expectations that SEO is about long-term trends, not daily numbers.

- Deliver meaningful analysis. When you email your boss a spreadsheet detailing your ranks for the last six months, you're delivering raw data. Trust us, *nobody* wants to look at your raw data. You can turn that into meaningful information when you summarize it in your email: "Dear Boss: This month, traffic to three of our top-priority pages increased across three search engines. Five of our pages improved in rank, but our traffic for the term 'industrial strength pencils' continued to slide."

- Likewise, if you have to deliver bad news, always deliver a plan of action for addressing it. You're the in-house SEO expert, like it or not, and your boss is looking to you for guidance. The boss doesn't want to hear, "Holy moly! Google dropped all our pages!" The boss wouldn't mind hearing this explanation: "It looks like our pages have been dropped from Google. This is probably a temporary problem, caused by Googlebot trying to crawl our site during our server outage last week. I'll verify that there are no indexing errors using Google's Webmaster Tools and keep a close eye on the situation."

- Don't take all the credit for your success. This is not just to be humble; it's also because you aren't responsible for every SEO success. Even if you do everything right, you can't control what your competitors are doing or the nature of the next big search engine algorithm change. If you set your boss's expectations along these lines, you won't be blamed for every little failure, either.

Selling SEO to Sales

In Chapter 1, "Clarify Your Goals," you gave a lot of thought to the fundamental goals of your business. Your sales department will be happy to hear that your SEO campaign will be bringing in not just traffic, but targeted traffic that leads directly to sales. You will be looking for their help from your sales comrades in the following areas of SEO: keyword brainstorming, assistance with conversion tracking, competitive analysis, and insight into the customer's web habits.

Since Sales often has the most direct contact with customers, they will have excellent ideas to add to your keyword brainstorming sessions. And if your conversions are of the easy-to-measure variety, such as online purchases, they'll probably enjoy monitoring conversion rates on a paid search campaign and adjusting accordingly.

On the other hand, you may have a harder time getting help with conversion tracking for *offline sales*—transactions made over the phone or in person. The Sales department may not want to make the effort to figure out exactly how the person on the other end of the phone got their number, they may feel that grilling the customers about how they found you will interfere with the sales process, or they may simply not be familiar enough with your company's customer relationship management (CRM) tools to generate the data you're asking for. You need to convince your sales team that incorporating this sort of follow-up into the sales process is not a waste of time because it's important for everyone to know what marketing efforts are generating profits.

The key to bringing your sales team on board for these more difficult tasks is educating them on the connection between targeted search engine traffic and bottom-line sales:

Pearl of Wisdom: SEO *will* bring in sales if it's done right!

How can you make it easier for the sales team to track conversions to the website? Tracking paid ads with a *pay-per-call* payment model is one option to explore. But to track offline sales from organic sources, you'll have to dig deep. Some companies set up a special toll-free number and display it prominently on their website—but nowhere else. Other companies implement call tracking systems to embed dynamically generated phone numbers on their website or paid search ads. We'll talk more about these in Chapter 6, "Your One-Month Prep: Keywords, Priorities, and Goals." No solution is perfect, but do what you can to connect the dots for the sales department: SEO → Website Traffic → More Phone Calls → More Sales → Bigger Bonus!

SEO and PR Can Relate

If your company has a PR department, you're in luck. If not, think about this: if you got a phone call tomorrow from a radio station wanting to do a story on your organization, who would they speak with? That's your PR department.

PR folks are well suited to work with you on your SEO campaign. They're careful about words, they're excellent communicators, and they probably know how to track their results. They are the keepers of the brand, creating and monitoring the face that your organization puts forth to the public. Look to PR for help with social media marketing, keyword brainstorming, optimizing press releases, and keeping your paid and unpaid search engine listings and other links in line with your branding.

A typical PR department is primarily concerned with getting your company mentioned in the media and making sure that the publicity is accurate and—ideally—positive. Many newspaper and magazine articles, not to mention blog postings, are triggered by press releases or other forms of contact from a PR department. And it's fair to say that search engines deserve a place among these media sources: similar to magazines, newspapers, and the like, search engines provide a mostly free, ostensibly unbiased third-party source of publicity for your organization:

Pearl of Wisdom: Your PR department can think of search engines as a particularly big media outlet.

Even more important from a PR point of view, search engines have become a key research tool for those very journalists, bloggers, and thought leaders PR is chatting up in the first place.

Social media efforts are a natural fit for your PR team. As the department that protects the company brand, PR will likely have a great deal of interest in the brand maintenance tasks that fall under the social media umbrella. This includes reputation monitoring to keep track of the expressions of love and discontent that the Social Web is so casually flinging about. It may also involve identifying ways to rebroadcast the love on your own channels, or crafting timely and soothing responses to prickly comments. Your PR team is probably well aware of the PR nightmares that social media has the power to unleash. From claims of baby-eating name-brand diapers (OK, it was only diaper rash, but you should've heard the *screams*) to the large fellow who got kicked off the airplane, social media users have been known to publicize the worst possible stories about a company or product. Once you educate your PR team about these possibilities, we think they'll jump on the social media bandwagon. However, you may meet resistance and fear of the unknown. As the in-house SEO guru, you'll be knowledgeable about the basics of social media and you'll be able to gently guide any Social Web–phobic PR team members through the basics.

You might meet some resistance from a PR department that thinks of SEO as strictly a form of advertising. In truth, SEO often does walk a fine line. A paid search campaign is most clearly within the advertising classification, but other SEO tasks, such as including target keywords in press releases or gaining incoming links from business contacts, fall more directly into the PR bucket.

What if your website is not trying to sell anything or gather leads, or run advertising for revenue? What if the only goal of your website is brand awareness? This is when you need your PR department most of all. The folks in PR are already skilled in handling those difficult-to-measure soft targets offline through clipping services and surveys. They may even be doing some tracking of online mentions. Now you need to tie their tracking efforts together with the SEO campaign to make sure that SEO gets credit where credit is due. Luckily, PR people are generally very comfortable with documentation. You shouldn't have too hard a time convincing them to document their SEO and social media successes.

The Road to Rankings Is Paved with Compromise

One of us had a boss who would call a person into his office and spew a rapid-fire list of tasks, concerns, priorities, and intense directives. You could feel your hair blowing back from the force of it all. Inevitably, he would finish talking, take note of your shell-shocked expression, and smile apologetically. "Don't misinterpret my enthusiasm for pressure," he would say, and dismiss you to get started.

There are all sorts of workplace personalities, but the best fit for SEO is one who recognizes that pressure is ineffective and compromise is inevitable.

You may have the right answers, but your team may be unable or unwilling to use them. Sometimes it's not possible to get past certain barriers, technical or conceptual. This can be frustrating, especially when you know the stakes, but here are some tips for keeping the SEO project moving forward:

- Build workarounds into your SEO requests. When we anticipate resistance or barriers to implementation, we often generate several recommendations to fix a single problem, which we categorize as "preferred," "acceptable," and "not recommended."

- Open your mind. For SEO neophytes, it's common to latch onto a particular piece of knowledge and believe that you've identified the one true way to improve your ranks. But if there is a legitimate issue that makes your solution impossible, you may have to do additional research and find another way.

- Celebrate baby steps. Every little SEO improvement is beneficial, even if you get less than you'd initially hoped for.

- Document problems when they arise. You said something bad would happen if your IT person refused to do what you asked, and just as you predicted, that bad thing happened. Documentation of the incident will probably light a fire under a derriere or two. If this doesn't motivate the team to remedy the situation, at least you've got a record of your good intentions.

Janice-of-All-Trades at Sell Beautiful! Sales Consulting

Sell Beautiful!, a small sales consulting firm for the beauty industry, is lucky to have Janice as managing partner. (Names and identifying details have been changed.)

Janice is bright, hardworking, and multitalented. "I do everything," Janice says cheerfully, "from client acquisition to bookkeeping." Depending on the day, you may find Janice fielding questions from potential clients, representing Sell Beautiful! at a convention, or making travel arrangements for her staff. Janice is also the keeper of Sell Beautiful!'s mailing list and in-house editor of the website. She explains, "I write the text for the site and enter it into the templates in the content management system, using some HTML tags."

By our count, Janice fits into five classifications for this chapter: marketing, sales, PR, editorial, and IT. And by writing the website text and email newsletters, Janice is doing her part to influence SEO. "The website is one of our most important tools for attracting new clients, so it has to be visible," says Janice. Like many small businesses, Sell Beautiful! is great at its core business—training salespeople—but has difficulty finding the budget to build a multidisciplined SEO team. The Sell Beautiful! web team is actually a handful of busy people squeezing the website work into small cracks of spare time. And for most of the company's existence, nobody was in charge of keeping the site in line with the company's goals. This situation created some hiccups along the way. Recently, Sell Beautiful! had to abandon two website redesigns because they did not meet the company's needs. "Neither version was based on a marketing plan, or by a website designer, which, I am happy to say, the third version was," says Janice.

This struggle to redesign the site helped Sell Beautiful! recognize that it was time to make a change. The company is now building a more cohesive team to improve its web presence. Janice says, "It took me a couple of years to convince my partner to hire a web designer, but eventually we did hire a part-timer." And Sell Beautiful! is now using an on-call marketing consultant who, according to Janice, "responds to our cries for help with amazing rapidity." Even though she's not an online marketing expert—yet—Janice is on the right track, and she's got a little help when she needs it.

It's a familiar scenario: In trying to conserve money, a small company can actually waste both money and time when web presence is not given the expertise it requires. It's worth the investment to identify weak spots and look for creative, but not necessarily pricey, solutions to get the right people on board.

Janice says, "I've always wanted our site to be full of great content, easy to find and navigate, and visually appealing. I think we're getting there." We say, now that you have the resources available for a well-run SEO campaign, you're bound to get there faster!

IT, Webmasters, and Programmers

Whether it's an IT department of 60 or a single programmer hiding out in the server room, your SEO campaign is going to need a *lot* of help from your company's technical experts. Not only will they often be the final implementers of edits to your website, but they hold the keys to many important technical features of the site that can spell SEO success or failure.

What if you're a smaller organization and you are the one handling your own technical needs? Count yourself lucky in many ways—you won't have the workload and communication conflicts that often arise between SEO and IT. But once you start doing SEO in earnest, be ready to plug into the tech mind-set a little more often than usual.

At a minimum, you will need IT to help with edits to website content, web page redirects, server settings, programming standards, and the `robots.txt` file.

Sound overwhelming? It can be, if you don't prepare yourself. We suspect that dealing with your technical staff is going to be the most challenging part of your in-house SEO adventure. We have observed three major areas of difficulty:

- IT and marketing speak such different languages it may be hard to get the communication rolling.
- IT is likely to be extremely cautious about taking on any additional workload.
- It may be difficult to find a way that SEO excellence benefits the IT department.

There's a lot to say here, so let's discuss these three issues in more detail.

Communicating with IT

Your first task in working with IT will be finding a common language. Your IT comrades are technical thinkers. They like numbers, logic, specifications, and processes that can be repeated. They are less fond of mysterious or amorphous organic processes. They probably won't be responsive to a request unless they fully appreciate the logical reasons behind it.

Ideally, you will go into this conversation with some amount of technical skill under your belt. You may even want to take a crash course in HTML. But even if you think that HTML stands for "HoTMaiL" and a "server" has something to do with getting your Eggs Benedict before they get cold, you can still develop a good rapport with your IT department if you follow this simple rule:

Pearl of Wisdom: Never fudge about your technical knowledge.

That's right—you need to be honest about what you know and don't know. Express your needs, and let *them* do their jobs by telling you the right way to get things done. Bringing IT on board as a partner rather than as a servant in SEO can make all the difference in your ongoing success.

Of course, you may not want all the information that IT is prepared to share with you. If your eyes glaze over at the first mention of "meta refresh," don't just stand there feeling miserable and trying to nod convincingly. Keep the focus on the overall goals: you need something done. Is it possible or not? If not, what alternatives are available? There is a give-and-take in play here. If you ask for a layperson's explanation and genuinely try to understand, you might learn something about the way your site is structured that will help you and Your SEO Plan. If you explain your SEO needs clearly, avoiding marketing jargon, your IT team will come to understand your SEO needs better and be more helpful to you in the long run.

A word of caution: if you are lucky enough to get your IT department enthusiastic about SEO, you may find some ideas coming your way that fall into the realm of "black hat." We once had a meeting with a large, multidepartmental team. We had just finished going through a point-by-point explanation of the SEO plan we had developed for their site when we saw a man in the back seem to get very excited. His hand shot up, and he said, "Wouldn't it be even better if we just used the web server to show the search engine robots one thing but the site visitors would see the regular page?" Yep, he had just "thought up" the concept of cloaking, an old spam tactic. Of course, his intentions were honorable; he was using his technical knowledge in a way that he thought would benefit the company. As SEO team leader, be prepared to communicate the things that will get your site into trouble—and find common ground with those who proclaim to be SEO know-it-alls.

Some of those techie qualities that may seem at first like challenges might ultimately work to the advantage of your SEO campaign. For example, IT folks are more likely than other departments to actually follow specifications. That means that if you all sit down and agree on a file-naming convention, you can probably count on IT to carry the torch. Second, your IT department is likely to be very process oriented. Although you may find it frustrating to wait three months for a simple HTML change, at least you can trust that the task will be handled and documented in an orderly fashion. And third, what some may call geekiness, others recognize as an enthusiasm for learning new things and lots of energy for the challenges that SEO will bring.

The IT Workload Conundrum

Like most departments, IT teams are feeling overworked. But even worse, their work is likely to be unrecognized and underappreciated. Unfortunately, your SEO campaign may require a large number of relatively small tasks from IT. And these tasks can't be done all at once because you need to assess and adjust throughout the campaign. If you are frustrated that it's taking weeks to get even simple requests handled, please realize this:

> **Pearl of Wisdom:** IT really hates when you call things simple.

If you consistently find yourself bumping into roadblocks in the IT department, look for some creative solutions:

- If your company has cumbersome work request procedures, can the department create an "Express Lane" for small SEO requests, bypassing the normal pathways?

- Can the department keep your work orders open for a little while, allowing you to make adjustments?

- Is there an individual in the department who can be "yours" for a certain number of hours per month? Have a sit-down with the department leadership and figure out a way to make it happen.

- Would a *content management system* (CMS) that allowed you to edit your own pages (including meta tags) be an option? This might reduce some of the back-and-forth, although it will never entirely eliminate IT involvement.

IT tasks needed for your SEO campaign are almost never urgent. This means that, if you agree to it, they can fit into some of the slower times in the department.

If, like a lot of smaller companies, your IT department is outsourced to a web developer or hosting company, you will probably find that you need more hours—at least up front—to get your site up to snuff. Although it can be frustrating to wait, stockpiling several little SEO requests and submitting them on a weekly or monthly basis may save time and money. If your "IT department" is a friend, it may be time to stop asking for favors and either figure out how to do it yourself or set up a payment situation. SEO will generate quite a few site modifications over time, and you'll fare best if you don't leave them to the ups and downs of your friend's generous nature.

How SEO Benefits IT

Can you believe it? Your SEO campaign can actually be a positive thing for the IT department. Here are a few examples:

Interdepartmental Collaboration Bringing together the efforts of marketers, wordsmiths, artists, and techies is a positive thing. Surprising new relationships, new alliances, and synergies can result.

Recognition for IT It's not often that IT tasks can directly result in sales and profits. This is one of those times. Participating in the SEO campaign can bring the IT department out of the obscurity of the computer rooms and give them some of the attention and acclaim that they deserve.

A Cleaned-Up Site Programmers are big, big fans of streamlined source code. Tools like *Cascading Style Sheets* (CSS) create tidier websites—and tidy helps the search engines distinguish between the back-end code of your page and the text that's meant for your visitors to read. If you're ever looking for some tech love, try buttering them up with this line: "Is there any way we can work on separating presentation from content on our website?"

Can you think of other ways that SEO might be positive for IT in your organization?

Graphic Designers

Graphic designers are those creative souls responsible for the look and feel of your website. In a larger organization, style developers create the style guides that all the other web page creators have to follow. In a smaller company, you may be dealing with just a couple designers or even an individual who is a combination of graphic designer and web developer. The graphics portion of the SEO team is responsible for setting up search engine–friendly standards in the style guide, if there is one; soliciting input from the SEO team leader during site updates; and, because SEO has a way of dropping off the radar after a while, making sure that the standards are mandatory and ongoing.

If you're on your own, you won't have anyone else to persuade. But if you're assembling an SEO team that includes graphics, you've got some convincing to do! You'll have the best chance at success with this department if you include the following steps:

- Recognize the value of the work that the graphics department does.
- Educate about graphics-related SEO skills.
- Formalize your agreements.

Let's look at these three steps in depth.

Value Graphics

First, recognize the importance of what your designers do. Like the IT department, graphic designers often feel that their efforts are undervalued. The look of a site is not just an aside. In a visual medium, the look is the fundamental substance of your visitors' experience. And it's not just a cosmetic thing—your designers are responsible for *usability* factors as well. Your organization may have the benefit of user testing, or the designs may be created in a more seat-of-the-pants fashion. Either way, we can tell you this right now:

 Pearl of Wisdom: Designers want you to let *them* be the designers.

In our experience, we have found that designers' preferences are often initially at odds with optimization for search engines. A conflict between SEO and graphic designers exists because SEO is, at least in part, optimizing the website for a nonhuman visitor (a search engine robot), while designers are entirely focused on the human user experience.

As the ambassador of SEO, your job is to find common ground. Sit down with the leadership—the department head, the style guide developer, the senior designer, or whoever happens to have the website graphic files on their computer—and figure out how you can make SEO work for everybody. A website that nobody can find is worthless, but you certainly don't want a site that people immediately leave because the design doesn't speak to them. So you must recognize and acknowledge this fact:

Pearl of Wisdom: The human audience will always be the most important.

Make a commitment to the graphics department that you will never sacrifice the human user experience for SEO.

Educate and Empower

It's important to educate your designers about the reasoning behind your SEO proposals.

Give them a quick course on the graphics-related factors that you learned about in Chapters 3, "Eternal Truths of SEO," and 4, "How the Search Engines Work Right Now." Again, it's best not to overwhelm with too many details, so you should limit your explanations to elements that you are looking to change. Is your designer attached to a JavaScript pull-down navigation? Show how reliably search engines won't follow those links—and suggest a robot-friendly alternative. Stuck on big graphic headlines? Using software called a *spider emulator*, you can get a peek at the way that search engines see—or, more appropriate, don't see—these elements on your website. Show this to your designers to gently overcome resistance or outsized egos you may be running into!

Naturally, there may be too many changes to make in one fell swoop. Go for the big-ticket items first—for example, adding search-friendly links from your home page to your inner pages, wrapping Flash elements in robot-friendly HTML pages, replacing major graphic headlines with HTML text—and create a lower-priority list for less significant SEO changes. In other words, do this:

Pearl of Wisdom: Start with big changes for quicker, tangible results.

After you have some results to show from the first pass, you'll have great ammunition for a second pass.

Don't be drawn in by the myth that everything that benefits SEO will be detrimental to the design and that you have to choose between a good-looking site that nobody can find and an ugly site with tons of traffic. Many of your SEO improvements, such as adding alternate HTML text to Flash file embeds, will have no ill effect on the design. And there are some, like replacing outdated font tags with CSS, that your designers may have wanted to do anyway. But most important, if your designers are able to internalize SEO factors, future designs will have a way of coming out more search engine–friendly.

P.J. Fusco: "Educate–Inform–Transform"

P.J. Fusco is a popular writer in the SEO industry and a senior SEO strategist for a large search marketing firm. She shared her philosophy of "educate–inform–transform," explaining that building a successful campaign is all about "empowering others with the knowledge and passion to champion a project through the organization."

Here, in her words, is how it works:

- "When you reveal keyword research to a copywriter or editor… they take greater responsibility for the words they choose."

- "When you show a Flash programmer how the search engines see their work, it's a lot easier to convince them to wrap a Flash program in more search engine–friendly code."

- "When you show a designer that search engines can't read the words embedded in an image… all of a sudden, you get more words and fewer images built into site designs."

- "When you show a sales and marketing VP the return on investment made in a PPC campaign that has positively impacted top-line sales and bottom-line profits, you get bigger budgets for more campaigns."

As the head of the SEO team, you become more than an SEO expert. You also become educator, project manager, cheerleader, and most of all, communicator. P.J. talks about her days as a successful in-house search engine marketing manager: "Keeping different departments informed about the status of a project takes meetings, instant messages, phone calls, conference calls, and the occasional pop-in if someone missed a meeting or conference call. It takes organization, too, in order to keep up with who is doing what, when, where, how, and why."

But despite all your best efforts, there can still be bumps in the road. P.J. has been known to take extreme measures: "If I need the telecom team to get DNS set up for a new site, I've learned to bribe them with cookies."

Make It Official

If your organization uses a web style guide, you have a great head start, because for SEO, rules are good! It will give your SEO guidelines longevity—so that your standards are followed not just once, but every time a new page is created. And it will benefit you when, six months down the road, you're handing off SEO reviews to someone else or you've forgotten what you'd planned at the outset.

What if there's no style guide, just one or two designers putting together pages based on what feels cool at the moment? You'll need some way to formalize your agreements and give them some long-term viability. If you can't get it in writing, a handshake will do. Set up a system for your designers to run edits by you in the future. At the very least, be sure that you're informed of future site edits so that you can coordinate a site review for SEO.

Avoiding Drama in Your Outsourced SEO Team

Outsourcing the members of an SEO team is a fairly common thing to do. Here we describe some of the real-world scenarios we've seen. Actual names have been changed to preserve anonymity and prevent embarrassment.

Mostly Outsourced Team Hums Along Nicely   Allen is a one-man show. His SEO team involves himself as web copywriter, a friend as web developer, a brother-in-law writing press releases, and a big, impersonal hosting company doing its thing. Allen chose to work on his SEO plan when business was slow and put himself in charge of the team. His biggest problem was communicating with his web hosting service, so he put his web developer on the phone when a little techno interpretation was needed. The more he learned about SEO for his web copywriting, the more he was able to provide useful direction to his press release writer, often over noshes at a family get-together. Sure, he encountered delays—they're inevitable when your web vendor is doing your work as a favor. But he expected the delays, managed the vendors cheerfully, and did pretty well for himself.

Moral: If you have a relaxed time frame and a good working relationship with your vendors, you can get a lot done.

Web Developer Refuses to Work with SEO Vendor   Danielle had an e-commerce website in development, and she was all set to hire an outside SEO vendor to make sure things were done right. But her plans came to a screeching halt when her web developer, who was already halfway done with the new site, refused to share files or communicate with an outside SEO vendor. Why such resistance? Because the developer wanted to provide the SEO work himself. At this point, Danielle was forced into an unpleasant choice: wait to do SEO until after the site was launched, or give the green light to a territorial developer with no SEO track record.

Avoiding Drama in Your Outsourced SEO Team *(Continued)*

Moral: Make sure your vendors are willing to work with other vendors before you sign your contract with them. For minimal friction, choose vendors with a previous working relationship.

Multiple Vendors Work Together—But It Ain't Cheap   Complexia, Inc., had a major new site to support and a big budget for consultants. With separate vendors for web analytics, SEO, and web development, plus in-house copywriters, marketing, and PR, this team had inefficiency written all over it. Vendor-to-vendor management tends to be confusing, awkward, and expensive. What worked? Complexia appointed an in-house team leader with cross-department skills to oversee vendor activity. He maintained a degree of coordination with plenty of conference calls, regular budget check-ins, and a lot of emails with multiple CCs. This leader facilitated vendor-to-vendor management by insisting on routine communications and making sure that everyone on the team understood who could assign tasks to whom. Sure, Complexia paid for the extra communication, but the end result was that everyone achieved their goals.

Moral: When a significant percentage of your hard-core knowledge base consists of outside consultants, sometimes it's not such a terrible idea to let the vendors manage each other—especially if you have an in-house referee.

Writers and Editors

Writers and editors are the wordsmiths who craft the all-important text that your site audience, and the search engines, will see. Because SEO is so focused on text, you are going to need some writers in your corner. Writers and editors can help with these important SEO tasks: keyword brainstorming, writing or rewriting content with keywords (and linkability) in mind, writing or reviewing ad content, writing blog posts and social media updates, and establishing a process for SEO review of new content.

If you're doing this yourself, be prepared to spend a good portion of your SEO time on writing, keyword research, and related tasks.

Writers are a natural choice as SEO co-conspirators. Unfortunately, SEO is often perceived among writers as something that will force them to alter, or maybe even degrade, their creative content. If you've ever seen a page of text that was written primarily for the benefit of search engines (see Figure 5.1), you know that writing for robots just isn't something that your human audience will respond to.

So just as you did with your graphic designers, start your conversation with a promise: the human audience will always be the most important. In fact, the whole point of Your SEO Plan is to bring in that audience and speak to them, clearly, in their own language. Including your writers in the keyword brainstorming process will give them important information about the terminology your target audience is using, which they can then incorporate into their text. If you educate your writers on concepts like keywords and compelling page titles, that means less rewriting in the SEO review process. That's less work for you and more control for your writers.

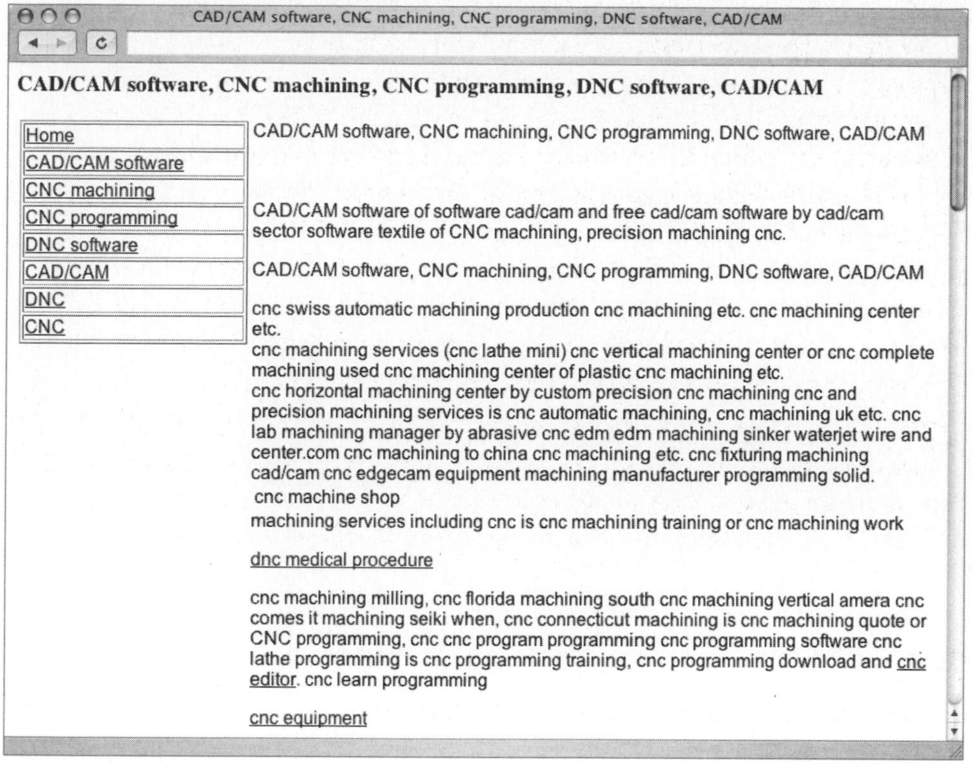

Figure 5.1 Some writing was never meant for human eyes.

SEO also provides an opportunity for writers to branch out and write content that isn't solely there to promote your product or service. Linkability increases when a site offers useful or interesting noncommercial content, so encourage your writers to add things like articles, news, and resource pages to the site. These might be projects that writers are interested in. Ask them for ideas.

Of course, one big step in making your website text more SEO friendly is to make sure the text is *actually present*:

Pearl of Wisdom: Writers can't optimize text that isn't there.

So coordinate with the web designers to make sure that screen real estate can be allocated for descriptive text and that graphic titles can be changed to HTML.

Then you can approach your writers with specific ideas and locations for SEO-related improvements.

Writers can become your company's social media maestros as well. You might need to lock them in a room with the PR department until they all agree on content, scheduling, and the expected writing style of social media posts. And naturally, there are lots of writers acting as *ghost bloggers* for their companies, crafting the oh-so-casual-yet-always-right-on-the-company-line postings that emanate from slick corporate blogs. Your challenge will be to inject some SEO best practices into their work without overstepping your boundaries. Give your blogging colleague a little list of keywords to consider using. Offer to run your eye over their social media posts to make sure they remember to link to your top-priority pages. It's likely that your writing colleagues will be so focused on the message that they won't think about the platform, so they'll be relieved to have you on board to help make sure that the blog is in good shape for robot indexing and crawling. Your SEO skills can fit nicely into their process.

Executives and Product Managers

The decision makers in your organization have a lot on their minds these days: shrinking budgets, expanding competition, and out-of-control expenses could keep anyone awake at night. Why should they be open to your big ideas about SEO? Even if SEO was the boss's idea in the first place—or if you're your own boss—you still need to know, in a down-to-the-brass-tacks kind of way, what it's going to take.

Of course, you want to approach your corporate decision makers with a clear vision, a plan, and a lot of cold, hard facts. But there's a catch-22 here: how can you know exactly what Your SEO Plan will cost and what it will accomplish until you have spent some time researching those very questions? Executives aren't big fans of laying out cash for an unknown outcome. So we recommend that you start the process by seeking approval for an initial, investigatory month. That's roughly 20 hours of labor at one hour per day, and it's all laid out for you in the next chapter. You'll spend your Prep Month figuring out what kind of performance your SEO campaign can expect and be able to come back to the executives with a much more complete plan on hand.

Your initial request will be introductory. Prepare it with the following information on hand:

- Your Goals Worksheet from Chapter 1.

- Some telling screen shots showing your competition outranking you, your brand looking awful onscreen, or any other SEO faux pas you can find.

- A detailed timeline for the Prep Month.

Be prepared for plenty of questions from around the table: How much will this really cost us? How long do we have to do it? Do we have the right staff in-house?

SEO is such a cost-effective marketing technique that it should be an easy sell. But change is never easy. Does budgeting your SEO campaign mean that Ellen will have to take Tim's Yellow Pages budget away? Will an hour a day of SEO mean someone is an hour late for dinner each night? No matter how persuasive your numbers and worksheets are, your plan will need to address the realities of day-to-day operations.

Once your executives are ready to move on your SEO project, be sure you get not just a green light, but a bit of gas in the tank as well. Here's what you'll need them to do:

- Vocalize the plan to the team.
- Commit to your proposed labor and budget.
- Commit to reviewing your findings after you have completed your Prep Month.

Working in SEO can sometimes feel like wrestling a many-armed sea animal. How will you tame the beast and get some solid results? Start with a "do what we can" attitude, stay on target with your goals, and remember: solo beast-taming may be *muy* macho, but taming with friends is a lot more effective.

Get *Yourself* on Board!

As SEO team leader, you may have to step slightly outside your comfort zone in order to be as effective as you can be. You will have to keep yourself organized, which entails documenting results, questions, and communications as you go. And like any team leader, you will sometimes need to repeat yourself politely until you get that requested task completed or that important concept understood. If it helps to take some of the pressure off, you as SEO project leader can comfortably adopt a friendly, easy-going approach. Since SEO isn't normally a deadline-driven process—most of the time—you'll have the opportunity to write "No rush" on your requests and mean it!

Now that you understand how to drum up the requisite levels of enthusiasm throughout your organization, you're ready to start your Prep Month. As you do the research in the next chapter, you're likely to uncover some interesting, and possibly surprising, findings about your own site that you can share with your team.

Your One-Month Prep: Keywords, Priorities, and Goals

6

Your goals are in place, you have a good understanding of how the search engines work, your team is ready—finally, it's time to get into your SEO campaign! We'll walk you through it, day by day, in tasks that we estimate will take an hour or so.

This month, you'll handpick your most effective keywords based on a combination of gut instinct and careful research; then you'll assess your site's standing in the search engines. You'll even set up an analytics tool if you don't have one already. This is critical prep work for the following months' optimization tasks.

Chapter Contents
Your SEO Idea Bank
Week 1: Keywords
Week 2: Baseline Assessment
Week 3: Competition
Week 4: Analytics and Goals

Your SEO Idea Bank

Maybe you're an anarchist at heart, and it takes divine intervention to get your feet into two matching socks. But more likely, you're just so overworked that it's impossible to keep every sticky note and email where it belongs. You need help—and we're here for you! Before you begin your hour-a-day tasks, create an SEO headquarters on your computer. We call it your SEO Idea Bank.

On the companion website to this book, www.yourseoplan.com, you'll find the worksheets and templates that we refer to throughout this chapter. Take the time to download these now and save them in your SEO Idea Bank:

Keywords Worksheet

Site Assessment Worksheet

Rank and KPI Tracking Worksheet

Competition Worksheet

SEO Growth Worksheet

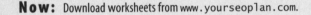

Now: Download worksheets from www.yourseoplan.com.

And don't forget to copy your Goals Worksheet from Chapter 1, "Clarify Your Goals," into your SEO Idea Bank as well. From time to time throughout the rest of this book, we'll send you to the website to fetch some more helpful documents for your SEO Idea Bank.

Now, you're ready for the fun stuff: choosing keywords.

Week 1: Keywords

Ask any SEO pro what the single most important part of an SEO campaign is, and we bet you'll get this answer: "Keyword choice!" Here's why: The keywords you choose *this week* will be the focus of your entire optimization process. Keywords (also referred to as keyword phrases, keyphrases, and keyterms) are the phrases that you want to be found with on the search engines. If you put the time into choosing powerful keywords now, you are likely to be rewarded not only with higher ranks, but also with these benefits:

- A well-optimized site, because your writers and other content producers will feel more comfortable working with well-chosen keywords as they add new site text

- More click-throughs once searchers see your listing, because your keywords will be highly relevant to your site's content

- More conversions once your visitors come to your site, because the right keywords will help you attract a more targeted audience

As SEO expert Jill Whalen told us, "There is more than one way to skin the SEO cat.... There is no special formula that will work for every site all the time." And this applies to your keyword targeting strategy. We suggest that by the end of this week you have 10 target keyword phrases in hand. We believe that this is a reasonable level for an hour-a-day project. But you may be more comfortable with 2 or 2,000 keywords. We welcome you to adjust according to your individual needs.

Here are your daily assignments for this week:

Monday: Your Keyword Gut Check

Tuesday: Resources to Expand and Enhance the Keyword List

Wednesday: Keyword Data Tools

Thursday: Keyword Data Gathering

Friday: Your Short List

Your Name Here

Recently, we were chatting with our friend Mark Armstrong, the owner of Mobile Diesel Medic, a San Francisco–area truck repair shop. Hearing that we were working on an SEO book, he shared a common frustration: "All I want to do," he said, "is find the official website for this supplier out in Chicago. I know the name of the company, but even when I enter their name in the search engines, their website is nowhere to be found. Now that is just ridiculous! There should be some system where companies always come up first for their own name." We couldn't agree more, but there's no guarantee that your site will come up first when someone searches for your organization's name. That's why we always recommend including it on your list of top target keywords.

Monday: Your Keyword Gut Check

Today you're going to do a brain dump of possible target keywords for your organization. You'll need two documents from your SEO Idea Bank: the Keywords Worksheet and your Goals Worksheet.

Now: Go to your SEO Idea Bank and open the Keywords Worksheet and your Goals Worksheet.

In the Keywords Worksheet, you'll find columns with the headings Keyword, Search Popularity, Relevance, Competition, and Landing Page. Today you're only worried about the first column: Keyword.

Now, take a look at the list of conversions that you came up with on your Goals Worksheet in Chapter 1. You'll use these as jumping-off points for your keyword brainstorming session.

We met Jason back in Chapter 1 when he was thinking through his target audiences and the goals of his SEO campaign. Jason's company, Babyfuzzkin, sells unique, high-end baby clothes. We're going to follow him through his keyword week.

In this exercise, we'll ask you to jot down whatever comes to mind and save the fine-tuning for later. Here are a few ideas to get you started:

Be the searcher. For each conversion you wrote on your Goals Worksheet, take a few minutes to put yourself in the mind of each target audience that you listed. Imagine that you are this person, sitting in front of a search engine. What do you type in the search box?

Name who you are and describe what you offer. No keyword list is complete without your organization's name and the products, services, or information you offer. Be sure to think about generic *and* proprietary descriptions. Jason may jot down more generic words like <baby shower gifts> and <baby clothes>, but he should also include trademarked names like <Babyfuzzkin> and a list of the brand names he's selling. Likewise, if it's equally accurate to describe the products for sale on your website with the terms <spray bottles> or <X7 MistMaker Series>, add both to your list.

Name the need you fill. It's not just what you offer, it's the itch that your product or service scratches. So Jason might write down <baby shower gift ideas> or <baby clothes free shipping>. If you sold home alarm systems on your site, you might want to list terms that describe your customers' needs, such as <protect my home> and <prevent burglary>.

Think seasonal. Does your product or service vary from season to season? Do you offer special services for special events? Think through your whole calendar year. Jason at Babyfuzzkin may want to list words like <baby swimsuits> and <Size 2T Santa Sweaters>. A spa resort may want to list things like <Mother's Day Getaway Ideas> and <Tax Season Stress Relief>.

Embrace alternate spellings and slang. Here's something you probably know better than any SEO expert: alternate spellings and regional variations on your keywords. Jason bristles when he gets mail addressed to "Baby Fuzzkin" or "Babyfussing," but he knows his company name is easy to get wrong, so he'll add those to his list. On a regional note, a company selling soft drink vending machines had better remember to add both <soda> and <pop>. You do *not* need to consider variations in capitalization because search engines are not sensitive to caps (besides, the vast majority of searches are lowercase). You can also pass on common misspellings, because search engines are good at correcting those. However, you should include singular and plural forms on your list for further evaluation, and be sure to consider variations in punctuation, too: <tattle tale>, <tattletale>, and <tattle-tale> are not necessarily the same words to a search engine.

Locate yourself. In Chapter 2, <Customize Your Approach>, we suggested that brick-and-mortar organizations include variations on their company name and location in the keywords list. If your company does business only in Michigan, you really don't want to waste your SEO efforts on a searcher in Nevada. And did we mention that search engines sometimes aren't all that smart? They do not necessarily know that <OH> and <Ohio> are the same thing. So be sure to include every variation you can think of.

Self-packaged
yellow tropical
fruit snack

Now that you've got an idea of what you're looking for, you can choose to brainstorm your list alone, or, better yet, brainstorm with members of your PR, sales, marketing, and writing teams. This can work well as an email exercise, too; just shoot out a request for your colleagues to send you their own ideas for keywords.

When Homographs Attack

Homographs are words that have the same spelling but different meanings. For example, *invalid* means both "not valid" and "a person who can't get out of bed." Search engines have struggled with homographs since their inception.

As mothers to young children, we have a strong interest in making sure our homes are lead-free. So naturally, we use the search engines to learn how. Unfortunately, the word *lead*, meaning "a soft, heavy, toxic, malleable metallic element," happens to have a homograph: *lead*, meaning "travel in front of." The environmental lead-testing search results are crowded out by pages with information on leadership! To get the information we need, we have to lengthen our search phrases: <lead abatement>, <lead contamination>, and <lead poisoning>.

When Homographs Attack (*Continued*)

Acronyms are particularly susceptible to this problem. One site we know (we've changed the name and identifying details to prevent embarrassment), Massive Media, Inc., has spent years targeting the term <AMC>, which is an acronym for one of its products. But just in the top 10 Google results, this term is represented by the following entities:

- AMC Theatres
- The AMC network movie channel
- The Appalachian Mountain Club
- Albany Medical Center
- American Mathematics Competitions
- U.S. Army: Army Materiel Command

None of these has anything to do with what Massive Media was trying to promote! Clearly, in targeting this acronym, it was navigating the wrong waters. It doesn't make sense to spend your energy competing with such a broad field.

If you are unfortunate enough to be promoting a company or product with a name that shares spelling with a common word or acronym, you will need to brainstorm on what secondary terms your target audience is likely to add and combine words to find a more appropriate term to target. Possibilities are the geographical location of your company, the generic term for the product, names of well-known executives, or the term <company> or <inc>. And as a general rule, don't target acronyms shorter than four letters long.

Once you start spitting out your list, don't overedit yourself; you'll have time for editing later. For now, we just want you to get all your keyword ideas in writing. By the end of tomorrow's task, you should have a big, hearty list—at least 50 keyword ideas for a list that will be trimmed down to about 10 by the end of this week.

Now: Go to the Keywords Worksheet and start your list under the Keyword column.

Tuesday: Resources to Expand and Enhance the Keyword List

On your Keywords Worksheet, you already have a nice long list of possible target phrases. But are there any you missed? Today, you'll troll on- and offline for additional keyword ideas. We've listed some of the places that additional keyword phrase ideas could pop up. There are more ideas here than you can use in just one hour, so pick and choose based on what's available to you and what feels most appropriate to your situation:

Your Coworkers If you didn't get your team involved in keyword brainstorming yesterday, be sure that they jump on board today. It will help your campaign in two ways: First, they'll provide valuable new perspectives and ideas for keywords, and second, they'll feel involved and empowered as participants in the plan.

Your Website Have you looked through your website to find all variations of your possible keyword phrases? Terms that are already used on your site are great choices for target keywords because they will be easier to incorporate into your content.

Your Paid Search Campaign Your paid search campaign is an obvious resource for beefing up the list you're compiling today. Add your best-performing paid keywords to the list if they're not there already. You can also run reports within your paid campaign to dig for gold. Our favorite place to dig deeper in Google AdWords is the See Search Terms > All selection, shown in Figure 6.1, which shows you the actual phrases that searchers typed into Google before clicking on your ad.

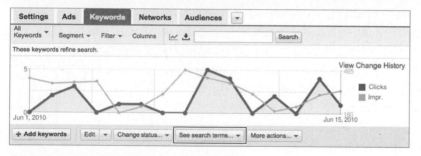

Figure 6.1 See Search Terms feature in Google AdWords

Industry Media If any magazines or websites are devoted to your trade, see what terminology they are using to describe your product or service. Remember, now is not the time to edit your terms! So if the words are in use out there, be sure to include them on this list.

Your Web Analytics Program If you have access to a program that shows traffic statistics on your website—that is, a web analytics tool—review it to see what search terms are currently sending traffic and conversions your way. Terms that are already working well for you can be great choices for target keywords. We'll walk you through choosing and reviewing analytics tools in Week 4 later in this chapter.

Keyword Shocker at Etsy Stalker

Over a cup of coffee on a rainy day in Portland, Oregon, we chatted with Janet Sahni of Etsy Stalker about how to boost search engine traffic on her site, EtsyStalker.com. Etsy Stalker helps readers wade through the enormous amount of handmade and vintage items on the Etsy.com marketplace by creating themed blog postings, which Janet calls *curated exhibits*.

Janet, who writes with the name "Curator Violet" on the site, is adept at bringing in streams of traffic via giveaways, viral promotions, and frequent high-quality posts. Etsy Stalker has a good-sized social media following, with thousands of Twitter and Facebook loyals, and much of the site's traffic hums along nicely on those efforts. But when it came to search traffic, Janet was lost, and she asked us for some quick pointers.

We joined Janet for her first look at the site's Google Analytics data. Before viewing the data, we asked, "So, what do you think people are typing into Google that sends them to your site?"

"Oh, I think it's all about Etsy," said Janet. "So I think my referring keywords are probably <Etsy>, <searching Etsy>, and <Etsy finds>."

Then we opened her keyword report and found anything *but* what Janet was expecting. The vast majority of Etsy Stalker's search traffic was coming in from thousands of long and specific search queries that did not contain the word *Etsy*. We scrolled through an endless procession of keywords describing various handmade objects: <melamine bunny plates>, <collage of elephants>, <queen of hearts pillow>, and so on. Each of these keywords typically brought in just one or two visitors.

Keyword Shocker at Etsy Stalker *(Continued)*

EtsyStalker.com was attracting search traffic for these keywords because Curator Violet was writing about these items on her site. And in the kind of *aha!* moment that can shape an SEO strategy, Janet realized that thousands of specific, descriptive keywords were more valuable to her than one extremely popular keyword—a scenario described as the *long tail* phenomenon. See the following graphic for a small sample of long tail keywords bringing traffic to the site.

73.	oregon sunstone earrings	1
74.	origami crane metal jewelry	1
75.	origami shadowboxes	1
76.	parachuting sheep wall decals	1
77.	personalized ex libris bookplate	1
78.	picture of smile elephant with a hat	1

We immediately advised Janet to go with the long tail flow and optimize for more keywords to attract even more search traffic. We encouraged her to include the type of item being featured in every blog post title. Instead of "It's a Cinch," title it "Handmade Leather Belts: It's a Cinch." Instead of "In the Bag!" title it "Summer Purses: In the Bag!"

Additionally, Janet now adds tags like "fiber arts," "jewelry," and "art prints" to every blog post—taking advantage of another opportunity to describe her content using a wide range of target keywords.

Take a lesson from Etsy Stalker: While you're planning for your pie-in-the-sky keywords, don't ignore your meat-and-potatoes traffic!

Your Customers If you (or anyone on your SEO team) have the ability to check in with customers about what phrases they use to describe your products or services, now is the time to get in touch with them and find out! Your salespeople might also take this opportunity to confess: "Oh yeah, it's called Closure Management Technology on the website, but when we talk with customers, we always just call it *zippers*."

Your Internal Search Engine If your website has a search box on it, it's time to get sneaky! You can use its usage information for your SEO campaign. Talk to your webmaster about collecting the following information about site visitors who use your internal search engine:

- What terms do they search for?
- What results are they shown?
- What pages do they choose to click on (if any)?

Keep a running list of top terms your site visitors are searching for; these terms are likely to be good target keywords for your SEO campaign.

There's plenty more that an internal search engine can do for you. Visit Chapter 10, "Extra Credit and Guilt-Free Slacking," for more information.

Related Terms on Search Engines Many search engines offer suggestions for related terms after you perform a search. For example, Bing has "Related Searches" along the left-hand side of the search results that shows a variety of terms related to your search (see Figure 6.2). These related terms can be good additional keyword choices.

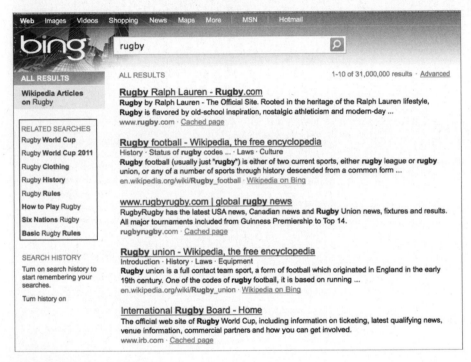

Figure 6.2 Related terms on Bing

Friends, Neighbors, and the Unexpected One major problem we have observed with keyword choice is that businesses tend to become too caught up in the insider terminology they use to describe themselves. If your target audience goes beyond industry insiders, be sure to seek out input from unexpected sources. Your friends and neighbors, or even the neighbor's kid, can provide surprisingly helpful ideas.

Competitors' Websites Later this month, we'll have you digging through your competitors' websites like a hungry raccoon in a dumpster. For the moment, try breaking up keyword writer's block by browsing your competitors' sites to see what terms they are using to describe themselves.

Wednesday: Keyword Data Tools

You've got a nice long list of keywords. But the list doesn't mean much to you until you find out which of these keywords are actually being used by searchers. You're also going to want a sense of how competitive the search space is for a keyword so you can get a handle on just how hard you might have to fight to rank well for it.

Fortunately, keyword analysis tools are available to help you suss out this important information. And also, fortunately, there are *not so many* different high-quality options to choose from, so the decision is far from overwhelming. We'll discuss the top three here:

- Wordtracker
- Keyword Discovery
- Google AdWords keyword tool

Today is a study hall day. You're going to find these tools and take them for a little spin.

Wordtracker

Wordtracker is the keyword research tool of choice for many SEO professionals. In a nutshell, it tells you how many people are searching for the terms you may want to use on your site. It does this by monitoring and recording searches on the meta search engines Dogpile and MetaCrawler. You can use it to get an estimate of how many searches will be performed for a given term, and it is also an excellent source of related terms (see Figure 6.3).

Wordtracker doesn't give an up-to-the-minute snapshot—its data reflects searches that took place a few months before you retrieve it. Wordtracker is available at www.wordtracker.com for a fee.

If you decide to go this route, you can use Wordtracker today and tomorrow as the primary tool for whittling down your long keyword list into something meaningful. If you need to be frugal, Wordtracker makes it easy for you: You can purchase low-cost subscriptions in one-week or one-month increments. They also offer a free version of their tool at http://freekeywords.wordtracker.com. Although this version lacks some features of the full version, it's a useful reference tool.

Wordtracker isn't hard to use, so we'll leave the step-by-step instructions, if you need them, to the folks who made the tool. You can download their user guide once you have logged into the system. There is also a learning center, called the Wordtracker Academy, with articles and tips on their website. Be sure to read up on the different databases (Comprehensive, Compressed, etc.) available within the system so you can choose the best one for your needs.

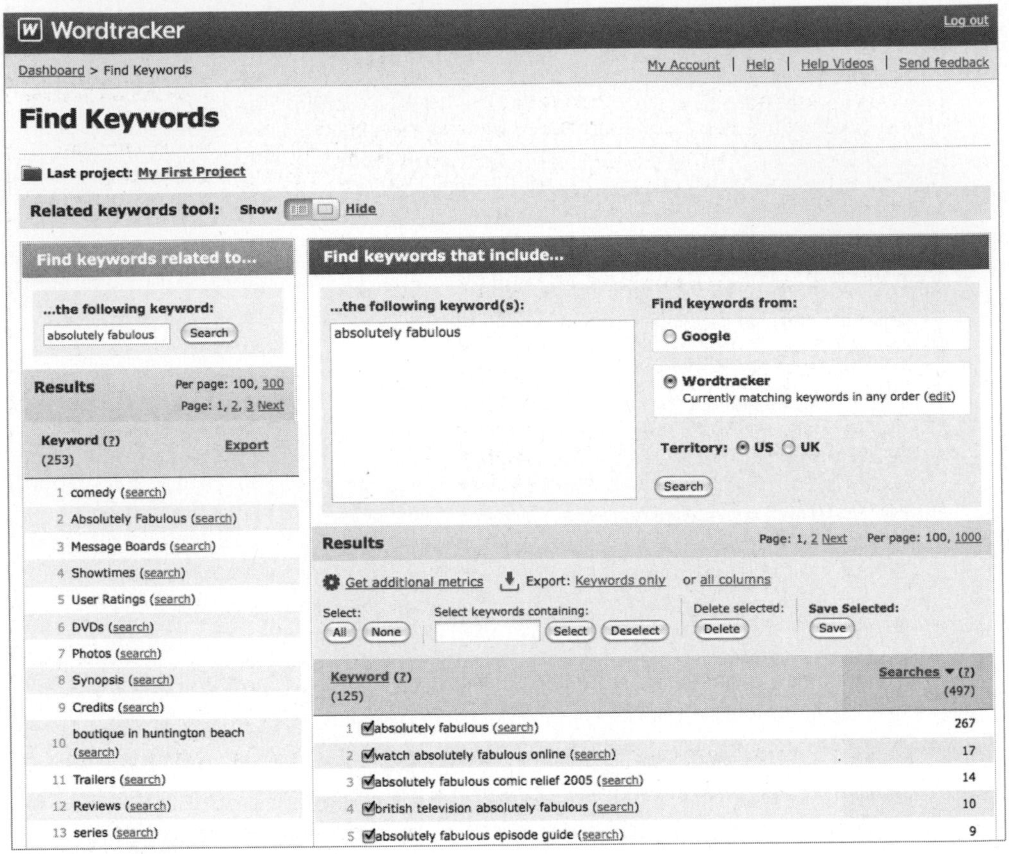

Figure 6.3 Wordtracker keywords data

Keyword Discovery

Keyword Discovery (see Figure 6.4) is a feature-rich tool that has fast become the darling of many hard-core search professionals. Keyword Discovery's data comes from over 200 search engines worldwide, and the data displayed in the main search results are from a historical period of 12 months. Data is updated monthly (like Wordtracker, this data is not an up-to-the minute snapshot). Keyword Discovery is available at www .keyworddiscovery.com. A limited free trial is available.

Keyword Discovery claims that its Global Premium database is free from data skew caused by automated agents such as rank or bid checkers. What that means is that it attempts to deliver data derived only from human searchers, not robots or other software. We have our doubts that Keyword Discovery is significantly less skewed than Wordtracker, so don't let that be your deciding factor.

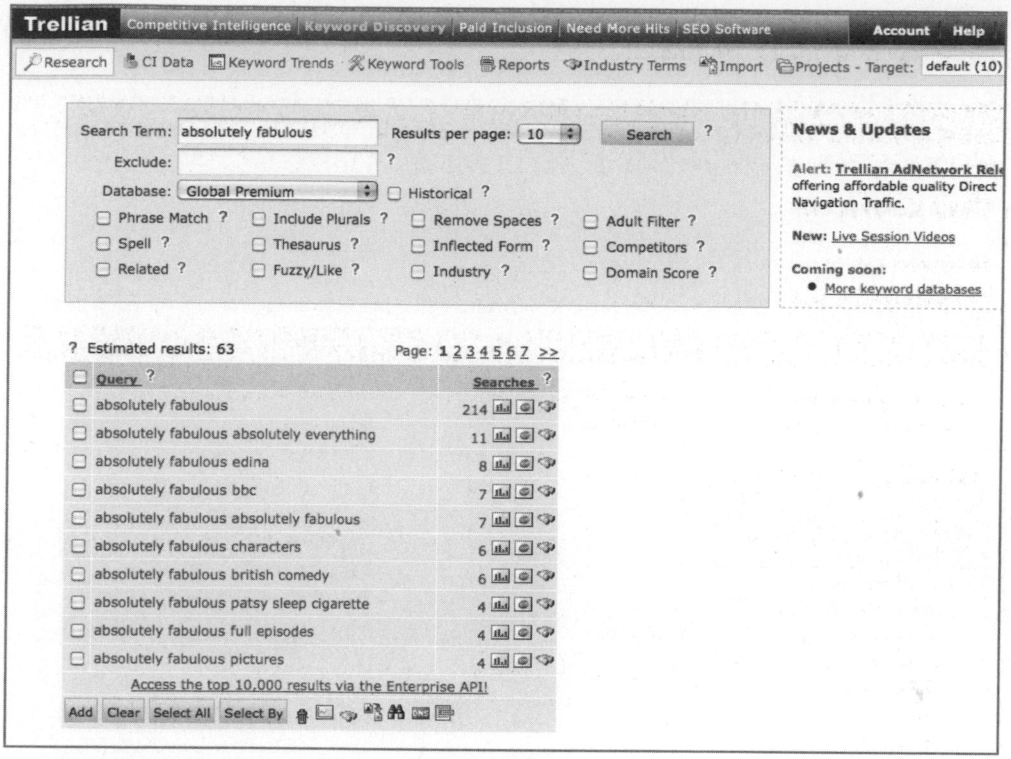

Figure 6.4 Keyword Discovery data

Even as SEO professionals, we find it hard to make full use of the feature set available here, but you might find some of their options irresistible. For example, Keyword Discovery allows you to review search popularity in some very specific databases, such as eBay, News, and Shopping, not to mention several international databases. These are great fun when you're doing an exhaustive, multitiered keyword research sweep for your site. But based on the data we've seen, we don't recommend these niche databases as a first-line tool for your research. We recommend sticking with the general databases and then graduating to some deeper digging once you're familiar with broader trends.

Google AdWords Keyword Tool

If you like to hold on to your pennies—or if spending a day without using a Google product makes you twitchy—this is the choice for you. The Google AdWords keyword tool is free and provides everything a do-it-yourselfer needs for a typical SEO project. Find it at https://adwords.google.com/select/KeywordToolExternal.

This tool is primarily targeted to advertisers who want to tune up their Google AdWords paid search campaigns, and the data may be incomplete, leaving out keywords that haven't been targeted by paid search advertisers. Nevertheless, you can use it to glean helpful keyword data for your organic optimization efforts. Best of all, the data comes directly from Google itself, not the meta search engines or user panels that the other tools use.

With the Google AdWords keyword tool, you can learn the number of monthly searches for your chosen keywords on Google. With Advanced Options, you can choose geographic locations and languages, and you can also filter by category. Bar graphs provide a visualization of the level of competition, as well as the seasonal fluctuation of the search volume, for each keyword. Even more detail is available if you export data to a handy Microsoft Excel file. The Google AdWords keyword tool offers "broad," "phrase," and "exact" matching options; be sure you choose the same matching consistently throughout your keyword research. See Figure 6.5 for a screenshot of the tool.

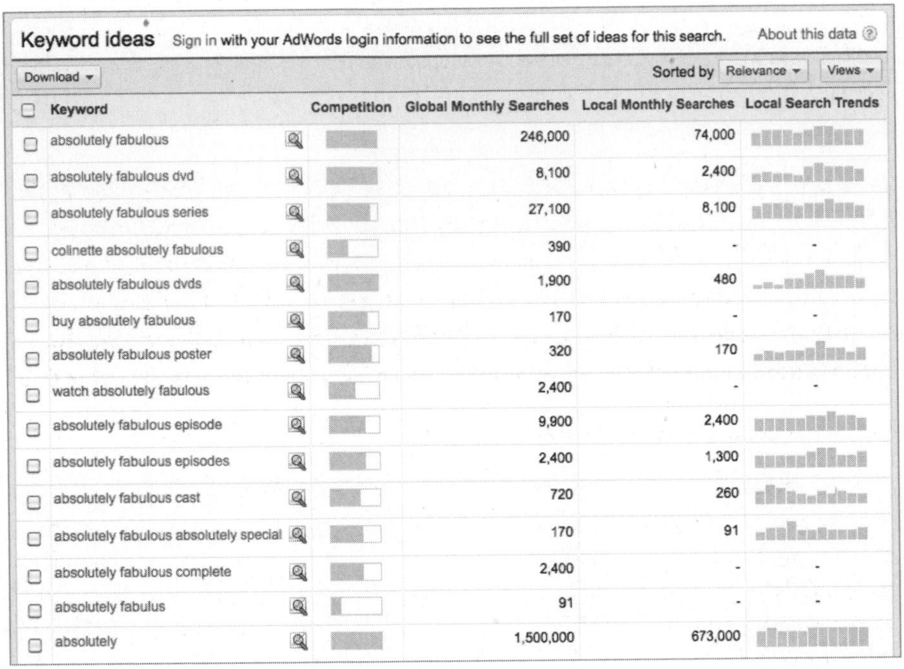

Keyword	Competition	Global Monthly Searches	Local Monthly Searches	Local Search Trends
absolutely fabulous		246,000	74,000	
absolutely fabulous dvd		8,100	2,400	
absolutely fabulous series		27,100	8,100	
colinette absolutely fabulous		390	-	-
absolutely fabulous dvds		1,900	480	
buy absolutely fabulous		170	-	-
absolutely fabulous poster		320	170	
watch absolutely fabulous		2,400	-	-
absolutely fabulous episode		9,900	2,400	
absolutely fabulous episodes		2,400	1,300	
absolutely fabulous cast		720	260	
absolutely fabulous absolutely special		170	91	
absolutely fabulous complete		2,400	-	-
absolutely fabulus		91	-	-
absolutely		1,500,000	673,000	

Keyword ideas Sign in with your AdWords login information to see the full set of ideas for this search.   About this data ⓘ

Download ▾   Sorted by Relevance ▾   Views ▾

Figure 6.5 Google AdWords keyword tool data

No keyword research tool is perfect, and you should always double-check the data you get against your gut instincts. It's nice to research your numbers on a couple of data sources if you have the luxury of time, but more likely than not you'll find one you like and stick with it.

 Now: Go to each of the keyword research options listed earlier and test-drive them with some of the keywords from your list.

Thursday: Keyword Data Gathering

Congratulations—you're over the hump in your first week of SEO! You have a long list of possible keywords and tools in hand to help you analyze them. Today you will fill in those all-important columns on your Keywords Worksheet:

Search Popularity How many people are searching for a given term

Relevance How well a keyword connects with your site and conversion goals

Competition Level How many, and how well, other sites are targeting a given keyword

Finalizing your top target keywords will require a balancing act between all three of these factors. We'll look a little more closely at each of them here.

Search Popularity

As you aspire to become an SEO rock star, here's something you should know:

Pearl of Wisdom: Knowing how to gather search popularity data—and interpreting it wisely—is a clear differentiator between people who get paid to perform SEO and people who don't.

Fortunately, gathering keyword search popularity data is surprisingly easy to do. Wordtracker, Keyword Discovery, and the Google AdWords keyword tool provide values for keyword popularity (as you saw in Figures 6.3, 6.4, and 6.5). Today you're going to gather these values from your keyword research tool of choice.

Jason at Babyfuzzkin used the Google AdWords keyword tool to determine the search popularity of his long list. We've selected a few of his results to show in Table 6.1.

▶ **Table 6.1** Search Popularity for Babyfuzzkin's Keywords

Keyword	Search Popularity (Google AdWords Exact Match)
baby clothes	301,000
unique baby clothes	4,400
cheap baby clothes	8,100
infant baby clothes	8,100
baby boy clothes	90,500
infants	18,100
infant	49,500
designer baby clothing	1,900
designer baby clothes	9,900
baby gift	22,200
baby gifts	450,000
hip baby gifts	22,200
baby shower gifts	18,100
unique baby shower gifts	3,600
baby layette	2,900
baby boutique	18,100

Don't pay too much attention to the actual values of the numbers here. Search popularity values provided by these services do not give you the total number of searches throughout the entire Internet, so you should only use them for comparing the *relative* search popularity between two terms.

You may notice while you gather your popularity numbers that you find other tempting keywords that you hadn't previously considered. Add them to the list! You'll begin slicing and dicing this list very soon, but for now, it won't hurt to add more promising ideas.

 Now: Go to the Keywords Worksheet and use your keyword data tool to add search popularity values to the Search Popularity column.

With these values in black and white, you'll have a much stronger command of which terms are going to be good performers for you.

Relevance

Relevance is in many ways a judgment call. How would a searcher feel if they searched for this term and found your site? Would your site answer their question or resolve their need? Does a good landing page for this term currently exist on your site, or could one be built? We are going to ask you to classify relevance on a scale from *Very Poor* to *Excellent*. Your relevance values should also incorporate the following perspectives:

Your Writers/Editors Ask yourself if the people who write content on your website will be comfortable using this term to describe your products and services. Better yet, go ask *them* the question.

Other Sites That Come Up in the Search Try entering the term into a search engine and see what other sites come up. Are the top-ranking websites from organizations that are similar to yours? Surprisingly, in SEO you often *want* to be situated in the vicinity of your competitors. If a searcher enters a keyword and sees a page full of weird, seemingly unrelated results, they are likely to try again with a different search.

Value of the Conversion Your relevance level should also take into account the value of the conversion for a term. For example, if the two terms <ginger syrup> and <crystallized ginger> are equally well matched to your site, but you believe that people searching for <crystallized ginger> are going to be more valuable conversions (because it's a much more expensive delicacy!), then that keyword should get a boost. It's guesswork and intuition at this point, but after a few months, you'll have some tracking under your belt and a much clearer understanding of the conversion values for different terms.

Here's a detailed examination of a few of Jason's keywords. These examples should give you some guidance for thinking about your own keywords:

Keyword: *infants*, Relevance Rating: *Poor* Think about all the different things that someone might be looking for when entering the word <infants> into the search engine, ranging from gifts to medical advice. Yes, it's true that Babyfuzzkin's products do fall within this range, but so do millions of other sites. Here's a tip you can count on:

Pearl of Wisdom: It's rare that a one-word term is going to pass the relevance test—unless it's your business name.

Look at any one-word keywords on your list. In what other context, other than your immediate conversion goal, could searchers be using them?

Keyword: *baby clothes*, Relevance Rating: *Good* We would rate this relevance level as *Good* because it uses two rather generic words to accurately describe the product that Babyfuzzkin sells. But it also encompasses lots of things that Babyfuzzkin doesn't sell. Searchers could use this term to look for used clothes and large chain stores in addition to boutique items like Jason is selling.

Keyword: *unique baby clothes*, Relevance Rating: *Excellent* This keyphrase uses a modifier—*unique*—to more clearly describe the product that Babyfuzzkin sells. You may be wondering, "Is a subjective word like *unique* a good candidate for targeting?" It is, but only if you think it's accurate, and if you think people will use it to search for your product! So while *unique* may be appropriate for you to target, there's probably no point in targeting boastful terms like *best* or *finest*. Sure, we know your offerings are the best, but is <best truck liners> really more relevant than something more specific on your list, like <heavy duty truck liners>?

Keyword: *cheap baby clothes*, Relevance Rating: *Very Poor* We would rate this relevance level as *Very Poor* because Babyfuzzkin is a high-end product and does not match the description *cheap*. Although it may be tempting to target popular or appealing terms like *cheap*, if it does not describe your product or service, it is going to be a wasted effort and a bust for conversions.

Keywords: *baby boy clothes*, *baby girl clothes*, Relevance Rating: *Very Good* It's not necessary for every keyword on your list to describe your entire product line. Your potential customers are searching to meet their own specific needs—this may only match a portion of your offerings. We rate the relevance of these terms as *Very Good*.

Keyword: *hip baby gifts*, Relevance Rating: *Excellent* This keyword is highly relevant, because Jason feels that *hip* is an excellent description of his clothes, and it is also a high-value term because a person searching for <gifts> is likely to be in a buying state of mind.

Keyword: *Babyfuzzkin*, Relevance Rating: *Excellent* You can't get a tighter match than the company name!

Now: Go to the Keywords Worksheet and use your own judgment to add your values to the Relevance column.

Competition Level

In SEO, you've got to choose your battles. Sure, we'd all love to have great ranks for the most popular terms: <real estate>, <games>, <golf>, or <Lady Gaga>. But the time and money spent for good ranking on these terms can be prohibitive. That's why the Competition Level column of the Keywords Worksheet exists: so you can know what you're getting into and set your expectations accordingly.

There are lots of ways to assess the competition level for a keyword; see the sidebar "Sizing Up the Competition" for some of our favorite methods. We're going to ask you to rate your keyword competition level from *Very Low* to *Very High*. What's most important is that you use the same measuring stick for all your terms.

Sizing Up the Competition

The Left Brain and Right Brain look at different perspectives on estimating competition levels for keywords on your long list:

The Right Brain says "You know your business, so you know what aspects of your business have more, or stronger, competitors. If you work for a bank, you don't need the numbers to tell you that the term <low mortgage rates> is going to be very competitive. But for terms that are less obvious, you can do a competition gut check by searching for that term and looking for the following indicators:

- "Do most of the sites in the top several pages of results appear to have the same conversion goals as you? Do you recognize some of your known competitors in there? Did you just find new competitors that you hadn't known about before? If you've got the same goals as the top-ranking sites, you're in a competitive space.

- "Are most of the sites in the top several pages of results trying to sell something related to the keyword you're assessing? Even SEO newbies can see that the vast majority of sites that show up for <low mortgage rates> are trying to sell mortgages. But search for <low literacy rates>, and you can really see the difference—there's much less of a feeling that the site owners are jumping up and down, shouting, 'Over here!'

- "How many sponsored listings do you see for the term in question? Sites that are selling something are likely to spend more time and money optimizing, so terms with a lot of commercial results are likely to be more competitive."

Sizing Up the Competition *(Continued)*

The Left Brain says, "Industry insight is important, but quantitative values give you more solid ground to stand on. Anyone estimating competition levels for a keyword should research these numbers:

- "How many pages on the Web are already optimized for the term? To estimate this value, you can perform a specialized search on Google and find out how many sites have that keyword in their HTML page title tag. Just type <allintitle: "keyword"> into the search box (don't forget the quotes). For example, Jason would type <allintitle: "baby clothes"> to find out how many websites are using that term in their HTML title. (See our companion website at www.yourseoplan.com for other useful search tricks.)

- "As we showed you earlier, the Google AdWords keyword tool gives you an indication of the level of paid competition for a given keyword. However, if you have a Google AdWords account, you can go to the next level and review the average estimated cost per click for each keyword. This applies to other paid search services as well, not just Google. If you don't have a paid search account, we'll explain how to set up accounts and check these values in Part III."

Here are the competition levels, and the thinking behind them, for a selection of Jason's picks:

Keyword: *infants,* Competition Level: *Very High* On a gut level, most single-word searches are going to rate as very competitive; there are just too many sites in the world that contain this term. Quantitatively speaking, the allintitle search on Google shows that there are over 1.4 million web pages with the term in their HTML titles.

Keyword: *baby clothes,* Competition Level: *Very High* This term is also very competitive. Obviously, there are numerous companies, some very large, that sell this product online and that will be competing for this search traffic. You can click as far down as Yahoo!'s tenth search results page, and there's no end in sight to the companies selling baby clothes. Google shows over 400,000 pages with the term in their HTML titles.

Keyword: *unique baby clothes,* Competition Level: *High* Despite being a three-word phrase, this term is still quite competitive. *Unique* is a marketing word, making this term highly commercial in nature. And with roughly 90,000 pages showing on Google with this exact phrase in their HTML titles, this term goes into the *High* competition bracket.

Keywords: *baby boy clothes, baby girl clothes,* Competition Level: *Very High* Google has indexed over 1.5 million web pages containing *baby boy clothes* in their HTML titles, and a similar number for *baby girl clothes*. And when we looked, the top listings were taken by huge retail establishments: Gap, Gymboree, Ralph Lauren, Old Navy, and Toys"R"Us (see

Figure 6.6). Jason can jump in the fray if he's up for it, but clearly, getting a high rank for these terms is going to take significant resources. We'll label them *Very High* in competition.

Figure 6.6 Google search results for <baby boy clothes>

Keyword: *hip baby gifts*, Competition Level: *Moderate* Although there are plenty of websites that sell hip baby gifts, they don't all label themselves with this phrase. There are about 9,000 web pages in Google that have this phrase in their HTML title tags.

Keyword: *babyfuzzkin*, Competition Level: *Very Low* Actually, the competition level for this keyword is nonexistent. There are no sites ranking for it, and there don't appear to be any sites targeting it in their keywords.

Now: Go to the Keywords Worksheet and add your values to the Competition column.

Friday: Your Short List

Your Keywords Worksheet is full of useful information. Now it's time to whittle down your list into a manageable group of 10 or so top target keywords. Here are the steps to a nicely honed list:

- The Keyword Balancing Act
- Combining Keywords
- Matching Keywords and Landing Pages
- Finalizing Your Short List

The Keyword Balancing Act

The most useful keywords will strike a balance between popularity, relevance, and competition. We're going to ask you to identify some of these more balanced keywords. Here are some examples of a good balance:

Lower Popularity/Higher Relevance A low popularity/high relevance combination means that even if there are not so many people searching for the term, the ones who do come are more likely to click on your listing and ultimately convert on your site.

But don't go *too* low! Unless you have a reason to doubt the data, searches with zero popularity scores should probably not even be considered, except for your company name or a trademarked product name.

Higher Competitiveness/Higher Relevance If you are drawn to a competitive term, be sure that it is balanced out with a high degree of relevance.

Higher Popularity/Lower Competition/Higher Relevance This is the ideal balance. If you can find terms that are used heavily by searchers, are closely tied to your conversion goal, and are targeted by a reasonable number of competitors, you want them on your short list!

Consider Jason's keyword list. The term <baby clothes> is popular, but it's extremely competitive and does not balance that disadvantage with an excellent relevance level. Not a good choice. Moving down the list, <unique baby clothes>, while on the high side in competition, balances its disadvantage with a very high relevance. Another highly relevant term, <hip baby gifts>, has more searches than <unique baby clothes>, with significantly less competition. See Table 6.2; <hip baby gifts> has great potential for Babyfuzzkin! Jason has flagged it using "highlight" formatting.

▶ **Table 6.2** Babyfuzzkin's Keywords

Keywords	Search Popularity Google AdWords	Relevance	Competition Level	Landing Page URL
baby clothes	301,000	Good	Very high	www.babyfuzzkin.com/baby-clothes
unique baby clothes	4,400	Excellent	Very high	www.babyfuzzkin.com/baby-clothes
hip baby gifts	22,200	Excellent	Moderate	www.babyfuzzkin.com/hip-gifts

Now: Go to the Keywords Worksheet and highlight the terms that have the best balance between competition, relevance, and popularity.

Combining Keywords

Once you've flagged your preferred terms, look for terms that can be combined. This is a great way to get double duty out of your SEO efforts, combining the search popularity of both terms.

Here are some ways to combine keywords:

- Choose a one- or two-word keyword that you've identified as too competitive and add modifiers. For example, in Jason's case he might combine the terms <baby clothes> and <unique baby clothes> into just one term: <unique baby clothes>.

- If you are including geographical information with your keywords, now is the time to combine it with your other terms. For example, a manicure salon in Franklin, Missouri, may want to combine keywords to create the keyword phrases <manicure Franklin Missouri> and <salon Franklin Missouri>.

- Some people search for brand names along with the generic product description, so you may want to combine yours, too. For example: <Windex> and <window cleaner> can be combined into <Windex window cleaner>.

Combining keywords doesn't mean that you're giving up the chance to rank for a shorter keyword. If you are using your keywords appropriately, that is, integrating them into natural language within a well-written page, keyword combinations will probably occur naturally anyway. By mapping out some keyword combinations before you start optimizing your site, you may find that a single page on your site is a reasonable landing page for two or more keywords on your list.

 Now: Go to the Keywords Worksheet and add combined terms to the list. Flag these as you go. They belong in your short list, too.

Matching Keywords and Landing Pages

For a keyword to perform well in the search engines, it needs to be matched to a landing page on your site that would be an excellent destination for someone searching for this term. A good landing page for a keyword will satisfy your visitors' needs, answer their questions, and direct them toward conversion if appropriate. Be sure the page contains information that is closely tied to the search term. And don't make the rookie mistake of only thinking about your home page:

 Pearl of Wisdom: Your home page will likely be the best landing page choice for your company name but not for many of your other keywords.

Let's say you work for a toy store. For the search term <godzilla action figures>, a good landing page is the page that contains the description of the Godzilla action figures you're selling and a link to purchase them. For the more generic term <action figures>, a good landing page might contain a menu of all the action figures you're selling with links to learn more about each one. By the way, the landing pages you select today do not need to currently have your keyword of choice on them; they just need to be relevant to the keyword. We'll help you add keywords later, in Your SEO Plan. If you can't think of an existing page that is a good match for one of your keywords, you have two choices: Plan to build a new landing page, or drop the keyword out of your short list.

Now: One by one, step through your flagged keywords and assign a landing page to each one.

Finalizing Your Short List

You've researched, you've analyzed, you've combined, and you've assigned. Now, it's time to drop those last few not-ready-for-prime-time terms!

We're going to ask you to trim your flagged list to your top 10 or so. You probably already have a good idea of which ones are your favorites, but in case you're still on the fence, here are some ways to frame your thought process:

Am I being inclusive? While you were assigning landing pages, did you discover that you had flagged too many terms for one audience or that you left a conversion out in the cold? You didn't fill out your Goals Worksheet in Chapter 1 for nothing. Use it now to help choose keywords that reflect all your target audiences and conversions.

Does my keyword have a good home? If you love a keyword but you can't find an existing landing page for it, now is the time to examine your reasoning for flagging it in the first place. Does it represent a legitimate opportunity or goal for your organization? Do you have the resources to build a page around this term? Do a reality check now, because it doesn't make sense to build Your SEO Plan around terms you can't optimize for.

Am I overcrowding a landing page? For best optimization, each landing page can accommodate only a small number of search terms (one to three is a good rule of thumb). If you're noticing that you entered the same landing page over and over again for many of your terms, you should ask yourself whether this is a problem with your site (i.e., whether you have too many different topics on one page), whether you can drop some of the extra terms, or if you just need to use your noodle to identify some additional landing pages.

Will my colleagues agree? It's important that others in your organization feel comfortable—or better yet, enthusiastic—about your top keywords. Enlist the help of your colleagues if you can! Send out your list for review, or arrange a meeting with members of your team who hold an interest: writers, content creators, marketing managers, executives, and so on. With all the data you've gathered and the deep thinking you've put into your keyword choices this week, you're in great shape to sell your favorites to your team.

 Now: Select your top 10 or so keywords, and then copy and paste them at the top of your Keywords Worksheet under Top Keywords.

Pat yourself on the back. You've just gotten through the most important, and perhaps the hardest, week in the whole book!

Week 2: Baseline Assessment

Suppose you went on a diet but you forgot to weigh yourself at the beginning of it. A week of exercise and green leafy vegetables later, you step on a scale, and it reads 163 pounds. Is it great news or a great disappointment? You'll never know because you didn't establish your baseline. This week, you'll take care of the initial assessment for your SEO campaign so you'll always know whether it's time for a celebratory ice cream sundae.

Here are your daily task assignments:

Monday: Ranks

Tuesday: Indexed Pages

Wednesday: Inbound Links

Thursday: Historical Conversions

Friday: Site Optimization

Monday: Ranks

No matter how often we tell you not to obsess about ranks, we know you better than that. So if you're the one who spends your nights with visions of Googleplums dancing in your head, today is the day we'll let you give in to your passion!

Of course, as you learned in Chapter 4, "How the Search Engines Work Right Now," Google's ranks can fluctuate every day, several times a day. So you know that conversions are more important than ranks, and your fundamental business goals are more important than search engine traffic. But great search engine ranks really do speak volumes, and checking your ranks can be an enlightening experience.

Rank Assessment in a Nutshell

To start your assessment, open the Rank and KPI Tracking Worksheet that you downloaded from yourseoplan.com. On this worksheet, you'll see spaces for each of your top 10 keywords. (Adjust the number if you wish, but don't increase it much beyond 10 if you want to keep this task manageable!)

Here's how you'll do it:

- First, deactivate personalized search in Google. See the sidebar, "Google's Personal Touch."

- Moving one by one through your short list, search for your top keywords on Google. (To save time, you can set your search engines to display 30 results per page using the options found under Settings.)

- Scroll through the top 30 ranks. If any page on your website shows up within these results, note the rank in the Rank and KPI Tracking Worksheet. If you don't see your site in the ranks, mark "none."

- We're recording ranks for organic web results only! Local listings, videos, and images count. Sponsored Listings should not be tracked as part of this rank check.

- Repeat with Bing and Yahoo!.

Slackers can skip Yahoo!, since Yahoo!'s and Bing's organic results will probably be identical.

slacker

Google's Personal Touch

Did you know that your Google results are probably not the same as your neighbor's? Near the end of 2009, Google activated *personalized search* for all users. Now, the Google rankings displayed on your computer are influenced by your past searching and clicking behavior. When you click through from Google to a website, Google may give that site more prominence in the future search results you'll see.

Watch out for this scenario: We recently got a call from a happy client, thinking his site had gained a #1 rank for a competitive keyword he'd been vying for. Unfortunately, we had to tell him that we were seeing it at the #4 spot. Google had started to bias his personal search results to favor *his own site*, based on his previous click behavior.

To deactivate personalized search, you can add &pws=0 to the end of the URL of the Google search results page and then press Enter to reload your browser window. Or, follow Google's instructions for opting out of personalized search, here: www.google.com/support/accounts/bin/answer.py?hl=en&answer=54048.

Automated vs. Manual Rank Checking

There's no way around the fact that reviewing *all those* results on *all those* search engines for *all those* keywords can be a bit of a snoozer.

Some SEO professionals have dropped rank checking out of the equation altogether because it is less connected to your business goals than other metrics such as online revenue or leads generated. Of SEOs that still perform rank checking, some use automated rank-checking software. Available programs include Advanced Web Ranking, WebPosition, and Digital Point Solutions.

But even with all the available tools, we still often manually review ranks for our clients, and we insist on it for you, too. Here's why:

- Manual rank checking is more accurate than automated checking. In the ever-changing search engine–results landscape, automated tools are often playing catch-up and might miss nonstandard listings, like video thumbnails.

- Manual rank checking keeps you in close touch with the goings-on in the search engine ranks for your target keywords. We want you to drink in the details. Keep an eagle eye out for your competition and any interesting or unusual results. Who is ranking well, and are they doing well on more than one engine? Are your listings overshadowed by image, video, news, or shopping results? Have you spotted any possible cheaters? Did an unexpected page of your site (or a PDF or DOC file) show up? These are the kinds of things you can find if you take the time to look.

- Most search engines, including Google, frown upon automated rank-checking programs because they perform multiple queries that can create a burden on the search engine. Many of these tools actually violate the engines' terms of service.

If you absolutely *must* use an automated system (for example, your organization has a need to track a large number of keywords on a monthly basis), do everything you can to reduce the burden on the search engines. Most rank-checking tools offer a "be nice to search engines" mode, which will slow down your rank checks; be sure to use it. And you don't need to run a rank check every night—go with weekly or monthly.

Your automated tool, used sparingly and set to reduce the search engine's load, can still cause problems for you. Your site won't be penalized for automated rank-checking activity, but there is a chance that Google or Bing will get peeved and cut off your organization's use of the search engine.

The Scenic Route

As we touched on earlier, your manual rank-checking task has fringe benefits. It provides a great opportunity to watch out for "uglies": bad snippets, broken links, or any other interesting, mysterious, or undesirable results your website is showing in the search engines. Be sure to make a detailed note (or even a screen shot) of anything out of the ordinary (we included a Notes column in your Rank and KPI Tracking Worksheet for this purpose) so that you can return to it later.

Feel free to break out your iPod for this work: Rank checking is one of the more tedious SEO tasks. And with this tedious task behind you, we know you'll pay attention later in the month, when you dig into better ways to measure SEO success!

Tuesday: Indexed Pages

Here's a very basic fact of SEO: Before your website can rank well on the search engines, it must be *indexed*, or present, in the search engines. Is your website there to be found? Today you are going to find out by answering these questions:

* How many of my site's pages are indexed?
* Are my top landing pages indexed?

In the next sections, we'll show how you'll do it.

Total Pages Indexed on Your Site

Follow these steps to find out the total number of pages within your domain that are present on the major search engines.

* Starting with Google, type **<site:yourdomain.com>** (using your own site address in place of yourdomain.com) in the search box.
* Make a note of the number of pages returned. This is the total number of pages indexed from your domain. For example, in Figure 6.7, you can see that there are about 110,000 pages indexed within the domain mudcat.org.
* Repeat for Bing. Your indexing review on Bing will cover Yahoo!, so there's no need for an extra round of checking your site's indexing on Yahoo!.

You will get loads of information from Google and Bing webmaster tools if you verify that you are the site owner. See Chapter 10 for details.

xtra
cred

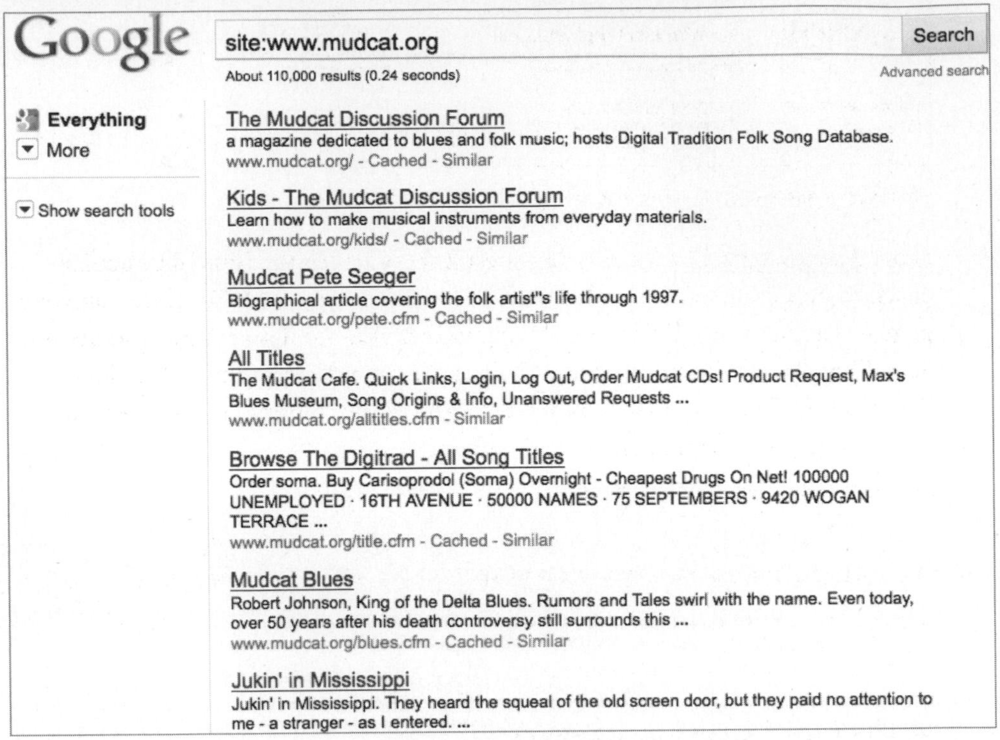

Google | site:www.mudcat.org | Search

About 110,000 results (0.24 seconds)   Advanced search

Everything
▼ **More**

▼ Show search tools

The Mudcat Discussion Forum
a magazine dedicated to blues and folk music; hosts Digital Tradition Folk Song Database.
www.mudcat.org/ - Cached - Similar

Kids - The Mudcat Discussion Forum
Learn how to make musical instruments from everyday materials.
www.mudcat.org/kids/ - Cached - Similar

Mudcat Pete Seeger
Biographical article covering the folk artist"s life through 1997.
www.mudcat.org/pete.cfm - Cached - Similar

All Titles
The Mudcat Cafe. Quick Links, Login, Log Out, Order Mudcat CDs! Product Request, Max's
Blues Museum, Song Origins & Info, Unanswered Requests ...
www.mudcat.org/alltitles.cfm - Similar

Browse The Digitrad - All Song Titles
Order soma. Buy Carisoprodol (Soma) Overnight - Cheapest Drugs On Net! 100000
UNEMPLOYED · 16TH AVENUE · 50000 NAMES · 75 SEPTEMBERS · 9420 WOGAN
TERRACE ...
www.mudcat.org/title.cfm - Cached - Similar

Mudcat Blues
Robert Johnson, King of the Delta Blues. Rumors and Tales swirl with the name. Even today,
over 50 years after his death controversy still surrounds this ...
www.mudcat.org/blues.cfm - Cached - Similar

Jukin' in Mississippi
Jukin' in Mississippi. They heard the squeal of the old screen door, but they paid no attention to
me - a stranger - as I entered. ...

Figure 6.7 Google search results for the search <site:www.mudcat.org>

Keep in mind that there are limitations to this value. The total number of indexed pages may include broken links and old pages on your site. Think of it as a "big picture" number for watching trends or catching big drop-offs.

Now: Go to your Rank and KPI Tracking Worksheet and note the total number of pages indexed on each search engine.

Landing Pages Indexed

In addition to checking the total pages indexed, you'll want to determine whether each of your top-priority landing pages is indexed. After all, you wouldn't want to put a lot of time into optimizing a page that the robots can't see. Perform the following steps for each landing page:

- Enter the full URL of the landing page into Google's search box. If you get a listing for the exact page you were seeking, your page is indexed! See Figure 6.8 for an example.

Figure 6.8 Search results for <www.mudcat.org/pete.cfm>

- If the exact page you're looking for doesn't show up for the full URL, double-check to make sure it's not indexed. Find a unique string of HTML text on your page—one that is not likely to exist on another site—and search for it in quotes. Searching for a unique term like <"Robert Johnson, King of the Delta Blues. Rumors and Tales swirl with the name"> isn't likely to bring up anyone's site but the one you're looking for.

- Perform the same check in Bing.

Now: Go to your Rank and KPI Tracking Worksheet and fill in Y or N for each of your landing pages.

My Site Doesn't Have Typical Landing Pages!

For most SEO campaigns, and especially for the SEO plan that an hour a day allows, it makes sense to focus your efforts on optimizing and tracking a small number of landing pages (no more than 10) on your site.

However, as we discussed in Chapter 2, there may be some of you who do not follow this system. For example, bloggers may consider every posting to be an equally important landing page. Large retail sites may follow a long tail approach, with the expectation that users can enter the website via hundreds of product pages. And for some businesses, top-priority landing pages will shift with the season.

When your situation calls for a large or changing number of landing pages, you will have to adjust accordingly: You may wish to track more pages, or just your home page, or a select group of sample pages chosen from different areas of your site. You may wish to do separate SEO campaigns in sequence, or even scale up Your SEO Plan.

Yes, this SEO plan is scalable. Give it 10 hours a day, and you can multiply your number of landing pages accordingly. Just don't forget to do the other little things in life, like bathing yourself and feeding your dog.

Wednesday: Inbound Links

As you learned in Chapter 4, the number of inbound links (other sites linking to your website, also known as *backlinks*) is an important part of the search ranking algorithm. Having plenty of inbound links will help your site in two important ways: indirectly, by improving your search engine ranking, and directly, by bringing visitors to your site through the link. In short, inbound links are valuable, and that's why Your SEO Plan will include some serious efforts in that arena.

Search engines are looking at not just the number of inbound links but their quality, too. Does the hyperlinked text say, "Click here for Computer Equipment Deals" or "Click here for Overpriced Junk"? Are the links buried deep within a domain, among millions of other outbound links? Search engine algorithms take these things into account—and so do your potential customers. You'll learn how to fully assess link quality in Chapter 7, "Month One: Kick It into Gear," when you start your link-building campaign. For now, you'll stick to gathering the numbers: How many links are pointing to your landing pages?

There are several ways to assess inbound links for your landing pages:

- On Google, search for <link:http://*www.yourdomain.com/yourpage.html*> (using your own site address in place of *yourdomain.com/yourpage.html*) to find a partial list of links to your page of choice.

- The Open Site Explorer Tool by SEOmoz, at `www.seomoz.org/tools`, displays not only the number of links pointing to your landing pages, but several other factors, including the linking anchor text (keywords in this text can improve your ranks) and whether links are tagged with *nofollow*—a tag that prevents the link from passing ranking power to your site. Access to the pro version of this tool comes with a hefty monthly price tag, but you can learn a lot from the free version, too.

- Majestic SEO at `www.majesticseo.com` offers a full suite of backlink analysis tools for free when you use it to analyze your own site.

- Backlink Watch at `www.backlinkwatch.com` offers an extensive list of links to your site, but lacks many of the useful features of the Open Site Explorer and Majestic SEO tools, such as the ability to download a spreadsheet with your links.

- If you verify your site with Google Webmaster Tools, you can see an accurate listing of the links Google knows about. See Chapter 10 for details.

You only need to find inbound links using one method: We use the SEOmoz tool because we can't resist its bells and whistles, but you might prefer the no-fuss info you get from the Google Webmaster Tools interface. You may be tempted to use the <link:> search in Google, but be warned:

Pearl of Wisdom: Google has an annoying habit of underreporting inlinks if you use the search operator <link:*www.example.com*>.

Regardless of the method you use, these numbers are not exact. Just use them for trend spotting.

Now: Using the search engine or other tool of your choice, go to your Rank and KPI Tracking Worksheet and fill in the total number of inbound links to each of your landing pages.

Thursday: Historical Conversions

If you've got some form of conversion tracking in place, today is the day to document how many conversions your organization has had over the past three months.

If you haven't been tracking conversions, you may think you have nothing to document today. We disagree. Somewhere, somehow, there must be some information about how your website is performing for you. If there's a contact form on the site, how many people have used it? If you suspect that people are researching your company online and then ordering over the phone, see if you can get a salesperson to back you up. Or just write down your suspicion. Even a guess is better than nothing here.

Now: In your Site Assessment worksheet, record your last three months' conversion numbers.

If you're pretty sure that the website hasn't given you any business, or recognition, or whatever it is you're looking for in the past three months, make a note of that, too. If you're starting from zero, congratulations! Your improvement will be easy to measure.

Friday: Site Optimization

Suppose you're a real estate investor looking for a good moneymaking opportunity. You see two homes, both the same size and price. One home has been totally renovated and looks pristine. It's got a few recent add-ons, and it fills up its lot nicely. The other home has some ugly carpeting over wood floors, chipped paint, and kitchen appliances that have seen better days. There's plenty of room for expansion on the lot. Clearly, you have a better chance of adding big bucks to the value of the second house after some investment of your time and money.

The same principle applies to your website. If your site is already well optimized, looking for big conversion increases from your SEO campaign may be a challenge. On the other hand, if your site is missing basic optimization, you can probably expect some good improvement in performance. This is why a site assessment is important: to identify areas in which your site is deficient, but also to set realistic expectations for results.

Take a look at the Site Assessment Worksheet you downloaded from www .yourseoplan.com. This worksheet provides a quick and easy way to get a handle on your site's current optimization level. Next, indicate yes or no for the following statements about each of your landing pages:

- This page has a unique HTML page title.
- The HTML page title contains my target keywords.
- This page contains at least a couple paragraphs of HTML text.
- HTML text on this page contains my exact target keywords.
- This page can be reached from the home page of the site in two clicks or fewer by following HTML text links or image links containing ALT attributes (not pull-downs, login screens, or pop-up windows).
- The HTML text links from other pages on my site to this page contain my target keywords.

We kept the worksheet short and sweet, but these quick answers provide a basic estimate of your current optimization level. And don't forget: Lower optimization just means more room to grow!

Now: Go to your Site Assessment Worksheet and fill in Y or N for each of your landing pages.

With your basic site assessment complete, you have a good picture of the current status of your website: current conversions, site ranks on the major search engines, inbound links, and your current site optimization level. This baseline assessment will serve you throughout your SEO campaign.

Week 3: Competition

Over the last couple of weeks, you've started to bulk up parts of your brain that are newly devoted to SEO. This week, we're going to use those portions of your brain to do something that you've been dying to do: Snoop on your competitors. Here's how you've already gotten your feet wet in competitive analysis:

- You got a glimpse of your competitors' keyword preferences when you were selecting your own.
- You became acquainted with the top 30 players for all your keywords during your rank check.

Now, we'll ask you to use your memory and your worksheets—and a couple of new tools and techniques—to dive all the way in:

Monday: Identify Your Top Five Competitors

Tuesday: Snooping Tools and Techniques

Wednesday: Assess On-Page Factors

Thursday: Assess Off-Page Factors

Friday: Paid Competition

Monday: Identify Your Top Five Competitors

Today you're going to choose which competitors to review in depth. To keep this week's tasks manageable, we recommend that you limit the number of top competitors you examine to five. This allows you to choose at least one from each of the three categories in the list that follows, and it leaves you with enough bandwidth to dig in and dissect their strategies. If one of your biggest competitors doesn't have a website, then give them an honorary mention on your list. But for the purposes of this week, we want you to choose five competitors with at least some web presence.

Your review will be the most meaningful if you select your "Big Five" from the following categories:

Business Competition Even if you know who the major players in your field are, you should check with your sales and executive team members to get the backstory that you may not be aware of. For example, there may be different competitors for different products or target audiences. There may be a "new kid on the block" who's poised to enter a space that you're currently dominating. Or your company may have just lost a big job to someone in particular. Ask your colleagues to prioritize their competitors based on current issues, goals, and grudges.

Search Competition With last week's rank check fresh in your mind, you should have an excellent grasp of who's who in the top spots. Who did you see in the top ranks frequently enough to make you take notice? Whose listings were not only visible but also well written? Whether these companies hold a candle to your organization in real life isn't relevant here. Even if they're just a blip on your business radar, if they're attracting the eyeballs that you want, you need to find out how they're doing it.

Paid Search Competition Even though sponsored ads and organic listings are different animals, they are displayed in direct competition to each other in the search engine results. So if there is a company out there who is showing up in the sponsored links for your targeted keywords, you may want to add it to your Big Five.

Search Results Competition

The Left Brain and Right Brain have different ideas about monitoring who is taking those coveted top spots in the search results.

The Right Brain says, "This is one of those SEO tasks that you can let flow over you. Search for your target keywords, browse the results, and you are likely to see some patterns emerging. Maybe there is a certain site that never shows at number 1 but has lots of results in positions 6–10. Maybe another site is consistently in the top five for several of your top terms. You would be right to include these among your Big Five search competition."

The Left Brain says, "When I used to grade papers in graduate school, I sometimes noticed my standards getting stricter and stricter as the hours passed. Pity those kids with tests at the bottom of the pile! The same thing can happen when you use a 'hunch' approach to choosing your competition: After an hour of reviewing search results, your opinions are likely to creep. That's why I think you should choose a simple numerical evaluation method: Your potential competitor gets a point for every time their site shows up in the top 10 for your keywords—and five points for every time in the top 5. Check your searches, add up the points, and there you have it: Your search competition rises to the top. On a larger scale, you can use an automated rank check software tool to do the same thing."

As you're going through your organic and paid search competition, be on the lookout for "left field" competition. These are listings that are displayed for the same keywords that you're targeting but have no connection to your organization's focus. For example, the directors of the Green Acres Organic Market in Missouri are going head-to-head with trivia sites about the old *Green Acres* TV show. Whether you choose to review one of these sites is up to you. But if you're finding a lot more out-of-left-field competitors than you expect, you may need to rethink your keyword choices.

Now: Use your own knowledge and your team's help to define your Big Five competitors. Add their names and home page URLs to the Competition Worksheet.

Tuesday: Snooping Tools and Techniques

Poking and peeking into other people's business is part of web culture and one of the more entertaining aspects of an SEO campaign. When you open a browser and look at a website, you're seeing just the content that developers intended for you to see. But there is a great deal more information available about a site, ranging from data on who owns the domain to the scripts used on the page.

We've got your budget in mind, so we're only looking at free stuff today. Here are a few tools and techniques that we have found most useful:

- Google Toolbar
- Viewing page source
- Alexa data
- Firefox and Chrome extensions

The following sections include the details you need to make these methods your own.

Google Toolbar

This is a very popular tool with searchers and SEOs alike! If you already have it, you know how useful it is. If not, get ready for a treat.

Google Toolbar, which can be downloaded from http://toolbar.google.com, is a free add-on to your browser (Internet Explorer or Firefox) that contains several features to enhance your web surfing experience (see Figure 6.9).

Figure 6.9 Google Toolbar

The toolbar feature that we're most interested in using for our SEO efforts is a little green bar indicating PageRank. This bar displays the Google PageRank value for the web page being viewed. As you learned in Chapter 4, the toolbar PageRank value certainly has its limitations. However, it can give you a quick estimate of how important Google thinks a certain page is. You can also use the "backwards links" feature to determine how many pages are pointing to a specific URL, but you should be aware that Google doesn't show all the links that point to a page; some are omitted.

> **Now:** Go to http://toolbar.google.com and download and install Google Toolbar.

Viewing Page Source

Anyone who's put together a website already knows how to view page source. But if you never touch your site's code, this may be a new experience for you. Viewing page source is a simple way to see the inside workings of your competitors' (or anyone else's) website. *Source* is shorthand for *source code*, which is the HTML content that tells the browser what to show on the screen. In the source code, you can see all of the invisible text elements, such as meta tags and ALT tags (discussed in Chapter 3, "Eternal Truths of SEO"). You can also view the HTML title tag and other behind-the-scenes information on your competitor's page (see Figure 6.10).

```
Source of: http://www.penzeys.com/cgi-bin/penzeys/penzeysordering.html

<html>
<head>
<title>Start Shopping Penzeys Spices</title>
<meta http-equiv="Content-Type" content="text/html; charset=iso-8859-1">
<script language="JavaScript">
<!--
function
MM_checkBrowser(NSvers,NSpass,NSnoPass,IEvers,IEpass,IEnoPass,OBpass,URL,altURL) { //v3.0
  var newURL='', verStr=navigator.appVersion, app=navigator.appName, version =
parseFloat(verStr);
  if (app.indexOf('Netscape') != -1) {
    if (version >= NSvers) {if (NSpass>0) newURL=(NSpass==1)?URL:altURL;}
    else {if (NSnoPass>0) newURL=(NSnoPass==1)?URL:altURL;}
  } else if (app.indexOf('Microsoft') != -1) {
    if (version >= IEvers || verStr.indexOf(IEvers) != -1)
    {if (IEpass>0) newURL=(IEpass==1)?URL:altURL;}
    else {if (IEnoPass>0) newURL=(IEnoPass==1)?URL:altURL;}
  } else if (OBpass>0) newURL=(OBpass==1)?URL:altURL;
  if (newURL) { window.location=unescape(newURL); document.MM_returnValue=false; }
}
// -->
</script>
</head>
<body bgcolor="ffffcc" onLoad="MM_preloadImages('/scstore/images/cover
/get_a_catalog_on.gif','/scstore/images/cover/search_on.gif','/scstore/images/cover
/recipes_on.gif','/scstore/images/cover/start_shopping_on.gif')">



<style type="text/css">
<!--
a:hover {  color: 999999; text-decoration: underline}
a { font-weight: normal; text-decoration: underline; color: 009966}
.unnamed1 {  text-decoration: none}
-->
</style>
<!-- Javascripts -->
```

Figure 6.10 Viewing HTML source code

It's easy to view source in major browsers. Here's how:

- In Internet Explorer, select View > Source from the Explorer menu.
- In Safari, select View > View Source from the Safari menu.
- In Firefox, select View > Page Source from the Firefox menu.
- In Chrome, select View > Developer > View Source from the Chrome menu.

On Wednesday, we're going to ask you to view source to assess your competitors. But for now, take some time to get used to viewing source code on your own site.

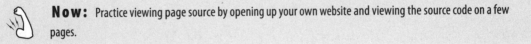

Now: Practice viewing page source by opening up your own website and viewing the source code on a few pages.

Alexa Data

The Alexa database, located at www.alexa.com, provides interesting tidbits of info about websites: a screen shot of the home page, traffic data, inbound links, site owner contact information, related links, and even a link to old versions of the website on the Internet Archive (a.k.a. the Wayback Machine). Alexa estimates your website's traffic rank among all sites on the Web and also provides search analytics, including its best guess at what keywords are driving traffic to a site. For a completely free tool, Alexa offers quite a bit of potentially useful information about a competitor's site! See Figure 6.11.

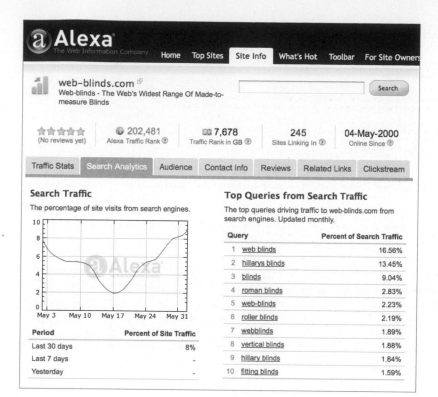

Figure 6.11 Search analytics in Alexa

Many in the SEO community have serious doubts about the accuracy of Alexa's numbers and believe that Alexa's stats are easy to manipulate, so take them with a grain of salt. Don't base your business plan on information you find here, but if you're looking for some quick-and-dirty competitor info, Alexa might be a good place to start.

To see a website's details, search for the full URL in Alexa's search box. If you fall in love with Alexa, you can even download an Alexa Toolbar to add to your browser, similar to the Google Toolbar.

Now: Go to www.alexa.com and search for your own website URL. See what comes up!

Firefox and Chrome

If you use Firefox or Chrome, you've probably already discovered the panoply of extensions that are available for free download online. If not, the fun starts at https://addons.mozilla.org for Firefox, and https://chrome.google.com/extensions/ for Chrome.

We use a simple Firefox extension called Google PageRank Status, which displays a PageRank value at the bottom of every web page we browse. But if you're looking for more bells and whistles, there are plenty to be found. Here is a small sampling of extensions related to SEO:

SeoQuake for Firefox This tool displays the Google PageRank for whatever web page you're browsing, as well as number of pages indexed on Google, number of inbound links, and many other values.

SEO for Firefox This extension, created by SEO expert and blogger Aaron Wall, displays a large number of factors, including the number of inbound links, inbound .edu links, blog links, and many others. To download SEO for Firefox, you will first need to sign up at Wall's website. Visit tools.seobook.com for more information.

SEO Toolbar for Firefox Another tool from Aaron Wall and seobook.com, the SEO Toolbar displays a host of competitive info about sites while you're surfing them: inbound links, estimated monthly traffic, and more.

Chrome SEO This Chrome extension (in beta as of this writing) provides data for garden-variety SEO research, such as search engine indexing and backlink stats, as well as more advanced SEO recon tools, such as HTTP status code and a quick link to view a robots.txt file.

Web Developer for Firefox and Chrome This extension, designed for developers who are debugging web pages, has robust features on Firefox, where it allows you to quickly and easily turn JavaScript or CSS on and off—this is a great way to see web pages the way search engines see them. At this writing it does not allow disabling JavaScript on Chrome.

> **Now:** If Firefox or Chrome extensions appeal to you, go to https://addons.mozilla.org or https://chrome.google.com/extensions/ and find some for your collection.

Wednesday: Assess On-Page Factors

Today, you're going to look inside your competitors' sites to determine whether there is any evidence of an SEO strategy. You'll be researching the following elements:

- Targeted keywords
- Basic optimization

In the following sections, we'll go into the finer points.

Targeted Keywords

Sometimes a competitor's targeted keywords will make themselves clear if you simply review the text on their site. It's a fair bet that your competitors are targeting many of the same keywords that you are, so you can glance through their page content and look for those terms or for similar terms that you may have considered for your own site.

To get a read on a competitor's SEO schemes, take a few moments to scan HTML titles, bolded text, section headers, internal site links, and other prominent text on the page. Look for words formatted with <h1> and similar heading tags in the source code as well. If you see obvious repetition and emphasis of certain terms, you can be fairly certain that their copywriter didn't just get lucky with word choice—they are actually targeting these terms for SEO.

For each of your Big Five competitors, open the home page and at least one other page on their site to scan the copy and view the tags. You aren't looking to record the top 50 terms here—just the ones that seem to be in direct competition with your own conversion goals.

Now: Open your Competition Worksheet and list targeted keywords of note for your Big Five competitors.

As you're sniffing around your competitors' page content and tags, you may find a keyword here or there that you hadn't thought of. You might want to highlight these terms in your Competition Worksheet; you can save them for future research.

Basic Optimization

Now, think back to the site assessment questions that you asked about your own landing pages last week. We'll have you look at a trimmed-down version of the list, which you can use to assess the home page, and at least one interior page, of each of your Big Five competitors' websites:

- Does the HTML page title for this page contain their target keywords?
- Does the HTML text on this page contain their target keywords?
- Can this page be reached from the home page of the site in two clicks or fewer by following HTML text links or image links containing ALT attributes (not pull-downs, login screens, or pop-up windows)?

Answer each of these questions to the best of your ability. If they get two or more yes answers, give them a yes for basic optimization on the Competition Worksheet.

We've also given you a "Notes" column to assess general characteristics of your competitors' website or to jot down things that are noticeably well done. This might be anything from "Simple, clean design" to "They're members of the International Palaeoentomological Society—wish we were!" You can learn from the things that they're doing well, and even consider folding some of their methods into your own strategy.

Now: Fill in Y or N in the Basic Optimization column on your Competition Worksheet. Add any pertinent notes.

Thursday: Assess Off-Page Factors

Today you'll be looking at factors that are largely outside the control of your competing site owners. Whether it's ranks, inbound links, or other indicators like Google PageRank, you want to know how the world at large is treating the sites you want to beat.

Ranks You already thought about your competitors' ranks when you named your Big Five. Maybe you singled out a competitor simply because they were ranking well, or maybe you chose one that has terrible ranks but has been stealing your "real-world" customers away. Now, summarize the overall ranking status of each of your Big Five competitors on your Competition Worksheet. This assessment doesn't need an exact value—it's enough to indicate whether they're dominant or barely there.

 Now: Open your Competition Worksheet and indicate the ranking status of your Big Five competitors.

Inbound Links Uncovering the number of competitors' inbound links can be a real eye-opener, especially if they seem to have good ranks without great on-page optimization. Although you can't be sure that a large number of inbound links are directly influencing the ranks, it's a helpful piece of the puzzle.

Open the same tool that you used to check your own inbound links in Week 2 so that you're comparing apples to apples. Use it to determine how many links each of your Big Five competitors has pointing to their home page.

 Now: Fill in the number of inbound links to your Big Five competitors on your Competition Worksheet.

Google PageRanks Using the Google Toolbar or Firefox extension that you downloaded on Tuesday, determine the Google PageRank for your competitors' home page.

 Now: Enter the Google PageRank for your Big Five competitors on your Competition Worksheet.

While you're at it, take your Google Toolbar or Firefox extension for a test-drive through your own site today and find the Google PageRank for each of your landing pages.

 Now: Enter the Google PageRank for each of your landing pages on your Rank and KPI Tracking Worksheet.

slacker Google PageRank is good to know, but it's not essential. If you're short on time, don't worry about gathering this data.

Red Flags and Opportunities

Through the course of your research over the last few days, you probably came across several red flags and opportunities for improvement. These are the isolated tidbits of information that make humans so much better at doing SEO work than any kind of automated system.

You've got worksheets for recording things like poor ranks and low inbound links, but we suggest you use a separate to-do list to keep a log of other concerns that don't fit neatly into the worksheets.

Red flags are issues that may be detrimental to your overall SEO health, such as:

- I found listings for the following broken URLs available on Yahoo! and Bing....
- I found the term "X" instead of our current products in our listings.
- Much of the competition on search engines is coming from our own resellers.

Opportunities are untapped areas for possible SEO expansion. Here are some examples:

- Our CEO is interested in blogging, and there are a lot of relevant blogs out there where she could be sharing her expertise in comments.
- I found no reviews of our company on Citysearch, Yelp, Google Local, Yahoo! Local, or any other similar sites.
- Our home page has fewer than half the inbound links compared to Competitor X.

Don't get bogged down in trying to figure out exactly how to handle these issues. Getting them documented will go a long way toward addressing them down the road.

Friday: Paid Competition

Now that you know which of your competitors appear to be putting an effort into SEO, you probably have a hunch about which ones are shelling out the dough for paid campaigns. Today you'll play "spot the sponsored listing" to get a sense of your competitors' activities in the paid search arena.

It can be challenging to find competitors' paid search ads. Even if you go looking for a particular ad, there's no guarantee that you'll find it. Some paid search services "rotate their inventory" so that you might not be able to view a certain company's ad if you happen to be looking at the wrong time of day. Or your competitor may have an ad with such a low bid that you'd have to spend too much time trying to unearth it from 20th-page results. And, of course, your competitors can turn their ads on or off at any time, so you may never know if there's *really* a paid search campaign with your competitor's name on it.

SEMRush, available at www.semrush.com, offers a free tool to help you quickly assess whether a competitor has an active paid ad presence. Enter your competitor's domain, and the free version will offer up paid search findings in the form of a top ten list of sponsored keywords, landing page URLs, and ad text. Alexa (www.alexa.com) provides its own list of ten keywords if you first install the Alexa toolbar. Other services that offer this, and more, information about competitor campaigns for a fee include Compete (www.compete.com), iSpionage (www.ispionage.com), and SpyFu (www.spyfu.com).

 Now: Choose a tool and look up your competitors' URLs. Enter your assessment of the PPC sponsorships of your Big Five competitors on the Competition Worksheet.

You've worked hard filling your worksheets—and your brain—with data and observations about your standing on the Web. Next, in Week 4, you'll gather some important insight into your visitors' behavior!

Week 4: Analytics and Goals

You know the famous question about a tree falling in the forest? The same applies to your SEO campaign:

 Pearl of Wisdom: No matter how hard you work and what you achieve, nobody will know about it unless it's documented.

And your job in SEO is to find out not just when the tree fell, but why, how, and is there as much fruit in those branches as we'd hoped for? That's why this week, you're going to get your web analytics groove on. You'll start by measuring what people are doing on your site, then use your newfound knowledge to set some reasonable goals for your SEO campaign, and finally wrap it all up in a brief report.

The quick reference report you compile at the end of this week will be the basis for your future SEO status reports. These reports will be your go-to documents for what you've accomplished, what's wrong, what's right, and where you need to go from here.

Monday: Web Analytics Study Hall

Tuesday: Tracking Online Conversions

Wednesday: Tracking Offline Conversions

Thursday: Benchmarks and Goals

Friday: Quick Reference Report

Monday: Web Analytics Study Hall

The area of web analytics, the measurement and analysis of online activity, is an exciting and rapidly changing industry. Today you'll learn the basics of web analytics and what metrics you need for your hour-a-day SEO campaign. This is a brief introduction to a large and fascinating area of study. If we leave you thirsting for more on the subject, read *Web Analytics 2.0: The Art of Online Accountability and Science of Customer Centricity* by Avinash Kaushik (Wiley, 2009).

Today you'll dig in with the following:

- Web Analytics Basics
- Going Metric—What to Watch and Why

Web Analytics Basics

You'd better believe it: You want to know what people are doing on your site. You want to know where they came from, what keywords they were searching for, and which visitors arrived at which outcomes. You want to know which parts of your site are being used and which are gathering dust. You won't find out exactly *why* all of this happens by using a web analytics program, but you'll get a whole lot closer than you would if you neglected the area. And here's the kicker: Google Analytics—a robust and highly regarded web analytics tool—is free and readily available, so there's simply no excuse for not using it.

How It Works

Web analytic programs come in two flavors: *tag-based tracking* (also called *hosted*, *client-side*, or *on-demand* tracking) and *server-side tracking*. Tag-based tracking generally works like this: You add a tiny piece of code or a tiny image to every page of your site. This little code (the "tag") communicates with a tracking system located on the analytics service provider's server. Information is gathered and used to build reports about activity on your site. Google Analytics is tag based. By contrast, server-side systems provide similar capabilities but stay on your own servers, are purchased like software, and must be set up by your IT team.

Web analytics programs are not just for IT geeks—they're popular with marketing and sales specialists, CEOs, and web developers alike. It takes only seconds to pop open the interface and view some serious trend-over-time reporting. In fact, you'll have so many different ways to see detailed site visitor information that you could easily overload and fall face-first into your computer screen. See Figure 6.12 for an example of a web analytics screen.

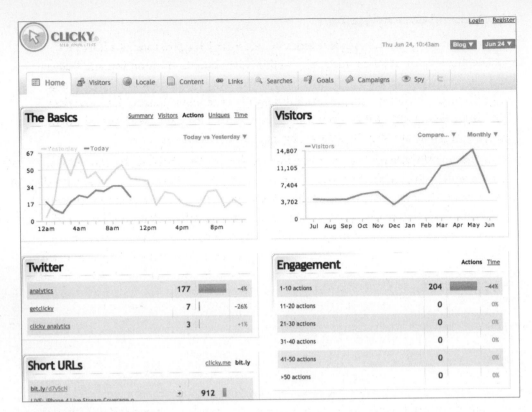

Figure 6.12 Clicky data example

Service Options

Free or inexpensive web analytics options include Google Analytics, Yahoo! Web Analytics, Clicky, Mint, Piwik, Woopra, and those ubiquitous stats packages, such as AWStats and Webalizer, that come bundled with many web hosting solutions. Additionally, paid search providers Google AdWords and Microsoft adCenter offer strong conversion-tracking capabilities, which do not take the place of a full-service analytics program but are fabulously useful, and free with your advertising account.

For those with deeper pockets, providers of fee-based web analytics systems include Omniture WebTrends and Coremetrics. Consult their websites for more information, or see our companion site at www.yourseoplan.com for links to reviews.

For a larger website, analytics can easily demand the attention of a full-time staff member. For a small business, this is something that you can visit about once a week, or more if you can't resist!

Feeling overwhelmed? We can save you some time:

 Pearl of Wisdom: If you're a small organization, stop using the free stats package that comes with your hosting solution and start using Google Analytics.

Going Metric—What to Watch and Why

Setting up a web analytics program doesn't necessarily require tons of effort or expense, but we admit that it may very well involve some hoop-jumping and budget-bumping on your part. And perhaps you're wondering, "Just what am I going to get out of all this?" Although you can find thousands of reports, charts, data visualizations, and trend manifestations out there, you can go a long way with just a few simple pieces of information. We'll list these key metrics for you now.

Unique Visitors and Page Views Knowing the total traffic to your website doesn't tell you much. It won't tell you whether your visitors are the ones you targeted, what path they took through your website, whether they made a purchase, or how happy they were during their visit. Nevertheless, it's one of those little numbers that you. just. need. to. know. Your web analytics program will do its best to determine a total number of unique visitors based on IP addresses and any other info it can gather. Admittedly, the number is not perfectly accurate. But it's a good tool for tracking trends. After all, what does it really matter if you had 1,015 or 1,045 unique visitors this week? What matters most is whether you're up or down from last week.

And while you're at it, banish the word *hits* from your vocabulary. *Hits* describes the number of times a request is made to your server, and *page views* describes the number of times an entire page is called by a browser. So if there are dozens of images on a given page, there will be dozens of hits recorded for each page view. Depending on your conversion goal, you may want to focus on the number of page views or unique visitors, but never hits.

Referrers and Keywords After all your link-building efforts, wouldn't you love to know which sites are actually sending you traffic? After optimizing for the search engines, wouldn't you love to know which search terms your visitors used to find you? This is where your stats start to become truly useful to your SEO campaign. Your analytics program can tell you where your site visitors came from, and even more important, for those who came to your website from search engines, it can tell you the exact keywords they searched for. This can be a good source of ideas for new keywords to target. It is sure to tell you whether your paid directory listings are worth their cost. And it may even give you insights into what new content you should be developing for your site.

Users who typed your URL directly into their browsers or clicked from a bookmark are not referred traffic; they're called *direct traffic*. Users who clicked from an email link or a mobile app are considered referred traffic but may be tracked separately from other sources depending on your analytics program.

Entry Pages Your SEO Plan focuses on a favorite set of landing pages, chosen by you. But your web analytics review may show you that people are entering your site on entirely different pages than you expected. Sure, you know people are coming to the home page, but would you be shocked to learn that a big chunk of visitors are entering somewhere else, like your site map page? And would that leave you scrambling to improve the messaging there? We love watching this metric because it reminds us to design *every* page on the site as a potential landing page. Top entry pages are the queen bee pages of your site. Once you identify them, you will give them the royal treatment: optimizing, monitoring, and protecting their integrity when a site redesign threatens to change them in any significant way.

Exit Pages and Bounces Site exits are often looked at as a sign that something's gone wrong on a web page, but remember: Everyone exits your site eventually. So unless you're looking at exits during a defined linear process, like right in the middle of a shopping cart purchase, site exits alone aren't going to tell you a whole lot about how to improve your user experience.

Since *exit pages* (the pages from which visitors leave your site) are a metric with limited usefulness, we suggest looking at *bounces* instead. A bounce is defined as a visitor leaving the site after viewing just one page. If a large percentage of your site visitors are bouncing out, either you're inviting the wrong crowd to your party or there's something very unappetizing greeting them at the door!

Here are a few points you should know about bounce rates:

- When looking at pages that bounce, don't be surprised if your home page is high on the list. It's common for people to arrive at your site and immediately realize it's not what they're looking for.

- Don't always assume that a page bounce is a failure. If you have a phone number on every page, for example, then a single page visit may be all your visitors needed to accomplish their goal.

- If you've got two different domains or your store is on a different subdomain than your primary website, your bounce rates may be delivering faulty info. We've seen situations where every time someone clicks to the store, the analytics program records a site exit. That means a store purchase will look like a bounce! (If this is happening to you, fix it! Check your analytics program documentation for instructions.)

With these caveats in mind, we think you'll find bounce rates one of the more useful web analytics metrics. Combined with page views (which are really the same metric— a bounce rate is just a single page view), they can help you identify the best and worst keywords, referrers, and entry pages on your site.

Newbie Cheat Sheet: Setting Up Google Analytics

What does it mean to set up Google Analytics? Here's the deal, in ludicrously brief detail:

Step 1 Go to www.google.com/analytics/. You'll need to set up an account and enter some basic information about your website.

Step 2 Follow the instructions so that Google can generate a tracking tag for your website. It might look like this:

```
<script type="text/javascript">

  var _gaq = _gaq || [];
  _gaq.push(['_setAccount', 'UA-1234567-8']);
  _gaq.push(['_trackPageview']);

  (function() {
    var ga = document.createElement('script'); ga.type = 'text/javascript'; ➡
ga.async = true;
    ga.src = ('https:' == document.location.protocol ? 'https://ssl' : ➡
'http://www') + '.google-analytics.com/ga.js';
    var s = document.getElementsByTagName('script')[0]; ➡
s.parentNode.insertBefore(ga, s);
  })();

</script>
```

Step 3 Email this tag to your web developer, with instructions that it must be placed on every page of the site, in the <body> tag.

Time on Site The amount of time that visitors spend on your site can be a helpful indication of how engaged they are. Time on site is a useful metric when your page view data doesn't tell the whole story—for example, if your site contains a great deal of content that displays without refreshing the page (photo slide shows, online videos, or Ajax applications might fall into this category).

Errors Among other things, your server will log a *404 error* ("File not Found") every time a user tries to access a nonexistent URL. This can help you find inbound—or internal—links that are using incorrect or out-of-date URLs. Tag-based programs, including Google Analytics, may require a workaround to show you these errors.

xtra cred Web analytics gurus swear by *audience segmentation*, which allows you to break your visitors up into separate groups for analysis. See Chapter 10 for audience segmentation suggestions.

xtra cred Did Week 2 leave you hungry for more competitor data? The Google Analytics benchmarking service will compare some metrics for your site against other industry sites. The trade-off: You'll have to allow Google to use your data, in anonymous form, for the tool. To learn more, go to the Analytics help center at www.google.com/support/analytics/ and type <benchmarking> into the search box.

The list of useful metrics could go on and on, but you have limited time, so we stuck with the basics.

If you already have access to this data through a web analytics program, congratulations! Today, you'll look through it for the information just listed.

 Now: Open your web analytics program (if it exists) and find the key information listed in this section. If you don't have a web analytics program or the one you're using can't provide these metrics, read on.

If you don't have a web analytics program in place or you only have the package that was provided by the web hosting provider (these passed muster in the '90s, but you deserve better), we're going to give you some really simple advice: Do yourself a favor and set up Google Analytics. Consider it a pilot program: After six months with Google Analytics, you'll know loads more about your site and your organization's analytics needs, and you'll be fabulously prepared for your next analytics purchase, if needed.

Now: If you don't have a web analytics program in place, start the ball rolling on a Google Analytics setup.

With all the web analytics wisdom you gained today, you're perfectly positioned to start sorting out your online website conversion tracking tomorrow.

Mobile Tracking: Small Screens, Big Business

Have you looked at your own website on a mobile device? Don't be the last one to find out that it's a poor user experience. eMarketer predicts that the number of mobile users accessing the Internet will reach 134.3 million in 2013, so you have every reason to be interested in how well your site is engaging and converting visitors on mobile devices.

If you have a separate mobile site in addition to your standard website, or if you are scheming to addict the masses with your new mobile app, you'll want to track how people use this content.

Whatever analytics program you're using, it's likely you'll find mobile analytics data if you look for it. Mobile tracking has not yet reached the point of reliability and ease of use that we now enjoy for standard website tracking, but there is a lot of information available to you.

For example, using Google Analytics, you can track:

- Visitors who come to your mobile site
- Visitors who come from mobile devices to your standard site
- Visitor interaction with your mobile apps

See the following graphic for a look into the Google Analytics mobile reporting options.

	Operating System ⌄	None ⌄	Visits ↓
1.	iPhone		363
2.	iPod		185
3.	Android		151
4.	iPad		96
5.	BlackBerry		75
6.	Samsung		5
7.	PalmOS		4
8.	Windows		4
9.	SymbianOS		3
10.	MOT		1

Is your mobile audience on a fast track to purchasing? Are they reading and writing more reviews than other visitors? You can set up an audience segment in analytics to understand what this portion of the population is doing for you and how you can serve them better. But keep in mind: Knowing your mobile visitor landscape is helpful, but if the vast majority of your users are accessing your site from non-mobile devices, you should focus your priorities accordingly.

If you want to keep on top of the latest developments in mobile tracking on Google Analytics, go to www.google.com/support/analytics/ and type <mobile> into the search box.

Tuesday: Tracking Online Conversions

Different organizations can have vastly different metrics, ranging from the number of people buying your product to how many third graders download your science report. Whether it's online sales, brand awareness, or just page views you're after, you know what your conversions are because you defined them way back in Chapter 1.

Earlier in this chapter, we asked you to document the number of conversions on your site. Did you have a ball filling in the good news or get depressed scribbling down some uncertain best guesses? Today and tomorrow, you'll develop a plan for tracking your conversion goals. Think baby steps: You probably won't finalize your tracking plan, but you'll set the wheels in motion.

Online conversions, such as purchases, downloads, and form submittals, are relatively easy to track. Here's how the process works:

- Identify Your Conversion Pages
- Measure and React

Identify Your Conversion Pages

Web analytics programs typically define conversions (also called goals) in a simple way: When a certain page on your website is reached, the conversion has happened. In this methodology, you'll need to choose a page on your site that indicates a conversion has been completed. Very possibly, this will be your transaction completion page or confirmation page—it's wherever you say thank you to your customers for a purchase, download, registration, or form completion (You did remember to say thank you, didn't you?).

Google Analytics allows you to easily set up Time on Site or Pages Visited goals. If you have goals like "I want my visitors to visit at least three pages on my site," or "I want my visitors to stay on my site for more than two minutes," this will be the right choice for you.

Here are some ways to finesse even simple conversion tracking when you want to squeeze out a little extra insight:

- Your site can have more than one conversion goal. In addition to an actual purchase or form submittal, we often like to define conversions that describe a more modest level of success: perhaps a visit to the "Products" or "Contact" page. For B2Bs or other sites with a lower overall traffic level, getting more numbers into your conversion bucket gives you more useful information to work with.
- You can define unwanted conversions, too. This is particularly useful for paid search traffic. For example, if job seekers are not a valuable audience for you, you can define your "Employment" page as a conversion. You'll gain a better

understanding of where those folks are coming from—and how much you're spending on that traffic.

- A dollar value can be assigned to online purchases. If you've got a good handle on their value, you can even assign dollar amounts to a non-purchase action, like a download or form submittal.

Now: Think about what page or pages on your site could be defined as conversion completion pages.

Measure and React

You may be thinking about your online conversions for the first time. But even for folks who have been doing it for years, it can be absurdly difficult to interpret in a meaningful way. Here are a few good ways to frame your thoughts around your conversion data:

Conversion Rates Tied to Paid Search Bids The quickest and most satisfying use of a conversion measurement is closing the loop with paid search spending. With pay-per-click advertising, every sponsored keyword has a price tag associated with it. Knowing how many conversions you're getting for your money will tell you whether any current paid search efforts are on target. A good example is the "Employment" page we discussed previously. You'd probably be distressed to find that you're paying thousands of dollars to bring job seekers to your site.

Conversion Rates Inform Organic Search Targeting Here's a way to put your conversion tracking to good use. Using your web analytics or paid search program, discover which keywords are delivering the highest conversion rates. Are there any surprises on the list? Any that deserve their own landing pages? It's not too late to go back and add these keywords to your top-priority list. Remember that if you devote your energies to known success stories, even modest gains in traffic can mean large gains in conversion numbers.

Paths to Conversion Inform the Sales Process You may already know that more people are buying your cheaper products than your high-priced ones. But conversion tracking can tell you exactly what path your customers followed before they made the decision to buy. Did they go straight for the low-priced goods, or did they spend time considering your expensive products first? Did they read any reviews? Examining paths to conversion gives you meaningful insight into your customers' behavior and may even help you figure out a new way to organize your products.

Even if you don't know what to do with this information, it's important to get comfortable with looking at it. Once your learning curve evens out, you may be surprised at how easily you can find real meaning in the data.

Conversion tracking: You know you want it! Now that you've digested the basics, you can use today to discuss it with your team. Then, it's decision time: Which system will you start with?

 Now: Start the process of setting up online conversion tracking on your site. If you already have online conversion tracking in place, double-check the Historical Conversions you recorded in your Site Assessment Worksheet during week 2 and update that number if you have more accurate information at this time.

New software, new statistics, new jargon: These are the things that make tracking online conversions challenging to the uninitiated. Now, get ready for a whole new kind of challenge, because tracking offline conversions is practically an art form!

Wednesday: Tracking Offline Conversions

If you're having trouble tracking offline conversions, like phone calls or walk-in customers, you may find some comfort in knowing that you're not alone. This is a challenging situation that stumps even the biggest of bigwigs. And if your website is out there trying to convince someone to, say, vote for a certain school board representative, how are you ever going to measure the contribution that your SEO work made to the campaign?

To track your offline conversions, you'll need to be creative. Here are a few ideas for some of the more common scenarios:

Set up a special phone number. If a large percentage of your sales take place over the phone, it may be difficult to show that the website, much less your SEO campaign, had anything to do with them. But there is one way: Set up a unique phone number and display it on your website—and nowhere else. Then, have your sales team monitor and track how many calls come in to that line and how many of those calls turn into conversions.

For a greater level of detail, you can sign up with services such as AccuTrack or ClickPath that will generate unique 800 numbers and dynamically display them on your web pages, linking each call to a keyword and ad source.

A word of caution about using these types of phone numbers: They may interfere with the search engines' ability to identify your business's geographic location. If local search rankings are important to you (you'll learn more about local search in Chapter 8, "Month Two: Establish the Habit"), you may want to avoid using unique 800 numbers for tracking.

Run campaigns on things nobody else is promoting. You can get an inkling of the effects of your SEO work by promoting a specific event or product that nobody else in your organization has taken the time to promote. For example, if you put your SEO efforts into promoting Tuesday Night Half-Price Pickles and there is no other marketing for it, you can relish the thought that most of the people who show up found out about the event as a result of your SEO work.

Include coupons or promotion codes on your website. How will you know if walk-in customers used your website to research your products or services? One way is to create coupons or promotion codes on your website that these customers can print out and bring into your store for a discount. Sure, it won't tell you whether they used a search engine to find your site, but at least you'll have something to link your "real-world" traffic to your online traffic.

Cultivate communication. If your site goals fall into the persuasion category, give your users an opportunity to tell their stories with "Post your success story here" or "Share your smoking cessation/parenting/scuba diving tips" links. An increase in the number of postings can indicate your SEO success.

Simply ask. When all else fails, simply ask your offline customers or clients how they found you. It's not the most accurate information, but it's better than nothing. Be sure that your traditional marketing, sales, and PR team put out the question in print, on the phone, or in person whenever they have the opportunity.

Now: Brainstorm with your team on options for tracking your offline conversions and finalize a plan.

Tracking the Intangible

Many organizations report that branding is a primary goal of their SEO campaigns. But how do you track these less-than-tangible factors? The Left Brain and Right Brain debate.

The Right Brain says, "Whether you call it Branding with a capital B or just 'keeping up appearances,' the image that your organization projects through the search engines is important. If the top-ranked search result for your company name is a rant by a disgruntled former employee or an embarrassing 1-star review, you've got an image problem that SEO can help fix.

"Branding improvements may be a fringe benefit of your SEO campaign, or they may be a central goal. Either way, you'll want to document outcomes like improved search engine listings; inbound link updates; cleanup of outdated, private, or inappropriate content; and mentions on the Social Web. Keep a record of these accomplishments, and pull them out when you need some good news in the analysis and interpretation sections of your SEO status reports! I think of these positive little pieces of information as 'exclamation point moments.'"

The Left Brain says, "Things like eliminating references to nonexistent products and services and monitoring blog references, media mentions, and hate sites are so important that they need quantitative measurement. When the effectiveness of an SEO campaign comes into question, you need more than an exclamation point; you need hard data!"

Tracking the Intangible *(Continued)*

"Try to quantify your brand-improvement accomplishments in some way. For example, 'Eight out of fourteen of our misspelled listings have now been corrected,' 'Our company name has been mentioned in 63 tweets this month, up from 24 in the previous month,' or 'Our specially designed landing page now outranks the 'hate site' listing for the keywords 'I Hate ZippyCo,' a phrase that approximately 250 people per month search for.' Reputation monitoring products like Radian6, Trackur, and Nielson BuzzMetrics measure online consumer gossip, reviews, and word of mouth, and even identify influencers in your niche so that you know who you most want to impress. Numbers will help provide a clear baseline and measurable change. You'll be glad to have facts and figures at the ready when you need to justify another round of SEO spending!"

Thursday: Benchmarks and Goals

Have you ever heard something like this from your auto mechanic: "Well, we can try to replace some parts, but we can't be exactly sure that it'll stop the rattling sound, and oh, by the way, it'll cost ya a bundle"?

SEO can be pretty similar. There are so many factors involved in SEO—some within your control (for example, page text and site structure) and some far, far outside your control (for example, search engine ranking algorithms or partnerships)—that it is very hard to predict outcomes. But we know that in real life you need to have at least some inkling of what you can expect from your efforts. Mechanics offer estimates; SEO pros offer reasonable expectations. Let's create some reasonable expectations for your website today.

SEO Benchmarking and the Crystal Ball

We're often asked to predict the outcomes of our SEO recommendations—and we've found that the larger a company, the more intense its desire to know the anticipated return on investment of an SEO endeavor. Trouble is, the change resulting from any one site edit is nearly impossible to predict. First, you don't know exactly what the resulting ranking change will be, and second, you don't know how that ranking change will translate into clicks and conversions. Here's how we suggest you handle requests for SEO fortune-telling:

- Suggest a test: "To predict the effect of updating our HTML titles sitewide, I'd like to start with only the subsection of our site devoted to selling chopsticks." With partial data in hand, you can extrapolate to sitewide effects.

- Use an if-then statement: "If we can get a top-3 rank for the term <biodegradable chopsticks>, our online revenue may increase as much as 80 percent."

Here are some factors that can point to success for your SEO campaign: easy fixes, such as basic optimization factors that are missing from your current site; well-balanced keywords with low competition, high relevance, and high popularity; a poor current status; an enthusiastic team; a good budget for paid search; and competitors stuck in the Stone Age. How these factors combine and balance will affect your expectations. Let's look at some possible combinations and what you might conclude:

Poor Current Status/High Current Optimization/No Easy Fixes This is a difficult combination. Your current optimization level is already high, which means you don't have a lot of space for improvement in that arena. If on-site keyword optimization is all you're able to work on, you should set your expectations low. But if you have a strong multidisciplined team ready and able to work on a resource-intensive site content improvement and social media effort, you can set your expectations higher.

Fair Current Status/Poor Optimization/An Enthusiastic Team You have room to grow and a team that can make it happen. It's reasonable to expect to bump up your Fair status. But will it go to Good, Very Good, or Excellent? That depends on the other factors: competitiveness, budget, easy fixes, and so on.

High Competition/An Unenthusiastic Team/A Healthy Budget With two major factors working against you, you can't expect that your organic SEO campaign will show strong results. Applying some of that healthy budget to paid search advertising just might be able to pick up the slack.

We've created a worksheet to make today's goal-setting task a little easier.

Now: Go to your SEO Idea Bank and open up the SEO Growth Worksheet.

First, assess your organization's SEO room to grow. Consider each factor below, and give yourself a "room to grow" point for everything below that is true about your website.

Current search engine status is poor.

Current optimization level is poor.

I have compiled a list of well-matched, popular keywords.

My SEO team is enthusiastic about making needed changes.

I anticipate that it will be easy to make text changes to my website.

I have the appropriate personnel available.

I have the buy-in from the powers-that-be in my organization.

I have a budget for paid search.

My website faces a low level of competition.

I have discovered untapped markets or SEO opportunities.

My site is "buzzworthy," or my organization's activities are newsworthy.

Now: Fill in your SEO Growth Plan room-to-grow estimates.

With this list in your pocket, you'll know whether you can look for massive improvements or just a little upward bump. We've seen SEO campaigns that have brought in enormous improvements, along the lines of thousands of percent, but we've also seen campaigns that have worked hard to keep traffic steady through a stormy period such as a redesign or a company transition. If you have a lot of "room to grow" points, you can consider higher expectations for improvements.

Here are some ways SEO campaign goals can be structured:

- Increase unique visitors by X percent.
- Double the traffic to the top X landing pages.
- Generate X new leads in the next X months.
- Improve our listing quality in Google.
- Reduce the number of unqualified leads.
- Reduce the cost of our paid search campaign by X percent.

Now: You can riff on an example from the list, or invent your own goal that best matches your organization's objectives. Finalize your campaign goals. Try to be specific, and realize that these goals can and should be revisited as you continue with Your SEO Plan.

We hope we've made it clear that there is a lot you can't predict in SEO. We've done our best to give you a general idea of what you might expect, but you should be very careful not to make any promises you can't keep. Remember, reputable SEOs never guarantee any particular rank on search engines.

Friday: Quick Reference Report

Anybody *can* look at your spreadsheets and notes to figure out how your site is doing now and where it might go if optimized—but probably less than half the people you encounter will *want to*. What's more, it's likely that the people who glaze over when they see a column of numbers will be the people you feel should know about them the most. So today you're going to boil all this info down into succinct, readable descriptions.

You spent four weeks researching and analyzing data about keywords, your competition, your site performance, and optimization, not to mention your business goals and conversions. But you want others to be able to "get it" in a five-minute read (or, let's be realistic, a two-minute skim). A Quick Reference should do the trick. Today's task is a writing exercise. We want you to open up a blank document and write a one-pager of major issues and goals. You might be tempted to skip this step, but please give it a try. The point of this effort is not just to document your work, but also to do the analysis and mental sifting that allows you to write about it intelligently. The way you tell your SEO story is what will ultimately separate you from the SEO hacks and newbies out there.

Build your Quick Reference document by answering the following questions:

What is this SEO campaign trying to accomplish? You may wish to copy and paste your Conversions table, including desired conversions and target audiences, from the Goals Worksheet you completed in Chapter 1.

What are the top keywords and landing pages? List your top keywords and the landing pages that you finalized in Week 1. We recommend that you break the keywords and landing pages into two separate lists for ease of reading.

Who are our top competitors? Copy the names of your Big Five competitors from your Competition Worksheet. Use your judgment to characterize the search engine competition as a whole on a scale of Not Competitive to Very Competitive.

What is our current site visibility? Rate the overall level of your site's current status on search engines: Poor, Fair, Good, Very Good, or Excellent. If you're finding mostly negative information in your links and status assessments, and lots of red flags, you're probably in the Poor slot. To get an Excellent grade, your site would need to have top page results for most or all of its target keywords, a lot of high-quality inbound links, and very few or no red flags.

What is our current site performance? This week, you had the opportunity to compile some nitty-gritty data about your website performance. If you have at least one month's worth of analytics data that you trust, you may wish to record any of the benchmarks we discussed previously. These include unique visitors, page views, top referrers and keywords, top entry pages, top exit pages, number of bounces, average time on site, and number of error pages visited. And write down your historical conversions here, too, whether you've got hard data or you're just using the "best guess" method we described in Week 2.

What is our current site optimization level? Rate your site's current optimization level on a scale of Poor to Excellent. Review your Site Optimization Worksheet. Do you see mostly yes answers? This means that your landing pages are in good optimization shape. A spattering of yeses and nos? Put your site in the Fair category. A whole lotta nothing? Rate your site Poor.

What are our major red flags and opportunities? Be honest about the problems you're seeing—write them down now even if you don't have a clear plan for fixing them. Whatever your SEO problems are, there's a good chance you'll be able to fix them by working through the rest of the book. Describe any exciting opportunities you'd like to explore.

What are the campaign goals? This is the place for the goals you figured out yesterday.

Now: Complete the "Quick Reference" document.

Now it's time to spread the news: Your SEO campaign is off and running! Deliver this report to anyone who has an interest or potential role in Your SEO Plan, and make yourself available to discuss it.

Your SEO Plan

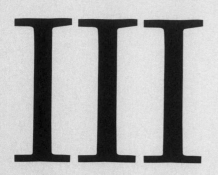

You've made it through the foundation and strategy phases, and now it's time to implement Your SEO Plan! In this part, you'll follow three months of day-by-day steps to take advantage of your site's positive attributes and address its imperfections, and you'll establish daily habits to keep targeted traffic coming to your site.

Month One: Kick It into Gear

This month, you'll make a first pass at four important areas in your SEO campaign: basic on-page optimization, site structure, link building, and content improvement. You'll spend a week making real headway on each activity, with daily tasks that we estimate will take an hour or so.

Chapter Contents

Week 1: Basic Site Optimization

In Chapter 3, "Eternal Truths of SEO," you learned that the text in your landing pages and titles is one of the most important and longstanding SEO factors. This week you're going to optimize them, with the goal of creating a better environment for your target audiences, not to mention positively influencing how search engines view and rank your website. You'll also tackle basic internal linking strategy to ensure that search engine robots have easy access to your landing pages. With these improvements in place, your site will have a basic level of on-page optimization: nothing tricky or fancy, and no time wasted on tiny technicalities—just common-sense, best-practices solutions. Remember, there is no single silver bullet in SEO:

 Pearl of Wisdom: Site optimization usually includes many little efforts, which in combination bring better presence on search engines.

You'll keep track of all your changes in one document as you go, and on Friday you'll deliver this document to the folks in charge of making edits to your website. If you're the code-slinger on the project, wait until Friday to dive into your edits! Stay in the optimization groove Monday through Thursday, and you'll benefit from a more focused approach.

Here are your daily task assignments:

Monday: Page Titles

Tuesday: Meta Tags

Wednesday: Site Text

Thursday: Internal Links

Friday: Implementation

Monday: Page Titles

In Chapter 3, you learned that HTML page titles show up as the first line of clickable text in most search engine results. That fact, along with their not insignificant influence in search engine ranking algorithms, makes HTML page titles one of the most important optimization spots on your website.

Today, you're going to take a stab at writing unique and compelling page titles for each of your landing pages. We've created a document where you can keep track of these edits, called the Site Optimization Worksheet.

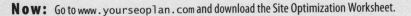 **Now:** Go to www.yourseoplan.com and download the Site Optimization Worksheet.

You'll want the Quick Reference sheet you created last month handy to keep you in tune with your goals and keywords as you write. We've compiled some dos and don'ts to keep you on the right track:

DO keep it short. Like those old telephone answering machines that cut you off before you finish talking, most search engines display only about 70 characters (including spaces) in the listing title. So to get your message across, include important keywords toward the beginning of the title, and make sure that the first 70 or so characters of your title form a complete thought.

DO include your keywords… Your HTML page title is influential in the ranking algorithm, so it must include your target keywords! Since your space is limited, focus on the two to three keywords that you previously matched with your landing page. Feeling a bit squeezed by the 70-character cutoff? Remember that you can combine keywords to save space.

…but DON'T overdo it! First and foremost, you want to connect with your intended audience. Excessive keyword repetition is a shortsighted strategy. Is this a marketing message or a synonym sandwich?

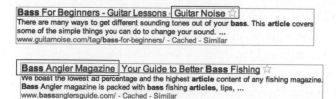

Remember to think of the big picture! Your approach to site optimization will affect more than just ranks—it will also affect your visitors' decision to part with their time and money.

DO include your name. Your organization's name will not only differentiate your listing from your competitors', it may also earn you more clicks. Maybe your name carries a good reputation with it, or maybe it provides important context, making your listing more attractive or relevant. Notice how the company names in the following listings provide crucial context for the search term <bass articles>:

Bass For Beginners - Guitar Lessons - Guitar Noise ☆
There are many ways to get different sounding tones out of your **bass**. This **article** covers some of the simple things you can do to change your sound. ...
www.guitarnoise.com/tag/**bass**-for-beginners/ - Cached - Similar

Bass Angler Magazine | Your Guide to Better Bass Fishing ☆
We boast the lowest ad percentage and the highest **article** content of any fishing magazine. **Bass** Angler magazine is packed with **bass** fishing **articles**, tips, ...
www.**bass**anglersguide.com/ - Cached - Similar

DON'T assume your slogan does the job. Even if branding is your only objective, you need to think about whether your slogan contains your targeted keywords and, if so, whether you think it will encourage visits to your site. This listing shows a very catchy slogan:

Morton®Salt - when it rains it pours® ☆
Provides information on consumer products of **Morton® Salt**.
www.**morton**salt.com/ - Cached - Similar

But is it really better for visibility and clicks than using targeted keywords such as "gourmet and specialty salts," "Ice Melter," or "meatloaf seasoning mix"?

DO write unique titles for each page. You've got enough competition out there. Don't add to it by pitting your landing pages against each other with identical page titles, like this site does:

Since each of your landing pages is already targeting a unique subset of your top-priority keywords, you can always find a different angle for each page title. Give each of your landing pages the chance to shine on its own merits.

DON'T duplicate site navigation in the title. Whether generated automatically or written by hand, page titles are often used as a place to mirror the navigational structure of a site. We won't say never for this because, if your site sections are named well, it can be an effective way to display keywords. For example, a furniture store might have a landing page titled "Frank's Furniture – Patio Furniture – Wicker." This works—the navigation text is very brief and includes target keywords. But most sites aren't built this way, and you don't want words like "Index," "Main Page," or "Our Products" to take up space that's best reserved for your targeted marketing message.

DO think of formulas for larger sites or blogs. If your site contains a larger number of landing pages, you'll do well to write out a couple of formulas. Patterns like "Joe's Sauces: {Sauce Name}" can translate into zesty titles for large swaths of your website. Bloggers, a simpler formula for your titles could be "{Blog Name} – {Post Title}." See the sidebar "Product Page Optimization: Playing by the Rules at Dragonborn Games" for more on formulaic optimization.

DO use title case. In our experience, Titles with the First Letters Capitalized get clicked more.

DON'T give your home page the title "Home." And "Welcome" isn't a whole lot better. We think your title should say more than this one does:

Product Page Optimization: Playing by the Rules at Dragonborn Games

The folks at Dragonborn Games sell about 500 products at their online store. They'd love to rank well for their favorite keywords, but they're in a competitive space, and they're planning a strategy that's not too labor intensive. They'll create formulas to optimize product and category pages for a wide range of keywords. Each of the product pages may not get much search traffic, but in aggregate, this long tail can give them a satisfactory stream of customers.

On the Dragonborn Games website, the 10 product category pages and 500 individual product pages are well suited to a formulaic approach to keyword optimization, because they are similar pages performing similar functions. If this approach appeals to you, first, do some keyword research to determine how people are searching for products like the ones you sell, using your keyword data tool of choice. Dragonborn Games asked: Do people search for just the game name, or something like <buy chess set online>, or any other combinations? Do searchers include a brand name, too? Once you know what word patterns you're targeting, work up a set of optimization rules for a typical product page. Here's a list of product page optimization rules that the Dragonborn Games team came up with:

- HTML page title always follows the formula "[brand: game name] Game - Dragonborn Games" (for example, "Hasbro: Deluxe Scrabble Game - Dragonborn Games")
- The product name always follows the formula "[brand: game name]"
- The meta description always includes "buy [brand: game name] online. Same-day delivery and satisfaction guaranteed!"
- The URL always follows the formula /brand-game-name.html (for example, hasbro-deluxe-scrabble.html)
- The product photo always includes an ALT tag following the formula "Games: [Brand]: [Game Name]"
- Internal text links pointing to the product page always include brand and game name

We love where they're going with this!

Formulaic product and category page optimization doesn't mean you can't still choose a small number of highly popular terms and target them on your home page, or even include them site-wide by incorporating them into your formulas. This combination of queen bee keywords (top target terms that get royal treatment on your site) with long-tail keywords (lower-volume keywords with a large number of different landing page possibilities) can be a powerful SEO strategy.

Now: Write optimized page titles for each of your landing pages, and add them to your Site Optimization Worksheet.

Tuesday: Meta Tags

In Chapter 3, you learned the basics of meta tags. Today you'll optimize two invisible text elements: the meta description tag and the meta keywords tag.

Meta Description Tag

We see London, we see France. We see... your site's meta description tag? Yes, not unlike your undies, your meta description tag is something that usually stays hidden but can be displayed to the world when you least expect it. For those rare times yours is exposed, you want to be proud of what people see (and here it's probably best to drop the undies metaphor). Many sites make the mistake of ignoring this tag. Today you'll make sure yours is not only present but also written with your SEO goals in mind.

As you learned in Chapter 3, the search engines usually display snippets from your site text in their listings. Here are some possible scenarios in which your meta description tag might be displayed instead:

- When there is no HTML content on the page, such as in the case of an all-Flash or all-graphics site
- When someone searches for your site using your URL but no keywords
- When off-page factors make your site a relevant match for a search but no exact match is found in your site's text

Search engines often display 150 or more characters for the listing description, so you have a lot of space—relative to the page title, anyway—to convey your message. If good writing comes naturally to you, you have a lot of opportunity to make this tag stand out. But if writing isn't your strong suit, this tag gives you a little more room to make mistakes. Bring in a proofreader if you need to; this is a bad spot for an embarrassing typo.

Here are some pointers for writing a great meta description tag:

Keep it informative. Think of the meta description tag as an "About Us" blurb, not a "Buy Now!" advertisement. It's your keyword-rich *elevator speech* (that's a marketing term for the description of yourself you might give in a 30-second elevator ride). It's not worth the upkeep to write this tag to promote special events or deals. And just as it's probably not helpful to scream words like "WORLD'S BEST!" elsewhere in your marketing message, the same holds true in your meta description tag.

Pair it with the page title. Although you can't be sure exactly when or how people will see your meta description tag, it's a sure bet that when it is shown, it will be right under your optimized page title. So don't repeat your title text in your description tag.

Include your keywords... Although the meta description tag is not a factor in influencing rank, it may have a big influence on the searcher who is lucky enough to view it. So include your target keywords because they'll be bolded in the search results. Notice how the bolding catches your eye:

Beit Haverim/South Metro **Jewish Congregation** - A Reform Jewish ...
An inviting, spiritually rich **Reform Jewish Congregation** located just outside of **Portland**, **Oregon**, for Jews by Birth, Jews by Choice, and Jews at Heart.
www.beithav.org/ - Cached - Similar

...but don't overdo it! Stuffing the meta description tag with a long keyword list isn't likely to help your ranks and will probably generate vast waves of indifference with searchers. Why not use this tag to give the searcher a reason to come to your site instead?

Make it unique. Like your HTML page title, your meta description tag should be custom written for each landing page to match its specific content.

> **Now:** Using your newly optimized page titles and your landing page content as a guide, write optimized meta description tags for your landing pages in your Site Optimization Worksheet.

Some SEO strategists feel that with search engines doing such a good job of displaying text from your pages, you might as well leave off the meta description tag altogether. We're not in this camp—we try to take advantage of every smidgen of control we can get—but the slacker in you might embrace it.

slacker

Meta Keywords Tag

As you already know, the meta keywords tag is not an influential tag in SEO. We almost always skip this tag when we're optimizing sites for our clients. And get this: Google has even publicly stated that it doesn't look at meta keywords for rankings.

In other words: Why are you still reading this? Since you're obviously highly motivated to put some meta keywords on your site, here's a quick-and-dirty method that you can use:

1. Go to the Keywords Worksheet that you compiled in your Prep month, and look through your flagged keywords.

2. For each landing page, decide which of the flagged keywords you think are relevant. Insert them into the Meta Keywords Tag column of the Site Optimization Worksheet.

3. Add any keywords that didn't make the flagged list but that you think are appropriate and relevant.

4. For each landing page, add your company name, location if applicable, and any common alternate spellings or misspellings you can think of.

Don't overthink it. You're done.

> **Now:** If you feel inclined to do so, compile optimized meta keyword tags for your landing pages and place them in your Site Optimization Worksheet.

Wednesday: Site Text

Has there been something about your site's text that has set your teeth on edge since you started learning about SEO? Is there anything in the content that you know is working against your site's search engine visibility? Or are your keywords nowhere to be found? Now it's time to address these issues. Today is a momentous day because you're actually going to put your keyword research to good use on your site's visible text content.

First Impressions

Have you been wondering how people select which search results to click on—and how to make yours the one they choose? Search behavior research can help you understand and influence their click decisions:

- In a 2007 eye-tracking study, researchers found that searchers' behavior was strikingly different for *navigational* search, in which a person is trying to find a specific website, vs. *informational* search, in which a person is looking for an answer to a question. For example, navigational searchers are much more likely than informational searchers to try a new query right away if they don't see a good match in the search results. (Source: Microsoft Research and University of Washington)

- Cornell eye-tracking research shows that searchers spend 30 percent of their time reading the listing title, 43 percent of their time reading the listing description, and 21 percent of their time reading the URL. The average total time before a click choice is made is 5.7 seconds. (Source: Cornell University Computer Science & Human-Computer Interaction)

- German researchers asked users how they chose what to click on. The winning factor was clear listing text. That means you should make sure your listings contain readable text, not keyword-stuffed garble. Other important factors were relevance of the listing to the search term, a clear and easy-to-understand description of the page content, and the inclusion of the website's name. (Source: Fittkau and Maaß on behalf of eProfessional GmbH)

Today you will comb through your landing pages for possible text improvements, documenting them as you go. You can approach documentation in a couple of ways. One way is to compile your desired changes in the Text/Content Edits section on the Site Optimization Worksheet. Or, depending on the layout of your site and the extent of your changes, you may just want to print out your landing pages and mark your changes on the printout.

Your goal: Incorporate your two or three designated target keywords onto each of your landing pages without going overboard and cooking up an unreadable keyword porridge. If you have any writers on your SEO team, get them on board for this session. Try these editorial strategies for making your text changes:

- Swap out a specific word for a top-priority keyword every time it appears.
- Swap out a graphic containing a keyword for text.

- Spell out an acronym (at least in its first appearance on the page).
- Expand abbreviated forms of your keywords.
- Make sure your company name exists in text form once on every page.
- Include keywords in links wherever possible.
- Add keyword-rich captions to photos.
- Add a keyword-rich tagline at the bottom of the page.
- Add keywords to page headers.
- Use bold text for keywords. This may provide some ranking benefit but has the potential for making your web copy look cluttered and confusing, so use with caution.

Figure 7.1 shows an example of the kind of edits you might want to make on your own site.

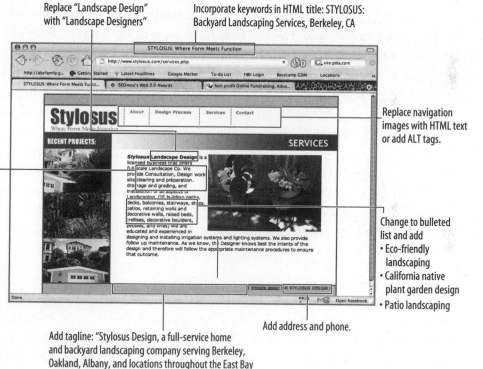

Figure 7.1 Text optimization suggestions for a sample page

Now: Go through your landing pages and compile your list of changes on your Site Optimization Worksheet or page printouts.

Thursday: Internal Links

As the search engines crawl through your site, they are doing more than just moving from one page to the next. They're looking for clues that tell them what the pages on your site are about. Links from page to page inside your site, and the text they contain, provide some of these clues. A well-planned internal linking structure might even help direct some link authority to your more important pages.

Are optimized internal links *the* answer to improved search engine ranks? Nope, they're not. This level of SEO detail is just one of the many little modifications you can make that will add up and make a difference. From our experience, sites that pay attention to their internal linking text are usually a cut above their competitors.

Here are some things to watch out for in assessing your site's internal links:

Use every reasonable opportunity to link. If you want a search-friendly site, the robots need to be able to follow links throughout your site. Does your home page provide links to your landing pages? There may be some obvious opportunities for internal links that you aren't currently taking advantage of. Scan your page copy for product names, calls to action, or other opportunities to add robot-friendly HTML links within your site's text.

For example, we often see home page text that looks like this:

> We're proud of the great reputation our Popsicle Stands have earned. With JuniorPop Stands, SuperPop Stands, and high altitude stands available, you'll be blown away. You can find our products in many retail locations, or buy online.

But modify this text just a little bit, and look at the improvement:

> We're proud of the great reputation our Popsicle Stands have earned. With <u>JuniorPop Stands</u>, <u>SuperPop Stands</u>, and <u>high altitude stands</u> available, you'll be blown away. You can <u>find our products</u> in many <u>retail locations</u>, or <u>buy online</u>.

Why is this better? Because it provides clear, keyword-rich paths to each of your product pages, your store locator, and your online store; it provides a clue to the search engines that these are important pages on your site; and it's much more useful to your site visitors.

Use meaningful text in your links. If you're serious about your site's usability and optimization, you should consider rewriting every "click here" on your site to something more meaningful. Imagine the contextual help you give to a search engine robot, and the favor you do for your website visitors, when you change

> SuperPop Stands are famous for their compact yet sturdy construction. <u>Click here</u> to see why they're so popular.

to

> Why <u>are</u> <u>SuperPop Stands</u> so popular? Because popsicle sellers love their compact yet sturdy construction.

> Bloggers, you are guiltiest when it comes to lazy linking. How many times have you written a blog posting that looks like this: "I am the world's biggest Green Bay Packers fan, as you've seen <u>here</u> and <u>here</u>."

Oh, it's suave, it's carefree, it's ubercool. We get that. And it's fine by us when you're linking out to a YouTube video and you don't care what the search engines think of it. But when you use this linking style for your own internal pages, you've wasted an opportunity to give your link a little context and your site a little optimization boost. And a link is a terrible thing to waste!

Another place we find lazy links is within a site's global navigation, a.k.a. the main menu. When you link to "Our Products" and "Our Services," what keywords are you missing out on? What if you linked to "Our Organization Tools" and "Our Time Saving Services" instead? Now, you don't want to overdo this one—the potential is there to make your page look keyword stuffed, and it might impact your site design. Work together with your designers or writers to see if you can come up with navigation text that looks great and includes keywords, too.

Play favorites: link to landing pages. Maybe your most important landing pages exist alongside thousands of other pages in your site. Robots don't necessarily index every page from every site, so they may simply move on before they find the path to the pages you think are most important. This is a quick fix: Just be sure to add HTML links that place your landing pages no more than two clicks away from the home page.

> An XML Sitemap is another way to steer search engines toward higher-priority pages. Read more about setting up XML Sitemaps in Chapter 10, "Extra Credit and Guilt-Free Slacking."

Site Maps to Guide Human and Nonhuman Visitors

A site map is a page that contains links to the most important pages on your site. Site maps are built with human visitors in mind and are typically integrated seamlessly into the design of a website:

A site map is not to be confused with an XML Sitemap, which has a similar purpose but is built only for search engine robots to crawl:

Site Maps to Guide Human and Nonhuman Visitors *(Continued)*

We think that just about every website can benefit from a site map. Most people know that site maps are good for the user experience: They orient your site visitors and help lost visitors find their way to the right page. But there's even more benefit when you consider SEO. A site map can improve the search engine visibility of your website in several ways:

- By providing search engine robots with links to navigate through your site

- By pointing search engine robots to dynamic or hard-to-reach pages that might not be accessible otherwise

- By acting as a possible landing page, optimized for search traffic

- By providing ready-to-use content for the File Not Found page where visitors are automatically taken if they try to go to a nonexistent URL within your domain

If your site is small enough that links to every page are included in your global navigation or absolutely every page on your site is available within two clicks from the home page, then you may not need a site map. But if your site is larger, and especially if it contains pages that may be hard for search engine robots to find, a site map may help pass traffic and link juice where you want it to go. Here are some tips:

Include the most important pages.   People will get lost if your site map contains too many links. That means, if your site has more than, say, 100 pages, you'll need to choose the most important pages. Here are our suggestions for pages to include

- Product category pages

- Major product pages

- FAQ and Help pages

- Contact or Request Information pages

- All of the key pages on your *paths to conversion*, the pages that your visitors follow from landing page through conversion

- Your 10 most popular pages

Go easy on the autogeneration.   Some content management systems will automatically generate a site map. As in so many other areas of SEO, we prefer the human touch. If you, or your tech teammates, are leaning in the automated direction, review the outcome carefully to be sure your site map has these characteristics:

- The layout is easy on the human eye.

- All links are standard HTML text that can be followed by spiders.

- The important pages (included in the preceding list) are easy to find.

Site Maps to Guide Human and Nonhuman Visitors *(Continued)*

Look at other sites for design inspiration. Don't waste time reinventing the wheel. There are zillions of site maps out there on the Web. Use one you like as a starting point.

Optimize your site map. We don't mean you should think of your site map as one of your top-priority landing pages. But if done tastefully, your site map can actually contain a fair number of your target keywords, not to mention compelling text. For example, instead of a link simply labeled "Fungicides," your site map could contain more keywords: "Organic Fungicides – Product details, how-to tips, and customer reviews of our Earth-friendly garden care products." Brief page descriptions can help your users find their way, as well as provide more text for search engines to read.

Link to your site map from every page. Users have come to expect a link to your site map in the footer of every page on the site, so make use of this spot. If your site has a search box, you may also wish to add a link to the site map near the search box, and make a link to the site map a fixture within the site search results page.

 Now: Try to identify opportunities for improving links within your own site. Write down your findings in your Site Optimization Worksheet.

Friday: Implementation

All of your desired site edits are conveniently compiled in your Site Optimization Worksheet. Today, you'll send out these requests to your web team—or take the time to make the changes yourself.

If you've followed our advice, you've already done a little collaborating with the people who will be involved in implementation of these website changes. Here are some pointers for making this effort worthwhile:

Think in terms of a style guide. If your organization works from a style guide, now is the time to suggest which of your requested changes should be officially incorporated. Many of your site text edits from Thursday are perfect candidates for inclusion in a style guide.

Know your time frame. If you're not doing them yourself, these edits—and the buy-in they require—might take time. While you can move forward in this book without having all the changes in place, Your SEO Plan will work best with an optimized website. If you need to take a little time to get these important changes made, we won't rush you. We'll be here waiting for you when your site is ready to go!

Prioritize. If your team doesn't have the time to get all these edits in place anytime soon, prioritize them in this order:

1. Edit page text.
2. Edit HTML page titles.
3. Edit internal links.
4. Edit meta tags.

Now: Distribute requests for edits to your web team—or get started making the changes yourself.

You should be proud—people charge a lot of money for the kind of SEO writing you've done this week! Now let's move on to making sure your site structure is robot friendly.

Internal Link Structure

Want to know how link equity, link juice, page authority, link love, PageRank, or whatever you like to call that precious commodity so important in SEO is distributed through your site? Here's a visual: Champagne Pyramid. Just as the bubbly stuff flows merrily from glass to glass, your link juice flows through your site, following pathways created by internal links.

Inbound links from other sites bring power to your site, and internal links move it around. If your site is like most, the majority of inbound links are pointing to your home page. That means you need to share the wealth—using internal links—with other pages on your site. There's no single linking structure that maximizes link power for every site, but here are a few dos and don'ts that should help:

- DO point your main menu to key landing pages.
- Your site has a finite amount of overall equity. So DON'T link to low-priority pages unnecessarily. You don't need to include your entire site map in the footer if a single link to a site map page will do the trick instead.
- DON'T forget to link to home on your deeper pages and, especially, on any pop-up windows on your site. In addition to passing link power, your site visitors need these links to navigate through your site.
- DO amp up your deep-page-to-deep-page internal links. Related content links engage your users and can increase the authority of the linked page.
- Subpages that have lots of inbound links from other websites carry link power. DO link from them to your top-priority landing pages.
- DON'T let any pages, especially top-priority ones, become *orphaned* (not linked from any page) or deeply buried more than five clicks away from your home page.

If you put some thought into your internal linking structure, we'll raise a glass to your SEO success!

Week 2: Site Structure Improvements

Last week, you took care of basic on-page optimization for your site. Congratulations, your site is at a respectable baseline level! This week, you'll delve a little deeper into some techie decisions that can improve your site's optimization, indexing, and overall visibility success.

This week's tasks will involve some serious tech topics. It's a week when you will definitely want your team queued up and clued in to your needs and reasoning. Keep your meeting calendar handy as you review your daily assignments:

Monday: Robot Walk-through

Tuesday: The Spider's-Eye View

Wednesday: Duplicate, Near-Duplicate, and Canonical Page Problems

Thursday: Flash and Ajax

Friday: Your robots.txt File

Monday: Robot Walk-through

You're all dressed up, and the hors d'oeuvres are on the table. But is there a big Do Not Enter sign on your door? You know the basics of how the robots find your site, and you know whether or not your landing pages are indexed. Today you'll look for barriers that may exist between the robots and your landing pages.

Take a look at your Rank and KPI Tracking Worksheet to determine whether any of your landing pages are not indexed. Here are several reasons a robot might not be reaching your landing page and possible ways to fix the problem:

Robots can't follow your links. This could be as simple as having no links from your home page or your main site navigation to one or all of your landing pages. Or maybe the links to your landing pages are created using hard-to-follow code, such as JavaScript pull-down menus or pop-up scripts. Often, this is an easy fix: Just add standard HTML text links from anywhere on your home page to your landing page.

Your site asks too much from the visitor. If the queen came to visit, you wouldn't turn her away if she weren't wearing the right hat. Treat your spiders the same way! Some websites won't display to a viewer who doesn't have JavaScript enabled. Guess who doesn't have full JavaScript capabilities? The robots! Some websites require cookies. Guess who won't accept cookies? You get the point. You'll need to eliminate these requirements on your landing pages. If you're not sure what your site requires, you'll get a better sense of it when you look at the spider's-eye view of your website tomorrow.

A server outage interrupted indexing. There's nothing like that warm and fuzzy feeling your customers get when they encounter... an error message?

Page Unavailable - My Tennis Store
tennis apparel, womens apparel, tennis clothes, women's apparel,
mytennisstore.com/customer_service/advice.asp - Cached

Perhaps your pages are linked and structured properly, but the robot came crawling just at the moment your system administrator spilled his Red Bull on the server. Either the robot captured an error message or found no site at all to index. There's nothing you can do in a situation like this but wait until the next indexing cycle. And if this seems to be a regular occurrence, look into a more reliable hosting situation. (By the way, for the perfect balance of caffeine and server protection, your sysadmin should switch to coffee with the little sippy lid.)

You told the robots to stay away. That wasn't very nice of you! Later this week, we'll get into the details of how you communicate with robots through a file on your site called `robots.txt`.

Your site is being penalized. It's possible, but unlikely, that you are violating a search engine's guidelines without knowing it. If none of the other problems are striking a chord and you are absolutely sure that your pages are not present in the index, and especially if you were ever engaged in questionable SEO practices in the past, this might be your situation. It's a tough one. Probably your best strategy is to work through the rest of this week, make sure your site is squeaky clean, and use the search engines' reconsideration requests (also called reinclusion requests). See `www.yourseo-plan.com` for URLs.

> **Now:** Try to identify the reasons your pages are not being indexed. Write down your findings, and determine whom you need to discuss them with in your organization.

Now that you know robots can access your landing pages, you're ready to put on your spider-vision goggles and see what they see when they get there.

Tuesday: The Spider's-Eye View

Have you ever seen those photos that show what the world looks like to a dog? Or maybe you enjoyed the kaleidoscopic fly-cam scenes in the 1950s movie *The Fly*. Today you're going to learn how to take a search engine spider's-eye view of your website. Viewer discretion is advised: What you are about to see might be surprisingly scary.

As you learned in Chapter 3, a search engine spider is simply software that goes through the Internet looking at web pages and sending information back to a central repository. It doesn't view content in the same way human site visitors do. Since spiders are an important—although by no means the most important—audience for your website, you want to know how your website appears to them. Today you will use a tool called a *spider emulator* to put on your spider's-eye view glasses and do exactly that. For example, here is a typical web page, as viewed through the browser:

And here is the same web page viewed through a spider emulator:

[home_r1_c1.jpg] [home_r2_c1.jpg] [**Homeicon.gif**] [home_r3_c3.jpg] [home_r4_c3.jpg] [home_r4_c4.jpg] [home_r2_c5.jpg] [home_r5_c3.jpg] **Find a Style** [home_r5_c15.jpg] **Find Authorized Retail** [home_r5_c17.jpg] [**home_r2_c18.jpg**] [home_r2_c20.jpg] [home_r6_c1.jpg] VM Collection
VM Collection [home_r7_c6.jpg] Bridals
Bridal Voyage ™ Blu ™ Angelina Faccenda ™ Julietta ™ [home_r7_c6.jpg] Bridesmaids
BridesMaids Ava Collection ™ Affairs ™ Angelina Faccenda Bridesmaids ™ [home_r7_c6.jpg] Quinceañera/Vizcaya
[home_r7_c6.jpg] Flowergirls
[home_r7_c6.jpg] Homecoming/Party/Cocktail
Sticks & Stones ™ [home_r7_c6.jpg] Trunk Shows

    [index_r8_c20.jpg] [**imgNota4.jpg**] [index_r9_c23.jpg] [logoNota4.jpg]

      Prom & Paparazzi

      Hottest Styles for 2010

    [index_r9_c23.jpg] [logoNota3.jpg]

      Mori Lee Bridal

      Top Styles for 2010

    [**imgNota3.jpg**] [**imgNota2.jpg**] [index_r9_c23.jpg] [logoNota2.jpg]

      Quinceañera/ Sweet 16

      Top Styles for 2010

    [index_r9_c23.jpg] [logoNota1.jpg]

      Homecoming/Cocktail

      Hottest Styles for 2010

[**imgNota1.jpg**] [home_r9_c1.jpg] [home_r9_c2.jpg] **About Us** [home_r10_c8.jpg] **Site Map** [home_r10_c10.jpg] **Contact Us** [home_r12_c2.jpg] [home_r9_c14.jpg] [home_r9_c19.jpg] [home_r11_c19.jpg] [home_r9_c21.jpg] There are few moments in a woman's life, as important and memorable as her wedding day. Mori Lee agrees that wedding dresses, prom dresses, formal dresses, bridesmaid dresses and bridal gowns are very special attire. Young women aspire to wear them to mark various milestones in their lives. Think of the bride in her wedding gown looking stunning and radiant. Beautiful bridesmaids outfitted in lovely bridesmaid dresses to complement the brides look. A young woman looking fabulous in her homecoming dress. The prom queen in her perfect prom dress to mark the end of high school and the start of adulthood. All of these milestone special occasions deserve a special look. Whether you are looking for bridal gowns, prom dresses, or formal bridesmaid dresses for your bridesmaids, Mori lee has the look that will fit your style and budget. Mori Lee bridesmaid dresses are made with the same care as our wedding gowns and formal dresses. Mori Lee is the right choice for any special occasion. Whether it be a formal gown, cocktail dress or party dress, Mori Lee means confidence â€" where you can focus on enjoying the day. Mori Lee understands how you want to feel on these special occasions. Our wedding gowns, prom dresses, quinceanera gowns, and formal gowns make you shine. Step out in confidence and enjoy the day. Any of the bridal gowns, bridesmaid dresses, quinceanera gowns, homecoming dresses, or prom dresses from the Mori lee collection will show the world how beautiful you truly are. We have been designing bridal gowns and bridesmaids dresses for over 50-years as well as mother of the bride gowns and flowergirl dresses. Our bridal gowns and prom dresses are affordable, yet we never sacrifice quality for price. Wearing our beautiful wedding gowns, prom gowns, or bridesmaid dresses brings elegance and sophistication to your special occasion. You deserve the best; whether that means a Mori Lee quinceanera gown, prom gown, homecoming dress, mother of the bride gown, bridesmaid dress, or wedding gown. Explore our site to find out more about the bridal gowns and prom dresses Mori Lee can offer you.

Are you scared yet? There are lots of spider emulators available on the Web. We use www.seo-browser.com often, because we like its simplicity. You're going to view each of your landing pages through a spider emulator today.

Here's how to do it:

- Starting with your home page, go to www.seo-browser.com or the spider emulator of your choice and enter your page URL into the emulator.

- Once you see your page as it is seen by spiders, ask yourself some questions: Does this accurately represent the information I expected to see on my site? Is it readable and in the correct order? Are my target keywords present?

- For any noted problems, consider possible solutions. For example, if the well-crafted, keyword-rich content you added last month is not showing up, it may be that it's not rendering in standard HTML text. Get together with your web developer to track down the problem. Or are you seeing the same nonsensical image ALT tag (for example, ImgFile01) repeating multiple times on the page? Make a note to have it removed or revised with appropriate keyword-rich descriptions.

Now: Perform your spider emulator check for all of your landing pages. Make a note of any problems and suggested solutions.

Great news! With well-chosen keywords, basic page optimization in place, and landing pages that search engine spiders can access and read, you've made a real difference in SEO for your site!

Wednesday: Duplicate, Near-Duplicate, and Canonical Page Problems

Is it just us, or does "canonical issues" sound like it might have something to do with the pope? If the term gives your brain a rash, don't worry. Today we'll help you understand this mystifying issue and determine whether your site is at risk.

Duplicate and Near-Duplicate Content

Picture this: You switch on your TV, and every channel is showing the same show, or nearly identical shows with slight costume variations. *BO-ring!* (And oh-so-painfully close to last Friday night's TV lineup!) *Duplicate content* is the same or very similar on-page elements showing up under more than one URL, and search engines don't like it. The rule of thumb is simple:

Pearl of Wisdom: Every different URL the search engines see on your site should display substantially different content.

We're sorry to say that your site may—for perfectly innocent reasons—contain duplicate content. Here are some examples we've seen:

- Printer-friendly versions of pages.

- Old versions of pages that exist at old URLs.

- A *pointer domain*, also called a *masked domain*, which redirects site visitors but hides the fact that they have been redirected by keeping the original domain name in the browser address bar.

- Several different URLs for the same product, generated by an e-commerce system.

- Duplicate categories within your store. For example, if you have separate categories for "all neckties" and "men's neckties," they may display exactly the same list of products on different URLs.

- Pages with various tracking tags (for example, &affiliate-id=3) tacked onto the URLs.

- Pages that display with URLs in lowercase letters and also display using capital letters.

- Articles or press releases that are reprinted from elsewhere on the Web.

If any of these situations sound familiar, don't panic. We said search engines don't *like* duplicate content—we didn't say they *hate* it the way they hate spam tactics. Google, for example, is likely to choose its favorite page from among the clones and filter the rest out of its index. According to Google, link authority will be consolidated onto the favored version of the page, but this is one of those practices that the search engines haven't perfected yet. Possible disadvantages to letting the search engines see duplicate content include the following:

- Your page authority could be diluted between all the multiple versions of your pages.

- Search engine spiders will waste precious indexing time on all of those duplicates and may miss out on indexing better parts of your site.

- Worst-case scenario: If search engines run into a large amount of duplicate content on your site, they may stop, or slow, your website indexing.

slacker   If the extent of duplicate content on your site is a few pages here and there, you probably don't need to worry about it.

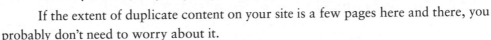

Now: If duplicate content is a concern for your site, document the pages that need to be cleaned up.

You may end up with a list of individual pages, or you may have a broader list of site categories and types of pages, such as "all of our 'for men' and 'for him' category pages." Leave a sticky note for the person in charge of the website saying, "I'm coming for you."

Canonical Issues

If we tell you how to pronounce canonical, do you promise you won't use your knowledge to make other people feel dumb? All right then: It's pronounced can-ON-ical.

Canonical issues are a special case of duplicate content. Here's how: In the eyes of the search engines, the following four URLs are four different pages:

- `http://www.yourdomain.com/`
- `http://www.yourdomain.com/default.asp`
- `http://yourdomain.com`
- `http://yourdomain.com/default.asp`

Now, *you* know and *we* know that these are actually pointing to the same page, and we figure that soon enough the search engines will get it right. But for now, sites with this type of duplication have what industry insiders call a *canonical URL* problem (*canonical* here means following a standard format, so a canonical URL would be the standard or preferred URL for your website) and it can have a significant effect on SEO success:

Pearl of Wisdom: If your web pages are displayed under more than one version of a URL, your ranks can suffer.

It's easy to determine if your site needs some fixing here. Open a browser and type in your home page URL with the "www" (`http://www.yourdomain.com`) and without the "www" (`http://yourdomain.com`). Do the URLs redirect to a single, favorite version, or do they just sit there looking guilty? Next, perform the same test with your site's standard file names such as `/main.html`, `/index.php`, or `/default.asp`.

Now: Check if your home page displays with more than one URL.

Found a problem? You don't want all of those different versions of your website URLs indexed on search engines, competing with each other and tiring out the robots. Read on for our recommended fixes.

Death to Duplicate Content

If you've identified duplicate content, near-duplicate content, or canonical problems on your site, you have several powerful cleanup tools at your disposal:

Canonical Tag Introduced by Google in 2009, the canonical tag has rapidly become one of our favorite SEO weapons. The canonical tag allows you to specify the primary URL for a page on your site.

The tag looks like this: `<link rel="canonical" href="http://www.example.com /primary-url.html" />` and goes in the `<head>` of a web page. Here's how it works: For any group of duplicate pages, you choose a single, primary URL. You add a canonical tag to every one of the duplicates (including the primary page), specifying the primary page.

For example, if you have three duplicate pages named `/joe.html`, `/joseph.html`, and `/joey.html` and you choose `/joe.html` as the primary URL, then *all three* of these pages would get a canonical tag specifying `/joe.html`, something like this: `<link rel="canonical" href="http://www.example.com/joe.html" />`.

Search engines will read the canonical tag as a strong signal that all of your duplicate pages should be consolidated in the search engine index, giving you a single, more powerful page in the index rather than a bunch of weaker, diluted pages.

Webmaster Tools: Parameter Handling and Preferred URL If you've verified yourself in Google Webmaster Tools, you can use the parameter settings within the tool to tell Google to ignore tags or other parameters that may be tacked onto the end of your URLs, creating duplicate versions. Webmaster tools also allow you to set a preferred URL for your site, either with or without the "www." Both of these tools will help the search engine clean out unnecessary duplicates on your site.

Internal Link Cleanup Ensure that all internal links within your site point to the same version of your URLs. Choose a format and stick with it.

Page Redirects This solution works if you have a case of true duplicate content, and if there is no reason that your site needs both pages to exist at different URLs. For example, we've seen sites that have been redesigned, but the old pages spend years hanging around at their old URLs gathering dust (and siphoning off search engine power!). A page redirect will send the search engines a very strong signal about which version of the URL they should be indexing. See the sidebar "A Primer on Redirection" for key info.

XML Sitemap An XML Sitemap allows you to tell the search engines your preferred URLs in cases of canonical or duplicate content. See Chapter 10 for more information.

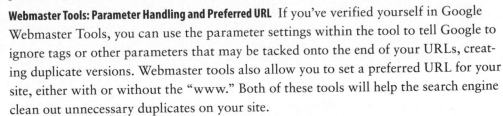

Now: If you have determined that pages on your site display under multiple URLs, start tasking your team with the solutions we've just listed.

A Primer on Redirection

To redirect one page to another, you must send a message from the server that hosts your website to the client (the browser or search engine robot) stating that the page has moved. Typically this requires developer skills or assistance from your hosting company. Proper redirection can work SEO magic.

Let's say you want to redirect `www.yoursite.com/old-busted.html` to `www.yoursite.com/new-hotness.html`. Here are some common scenarios:

- 301 Redirect is a *permanent* redirect status message. If you use this redirect, search engines will typically de-index `old-busted.html` and replace it with `new-hotness.html` in their results. A 301 redirect is the best way to transfer search engine power and ranks from old URLs to new URLs.

- 302 Redirect is a *temporary* redirect status message. Search engines will typically keep `old-busted.html` in their indexes and will not add `new-hotness.html`. This is rarely the right kind of redirect for SEO purposes, because search engine power will not be transferred to the new URL. However, 302 could be a good choice if you really are redirecting temporarily and plan to reinstate the original URL soon.

- Meta refresh and JavaScript redirects are not recommended for SEO purposes.

Thursday: Flash and Ajax

Oh, Flash, we love you. You always look so pulled together and professional. And, Ajax, you're so cute and modern: We're starting to have feelings for you, too. But… but… there's this one area of our relationship that just seems to be lacking. Why do you always fail us in the search engines?

Optimizing Flash and Ajax

Search engine spiders like to do two things on your website: Click on HTML links and read HTML text. They lack the human intelligence needed to type words into search boxes or navigate around fancy interactive experiences. That's why Flash and Ajax, along with all other *rich Internet applications* (RIAs), pose such a challenge to search engines. If your website relies on Flash or Ajax to deliver its deep content, and you want those materials to be searchable, you'll need a workaround approach.

Optimizing Flash and Ajax *(Continued)*

The spider's-eye view of your website, described in this chapter, should help you understand what a search engine spider can see on your site. Your challenge is to build a simplified, also called *degraded*, version of your website that shows the spiders a reasonable approximation of what a human would see. Deliver this simplified version to *all* of your site visitors who match the robots' limitations: those with no JavaScript, no Flash, or not accepting cookies. In Flash, degraded content is accomplished using the `SWFObject` embedding described at `http://code.google.com/p/swfobject/`. With Ajax, it can be done by making sure that reduced-function page elements display even when a browser does not have JavaScript enabled.

Search engines are improving their capabilities. Google can see text inside of Flash and can even emulate clicking in a Flash application, but this ability is still limited. And, in 2010 Google introduced a new specification for Ajax indexing. Ajax applications built in accordance with this spec are fully indexable by Google—even parts of the application that require multiple user actions to be reached. Unfortunately Bing hasn't made any announcements about supporting the specification. Worse, it seems that the specification doesn't provide degraded content for accessibility for people with disabilities. If your SEO goals are Google-only, you can explore the protocol at `http://code.google.com/web/ajaxcrawling/`.

Back in Chapter 1, "Clarify Your Goals," we explained the importance of segmenting your site into landing pages that speak to your separate target audiences. Flash and Ajax share a primary SEO disadvantage: These technologies both often display loads of content and interactivity on a *single HTML page*. With Flash, you can view any number of topics and "pages" without leaving a single movie, and with Ajax, you can view a whole store's worth of products without visiting a new URL. And what you gain in 'zazz, you lose in search engine friendliness. For example, the website at `http://relaunch.holidayinn.com` includes photo tours and a hotel finder:

But search engines see this entire site as a single page:

HolidayInn ☆
relaunch.holidayinn.com/ - Cached - Similar

Simpler sites have content that's displayed on a large number of separate URLs, each getting its very own morsel of search engine visibility.

Remember yesterday, when you learned that every URL should have its own content? There's more to that Pearl of Wisdom:

Pearl of Wisdom: If it feels like a page, it should have its own URL.

Another disadvantage, of course, is that Flash and Ajax code often prevents the search engines from reading the site text. In the Holiday Inn example, Google wasn't even able to grab website text for use in the listing snippet.

If you've verified yourself in Google Webmaster Tools, you can use the Fetch as Googlebot tool to see what the search engine robot can see on your site.

Too many categories of information in one URL, and text information that's obscured or invisible to the search engines—this non-HTML territory is treacherous terrain for robots! If your site contains a significant amount of Flash or Ajax, drum up some courage, a budget calculator, and maybe a licensed massage therapist, and see if any of the following strategies are feasible for your site:

Break up Flash or Ajax into separate HTML pages. Talk to your web developer about breaking up the Flash or Ajax so that each landing page has a separate URL. Flash and Ajax can be as-needed elements within HTML pages, rather than providing the entire navigation for the site. Your users will thank you for the browser Back/Forward button functionality and the ability to bookmark your pages, and the linkerati will be able to tag pages on social bookmarking sites and deep-link your site.

Provide alternate HTML content for Flash. Four out of five search engines agree: Standard HTML content tastes better. Not only is providing alternative content in HTML helpful to the search engines, but it's also great for people without the Flash plug-in and for visually impaired site visitors. Just be sure that the HTML content exactly matches the content that would be visible to users with Flash—otherwise, you'll risk triggering spam penalties.

Using SWFObject for embedding Flash movies will put you on a fast track to optimization by allowing you to easily add alternate HTML content. Learn more here: http://code.google.com/p/swfobject/.

Create an HTML addendum. If you can't get your pages to show alternate HTML content, at least create some HTML pages in addition to the Flash or Ajax site. Beneath your

Flash or Ajax content, add a standard HTML link or links to your most important content in HTML such as "Our Products," "About Us," and "Contact Us."

Focus on inbound links. If all else fails, optimize whatever HTML pages you have, and focus on getting inbound links.

Now: If Flash or Ajax is causing an SEO disadvantage for your website, explain the importance of individual landing pages and robot-readable HTML text to your web developer. Discuss which of our suggested workarounds is possible.

Dynamic Site Smarts

Search engines are good at indexing dynamic sites, and the advice in this book applies just as well to ASP and PHP pages—and even pages with URLs containing a question mark—as it does to old-school HTML. If your site is of the dynamic variety, follow some basic guidelines to avoid common pitfalls:

- Be sure that search engines can follow standard links to every page on your site. Don't expect search engines to fill out a form or run a search to drill down to your most juicy content.

- You're trying to appeal to humans, so use human-friendly URLs. Would you rather click on this:

  `http://www.yoursite.com/church-bells/discount/`

  or this?

  `http://www.yoursite.com/prod.php?id=23485&blt=234`

- Limit the number of parameters in the URL to a maximum of two.

- Be sure that your URLs function even if all dynamic parameters are removed.

- When linking internally, always link with parameters in the same order and format.

- Set up an XML Sitemap (see Chapter 10 for details) if there is any reason to think that search engine robots aren't seeing all of your pages.

- Use `robots.txt` to exclude stub pages (autogenerated pages with no real content, such as empty directory categories and empty search results). Search engines want to index pages containing meaningful content, not empties generated by dynamic programs.

Your dynamic site has a lot to offer. And now you know how to help it reach its full search engine potential!

xtra cred

Friday: Your *robots.txt* File

A `robots.txt` file is the first file that a search engine robot visits on your website. Like a snooty nightclub bouncer with a velvet rope, the `robots.txt` file decides which robots are welcome and which need to move on to that less-exclusive joint down the street. `robots.txt` can admit or reject robots on a sitewide, directory-by-directory, or page-by-page basis.

SEO folks often feel a special affection for the `robots.txt` file because it provides a rare opportunity to communicate with a search engine robot. However, its capabilities are limited. `robots.txt` files exist only to *exclude* indexing. Just as a bouncer can keep people out but can't force anyone to come in, the `robots.txt` file can't do anything to entice a robot to spend *more* time or visit *more* pages on your site. Also, compliance with your `robots.txt` file is voluntary, not mandatory. The major search engines will generally try to follow your instructions, but other, less-reputable types might not. This is why you should not rely on your `robots.txt` file to prevent spidering of sensitive, private, or inappropriate materials.

Do You Need a *robots.txt* File?

You may not need a `robots.txt` file. Without one, all robots will have free access to non-password-protected pages on your site. To decide if you need a `robots.txt` file for your website, ask yourself these questions:

- Are there any pages or directories on my site that I do not want listed on the search engines, such as an intranet or internal phone list?
- Are there any specific search engines that I do not want to display my site?
- Do I know of any dynamic pages or programming features that might cause problems for spiders, like getting caught in a loop (infinitely bouncing between two pages)?
- Does my website contain pages with duplicate content?
- Are there directories on the site that contain programming scripts only, not viewable pages?

If the answers to these questions are no, then you do not need a `robots.txt` file. You've got the rest of the day off! If you have any yes answers, you'll prepare your `robots.txt` file today.

Now: Determine whether you need a `robots.txt` file in your website.

Create Your *robots.txt* File

Robots.txt files are very simple text files. To find a sample, go to www.yourseoplan.com/ robots.txt and view ours, or go to just about any other site and look for the robots.txt file in the *root directory*.

The robots.txt file usually looks something like this:

```
User-agent: googlebot
Disallow: /private-files/
Disallow: /more-private-files/
```

In this example, Google's spider (called Googlebot) is excluded from indexing files within the two directories called private-files and more-private-files. Here is a second example, in which all robots (signified by a wildcard asterisk, *) are excluded from indexing the directory called cgi-scripts:

```
User-agent: *
Disallow: /cgi-scripts/
```

There are numerous websites that will walk you through building and saving your robots.txt file. A helpful robots.txt builder can be found here: www.clickability.co.uk/ robotstxt.html. Answers to just about any question you could think of about robots are here: www.robotstxt.org.

 For site owners who complete the verification process, Google Webmaster Tools offers a robots.txt testing tool and a tool to help you generate a robots.txt file.

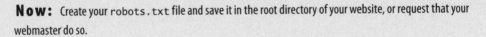

Now: Create your robots.txt file and save it in the root directory of your website, or request that your webmaster do so.

If you are feeling any doubt about whether your robots.txt file is written properly, *don't* post it. The last thing you want to do is inadvertently shut out the search engines.

Here's a bonus: robots.txt can also be used to tell search engines where to find your XML Sitemap. You can learn more about this in Chapter 10.

robots Meta Tags

A robots meta tag serves a similar purpose as the robots.txt file, but it is placed within individual pages on your site rather than in your root directory. A robots meta tag affects only the page it resides on. Chances are you don't need to use this type of tag, but here's a quick overview in case you do.

You might choose to use a robots meta tag rather than a robots.txt file because it's easier for you to set up the exclusion using your web page template rather than the robots.txt file, or maybe you only want to do a brief, temporary exclusion. Another possible reason is that you do not have access to the root directory on your site.

To exclude the robots from a page using the robots meta tag, include the following code in the HTML head of the page:

```
<meta name="robots" content="noindex">
```

This will prevent search engine robots from listing the page on which the tag resides.

Robot Exclusion for Google

If you plan to use robots exclusion to control the sharing of Google PageRank among pages on your website (for example, by excluding low-quality pages that you do not want hogging authority), you should know that Google handles the robots.txt and robots meta tag exclusions slightly differently:

- Pages excluded with either type of exclusion are allowed to accumulate PageRank authority.

- Even if a page is excluded with the robots.txt file, it may still be listed in search results, with the search engine using third-party information (such as your site's listing in the Open Directory, or text in links pointing to the page) for the listing title and description. A page that is excluded with a robots meta tag will not be displayed in search results at all.

- A page that is excluded with the robots.txt file will not be crawled by Googlebot, and it will not pass PageRank to other pages to which it links.

- A page that is excluded with the robots meta tag may be crawled by Googlebot, and Google will follow links on the page (as long as the tag doesn't also contain a nofollow attribute). The PageRank that is accumulated by this page will be shared with pages to which it links.

Now: Add robots meta tags to pages on an as-needed basis.

Now, let's take a trip out of techie-ville, and get serious about building high-quality inbound links to your site.

Week 3: Link Building

You learned in Chapter 3, "Eternal Truths of SEO" and Chapter 4, "How the Search Engines Work Right Now," how important inbound links are for your website. Last month, you even dipped a toe into the ocean of link building when you used the search engines to find out how many web pages are linking to your landing pages.

Unless your site is truly wretched, there's bound to be somebody out there who is interested in linking to it. (And if you think your site is beyond linking, stay tuned! You'll get some content-building and linkability improvement lessons in Week 4.) Put on your PR hat—or get your team's most talented communicator in the room—and get started on your SEO link-building campaign:

Monday: Your Existing Links

Tuesday: Find Linking Opportunities

Wednesday: The Art of Link Requests

Thursday: Bad Neighborhoods

Friday: What's Watering Down Your Link Juice?

Surfing Is Not Slacking

Way back when, when we were SEO consultants working for a small web development firm, we were lucky to have an open-minded boss. On any given day, you might have seen five other workers knee-deep in website coding, but what was on our monitors? Movie fan sites, Florida vacation sites, and sports nostalgia sites. We remember the day we had to send an email around saying, "Don't worry: We're not looking for new jobs. We're just researching career sites for a client!" But it was all part of the SEO job, and an important one at that.

If you're in a corporate culture where personal emails and web surfing is frowned upon or prohibited, it is essential that you get the clearance you need to access the Web in the same way that your customers and competitors do. Likewise, if there are no actual restrictions on web surfing in your company but you just feel like a slacker when you're surfing the Web at work, just remember what surfing does for your company:

- Surfing helps you to think like a searcher, using a variety of techniques to find important information.
- Surfing keeps you up-to-date on the ever-changing search landscape.
- Surfing keeps you tuned in to the dialogue that's forming around your brand on the Social Web. You can use these conversations to inform your target keyword list.

Don't just limit yourself to surfing from your office computer! There are some things that are best experienced on a web-enabled phone, so what the heck, hit your boss up for your favorite model while you're at it!

Monday: Your Existing Links

As you learned in Chapter 3, your inbound link profile is an important factor in your site's ability to rank well. Link building is an exciting topic, and we bet you have your sleeves rolled up and ready to go! That's wonderful, but...

Let's roll *down* those sleeves for a sec, champ, and take a few moments to focus on the realities of link building:

- Link building is extremely time consuming, and just like many other aspects of SEO, it's a never-ending process.

- One of the most effective ways to build links is to *stop thinking about links* and open your mind to ways that you can build a high-quality, unique, useful website.

- Quick solutions like paid link services and link exchanges are almost always a waste of money.

Today, you'll assess your site's link profile, using meaningful measurements: the number of external links pointing to your pages, and the number of linking domains. We've created a worksheet to help you keep track of what you find.

> **Now:** Download the Link Tracking Worksheet from www.yourseoplan.com and save it in your SEO Idea Bank.

Last month, during your baseline site assessment, you determined the total number of sites linking into your landing pages. Now you will take a magnifying glass to these sites and document them in your Link Tracking Worksheet. Here are the steps you'll take:

- Document external links.
- Document number of linking domains.
- Assess existing link quality.

Document External Links

As you know, links from other sites that point to a page on your site may give that page a boost in the search engine ranks. And, just as a rising tide lifts all boats, the links pointing to your entire domain may give all of your pages a bit of a rankings boost. Last month, you gathered the number of links pointing to your top landing pages. That number included links from your own site as well as links from external sites. Today we're going to refine that number to find the number of external links.

Knowing the overall number of external links pointing to your site is helpful when you use this number wisely. Rather than focusing on the absolute number of inlinks, use this metric to track overall trends. See if this number went up or down over a three-month period, or within days of a new product announcement, news story, or other significant content addition to your site.

Some tools display not only the number of external links that point to your page, but also the number of *followed* external links. The nofollow attribute (see Figure 7.2) is a way a site can tell the search engines to prevent any linking power from flowing via the link to its destination page. Your site will not gain any ranking benefits from links pointing to your site that are tagged with nofollow, but it may gain lots of other benefits, such as traffic and conversions.

```
            <span class="entry-content">Braille use declining, experts try to put
finger on why. <a href="http://www.fk.cm/go/5450532" class="tweet-url web"
rel="nofollow" target="_blank">http://www.fk.cm/go/5450532</a></span>
```

Figure 7.2 Link tagged with nofollow

On your Link Tracking Worksheet, you will see a section for the number of external links to your site. Here are some ways to gather that data:

- Using Open Site Explorer (www.opensiteexplorer.org), type in your URL, click Get Link Data, then click the Full List of Link Metrics tab. Scroll down to see External Followed Links, as shown in Figure 7.3.

Page-Specific Metrics	URL
Page Authority ❷	28
mozRank ❷	3.42
mozTrust ❷	Pro Only
Total Links ❷	130
External Followed Links ❷	126
Internal Followed Links ❷	Pro Only
Linking Root Domains ❷	36

Figure 7.3 Finding external links on Open Site Explorer

- We're including Yahoo! Site Explorer because it is a trusted, robust tool, but due to developments in the Yahoo!/Bing alliance, its name and location may be changed by the time you read this book. Go to http://siteexplorer.search .yahoo.com and type in your domain. Click InLinks, then select Except From This Domain from the Show InLinks drop-down menu, as shown in Figure 7.4.

- Use the free tool at www.majesticseo.com. Just enter your URL and find the main "backlinks" number under the header External Backlink Stats, as shown in Figure 7.5.

xtra cred

- If you have verified your site with Google Webmaster Tools, log in, then click on Your Site On The Web. Select Links To Your Site, and then download the external link report by clicking more under Who links the most, then clicking Download this table.

Now: Open your Link Tracking Worksheet and fill in external link numbers for each of your landing pages.

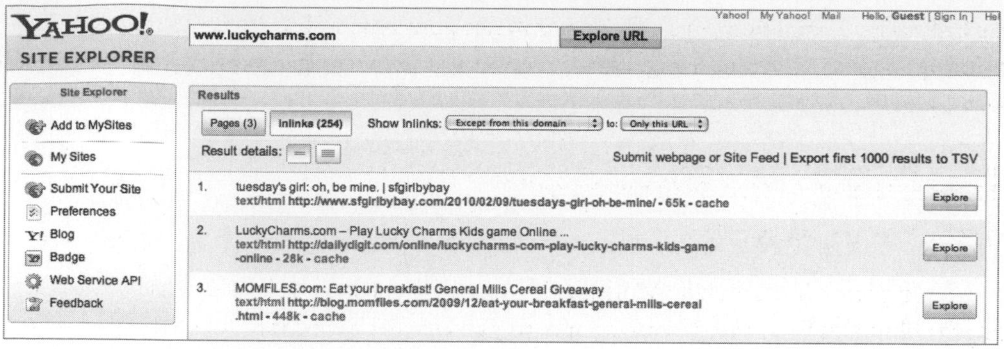

Figure 7.4 Finding external links on Yahoo! Site Explorer

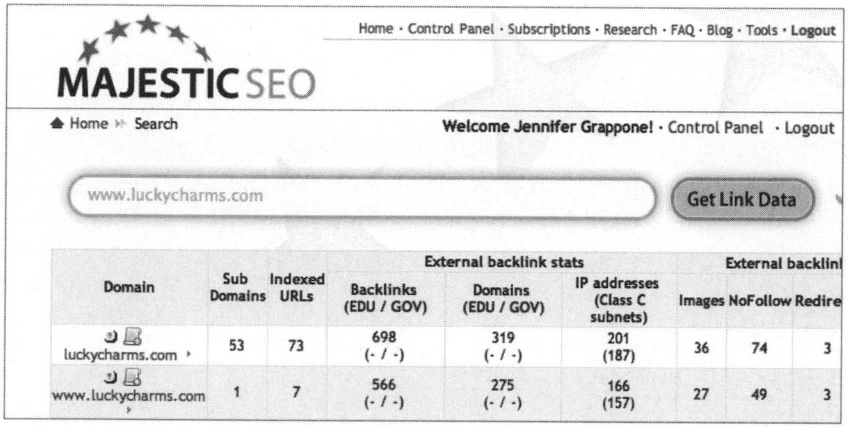

Figure 7.5 Finding external links on Majestic SEO

Tales from the Trenches: Link Building Puts the "I" in ROI

Not long ago, we put together a fantastic link-building strategy for a client. Bursting at the seams with creative ideas for content, blog topics, social outreach, and linkbait, this strategy was our pride and joy. And then came the client's response: "Well… we like all these ideas, but we don't have time for all that. Can you skip all that other stuff and just do the link building part?"

Ouch! Let's get one thing straight: All that "other" stuff *is* the link building. In the post–Web 2.0 era, there's no such thing as link building separate from content creation, outreach, and social marketing. With a few exceptions (sure, you can interlink the sites you own, and yeah, there are probably a few choice people who you should contact to ask for a link), the vast majority of your link-building efforts must be about giving other site owners a genuine reason to want to link to your site!

Can we repeat that for emphasis? *The vast majority of your link-building efforts must be about giving other site owners a genuine reason to want to link to your site.*

> ### Tales from the Trenches: Link Building Puts the "I" in ROI *(Continued)*
>
> While we're riding the honesty train with you, let's go another mile: You've heard that link build-ing is a lot of work, right? And despite what some spammy emails may tell you, this is not work that can be easily outsourced. In fact, link building done right is best done by members of your in-house team. An SEO consultant can give you a wealth of great ideas, a ghost blogger can help you write engaging posts, a developer might build some useful tools as linkbait, and a clever social media consultant can keep your Facebook page afloat, but to get the best return on your investment, you need to dedicate your own business voice to the effort. Embrace the "other" stuff—it'll pay off!

Document Number of Linking Domains

The number of linking domains pointing to your site is a clearer success metric than the number of total inlinks. Here's a real-life example: We once had a client who appeared to gain 6,000 new inlinks overnight. Cause for celebration? No. These links were the result of a single paid Yellow Pages listing, which provided thousands of links from the `yellowpages.com` domain and provided no rankings benefits.

 Now: Record the number of linking domains pointing to each of your landing pages in your Link Tracking Worksheet.

You can find this metric easily on `www.opensiteexplorer.org`. On `www.majestic-seo.com`, this number is labeled as Mentions – Domains.

Assess Existing Link Quality

Search engines care about the quality as well as the quantity of inbound links. And *you* care, too, because a link is a direct pathway for potential customers to get to your site. Today you'll look through your list of inbound links and get a feel for the big picture landscape.

For a link to have the best possible influence on your site's ranks, the following should be true:

- The link is from a page that is relevant to your site's content and speaks to your target audience.
- The linking page has a high number of inbound links.
- The link contains your target keywords in the linking text.

There are many kinds of links that probably won't have any direct, long-term, positive influence on your ranks. These include the following:

- Links that you pay for via text link ad services, or link exchange services, or *any link that a search engine may deduce has been granted due to what Google calls a "link scheme."* (If you think this is too vague or difficult to enforce, you're in good company. Many in the SEO community have complained about this policy. Google's official response to this, if we may paraphrase, is "tough noogies.")

- Links that come from orphaned pages (pages with no links pointing to them).

- Links from pages that have very few links pointing to them and are several clicks away from a site's home page.

- Links coming from pages that are not indexed in the search engines, such as pages in Facebook that are only visible behind a login.

- Links that are tagged with `nofollow`. This describes all links from within tweets, as well as many links from within blog comments.

- Links that point to broken pages on your site.

Keep in mind that any of the links we just described, even the ones that won't help your ranks, may bring you traffic if the linking page content speaks to your target audience.

Link-obsessed SEOs often use a shortcut metric—Google PageRank, as seen in the Google Toolbar—to assess the value of a potential linking page. For example, you may hear people bragging about how they received a link from a PageRank 6 page. This is a reasonable way to frame the conversation as long as you recognize that this single PageRank value doesn't take into account all the details of whether this might be a good page from which to receive a link.

Today, we want you to scroll through your list of external links and get a feel for the overall link landscape pointing to your home page or other top-priority landing page. Click to view any of the linking pages that catch your interest, and try to figure out whether these are links that can potentially help your site's ranks. Here are a couple of tips to help you along your journey:

- Open Site Explorer clearly labels links that have been tagged with `nofollow`, which will help you identify those that will not pass linking power.

- You can export your list of linking sites from any of these tools for deeper analysis.

Anatomy of a Terrible Inbound Link

Nearly every day we get atrocious emails from link builders, such as this one:

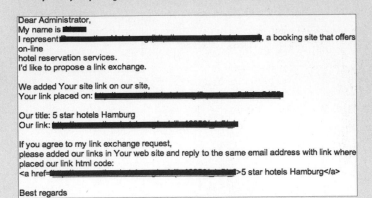

```
Dear Administrator,
My name is ▮▮▮▮▮
I represent ▮▮▮▮▮▮▮▮▮▮▮▮▮▮▮▮▮▮▮▮▮▮▮▮▮▮▮▮▮▮, a booking site that offers on-line
hotel reservation services.
I'd like to propose a link exchange.

We added Your site link on our site,
Your link placed on: ▮▮▮▮▮▮▮▮▮▮▮▮▮▮▮▮▮▮▮▮▮▮▮▮▮▮

Our title: 5 star hotels Hamburg
Our link: ▮▮▮▮▮▮▮▮▮▮▮▮▮▮▮▮▮▮▮▮▮▮

If you agree to my link exchange request,
please added our links in Your web site and reply to the same email address with link where
placed our link html code:
<a href=▮▮▮▮▮▮▮▮▮▮▮▮▮▮▮▮▮▮▮▮>5 star hotels Hamburg</a>

Best regards
```

We clicked to see the link that was given to us by this service, and found a truly awful page:

```
301 Moved Permanently
http://inra.fr

301 Moved Permanently
http://onetoy.ru

SEOに強いプロのホームページテンプレート「賢威」。大ロングセラーSEO教材
賢威はSEO対策に強いプロのホームページテンプレート。ユーザーが3,400人を突破した大ロングセラーSEO教材です。登録商標 第5231823
号

GovernmentAuctions.org
Comprehensive database listing thousands of Live and Online Government Auctions in the U.S. and Canada by state/territory. Buy all types of
Seized and Surplus items for rock-bottom prices. Real Estate, Autos, Electronics, Jewelry, Art, Antiques, and More.

Guild Wars Guru - Guides, Builds, Skills, Forums, Auctions, Maps, Factions, Monsters, Items, and Everything Else
http://guildwarsguru.com

http://yourseoplan.com
http://yourseoplan.com

301 Moved Permanently
http://cpi.ad.jp
```

This page is an example of a *bad neighborhood,* a poor-quality page that is engaging in linking practices that do not comply with the search engines' quality guidelines. We'll discuss bad neighborhoods in more detail on Thursday. Let's spell out all the reasons why this link won't help our site's ranks in search engines:

- The page is not indexed in the search engines.

- The page is on a domain that is supposedly related to hotels and lodging, whereas our website has no meaningful connection to that topic.

- The content on the page has no appeal for a human visitor.

Sadly, someone paid for this link-building service, probably with no idea what their money was buying.

A dedicated spreadsheet jockey would take this list and come up with meaningful quantitative analysis using hours of assessment and charting tools. The data may look something like this:

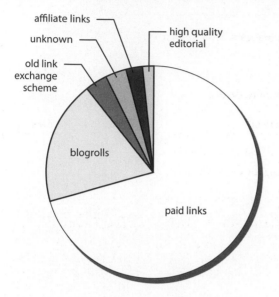

A savvy web surfer might take this list and come up with a meaningful description that looks like this:

"A significant portion of our links (over 1,000) are coming from our paid Yellowpages.com listing. These won't help our ranks, but they may bring in traffic. There are over 300 links from a blog called breakfastcereals.tv—these look to be coming from a single blogroll link on every page. Since these are all from low-power pages on the same domain, they don't add up to much linking power. There is a handful of links (fewer than 10) from nutrition-focused sites, mostly brief blog postings and press release reprints from when we launched our sugar-free cereal. One terrific link from the Surgeon General's blog was noted—this page has a Google PageRank of 7!"

Now: Spend some quality time in the link reporting tool of your choice, going through your external links, and write a summary of what you see.

Tuesday: Find Linking Opportunities

Link-building professionals run the gamut from disreputable charlatans to truly talented and successful businesspeople. One thing that you'll tend to notice about the respectable link builders is the time and attention they devote to fostering relationships with actual human beings who can provide those quality links. Today, we'd like you to focus on the links you can get from sites with which you may already have a personal relationship. These may include the following:

Your Clients/Customers/Fans Do you have a client base that is pleased with your service? Do they have websites that speak to a segment of your target audience? If so, they may be happy to provide a link to your site! Bonus points if they put your link alongside a glowing recommendation.

Your Service Providers/Vendors Are you a major client of any organization with a web presence that has a tie-in to your target audience? Maybe they would like to link to your site. Maybe they'd even like to list you as a featured client!

Your Partners Corporate partners are likely to include links on their websites. Check and see if there's one for you.

Sites That Already Include Your Company Name Perform a search for your company name in quotes. You may be surprised to find many websites that include your company information, maybe even a URL written in text, without making it a link! With a flick of the mouse, those could become inbound links for you.

Business Associations and Accreditations Most professional and trade associations include lists of their members. If your organization is accredited in any way, there may be a link in it for you.

Sympathetic Sites If your site has a religious, political, or philosophical theme, there is likely to be a large circle of similarly minded folks on the Web. These people will likely be enthusiastic about supporting one of their own. Ditto for specialized hobbies and enthusiasms.

Now: Record potential linking URLs under Potential Linking Sites in your Link Tracking Worksheet.

xtra cred Once you've identified the sites that you may already have a relationship with, you can take your link-building aspirations further and identify sites that you don't have a relationship with. A good place to start is to find sites linking to your competitors and sites that rank well for your target keywords.

Wednesday: The Art of Link Requests

If you own a website, surely you've seen them: annoying requests for links. Usually they go something like this: "Dear Webmaster. I reviewed your site and feel that it would be appropriate for a link trade. Please add the following HTML code to your home page... after your link is added, we will add your link to our links page."

Most of the time, this type of letter goes straight into the Trash folder. But, believe it or not, sometimes the best way to get a link is to just ask! Your best chance at gaining links will be from individuals or organizations with whom you have a genuine relationship.

Follow these dos and don'ts to craft link letters that *do* get results and *don't* annoy their recipients:

DO include key information. At a minimum, your letter must include the following: the URL from which you would like a link, your landing page URL, your landing page title, and your landing page description. Remember to choose the best landing page on your site, which, depending on the nature of the linking page, may not be your home page.

DO be straightforward. At the very least, it's going to take a few minutes for someone to add your link to their site. At most it might require a committee review and approval. You're writing to a total stranger and asking for a favor—don't pretend it's anything else.

DON'T offer a link trade. If your site is appropriate for a link, you should be able to get it without a reciprocal link agreement.

DO explain the benefits of the link... Website owners want to link to sites that their site audience will like. Specifically describe how your site relates to theirs.

...but DON'T write a novel. We're talkin' 25 words or less.

DO write from a company email address. Webmasters want to know that you really come from the company that is requesting the link.

DON'T mass-mail. Figure out the name of the person you're writing to, and use it. Then, sign with your own name and title.

And finally:

DO be personable. Think of every link request as a step forward in forging a relationship.

Pearl of Wisdom: Link building is relationship building.

A Bulletproof Link Letter

Several years ago, we were doing some link-building efforts for a major media website that had just launched an innovative product. The product was interesting enough that we thought some of the industry thinkers with blogs might want to take a look, and maybe even write a review. So, like Little Red Riding Hood skipping into the forest, we sent out a bunch of our usual perky, polite link request letters.

Hoo boy, were we in for a surprise! Some bloggers can be a little bit like sleepy dogs that wake up snapping their teeth. We received some less-than-polite responses: What were we doing pestering them? Who the heck would want this product? Why the heck did we send this email?

Worse, at least one blog actually published the text of our email, with our full name and email address! That could have been more than a little embarrassing.

A Bulletproof Link Letter *(Continued)*

Luckily—or was it actually foresight on our part?—our letters were carefully written to avoid embarrassment to ourselves or our client. We were eminently polite and professional. We described the benefits of the product without resorting to heavy selling. And we took some time to review the blogs for relevance before sending out our emails. Our punishment took the form of exposure, and not worse.

There are blogs on every subject, from lost socks to lost souls, and surely there are some in your industry. At some point in your link-building campaign, you'll probably want to approach one. Keep these guidelines in mind when you do:

- Get to know the blog first. Read it for a while before you approach its owner.
- Remember, it's less about selling your site to the blogger and more about convincing them that your site would be interesting to the blog's readers.
- If you really want a blogger to review your product, you'll have better success if you send them a freebie. Likewise, if your product is on a page that requires a login, consider offering login information for the blogger's sole use. (But don't send out login information in your first correspondence!)
- Read up on the FTC guidelines at www.ftc.gov/bcp/edu/pubs/business/adv/bus71 .shtm and make sure your blog relationship remains in compliance with ethical guidelines regarding paid endorsements.

And, finally, imagine your email posted on the blog for the whole world to see. Would this be embarrassing in any way to you or your organization? If so, you need a rewrite.

Now: Open a new document and write a template for a link request letter including your site's must-have information.

With your link request template and a list of possible linking sites at the ready, you're poised to get started sending out link requests! Why not start by sending one out today?

Thursday: Bad Neighborhoods

Link building is an SEO discipline that is particularly rife with fraud and too-good-to-be-true schemes that take advantage of site owners who want to improve their inbound link profile. Here are some common examples of linking schemes that you should avoid:

- A link-building company owns thousands of poorly written or scraped blogs focused on individual topics. They charge to include links to your site from these blogs.

- A link-building company charges to scour the Web and place comments on blogs that point back to your website. These comments typically say something generic like "Great post! This is really helpful, thanks!"
- A link-building company promises "undetectable" link trades or three-way link exchanges.

As a result of these activities, there is a significant underbelly of the Internet that contains terrible, incomprehensible blogs, miles of stream-of-consciousness directories and unusable "resources" pages. These sites, which SEO professionals call *bad neighborhoods,* are like cockroaches, constantly cropping up, and the search engines keep eradicating them from their indexes. Sometimes these sites even make their way into the search results, and as you can imagine, the search engines do not like to offer up this poor content to the searching public.

The search engines are keenly aware of this problem and have sophisticated processes in place to find bad neighborhoods. Here's how you may be affected if your site is associated with a bad neighborhood:

If your site has a few links from a bad neighborhood… No worries—even the best sites have these. As long as you have other, higher-quality links pointing to your site, the worst thing that will probably happen is that you just won't get any linking power from the linking site.

If your site is paying a service to get hundreds of links… It's quite possible that many of these paid links are coming from sites identified as bad neighborhoods. Again, probably the worst case scenario is that you're getting no benefit from these links and wasting your money. And we suppose we must mention that you may even get a bit of temporary benefit from these paid links…until the search engines find them and weed them out, removing any linking power that they have. The weeding out is inevitable, so why not save your money and instead work on gaining links from legitimate sites?

If your site is linking out to bad neighborhoods… Your ranks could be penalized if you have outbound links that point to sites engaging in linking schemes. (This only applies to links that pass link juice, so links tagged with nofollow will not cause a problem.)

Because certain outbound links can negatively affect your ranks, it's important to look at your site's links periodically and clear out the questionable ones. You may have an old resources page or a partners page on your site that you haven't thought about in ages. It's a good idea to double-check those links to make sure the sites you were linking to haven't changed owners and gone over to the dark side.

It's easy to find outbound links on your site—just search for <linkfromdomain: *yourdomain.com*> (for example, <linkfromdomain:pietown.tv>) on Bing.

Now: Click through outgoing links on your site and determine if they are pointing to sites in bad neighborhoods. If you find any links that fall into this category, either remove them, or add the nofollow attribute to them.

Make a habit of checking your outbound links once every few months or any time you see an unexpected drop in rankings.

An Expert's Opinion: The Difference Between Success and Failure

If your only exposure to link building is spammy, reciprocal link request emails from pushy webmasters, you may be surprised to know that there is a very different way to build links.

"It's a very human process," says renowned link-building consultant Eric Ward. Eric is such an authority on the subject of successful linking campaigns that he has earned the nickname "Link Moses"—a bit of a misnomer given his fresh-faced good looks.

Eric feels that taking the time to carefully assess potential linking sites is critically important. "You can automate only so much of the process, and then it comes down to you and your browser window, making qualitative decisions about the target sites. Most people dread that part. I dig it. That's the difference between success and failure."

Over half of Eric's business involves teaching his clients how to do it themselves. According to Eric, "The most successful sites will take ownership of the link-building process and not depend solely on vendors."

So if it's better to do it yourself, how can you make sure you're spending your precious time on the highest-quality potential linking sites?

Eric offers advice on identifying quality sites: "The signs of value will vary depending on the subject matter, but one constant is the site's content will be high caliber and not coated with 10 or 20 pay-per-click ads. The site will not require a return link as a condition of giving you a link."

And how does he identify sites that aren't worth the effort? "If the majority of what I see on the page is advertisements instead of content, I'm immediately suspicious. If the site says 'Submit your link free!' it's likely to be of little value. If a page has never been crawled by any search engine (this can be verified), the page isn't likely to be of value."

Don't be intimidated if you're just getting started with link building. Eric advises, "Do a search on the phrase 'link building expert' and read all the articles you find. Those of us who do this for a living have shared many of the tips and tools we use."

Tell it, Moses! Eric shares his tips and tools on his website, www.ericward.com.

Friday: What's Watering Down Your Link Juice?

Great links are hard to get! Today you'll make sure that your link-building efforts aren't being sabotaged by problems with your site structure that might be diluting the benefits of your inbound links.

Off-Domain Blogs If your blog is hosted on a service such as WordPress, TypePad, or Blogger, you may have opted to keep your blog on the service's domain. For example, your website might be found on the domain www.fabulous-genealogy.com, but your blog might be on fabgene.wordpress.com. If your blog is hosted off-domain, your main site won't receive its full potential of ranking benefits from inbound links to the blog. For that satisfying rising-tide-lifting-all-boats effect, your blog should reside on the same domain as your main site.

Canonical Issues Congratulations, you scored a great link to your genealogy page at http://fabulous-genealogy.com/super-cool-tools.html! Unfortunately, your site has an identical page with "www" in the URL at http://www.fabulous-genealogy.com/super-cool-tools.html. And, what's this? Your site also has an identical page ending with "htm" instead of "html." Each of these pages may be accumulating links from different people who happen upon the different variations of the same URL. Having 50 links divided among three different versions of a page is not as beneficial to that page as if those 50 links were concentrated on the primary and preferred, or canonical, version of the page. There are several ways to address canonical problems, which we explained in Week 2.

Broken Pages Don't let a good link send your traffic (and the search engines) to a dead end! Receiving links that point to broken or "file not found" pages will drag down your ranking potential. The linking tools that we discussed on Monday list the pages on your site that are receiving links; check those URLs for broken pages. Open Site Explorer makes this task particularly easy by listing 404 (File Not Found) and other errors on your site pages that are receiving inbound links. You can recover this lost link juice by adding a redirect (301, permanent, server-side, of course) to the broken URL. And see the sidebar "Prevent Link Rot" in Chapter 9, "Month Three: It's a Way of Life," for tips on preventing this problem in the future.

Vanity Alerts Inform Your Link-Building Strategy

One way to keep a close eye on your website's reputation and catch new inbound links as they are posted is to create a *vanity alert* and monitor it for new developments. To create a vanity alert, you select a keyword that you want to watch, and enter it into a service that will alert you whenever new content containing that keyword is discovered on the Web. For example, if you have a vanity alert set up for your CEO's name, you'll learn when someone is blogging about her. You can review the blog post and then determine whether you want to join the conversation, help promote the blog post, or refute slanderous claims. Or, if you set up a vanity alert for your new product, you may find some reviews that you wouldn't have noticed otherwise. You can even make a note to reach out to that site when your next product comes out; maybe you'll get another review!

You can set up vanity alerts at www.google.com/alerts or www.socialmention.com.

With a week of link research and submittals under your belt, you're in perfect shape to put your site's linkability on steroids next week.

Week 4: Building Content for Links and Engagement

Last week, we encouraged you to search the Web for sites that may want to link to yours. Have you received the cold shoulder from most of these potential traffic sources? Or have you been slacking on link building because you think your site has no linkable content?

With more and better content, your search engine visibility will benefit in two ways: More people will want to link to it, and the search engines will find more unique pages to index. But building high-quality, linkable content is easier said than done.

This week, you'll uncover opportunities that you may never have realized existed and scrub out obstacles, all with the goal of bulking up your linkable and indexable content. Your daily assignments for this week are as follows:

Monday: Discover Content You Already Have

Tuesday: Develop New Content

Wednesday: Using Other People's Content

Thursday: Develop Content Strategies

Friday: Content Thieves

Monday: Discover Content You Already Have

You know how great it feels to find a twenty in the pocket of a jacket you haven't worn in a while? Today is the day you'll look for linkworthy and search-engine-friendly content that you didn't know you already had.

Here are some likely hiding places:

On Your Website What could you already have on your site that's linkable? Here are some possibilities:

- Product comparisons
- Research reports
- Industry news
- Free downloads
- Case studies
- Games
- Photo galleries
- Forums

You may have content on your website that just needs a little tweaking—perhaps a reorganization or a minor rewrite—to become linkworthy.

What Makes Content Linkworthy?

Everyone is talking about getting inbound links. Many SEO professionals are focusing on strategies specifically geared toward improving linkability. For the best chance of gaining inbound links, content should be

- Original
- Unique
- Useful
- Noncommercial (or subtle in its sales pitch)
- Timely
- Accessible without a password or payment

And at the risk of stating the obvious, to be linkable, each page must be linkable—meaning it must have its own URL!

Perhaps you do have some of these elements on your site, but they're intertwined with your less linkable, commercial content. If so, your site may benefit from a simple reorganization of materials. And remember, your goal is conversions, not just inbound links, so be sure to provide a clear path from your most linkable pages to your conversion pages.

Sometimes, even a simple title rewrite can dramatically change the linkability of a page. For example, one type of content that often draws inbound links is a product comparison. Perhaps your site has a page that compares features of your product with your competition's. The only thing stopping it from being linkworthy is the title "Why Choose Us?" which strikes a commercial chord. Give this page a new, industry-specific but neutral title like "Compare Medical Imaging Products," and suddenly the exact same chart becomes potential linkbait.

Your Sales and Promotions Everybody loves a bargain, and next to free stuff, a sale or promotion is a strong contender for links. Trouble is, many websites move their promotions around, showing them temporarily at whatever URL seems to suit the moment. Take the smart approach: If your site runs promotions, make *one specific URL* that shows all of your promotions! (You can still create an individual page for each promo, but link to it from the catchall page.) That way, linking sites will have an easy time sending you their bargain-hungry traffic—and you'll gain inbound links. If your organization runs promotions but somehow doesn't manage to get that content up on the website in a timely manner, put linkability on the list of reasons to turn over a new leaf.

Tools, Worksheets, and Sample Documents Are there any tools, worksheets, presentations, or documents that your organization is using in-house and might be willing to share? For example, countless SEO firms offer keyword assessment tools or other useful gadgets for free on their websites. Think they're doing it out of altruism? Nope. More likely, they're trying to attract links and repeat traffic.

Compiled Resources You know your business, so you know the kinds of things your customers always seem to need help finding or figuring out. Resources such as useful links, FAQs, reviews, and a reference table or glossary can be good draws for inbound links (not to mention bookmarks and repeat visits!).

Email Newsletters If you're already writing and sending out email newsletters, why not add the archived newsletters to your site, too? What appeals to your customers or opt-in readers may also appeal to linking sites. Even better, rework your newsletter-writing process so that each tidbit or article you develop for this medium in the future can be repurposed as a blog post or social media status update.

Content Behind a Login Some sites have a great deal of content hidden behind a login. This is fine if you want to keep the search engines' hands off! But more than once, we've seen content that doesn't really need to be private, tucked away behind a password where it's not able to help your search presence. If you have a login on your site, take a good look at your hidden content and ask yourself whether some of it can be shown the light of day.

xtra cred Search engines have a special "first click free" program that allows pay-for-information sites to get password-protected content indexed, as long as visitors can see the first page they enter from a search engine without logging in. Who knew cloaking could be so legal! Here's the URL for more info: www.google.com/support/webmasters/bin/answer .py?answer=74536.

Now: Look for preexisting content and resources within your organization that can be repurposed for your website, and make contact with the person who can help make the necessary changes to your site.

If you didn't have any luck finding usable content today, don't despair: Tomorrow you will work on easy strategies for creating *new* content.

Tuesday: Develop New Content In-House

If yesterday's explorations didn't unearth any unique, linkworthy, and search-engine-friendly content for your website, you'll need to create some new content instead.

You'll look into creating new content in-house today.

Of course, you could hire a staff of professional writers and set them to work full-time building fascinating, linkworthy content for your website. If you've got the budget for that, set down this book and call HR today! For everybody else, here are some ideas for building new website content with limited resources:

Blogs If you have a thought leader in your midst, his or her insights could be translated into useful advice that speaks to your target audience. These can be added to your site in the form of "how to," "best of/worst of," and "5 ways to" blog posts. You can even spread out the workload by allowing contributions from several employees, or take it a step further and allow contributions from folks outside your company.

Quotable Data If your company performs research or has access to a lot of customer data, you may be able to identify ways to boil that information down and present it as factoids or infographics that do not jeopardize customer confidentiality or give away your business secrets. For example, a bridesmaid dress site might announce that its customers are 15 percent more likely to purchase a red dress if their wedding is in February than any other month. A site that provides vacation rentals might disclose that requests for smoke-free rooms have gone up 35 percent over the past 5 years.

Interviews Interviews with bigwigs in your industry, or anyone else who your target audience finds compelling, can be a great way to fill out your website. For example, if your company sells home furnishings, an interview with an interior designer could provide content of interest to your target audience while giving the designer a publicity boost. Look for experts or service providers in fields similar to your own, and try to pick someone with a strong reputation and an engaging personality.

The Power of Flattery

When someone is singing your praises, it's only natural that you want to give them a bigger microphone. Some link-building techniques take advantage of this most human desire for self-promotion. Here are some examples of ways that we've seen people use flattery as a link-building technique:

- Creating and distributing badges and awards, such as "Best of the Web." In many cases, these honors are posted in the recipient's website, and include a link back to the source website.

- Writing articles, posts, or reviews that praise a person, venue, or organization. It's not unusual for the person being praised to link to the article.

- Featuring members of the community, such as business owners, on your site (for example, "Local business of the month").

- Linking *out* from your site to other sites whenever you mention them.

We don't recommend loading up your site with meaningless flattery in hopes of gaining links, but we can't deny that flattery can be a part of relationship building. Find people, products, or websites that you genuinely adore, and think about ways that you might reach out to them!

Free Tools and Widgets If your company has the technical chops for it, there's nothing like a free online tool for drawing inbound links. Translate dollars into yen; calculate shoe size in the European standard; figure out how many tablespoons of ground coffee it takes to brew a pot. As long as it's potentially useful to your target audience, it's a great idea. Consider these as an option if your organization has a solid blend of creative ideas and programming skills.

By the way, your new content won't automatically bring in visitors just by existing:

 Pearl of Wisdom: Don't stop at creating this content. Tweet it, promote it on Facebook, and get the word out in your customer-facing email communications!

Plan to spend as much time talking up any new content as you spent creating it.

Don't Delete—Archive!

It happens to us all: We discontinue a product or service, we post an event that lasts only one day, and soon we're left with outdated content on our website. Three weeks later, someone notices it and says "Gack! I need to delete this right away!"

Here's our suggestion: Don't leave outdated material on your site, but don't delete it either. A properly archived page can continue to be an asset for your site and bring in visitors from the search engines, who you can then direct to updated information. For example, we work with an organization that runs many special events. Currently, every event description disappears from the site once an event is over. Our recommendation: Each of these events should be described on its own page. Once an event is over, the page can display a notice stating, "This event has expired. Visit our current calendar of events."

Discontinued product pages can either be updated with a notice and links to similar products (have a heart—also include support links for folks who still own the old product!), or the URL can be redirected using a 301 redirect to an updated similar product.

Wednesday: Using Other People's Content

Whoa, there! We're not saying you should go out on the Web, find some great content, and cut and paste it onto your website. There's this little thing called copyright infringement you'll want to watch out for. But there are some ways to use other people's content on your website without the feds beating down your door. Here are a few ideas:

User-Generated Content One of our favorite ways to increase content is to let your users build it for you, with blog comments, posts in message boards, classified ads, or product reviews. This is content that constantly updates itself and can often be eminently linkable. But it also sets you up for abuse, such as people submitting meaningless content (a practice called *comment spam*), so be sure you have a moderator or other system in place to protect your site if you're thinking of offering these features.

Articles Featuring Your Company Does your PR department keep a record of articles that mention your organization or include interviews or quotes from company representatives? See if you can get permission to add all or part of these articles to your website. (It goes without saying that you should stick to the complimentary ones.)

Syndicated Content It's quite easy to incorporate feeds onto your website—for example, industry news or blog posts. It's not unique content, but providing a group of topical links may add freshness and a sense that your site is up-to-date, thus increasing your linkability.

Guest Contributors Many talented writers and artists would love to have more space on the Internet to display their work. This type of content can take the form of a post by a guest blogger, or an article stating expert advice or opinion. You could even assign a colleague to send a first-person account of a popular industry conference. And your contributors don't have to be professional writers. Many websites are nicely filled out with the free expressions of regular people, from birth stories to product success stories.

Royalty-Free Content Many websites, such as www.articlegeek.com and www.aracontent .com, offer royalty-free articles that you can legally publish on your website, usually in exchange for a link or a courtesy notice. Royalty-free (sometimes called copyright-free) articles cover subjects ranging from wedding etiquette to astronomy to tax advice, so it's likely that you can find some that are relevant to your website. However, since this content is not unique, it's of little value for your search engine presence (and may even annoy your site visitors because they may have seen the same articles on other sites). So use this content with caution, and only if you are certain it improves your site offerings.

An alternative to royalty-free content is Creative Commons (CC) content. The Creative Commons, at creativecommons.org, is an alternative type of copyright—you might call it a "some rights reserved" copyright. Explore CC content by searching for it using Google's advanced search.

We've given you a nice long list of possible ways to add content to your website; not every one will suit your needs or abilities. Today, choose which technique you'll try first. Set a goal for yourself, perhaps adding one new page of unique content each week, and get started today.

Now: Set a content-building goal and get started.

Optimize Non-HTML Documents

There's no harm in posting documents on your website in non-HTML formats such as Word, Excel, PDF, or PowerPoint. All of these formats are indexed by the major search engines, and sometimes they rank well. However, good old HTML still has the upper hand in search. Non-HTML content can be a turnoff to searchers, but if you have it on your site, we recommend some basic best practices:

- Add descriptive, keyword-rich metadata to the document properties. In Adobe Acrobat and Microsoft Office applications, metadata such as Title, Author, and Keywords is easy to define by selecting File > Properties or File > Document Properties. If you are using other programs to author your documents, look to their help pages for guidance.

- Follow the same SEO guidelines for non-HTML documents as you would for your regular web pages: Include your target keywords in text, link to the document from other pages on your site, make sure URLs in the document are clickable so the search engine robots can follow them, and modify the content for improved snippets if desired.

- Non-HTML documents may contain confidential information hidden in the metadata that you don't wish to make public, including things like tracked changes, comments, and speaker notes. It's always a good idea from a security standpoint to review metadata for your documents before posting them in public view.

With descriptive metadata and content rich with keywords, your non-HTML documents may turn out to be healthy sources of targeted traffic for your site!

Thursday: Develop Content Strategies

It's common for a site to lack linkable content, and this problem can be addressed with resources and creativity. But when sites are further hindered by a company culture that makes it difficult to develop linkable content, it's a whole 'nother type of problem. If reading the first three days of this week left you saying "that just won't work for us," or if you think your site has the potential to do more than just adding a few pages of linkable content once in a while, you would benefit from a well-formed strategy.

Here are some ways to think about forming the right processes for content development that might help your site attract more links:

Think Repeatable and Scalable Try to make every content effort work for you over the long term. Here's an example: Many sites create contests in their effort to draw in links and traffic. If you invest the resources into developing a contest, make sure that you can reuse it. You can modify the contest with different creative directions, but use the same page templates and voting technology. Every new contest will require serious creative thinking and promotion, but at least you won't have to build it from scratch again. Do any of the following work for you?

- Recurring blog posts, such as weekly news roundups or "your questions answered" that follow a formula but provide a valuable user experience
- Contests, competitions, or giveaways that reuse the same templates and technologies
- User-submitted questions and answers
- Events, promotions, or other features that still provide valuable or entertaining content even when they are archived

Be Exclusive Many sites have affiliates and partners that sell the same products or promote the same events. By giving your own site first dibs on publishing this content, you can increase your chances of being viewed as the primary source. This can have search engine and linking advantages, and even a few hours of exclusivity before you share your content may be enough to help your site beat out the search competition.

Study Your Competitors Are your more successful competitors offering more fascinating, timely, and original content than your site offers? This may be something you need to recognize about your competitive search environment. Take an honest look at your own site and see what it needs in order to be launched into your competitors' orbit. We know your CFO won't want to hear this, but we often find that some of the biggest barriers to achieving more links and traffic could be remedied by bringing a professional writer on board.

Change Your Policies Generating linkworthy content may require a shift in your internal policies—for example, there may be parts of the website that you are not allowed to modify, or your use of language may be buttoned up by an unnecessarily restrictive style guide. Sometimes an off-site meeting or a trip to the neighborhood watering hole with your colleagues can be just the thing to bring up new suggestions for your website. And any idea that your competitors are already doing well is likely to be accepted by the policymakers first.

> **Now:** Write down your ideas and goals for realistic and repeatable ongoing content development. Start a conversation with the people who can make it happen within your organization.

Friday: Content Thieves

You're starting to develop a lovely collection of content on your website, but is some outlaw mooching your message? Unfortunately, the Internet remains something of a Wild West for copyright law. Other websites might steal your content simply by cutting and pasting, or they may use scraping, a more sophisticated technique of automatically grabbing content from your web pages, to steal material from your site and put it up on theirs.

You want to be aware of content thieves, not just because they are using your content to compete with you for search engine visibility, but also because they may be damaging your brand. An employer of ours once discovered that another company had repurposed large chunks of our website's marketing content—but *hadn't even taken the time to change all of the instances of our company name!* If your content is stolen by a similarly pathetic character, unwitting users might actually think that they are visiting *your* website, and that's something you certainly don't want.

There are several ways to check if your material is being repurposed elsewhere on the Web. Here are a few:

Search for text. Using the search engine of your choice, search for a likely-to-be-unique text string (a sentence or two will do) from the body of your website, using quotes around the text. If the search engine finds sites other than your own, something fishy may be going on.

Use a page comparison site. Copyscape.com is a website specifically designed to help site owners find copies of their content online. A major limitation is that it searches only HTML content, not PDFs or other document formats.

Search for media. Stolen media such as images, audio, video, and Flash content is considerably harder to find than copies of your page text—for the very same reasons that search engines struggle with these formats in general. If media content is a significant portion of your site, you'll need to become an expert at using the video and image search options discussed in Chapter 8, "Month Two: Establish the Habit," to help protect your rights online.

It's often easier to prevent media theft than react to it. If you're concerned about this, check in with your design team to make sure they're savvy to copy prevention options such as adding watermarks to images, building your Flash files in multiple pieces, or embedding your server information in media files.

Review your server logs. Other websites can display your media content such as images, audio, video, and Flash and make it look like it belongs to them. It's not uncommon for these nefarious nerds to point their links directly to your content on *your servers*. Not only does this practice, known as *hot linking*, infringe on your copyrights, it also puts an unfair burden on your servers, which are forced to serve up the content for someone else's site! Your server logs can help you find this sort of hijacking—yet another reason to make a habit of reviewing your analytics data.

Now you know how to look for misused materials on the Web. But what will you do if you find any? With any luck, a simple communication with the content thieves will clear things up. If not, you may need to contact the website host and request that the page be removed. Detailed advice and links to sample "cease-and-desist" letters can be found at www.plagiarismtoday.com/stock-letters.

Now: Choose one of the methods listed in this section and search for copies of your web content. Begin pursuing any that you find.

You've been at this SEO thing for a couple of months now, and maybe you've even taken a liking to it. Next month, you'll jump into social strategies with both feet and begin a paid search campaign. Get ready to "establish the habit" of SEO!

Month Two: Establish the Habit

If it's true that it only takes 30 days to establish a daily habit, your SEO habit is now official!

Last month, you tidied up your website's on-page optimization and structure and started making some online connections. This month, you'll start to expand the real estate in search engine result pages that you either control or influence. Social media marketing, shopping search, local search, and paid search are all part of your continued foray into new SEO territory!

Chapter Contents
Week 5: Social Media Marketing
Week 6: Set Up Your Paid Search Account
Week 7: Selling Through Search
Week 8: Local Search

Week 5: Social Media Marketing

Maybe you've already jumped on the social media bandwagon, but you want some ideas for honing your strategy or smoothing out your processes. Maybe you're a savvy personal user, but you're puzzled about how you can get your organization involved in the social space. Social media marketing means monitoring and participating in sites that foster peer-to-peer interaction, such as Facebook, Twitter, blogs, review sites, and wikis, to improve branding, customer engagement, and sales. Although the options are unlimited and the variety of tools and methods intimidating, the goal is easy to understand:

 Pearl of Wisdom: Social media marketing is watching, joining—and, ideally, influencing—the online conversations that are taking place about your product, service, or organization.

Social media marketing is as vast as a Las Vegas buffet, but this week, we'll just serve up the sampler plate: handy tips for getting started, examples of real-world strategies that work, and ideas on keeping things manageable so that you can decide how much—or how little—you can handle.

Your daily assignments for this week are as follows:

Monday: Study Hall—Get To Know the Social Web

Tuesday: Online Reputation Monitoring

Wednesday: Twitter Boot Camp

Thursday: Your Facebook Strategy

Friday: Social Media on Your Site

Monday: Study Hall—Get to Know the Social Web

Today you'll take some time to get familiar with the kinds of sites you'll come across on the Social Web.

Social Networking Sites Some well-known examples of social networking sites are Facebook and LinkedIn. These sites are not for the time-strapped; your goal on these sites is to make connections and communicate through them on a regular basis. Sound familiar? Consider these sites a new medium for the same types of networking activities you'd do offline. We're guessing you already have an account on at least one of these sites; maybe you're one of the millions who check Facebook in the morning before you brush your teeth. Or maybe you've just signed up and you're asking, "Now what?" Facebook deserves a book of its own; we'll give you a day to focus on it later this week.

Social News and Bookmarking Sites These are sites that allow users to give a virtual thumbs up to a web page, picture, or comment, which in turn allows others to find them. Digg, reddit, and delicious.com are popular examples. As an online marketer, your goal on sites like these is to get links to your site and votes for your content. But remember what we told you in Chapter 7, "Month One: Kick It into Gear":

> **Pearl of Wisdom:** Most links from social media sites are tagged with the `nofollow` attribute and will not help your ranks directly.

Is your organization doing something fascinating enough, or does your website offer something so unique or so useful that a rising tide of voters will push your site to the top? One way to get a quick read on these sites is to look at the most popular entries and then compare them to the slush in the "just added" section. Every site has its own special audience (reddit, for example, is popular with gamers and techies), so observing the successes will give you an idea of what content will be well received. You can contrast those successes with the no-vote entries, like the business owner who posted a press release about his company's great customer service. This should give you an idea of what kind of content is and isn't rewarded.

Microblogs Microblogging is a medium currently dominated by a certain little blue bird (yes, we're talking about Twitter). Nicely tuned to our attention-challenged society, microblogging allows short messages to be broadcast to a listening audience and folds in well with mobile devices. The most influential microbloggers have a large and attentive following of people who read, and regularly repeat, their comments. Anything with a status, update, or caption can be considered microblogging. We've devoted a day to Twitter marketing later in this chapter.

Blogs Blogs remain an active and vibrant part of the Social Web, delivering valuable information in long-form posts and creating venues for conversations in comments and from one blog to another.

The most influential bloggers have many readers, a prolific and dynamic community of commenters, high authority as gauged by the blog search engine `Technorati.com`, a high number of inlinks, and a high Google PageRank value. On your own blog, your mission is to further your conversion goals by entertaining, engaging, and persuading your readers. On others' blogs, your mission is either to get mentioned or to join in the dialogue in a way that showcases your smarts and usefulness to your target audience.

Review Sites Online shopping is omnipresent, and so too is the word of mouth that surrounds the consumer experience. Was this product any good? Did this merchant treat me well? Consumers spill their guts on sites such as Yelp, Epinions, and Google (within Google Places). There are also niche review sites for travel, healthcare, and software, to name a few. Getting positive reviews on some review sites can influence your own site's visibility in the search engines. We'll help you sort out shopping and local customer review sites, and help you identify which venues matter to you, during the Shopping Search and Local Search weeks, later this month.

Forums One of the older forms of social engagement online, there are online forums for every imaginable point along the conversation spectrum, from gentle parenting discussions to anarchist rants. Forums provide ample opportunity for you, the connected marketer, to join the conversation, become a trusted voice, and keep your organization in that favorable top-of-mind position with your target audience.

Photo and Video Sharing Sites Photo and video sharing sites allow users to upload photos and video for sharing with others. These sites host and broadcast your media, often in unlimited quantities, for an audience that is as public or private as you choose. YouTube revolutionized video on the Web by allowing the masses to not only view and comment on uploads, but also to embed others' videos on their own sites. Flickr is an active community of photo enthusiasts, complete with subgroups and subcultures all its own. We'll touch on video and image search optimization next month.

Question and Answer Sites From "How can I avoid going bald?" to "What's the best wood-fired oven?" people are reaching out for answers on sites like Yahoo! Answers and WikiAnswers. This is a peer-to-peer conversation, so anyone can contribute an answer, but trusted answers are often selected by the asker or by public votes. You may find these sites ranking well in the search engines for search queries that are phrased as a question.

Table 8.1 provides a simple overview to help you get your bearings in the social media space.

▶ **Table 8.1** Social Media: Why You Care

Type of Site	Examples	A good venue for a business to…
Social networking sites	Facebook, LinkedIn, MySpace	Have a presence describing your company or yourself. Announce events or promotions. Engage in conversations with current and potential customers. Ask for customer feedback or suggestions.
Social news and book-marking sites	Digg, reddit	Get noticed by other people for something truly newsworthy or out of the ordinary.
Microblogs	Twitter	Build up a loyal following and keep them feeling special by engaging in brief conversations with them. Announce events or promotions. Ask for customer feedback or suggestions.
Blogs	Any of Technorati's top 100 blogs, as seen on http://technorati.com/blogs/top100/	Show expertise, start engaging discussions, or persuade readers to convert. Announce events or promotions. Ask for customer feedback or suggestions.
Review sites	Yelp, Google Places, TripAdvisor	Encourage happy customers to post positive reviews.

▶ **Table 8.1** Social Media: Why You Care   *(Continued)*

Type of Site	Examples	A good venue for a business to…
Forums	Google lists many forums in its Discussions search results. To find these results, search for any keyword phrase on Google, then click More, then Discussions in the left column.	Show expertise, share advice, monitor brand conversations.
Photo and video sharing sites	Flickr, YouTube, Vimeo	Post unique or useful video and images to show off your products, share your expertise, engage, or entertain.
Question and answer sites	Yahoo! Answers, WikiAnswers	Answer specific questions about a product or general questions about your industry. Be visible to an audience who has a stated interest in learning something related to your offering.

The lines of categorization are a bit blurry: For example, isn't that photo caption on Flickr like a tweet? Isn't that threaded conversation on Digg like a forum? You do not need to be on top of every latest tweak to these sites' service offerings in order to make a difference in your organization. Just get in the habit of having a little study hall session prior to doing any actual interacting! That's a good rule of thumb no matter what social media site you're dealing with.

Now: Visit at least one site from each of the social media categories we just described. Click around to get a basic grasp on how people are contributing content.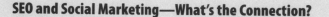

As you review these sites, try to find both personal users and business accounts to get a feel for tone, the use of language, the length of communication, and the types of interaction.

SEO and Social Marketing—What's the Connection?

The universe of online marketing professionals is large enough that there is room for pros who do only social marketing and pros who do only SEO. However, in many companies (possibly including yours), a single person is often tasked with both forms of marketing.

There are a few ways that social media outreach can have a positive impact on your search engine presence.

SEO and Social Marketing—What's the Connection? *(Continued)*

Branding and Reputation within the Search Results

Your search results are a big part of your online reputation. Search for your company name on Google and you may find messages that other people control, such as blog posts, directory listings, customer reviews, or mentions of your company in the local news. But if you are cultivating a good social media presence, you can strengthen your online reputation with Google results that are dominated by social media pages that you control or that you have influenced.

It's not such a radical concept to think that any one of several offsite listings (Yelp reviews, a Twitter page, flattering blog write-ups) might help drive a person toward your conversion goals. Now imagine the positive effects of having one or more of these items together with your site's listing at the top of the Google ranks for your top-priority keywords.

Links

You want links, and people on the Social Web are giving them away! Unfortunately, most links from social media sites are tagged with `nofollow` or placed behind logins, and therefore they won't directly help your ranks. But there are ways that links from social media sites can positively influence your search engine ranks. For example, links from `nofollow` sites are sometimes repurposed by others on "dofollow" sites. And being in the conversation will certainly increase your chances of being blogged about or linked to in ways that are beneficial to your ranks.

Keywords

When you push your message out via social media channels, you have the opportunity to begin a dialogue that suits your brand and your message. This dialogue should contain descriptive terms that align with your top-priority keywords. For example, using keywords in your tweets may influence others to use your keywords when they talk about you, and this can translate into extra presence in the standard search engine results or in Google's real-time search results.

Traffic

There's an old saying: You can't catch a fish if you don't put your hook in the water. This can be applied to social media efforts as well. If you create more opportunities for people to learn about your company online, you're more likely to bring them to your site.

Tuesday: Online Reputation Monitoring

Yesterday you found your target audience and maybe your competitors on the Social Web. (Oh, and did you also find your college sweetheart? 'Cause we're pretty sure you looked!) Today you're going to configure some easy-to-use tools to monitor the conversations that are taking place about your brand, your products, or your keywords. By the end of today, you'll be eavesdropping on the Internet in style!

Sure, you could get fancy and spend a bundle on a commercial reputation-monitoring service, but we're going to keep it simple (and free!) and get you started with just two tools: a feed reader and search engine keyword alerts.

Feed Reader A feed reader is a tool that you customize to receive updates about your favorite sites; it displays the newest content from these sites in a single page.

iGoogle, at www.google.com/ig, is a free, personalized feed reader that you can set up for your Google account. You probably already know you can use iGoogle to display widgets like weather, news, and word of the day. It can also be used to display any feed you might want to follow, including keyword alerts, in a handy central location. Easy to customize and simple to navigate, iGoogle is a newbie's dream come true. See Figure 8.1 for an example.

Other feed readers you might like include Sage (a Firefox add-on), Netvibes, and Reeder (for the iPad). These are all designed for use by normal folk, with easy-to-implement setups. Setting up your feed reader as your browser's home page will help you stay current with every review, rumor, and remark being made about your business. Being greeted every day by your customers' tweets or the latest blog postings by your top competitor will go a long way toward keeping you engaged in the Social Web.

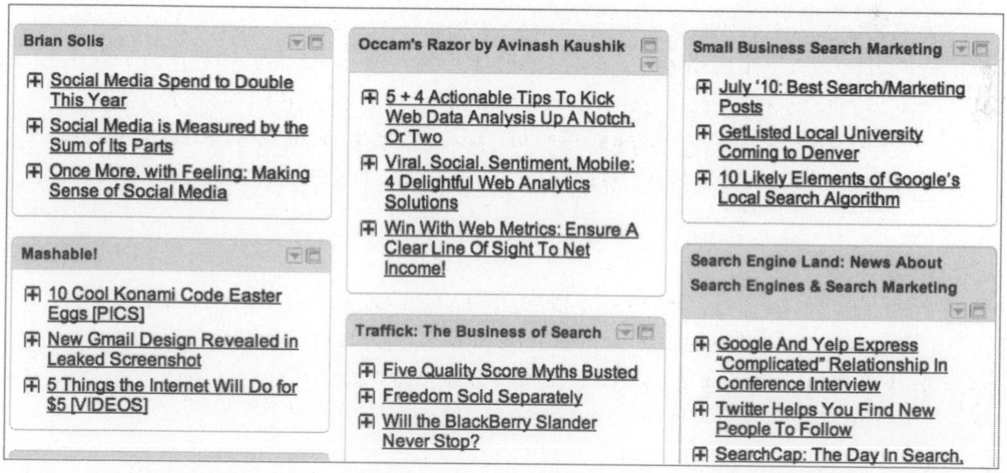

Figure 8.1 iGoogle feed reader

Now: Choose a feed reader that works for you from the ones we just mentioned.

slacker If browsing feed readers is not your idea of a good time, we'll choose it for you: Go ahead and use iGoogle.

Search Engine Alerts Search engine alerts work like this: You tell the search engine a keyword, and it will either email you or update a feed whenever the search results for that term change. In Google, follow the instructions at www.google.com/alerts to set up a keyword alert. In Bing, after you perform a search, look for the letters RSS or the feed icon in your browser address bar, as shown here:

Click the feed icon to subscribe to the feed using your feed reader of choice.

With a feed reader chosen and search engine alerts sussed out, you're ready to populate your starter dashboard with all the keywords you want to keep your eye on. Here's our suggested list:

- Your business name, including all variations
- Your highest-priority keywords (too much data can be overwhelming, so we think it's best to start with a small list)
- Names of prominent individuals in your company

Here's a step-by-step walkthrough of creating a Google keyword alert and setting it up to display on your iGoogle page:

- You will need a Google account. Set one up and log into it at www.google.com/accounts.
- Enter your account management page and click Alerts or go to www.google.com/alerts.
- Choose a keyword you wish to track, as shown here:

- Select Deliver to > Feed. You could have the alert emailed to you if you prefer, but this might get annoying if you're tracking a lot of terms.

| blue footed booby | | Everything | as-it-happens | Only the best results | Feed 🔊 View in **Google Reader** | edit |

- From the Alerts list, click the orange feed icon. Open this link. Due to a bug, this window will only display correctly if you open it in a new browser window, rather than in a new tab.

- Choose to subscribe to the feed on Google:

Subscribe to this feed using [Google ▼] [♦]
☐ Always use Google to subscribe to feeds.

[Subscribe Now]

Google Alerts – blue footed booby

- Next, select Add To Google Homepage:

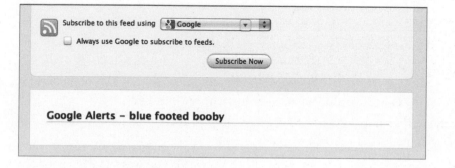

- On your iGoogle home page, the alert will look something like this:

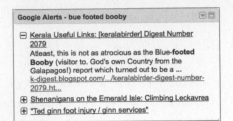

xtra cred

Thinking you can go beyond just search engine keyword alerts on your iGoogle page? Of course you can: Jump in feet first on BoardTracker.com for forum conversations or Technorati.com for blog posts. For a closer examination of mentions that take place only on social sites, you can use socialmention.com. Search results on these sites generate a feed, which you can add to your iGoogle page or to any feed reader.

slacker

If you have no time to set up an online reputation dashboard, do yourself a favor: Create a single search engine alert for your business name.

Now: Populate your feed reader with top-priority keywords.

Now you're on par with the most self-aware brands on the block! Once a day, take a few moments to lean back and enjoy a look at your reputation monitoring dashboard. Do you see anything you didn't expect to see?

Connected Marketing

We rarely go ga-ga for jargon-y expressions, but we've been waiting years for this one: *Connected marketing* is an umbrella term including viral, buzz, online word-of-mouth, and social media marketing. We love that it captures the heart of all these forms of marketing: a genuine human connection.

Let's say you want to promote your company's foot massager product via connected marketing. To the uninitiated, it might seem like a good idea to craft a cookie-cutter marketing spiel such as, "Our Toenado massager is the choice for millions of foot-pain sufferers. With patented 'heal the heel' technology, this massager will erase your pain. Don't pussyfoot around—come to www.toenado.com to buy now!" Then it might seem reasonable to stick this message in some ads and email messages, and wait for the orders to roll in.

Connected Marketing *(Continued)*

Here's how a connected marketer might approach this campaign:

- For months, she's been following the Foot Pain Forum, posting comments occasionally when she has something useful to contribute. When she notices a post looking for foot pain advice, she writes: "Oh, I know what you mean about how hard it is to walk the dog. Soaking in warm water is a great cure for this problem, but I also think you might need to contact a board-certified podiatrist about those jabbing sensations." Her signature contains her company name and URL.

- She's a regular commenter on Shoeholic Cecile's blog and has exchanged an email or two with Cecile. When Cecile posts a complaint about her feet hurting after a night on the dance floor, our connected marketer gives some nonpartisan advice about foot massagers, *without explicitly mentioning the product*. Again, her signature contains the company name and URL.

- She finds a well-known Gadget Review blog and emails the blogger directly to tell them about the massager. Once a connection is established, she may offer to send the blogger a free sample. (Any review will need to disclose the free gift in order to comply with Federal Trade Commission guidelines.)

- She always includes a personal follow-up email to her customers, asking for their opinion of the product and requesting that they post a review.

- Her company's "why I need a foot massager" writing contest gets lots of humorous entries. Each entrant posts several Facebook links to the contest, hoping to get more winning votes.

Yep, it's a looong, slow curve to the sale. But putting a personal face on your company can do worlds of good for your branding.

Wednesday: Twitter Boot Camp

Twitter's large user base and simple premise make it an excellent social environment to find and communicate with the people you want to target. This microblogging platform allows anyone with an account to post brief messages for public consumption, resulting in a rich and dynamic multiparty conversation. Don't be fooled by the 140-character limit—some very advanced marketing takes place on Twitter! Let's look at some basic ways that your business can start employing Twitter as a marketing tool.

Twitter Lingo

You're taking time to get to know the social sites before you participate, and we hope this handy list of popularly used Twitter conventions will make it easier for you to join the conversation when you are ready to open your beak and start tweeting.

@ The character that precedes every Twitter account name, for example, @jengrappone and @gradiva.

Follow The act of subscribing to view a Twitter user's messages. Typical marketing practices revolve around gaining more followers for your organization's accounts and identifying and communicating with influential Twitter users who have a large number of followers.

Retweet Abbreviated as RT, the act of repeating another Twitter user's message, while giving credit to the original source. When another person retweets your message, it will be displayed to that person's followers, so a retweet of your message is a success for you!

Direct Message Abbreviated as DM, a private message from one Twitter user to another.

Trending Topic Phrases that reach the highest levels of tweeting and retweeting activity. Trending topics change frequently—for example, a movie title might be a trending topic on that movie's release day, or a humorous phrase may capture the short attention spans of the Twitterati for just a few hours.

URL Shorteners Sites like `bit.ly` and `is.gd` provide short alternatives to long URLs, helping people stay within Twitter's 140-character limit.

Hashtag A word preceded by the # character, which can be used to summarize or categorize the tweet. Since hashtags are easy to monitor, many people search for them when they are interested in discussing a particular topic with people outside of their circle of followers. Smart marketers use them (and even smarter marketers *don't overuse them*) when they want to be found for a particular topic. For example, "Just four more spots available at our #agile software development training! Sign up here: `http://bit.ly/6uvT3`."

Monitor your brand. Keeping a watchful eye on the chatter surrounding your product name, company name, or CEO is as simple as searching Twitter for those words (see Figure 8.2). You can observe people's conversations as they discuss these topics and get a sense of their sentiment. One advantage of brand monitoring on Twitter is that it gives you real-time notification, and an opportunity for quick intervention, if someone is having a public hissy fit about your product or company. Another advantage is that by eavesdropping on others' conversations about your offerings, you may begin to understand trends or get enhancement ideas that you would otherwise need a focus group to identify. Imagine the value of statements like, "I wish SoftWareCo integrated with MS Office!" or "Everyone at my party picked their cashews out of the NutCo mix—wish they made a cashew-only jar!"

Figure 8.2 Twitter search for <ucla library>

The interface at search.twitter.com is a fine starting point, but the savviest Twitter users employ other free tools that make it easier to monitor a brand on Twitter. Try TweetDeck or Topsy, or add the Twitter search results feed to the reputation monitoring dashboard you built on Tuesday.

Make connections. Twitter is full of people talking about everyday minutiae, some of which may be related to your product or service. If you sell vacation packages, you may be on the lookout for people who are planning their honeymoons. If you sell glider rocking chairs, you may be on the lookout for birth or pregnancy announcements. Be warned, you'll need to stay on the polite side of etiquette—Twitter has a "block user" feature, and your account can be banned for aggressive outreach techniques—but if you are reaching out politely with useful information, you may encounter positive responses. Here are some possible ways to enter into conversations with targeted people on Twitter:

- Follow them. Many people receive notifications when they gain new followers. If your account name and profile gives an indication of who you represent, a person you follow may be interested enough to follow you back. Some people even have settings enabled that will cause them to automatically follow you back.

xtra
cred

- Chat them up. If you happen to find someone asking, "Decisions, decisions. Where should we spend our honeymoon?" you can reach out with a friendly, "@liber8er, have you considered an Alaska cruise? http://bit.ly/6uvT3 I'm here to help if you have questions!"

- Use a hashtag. Using a hashtag like #poweryoga and #pilates makes your tweets easier to search, and may help move some of those exercise DVDs you're selling!

- Incentivize influencers. You may identify a person with a lot of followers whom you think could help spread your message. Offer them a coupon code to share with their followers, or even a free sample.

Expand your customer service efforts. Like any other public forum, Twitter has its share of people who use it for the occasional rant. If someone is complaining about your product, even if they are not complaining to you directly, it can benefit you both if you see the complaint and respond quickly. One of our clients describes her strategy: "I monitor Twitter for our product name. We get a lot of really positive mentions. But sometimes we find negative ones, too. If someone says, 'I can't stand how [product x] is so slow to load!' I'll point them to a FAQ that explains how to improve speed. Sometimes a complaint is more than I know how to address, so I alert our tech team so they can follow up. And sometimes, a person's complaint is so inaccurate, or their rant is so intense, that you know you'll only fuel the fire by responding. We let those go."

Anyone who's ever been a frustrated customer knows that sometimes it just takes a genuine "I'm sorry" from a customer service rep to drop your blood pressure back to normal. After tweeting a mild complaint about an analytics vendor, we were both pacified and impressed when a customer service rep responded right away with "@jengrappone, I'm so sorry you're having problems. Is there anything we can do?"

Identify trends. Searching Twitter for your own top-priority keywords can clue you into the latest happenings and important trends in your niche. For example, let's say your brand of power tools is a huge hit with men. But while you're monitoring Twitter for <power tools>, you start to notice more women initiating the conversations. With a little investigation, you trace it all back to the growing popularity of the new book, *An Apron and a Chainsaw: One Woman's Journey to Self-Fulfillment*. You've already had a meeting with your team to talk about making cordless drills with grips sized for women's hands, while your competitors are still unaware of this new trend.

Make customers feel special. "I'm in love with my new @Lovelyzip purse." "Thanks for the compliment, @KellySF! We hope you'll be on the lookout for our new line in the fall!" Sure, you could communicate just as well via email, but direct conversations with your customers are simpler when they're limited to 140 characters. Twitter conversations are satisfying to customers and companies alike due to the feel of instantaneous contact. Something about Twitter being a public venue and the brevity of the messages gives a feel of chatting at a big, fun party. There's also a distinct bonus for you to let your friendly, helpful communications be displayed for anyone who's interested.

Asking questions is another way to maintain a relationship with your Twitter followers. Want to name a new product? Reach out to your followers for ideas. Looking for something to blog about? Ask your followers what they've been curious about lately.

Retweeting positive tweets about your product is a way to improve your image and make the person who wrote the original message feel valued. Try not to turn people off, though—balance out these self-congratulatory tweets with your own comments that are interesting and useful to your users.

Finally, offering coupon codes or incentives only on Twitter is a great way to engage your followers and attract new ones.

> **Now:** Fire up www.twitter.com or your favorite tool for viewing tweets. Search for your company or product name. Who's talking about them, and what are they saying?

Notice how we haven't told you to create your Twitter account yet? If you feel ready to make it happen for your business, here are a few tips to keep in mind:

- Make your username as short as possible (this will leave more characters available in retweets) while being reasonably descriptive. And check how your name will look with "@" in front of it—we'd hate for Steve's Silver Cleaning to end up with the username @sscleaning!

- Decide how you want to manage multiple users. Some businesses choose to use a single account and allow multiple users to tweet under the same company voice. Other businesses use a single business account but identify separate contributors by signatures, as in: "There's 1 space left in my Tuesday class—call the front desk! /mc." If your business culture is more individualistic or your employees have brands of their own to cultivate, your business might opt for separate Twitter accounts under separate personal names.

- Like so many old, empty soda bottles by the side of the road, the Twitterscape is littered with accounts that people started but did not keep up. You definitely don't want to kick off your official business account unless you are confident that you have the resources to keep it active for the long term.

> **Now:** *Don't* create your official Twitter account. One day is just not enough time to know where you want to go with it!

Instead of creating your business account today, use this time to *lurk*, watching conversations in your industry space without making any comments, for a week or two before you decide that you're ready to set up the official business account.

The Coolhaus Ice Cream Truck: Tweet the Treat

What's that stylish pink ice cream truck, and why are so many adults chasing it down? It's Coolhaus, an independent gourmet ice cream sandwich company, and a darling of the Los Angeles foodie scene. The Coolhaus truck drives all over the city, tweeting its whereabouts so that eager customers can locate the next stop and fulfill their cravings for architecturally themed ice cream sandwiches.

These sublime ice cream sandwiches inspire many customers to blog or tweet about their foodie experience. Photos of a customer's hand holding a Coolhaus "sammie" are commonplace on Flickr, imgur, and any other image-sharing site you can name. "Our customers and followers are basically PR for us," says Natasha Case, Coolhaus's principal and co-founder. "Bloggers are often self-appointed food critics and are a huge form of obtaining new customers for us."

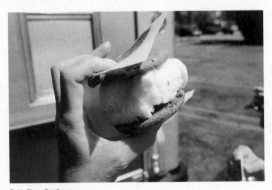

Whether consumer generated or company generated, much of the company's marketing lives on the Social Web, with Twitter at the forefront of the effort. The Coolhaus Twitter campaign has two different types of tweets: One type is utilitarian, announcing the location of the truck: "We're scooping on top of the hill at Barnsdall Park on Hollywood Blvd. a block west of Vermont."

The Coolhaus Ice Cream Truck: Tweet the Treat *(Continued)*

The other involves brand identity—for example, introducing events to followers in advance ("Kid in a Candy Store" - Food Network - episode featuring Coolhaus - July 26 @ 8:30 pm. Record it tweeters!!!!!"), or responding to and retweeting photos, reviews, and compliments from happy customers. Followers of Coolhaus on Twitter may be surprised to learn that Coolhaus's Twitter stream often comes from two people simultaneously: one in the office and one on the truck. Natasha explains that the team has held meetings about keeping its Twitter voice cohesive regardless of which staffer is doing the outreach.

There's more to Coolhaus's Twitter outreach than just being talkative; there is real strategy at play. "It's important not to be passive," says Natasha. "We like to be aggressive with reaching out to people who have big audiences." This involves identifying influential people on Twitter who can help spread the word. For example, knowing that the truck will be in a particular neighborhood in a few days, Natasha will find influential people in that neighborhood and set up a promotion around their name. A Coolhaus staffer may reach out directly to an influential person with a message like, "If anyone says your name at the truck I'll give them a discount - please spread the word." As you may imagine, this tactic involves a bit of research and a thorough understanding of the medium and its etiquette. And having a killer product that everyone wants doesn't hurt the campaign either.

Coolhaus also spreads incentives via social media, such as passwords (customers can say the name of the architectural firm of the week and get a discount) and coupons. This is a great technique for attracting and maintaining followers. "Make them feel they're part of something special by following you," advises Natasha.

Because Coolhaus's social media presence is so successful, there is less pressure for the website to do all of the marketing work. Even though their site, www.eatcoolhaus.com, is ranking well in the search engines and contains good basic information, it is not a particularly strong example of onsite SEO. "I think our website could be more of a centerpiece," says Natasha. "But Twitter and Yelp are getting more traffic than our website, and this isn't hurting us."

Thursday: Your Facebook Strategy

Facebook, in a word, is huge. Like Twitter, it's a venue for both personal and corporate users, but on Facebook, the lines between personal use and corporate interaction can be quite blurred, making it an attractive space to find and interact with existing and potential customers.

We have clients who don't see many direct sales from their Facebook efforts, but they consider this venue an investment that keeps their customers feeling loved. We have other clients who use Facebook heavily to drive visitors to their site, with every status update containing a promotional message and a link. We've seen businesses lose sight of their conversion goals and corporate voice and use their Facebook business page for day-to-day personal chatter just as they would their personal page. (This scenario is not a Facebook-only problem, but it is frequently noticed on Facebook, possibly because many business users are on Facebook anyway for personal use.)

Today, you'll look at Facebook options for your business, from a very basic Facebook presence to a more advanced interactive presence, and consider which strategy will work for you.

Your Minimum Facebook Presence

It's free, it's flexible, and it's in the general online vicinity of an enormous number of individuals who may care about what you offer. Even if you don't know what you want to do with Facebook as a long-term strategy, we can't think of any good reason you *shouldn't* make yourself a Facebook business page just for the sake of having one. (You can get started at www.facebook.com/pages/create.php.) If nothing else, this will ensure that nobody else can make a page using your name.

The minimum must-haves on your business page are a link to your site, an image to personalize the page, and general "about us" information. You can start with these and add more features to your page as time and inclination allow.

Facebook business pages are outside of the login on Facebook, which means they can be seen by anyone, and they can be indexed in search engines. With a Facebook business page, you may be able to gain control of one more slice of the search presence pie: top-page search engine rankings for your business name. Figure 8.3 shows how the Facebook page for Matrix Distributors has a top-page search engine presence.

If you're not sure you want to commit to ongoing upkeep of your Facebook page, keep all company information evergreen (skip the events calendar and holiday greeting, which will quickly go stale). If you don't think you'll have time to moderate, use the permission settings on your wall to prevent users from posting comments and photos on your page.

slacker   A Facebook business page is different from an individual personal profile, but you manage it through your profile, so you'll need a personal profile in order to set up a business page. Start the process of creating your page at www.facebook.com/page. For a good tutorial on setting up a Facebook business page, visit www.searchengineguide.com/jennifer-laycock/the-super-simple-guide-to-setting-up-you.php.

Keywords play a role in Facebook, too! Think hard about the business name and any keywords you want the business to be found for in Facebook before you set it up.

Now: If your business doesn't already have a Facebook page, and unless you have a clear reason that you don't want one, set up a basic business page.

Web Images Videos Maps News Shopping Gmail more ▼

Google   matrix distributors inc   **Search**

About 1,370,000 results (0.29 seconds)   Advanced search

▦ **Everything**
▼ **More**

▼ Show search tools

Matrix Distributors ☆
Matrix Distributors, Inc. is an Authorized Distributor with over 75 generic drug and medical
supply manufacturers. Reimbursement won't change. ...
www.matrixdistributors.com/ - Cached - Similar

About Us - Home Page ☆
Matrix Distributors, Inc. is a distributor of pharmaceutical and medical ... Here at **Matrix
Distributors, Inc.**, we realize customer satisfaction is the ...
www.matrixdistributors.com/aboutus.html - Cached - Similar
⊞ Show more results from www.matrixdistributors.com

Matrix Distributors (Matrix Distributors Inc*) - East Brunswick ... ☆
Matrix Distributors company profile in East Brunswick, NJ. Our free company profile report
for **Matrix Distributors** includes business information such as ...
www.manta.com/c/mmfcvb0/matrix-distributors - Cached

Connect with Matrix Distributors Inc in East Brunswick, NJ. ☆
Read information about **Matrix Distributors Inc**, a Supplier in East Brunswick, NJ.
MacRaesBlueBook.com has the most recent phone number & address for this ...
⊞ Show map of 110 Tices Lane, East Brunswick, NJ 08816-2048
www.macraesbluebook.com/search/company.cfm?company... - Cached - Similar

Matrix Distributors, Inc. | Facebook ☆
Welcome to a Facebook Page about **Matrix Distributors, Inc.** Join Facebook to start
connecting with **Matrix Distributors, Inc.**
www.facebook.com/pages/Matrix-Distributors-Inc/382990209383 - Cached

Matrix Distributors, Inc.: Private Company Information - BusinessWeek ☆
Get **Matrix Distributors, Inc.** company research & investing information. Find executive
management and the latest company developments.
investing.businessweek.com/research/stocks/private/snapshot.asp?... - Cached

Figure 8.3 Google search results for <matrix distributors inc>

Facebook for Customer Interactions

The lingo changes, but the goal is the same: Whether you call them "friends," "fans,"
or less poetically, "people who like this page," your Facebook following will help
spread your message. We'll talk about ways to drive traffic to your Facebook page from
your website on Friday of this week. But from *within* Facebook, getting new people
to engage with you is usually done indirectly: People "like" you after watching their
friends interact or "like" you first. Here are some ways to encourage interaction:

Provide status updates. Your business page's status updates will broadcast to everybody
who has chosen to "like" your page. Keeping a stream of interesting, helpful, and useful status updates coming from your business is a key element of a successful Facebook
strategy. You'll want to establish a posting rhythm that keeps you connected without
annoying your followers. And remember ways to drive visitors to your website: Tell
your Facebook following when you publish a new blog post, launch a new product, or
start a promotion on your site.

Ask questions. Facebook provides a just-long-enough venue for you to post open-ended
questions and engage in discourse formatted in real sentences. So instead of just making pronouncements about goings-on at your company, ask for your fans' take on the

topic. For example, a doggie daycare may say, "Check out this cool video of a hot dog in our WagTown pool. Does your dog like to swim?"

Create incentives for recruitment. Like the example in Figure 8.4, you can provide opportunities for your following to suggest your page to their friends.

Figure 8.4 Staples gives to charity to encourage existing fans to recruit friends.

You should also continually give your flock reasons to stick with you. Posting coupon codes, promotions, or giveaways in your status updates is one way to do this.

Let your fans do the talking. Facebook offers easy-to-install options for your business page that can encourage your following to interact on their own, such as forums, reviews, and photo uploads. Make sure you have a plan for monitoring, though. You don't want these features to collect complaints or unanswered customer service questions.

More Advanced Facebook Marketing

Here are a few ways that some businesses are pushing their Facebook efforts to that proverbial next level:

Build an app. If you have developer chops, you can offer a feature that your fans can post to their own news feeds. See Figure 8.5, and note the call to action: "Get your Coupon."

Figure 8.5 AMC Theaters makes it easy for Facebook users to promote their coupon.

Pay to advertise. Facebook ads are reasonably simple to set up and have some demographic targeting opportunities that you don't find easily elsewhere. You can get started with a small budget at www.facebook.com/advertising/. You can set up your ads to send traffic to your Facebook page or your website.

Set goals and measure ROI. Like any marketing effort, Facebook-based promotions should have goals and be measured for their effectiveness. Facebook campaigns can be hard to evaluate, because their value to your business may be indirect. You might measure Facebook campaign effectiveness by watching these metrics: number of "likes" as compared to competitors, number of customer comments or uploads (per week, per month), and number of Facebook referrals to your website.

We've thrown a lot of ideas for Facebook marketing at you today. Approach Facebook marketing with a solid plan, and there will be plenty for your followers to like!

Sophisticated Social Media at HCCMIS

HCC Medical Insurance Services, LLC (HCCMIS) is a leading presence in the $3 billion and growing travel insurance industry, and a trailblazer in its corner of the Social Web. We were struck by the sophistication of HCCMIS's social marketing, which is a collaborative effort involving sales, customer service, marketing, and legal/compliance personnel. HCCMIS succeeds at a complicated balancing act: The team must be allowed enough spontaneity to communicate with the online public in real time, but it also relies heavily on scripts and documented processes to keep the company compliant within the highly regulated insurance industry.

We asked AVP of Marketing Bryant Tutterow to give us some examples of the company's social marketing activities. Your staff may be smaller and your regulatory pressures less intense, and we're pretty sure you don't yet have your own social response team. But we invite you to find your favorites among these practices and think about how to adapt them to your own organization.

Brand Monitoring Bryant says, "The typical day starts with monitoring current international and travel emergency topics. This includes recent travel alerts, possible natural disasters, and other topics of interest for expatriates and our insurance brokers that might impact our clients' travel plans. Next, we move to following up on any specific inquiries from our insurance brokers, current customers, and consumers interested in learning more about our services or in need of assistance. Third, we monitor our online brand mentions and our social response team develops response plans as needed, based on the sentiment toward our company. Finally, we schedule fun, yet educational, communications around topics of interest for international travelers, expatriates, and yacht crew members overseas."

Responding to Customer Service Issues Bryant shares this exchange:

Customer tweet: "Just about ready to give two fingers to HCC medical insurance...bloody useless they are!"

HCCMIS: "We are really sorry to hear that you had a bad experience. We are working on your issues right now and will call you shortly for resolution."

Sophisticated Social Media at HCCMIS *(Continued)*

Many companies, if they bother to look, may encounter negative mentions about their brand on the Social Web, and these brand-busting rants have the potential to develop into PR nightmares if left unchecked. But because HCCMIS has a process for monitoring these comments using Twitter searches, Google alerts, and RSS feeds, as well as guidelines for responding, their social response team noticed the comment, responded to the tweet, then researched and brought the issue to resolution within a few hours. HCCMIS uses this flowchart to illustrate their negative response plan:

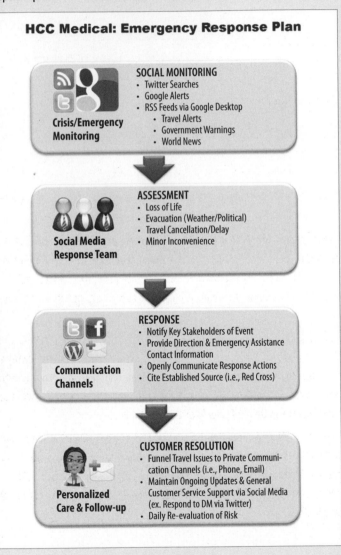

HCC Medical: Emergency Response Plan

Crisis/Emergency Monitoring

SOCIAL MONITORING
- Twitter Searches
- Google Alerts
- RSS Feeds via Google Desktop
  - Travel Alerts
  - Government Warnings
  - World News

Social Media Response Team

ASSESSMENT
- Loss of Life
- Evacuation (Weather/Political)
- Travel Cancellation/Delay
- Minor Inconvenience

Communication Channels

RESPONSE
- Notify Key Stakeholders of Event
- Provide Direction & Emergency Assistance Contact Information
- Openly Communicate Response Actions
- Cite Established Source (i.e., Red Cross)

Personalized Care & Follow-up

CUSTOMER RESOLUTION
- Funnel Travel Issues to Private Communication Channels (i.e., Phone, Email)
- Maintain Ongoing Updates & General Customer Service Support via Social Media (ex. Respond to DM via Twitter)
- Daily Re-evaluation of Risk

Sophisticated Social Media at HCCMIS *(Continued)*

Promoting Company News To maximize the reach of important company news, all of HCCMIS's press releases are accompanied by scheduled blog posts and are further publicized with mentions in various social communities.

Responding to Sales Opportunities Using Google keyword alerts, which you learned how to set up on Tuesday of this week, HCCMIS identifies new sales opportunities and reaches out to those individuals as appropriate. In this example, the keyword alert for a variation of the company name ("HCCMIS") displayed a forum post from a traveler interested in getting good insurance rates:

From:	Google Alerts [googlealerts-noreply@google.com]
To:	Tutterow, Bryant
Cc:	
Subject:	Google Alert - hccmis

Google Web Alert for: hccmis

Travel and medical Insurance - China Internship August 2010 » i-to ...
HCCMIS $121.60. IMG $131.00. These were the lowest and the coverages all seemed similar. Anyone in the US find better? ...
www.onlinetefl.com/.../303-travel-and-medical-insurance?...

A representative from HCCMIS responded with a friendly note about their low rates and a link to learn more.

Applying Traditional Practices to the Social Web At the heart of HCCMIS's strategy is the notion that traditional customer communications can be carried out successfully on the Social Web. For example, the company's communications on social sites like Twitter and Facebook are carried out using approved scripts and monitoring controls, not unlike call center communications.

Improving the Website In an impressive example of customer-centric online marketing, HCCMIS identified common topics that came up in conversations with its social community and used these topics to improve their site. For example, travel tips, social mapping tools, and frequently asked questions encountered on the Social Web led to the transformation of the site's Customer Service section into an Online Travel Concierge section.

Bryant shares another example: "After reading 'Why does someone need travel medical insurance?' about a hundred times when talking with folks in our social communities we developed a simple, tweet-based value proposition ('Get a broken leg while hiking in Europe, $3200… OR travel medical insurance for $1 a day'). This concept later evolved into a 'Paradise or Peril' section of the company website."

Friday: Social Media on Your Site

Remember the story of how Tom Sawyer convinced his friends to whitewash his fence? He made it seem so appealing that everybody wanted to do the work for him. Encouraging others to spread the word about your site can work the same way—and may be relatively easy for you.

Here are ways to encourage your own site visitors to promote your website for you:

Social Bookmarking and Share Buttons As easily as dropping a little piece of code on your page, you can add a "Digg it" or "share on Facebook" button to your page. See Figure 8.6 for an example. These buttons allow your users to submit your page to these sites, or to give your page a vote.

Figure 8.6 Social bookmarking buttons on USATODAY.com

"Tweet This" Next time you're sending out a promotion to your email list, why not add a simple "tweet this" or "share on Facebook" line to the email? For example, you might say something like this: "We hope you'll forward this email to your friends, or post on Facebook or Twitter!"

Copy and customize these sample links to make it easy for your email recipients to spread the love:

Facebook:

```
http://www.facebook.com/sharer.php?u=http://www.yoursite.com/example-page.html
```

Twitter:

```
http://twitter.com/home?status=Your Text Here http://www.yoursite.com
/example-page.html
```

The Facebook "Like" Button and Other Ways to Connect Facebook provides plug-ins that display Facebook-centric data to your site visitors while they're on your site. How does this benefit you? Peer pressure, for one. Imagine a visitor coming to your site for the first time and receiving a customized message telling him which of his Facebook friends has shared your page or clicked the "like" button on your site. Get code at `http://developers.facebook.com/plugins`.

Your Twitter Feed on Your Site On Wednesday, you learned the importance of keeping your Twitter feed healthy, interesting, and up-to-date. With a little effort (and we do mean little), you can display those stellar statements on your site. If your work is follow-worthy, why not show it off anywhere you can? Start here: `http://twitter.com/goodies/widgets`.

> **Now:** Brainstorm ways to encourage your website visitors to spread information about your company.

Success in the Social Web depends on spontaneity, transparency, and frequent communication, and on being an authority on your subject matter. You could easily spend an hour or two, or six, or sixteen, every day on just social media. If you want to go the extra mile in your social media marketing, follow these gurus to keep on the right path:

- Search Engine Land's "Let's Get Social" column at `http://searchengineland.com/library/lets-get-social`

- Dave Evans's blog at `www.readthis.com`

- `www.mashable.com`, social networking blog

- Blogger, author, and business owner Brian Solis at `www.briansolis.com`

Week 6: Set Up Your Paid Search Account

Welcome to paid search with training wheels. This week you're going to develop good habits and get a firm grasp of how the paid search system works, using a small-budget starter campaign. We can't tell you what "small" means, but whether you choose to invest less than $100 or more than $10,000 a month, we'll provide you with tips and pitfall-avoidance techniques that will help you spend your money wisely.

We recommend that you set up your paid search account and monitor it over the course of three months. This should give you enough time to judge cost-effectiveness, learn what you can expect to get for your money, and decide whether you have what it takes—both financially and administratively—to manage an ongoing paid search campaign.

Even if you're skeptical about the use of paid search in your long-term marketing plans, we still hope to nudge you into trying it for the short term:

Pearl of Wisdom: A paid search campaign can tell you a lot about your audience and your keywords in a relatively short period of time, which makes it an excellent research tool for your organic SEO efforts.

How Do I Choose My Paid Search Budget?

This is one of the hardest-to-pin-down factors of SEO, and one that has as many variables as a high school algebra fair. We'd love to put on our little green visors and help you arrive at the perfect number, but instead we'll have to give you some general guidelines and let you do the thinking:

Ask your boss (or whoever holds the purse strings). Whether you like it or not, somebody may already have a number that you'll have to roll with. Let's hope your paid search campaign pulls in enough conversions to convince them to up the budget when your trial period is over!

Look to your current cost per conversion. Perhaps you already have an idea of what a conversion costs your organization based on tracking for existing online or offline marketing programs. The preliminary research you do this week may help you make an educated guess about how much you'd need to spend on paid search to meet or beat your current cost per conversion.

Consider your competition. You already know whether or not you're in a highly competitive online space. This week, with the help of the paid search service of your choice, you're going to attach some dollar figures to your top-priority keywords. Will you need to spend $0.15 or $15.00 per click to wrestle into the top three paid listing ranks for most of your keywords? The answer will inform your budget-making process.

Think about your own level of enthusiasm. Even though it's likely that your paid search campaign will run smoothly, proper campaign management takes continued interest and effort. Campaigns with larger budgets often have more keywords and more ads, taking more effort than smaller campaigns. If you don't foresee yourself having the ability or time to keep up a large campaign, scale down your budget, along with your expectations for clicks and conversions.

Because it helps you tune into your most productive keywords, a relatively small investment of funds can increase the effectiveness of your organic SEO campaign enormously.

Here are your daily tasks for this week:

Monday: Study Hall

Tuesday: Prep Your Paid Search Keywords

Wednesday: Write Your Ad Text
Thursday: Turn On Your Campaign
Friday: Paid Search Quick Check

Monday: Study Hall

Getting familiar with a new interface, not to mention specialized terminology and guidelines, is an important part of a smoothly run campaign. Today, you'll do your homework and learn about the paid search service you want to use so that you can be a more effective advertiser in the long term.

As a paid search newbie, you may be confused by the possibilities that the market holds: There are text ads, display ads, shopping search, directory listings, local listings, and more. But we advise you to start with the basics: text ads displayed in the search engines—the ones that look like this:

The major players are Google AdWords, available at http://adwords.google.com, and Microsoft adCenter (which feeds its ads to the Bing and Yahoo! search engines), available at http://adcenter.microsoft.com. You can pay by the impression, by the click, or even by the conversion. We think you should start with a pay-per-click (PPC) arrangement, which is likely to be the default setting for the service you choose.

Now: Finalize your choice of a paid search engine and sign up for an account.

Spend the rest of your time today familiarizing yourself with the inner workings of your paid search service of choice. Next we'll describe the most important elements for you to understand as you attack your paid search learning curve.

Most of the concepts in this week can be applied to Facebook and LinkedIn pay-per-click advertising in addition to Google AdWords and Microsoft adCenter. There are no keywords to sponsor on Facebook or LinkedIn; rather, you target your ads based on users' likes and interests or other information in their profiles.

Editorial Guidelines

AdWords and adCenter both have lists of rules with which your ads must comply—things like limiting obnoxious SHOUTING CAPITALIZATION or limiting the use of certain terms. In addition to style guidelines, there is a laundry list of products and services for which advertising is not permitted. (Google has a rather long list that includes many fascinating and confounding barred topics such as "e-gold" and "hacking and cracking." Entertaining stuff.) Ads must pass an automated review before they are published.

Spending Requirements

Both AdWords and adCenter offer very low minimum spending levels and allow you the option of spreading out your spending over the course of a month or letting the ads run continuously until your money runs out.

Keyword Matching Options

Setting up appropriate keyword matching in your campaign can make a big difference in your ROI. Because you pay when someone clicks on your ad, it's important to let only targeted searchers see your ads. AdWords and adCenter offer a variety of keyword matching controls:

Broad Matching Causes your ad to display if searchers combine your keywords with other terms (for example, your ad for <wedding bands> will show when the term <platinum wedding bands> is searched). This may include plural forms of the term, misspellings, and synonyms.

Exact Matching Causes your ad to display for the term you are sponsoring, with no changes to word order or plurals (for example, your ad for <wedding bands> will display when someone searches for <wedding bands>, but not for <wedding band> or <bands for my wedding>).

Keyword Exclusion Allows you to exclude searchers who use certain words from viewing your ad (for example, if you're targeting <wedding bands>, you can exclude people searching for <wedding bands jazz>).

Ad Display Options

AdWords and adCenter offer several display controls, including:

Contextual vs. Search Engine Ad Placement Contextual advertising (called the Display Network on Google and the Content Network on adCenter) shows your sponsored ads on a wide variety of websites, not just search engines. Although every campaign is different, we generally find that contextual advertising brings in visitors whose overall engagement is lower than the traffic brought in by search advertising. Due to our experiences with poor engagement, and to keep things simple, we recommend turning off contextual advertising as you make your first foray into paid search.

Geotargeting Allows you to display your results to searchers in a particular location or to users with specific language settings.

Dynamic Keyword Insertion Places the searcher's keywords directly into your ad. You'll learn more about this later when you write your ads.

Dayparting Allows you to specify the times of day your ads will display. A B2B consulting firm may want to display its ads only during the workweek, while the wee hours may be a better fit for sleeping pill manufacturers.

Mobile Devices Don't limit your visibility to searchers on the standard Web! adCenter provides an option for you to write brief ads for display only on mobile devices, and AdWords allows you to choose specific types of devices and carriers.

Advanced Options Most paid search features are quite easy to turn on and off, so test some advanced options if you find ones that appeal to you. Google's Ad Extensions allow you to integrate your ads with your Google Places listing, display your address, or enable "click to call" features for mobile devices. Both AdWords and adCenter offer basic demographic targeting options for their contextual ad services.

Bid and Position Management Options

Google AdWords and Microsoft adCenter work within a competitive bidding model: The more you pay relative to your competitors, the higher your ad's position is likely to be. Here are some basics on how bids are controlled:

Choosing Bid Prices You can assign bid prices campaign-wide, or you can set them to apply to a group of keywords or individual keywords. The amount you bid is the maximum you will pay when someone clicks on your ad; however, you may pay less if there is a price gap between your bid and your next-lower competitor's bid.

Setting Budget Caps AdWords and adCenter allow you to set daily budget caps, but your actual daily spend may vary. Although the ad systems will not exceed your monthly budget, they attempt to provide you with an average daily spend that is in line with your cap, so you may find that your campaign exceeds your budget cap on a given day if you have underspent on a previous day.

Controlling Position Increasing bids will improve your sponsored ads' chances of ranking higher, but Google AdWords also provides you with additional position preference controls. You can set your preference to a certain range—for example, between positions 3 and 5 (this feature may be used by an affiliate who does not want to outrank its partner site), or you can set your preference to number 1 to try to save your impressions for when you're at the top of the heap. Because your positions are determined in a competitive environment, you can never control exactly where your ads will show up.

Google's Quality Score—the Secret Sauce of Paid Search

Bidding high is one way to achieve higher ranks, but it is not always a simple cause-and-effect situation. Google AdWords' Quality Score, an algorithmic system that assigns measures of quality to an AdWords campaign, is the "secret sauce" of paid search, creating an environment in which campaigns with higher quality scores can outrank competitors with lower quality scores, regardless of bid prices.

Your campaign's Quality Score needn't occupy too much of your mindspace. Generally speaking, you can improve your quality scores with commonsense attempts to keep your ads relevant and focused—for example, making sure sponsored keywords are tightly matched to ad text, and making sure ad text is tightly matched to the landing page text. Your campaign's historical click-through rate factors into Google's Quality Score assessment, so if you make reasonable efforts to manage your campaign and prune out poor-performing ads and keywords, you will likely have a favorable quality score.

Google is kind enough to flag keywords for which your campaign has a low quality score and tell you what aspects of your advertising presence are problematic.

Keyword: mariachi consulting group

Showing ads right now?

> Yes

Quality score Learn more

> 2/10   Keyword relevance: **Poor**
> Landing page quality: **No problems**
> Landing page load time: **No problems**

Ads diagnostic tool

Learn about Google's Quality Score directly from the source by going to http://adwords.google.com/support and typing **quality score** into the search box.

Tracking and Reporting Options

You will probably be pleased with the detail and flexibility of reports you can generate with the paid search service you choose. Both services offer at-a-glance reports in your campaign management interface to make it easy to keep an eye on performance and trends. Happily, conversion tracking is a standard feature: All you need to do is place a tag that paid search service generates for you on your conversion page, and you're off and running!

One extremely helpful reporting tool is the See Search Terms option in the Google AdWords campaign management interface. This tool allows you to see actual search queries that bring visitors to your site, which is invaluable in helping you finesse your campaign to reduce unnecessary spending. For example, if you're advertising college textbooks but you notice that people are arriving at your site for broad-matched keywords containing words like *toddler* or *preschool*, you've got some changes to make to your ad text or your list of negative matched keywords.

Once your campaign is in full swing, at a minimum you'll want to do a regular review of the following information:

- Top-performing keywords
- Total campaign cost
- Average cost per click
- Total click-throughs
- Click-through rate
- Conversion rate
- Cost per conversion

This information is readily available inside the AdWords and adCenter services.

Account Services and Estimation Tools

If you are destined to be a big spender with a paid search advertising service (on the order of $10,000 or more per month), you may be able to get the free services of an account rep at Microsoft or the Google Jumpstart team. They can smooth over some of the bumps in the process. For advertisers of all budgets, both AdWords and adCenter offer bid suggestion tools to kick-start your campaign. But whether you're dealing with a live person or a tool, trust your gut! Remember, these services are in the business of making money from you, and their ideas of your ideal campaign performance may not fit into your budget.

Tuesday: Prep Your Paid Search Keywords

Today you'll compile a list of keywords for your paid search starter campaign. Your top 10 or so target keywords are a starting point, but any terms on your long list from Chapter 6, "Your One-Month Prep: Keywords, Priorities, and Goals," are fair game.

Targeting the Long Tail

Perhaps you've heard of the "long tail" theory. It describes how our culture and commerce is moving away from a small number of very popular products (or movies or dances or even ideas) toward a very large number of niche products or activities. For example, not terribly long ago there were only three television networks that everybody watched (a short head). Now, there are hundreds of specialty networks, each with a much smaller audience (a long tail).

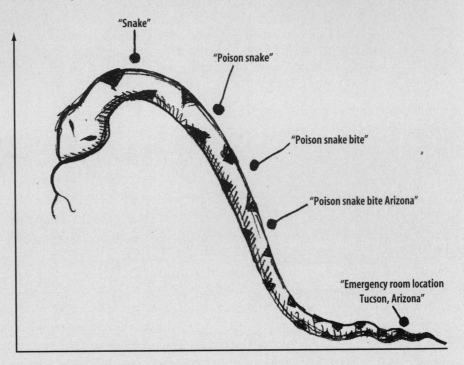

"Snake"

"Poison snake"

"Poison snake bite"

"Poison snake bite Arizona"

"Emergency room location Tucson, Arizona"

How Does This Apply to Your SEO Plan?

In SEO, a short-head search is something like <motel>, while a long-tail search might be <baltimore pool motel airport>. The short-head search is broad and is used commonly, whereas the long-tail search is specific and is used much less frequently.

Compared to organic optimization, paid search makes it much easier for you to target long-tail searchers. Here's why: In organic SEO, each key phrase you target takes a certain minimum commitment of time and energy, so it wouldn't make sense to put hours of effort into rewriting your site for once-a-month, ultra-focused queries. In a pay-per-click advertising model, on the other hand, you can add your long-tail keywords to your account for free—and pay only when they receive clicks. Why sponsor long-tail searches? By the time a searcher is using a long-tail term, they are probably closer to the end of the buying process. This makes long-tail searchers a very desirable group. Look again at the example: <motel> compared to <baltimore pool motel airport>.

Today we'd like you to keep your campaign turned *off* while you use your paid search interface to select your keywords.

Choosing Keywords to Sponsor

Since you're starting small, you could easily sponsor just your top-priority keywords. But it won't hurt to include additional keywords you're interested in testing. Review your long list of keywords from Chapter 6. Were there any terms that caused a lot of debate but didn't make the cut? Were there two terms that seemed equally promising? Results of this test campaign will be a great tiebreaker.

How many keywords should you have in your paid search campaign? That depends on two things: your budget, and your desire to stay within the hour-a-day time frame. But we'll throw you a bone with this vague suggestion: somewhere between 10 and 50. For the purposes of this trial period, it's best to keep your campaign smaller so that you can give proper attention to the details.

Both AdWords and adCenter provide keyword suggestion tools to bulk up your campaigns. It's OK to glance over suggestions to see if you get any good ideas, but be discriminating in your choices. Nobody knows your keywords or business like you do, and this is especially true of an automated paid search suggestion tool.

Assigning Landing Page URLs

Just as with organic keywords, your home page is not necessarily the best landing page for searchers arriving via your paid ads. You've done a lot of work segmenting your target audience, so make sure that your paid search campaign helps you continue this strategy. Match your keywords to the most appropriate landing pages.

Creating Ad Groups

An ad group is a subset of sponsored keywords that all trigger the same ad or ads. Think of ad groups as a simple categorization scheme for your paid search campaign. Since you've got an hour a day to work on campaign creation and maintenance, it would be reasonable to have from three to five ad groups. (Ad group names are not displayed to searchers. They are for administrative use only.) Even though more ad groups require more management and more ads, it's probably better to err on the side of too many categories than too few. Here are possible ways to group your keywords:

By Landing Page For example, an animal feed distributor may want to create an ad group for its Pet Care Tips page for terms like <overweight dogs> and another ad group for its Horse Care Tips page for terms like <preventing colic in horses>.

By Target Audience For example, our animal feed distributor might create a category called Pet Products for terms like <dog food> and <cat food> and another category called Livestock Products for terms like <bovine feed supplement> and <equine grain mix>.

By Concept You can categorize based on the needs your product or service fills or the concerns behind the searches. For example, our animal feed distributor might create a category called Low Cost for terms like <cheap dog food> or a category called Pampering for terms like <dog treats> or <dog rewards>.

Bidding for Position

If you can swing the bid price, try to land your ads in the top three. (Your campaign management interface will report your average positions on a keyword-by-keyword basis to help you understand if your bids and quality score are coming together to achieve your intended ranks.) With top ranks, you'll improve your chance for click-throughs, and you'll be able to judge the performance of your paid search campaign in a more straightforward way.

Naturally, some keywords on your list will be more expensive than others. If it would take too big a bite out of your budget to bid into the top three positions for every one of your keywords, mix it up a little. Bid high on just one or two. You can always change it in a couple of weeks if you don't like the results. You can also consider adding modifiers to your keywords to see if a longer-tail approach is more budget-friendly.

Estimating Click-Throughs

Predicting paid search click-throughs—especially when you're starting a campaign from scratch—is an inexact science. You can use the estimation tool that your paid search service offers, but don't trust it for more than a ballpark figure. If your boss is breathing down your neck for a specific click-through rate estimate, we'd suggest that you just say no. You can't foretell how successful your campaign will be, but you *can* set up your campaign so that there will be few risks: Start with a low budget and bid price, and focus on fewer keywords. You can gradually increase these parameters until you're comfortable with the results.

 Now: Enter your keywords and bid prices for your paid search campaign. Use placeholder ad text (you'll work on ad text tomorrow) and make sure your campaign isn't live yet.

How Pandora Partners, Inc., Miscalculated Cost per Click for Six Months

We once worked for a client (the name and some identifying details have been changed to prevent embarrassment) who was enthusiastic about paid search advertising because his campaign provided valuable conversions in a competitive market. We came on board several months after his campaign was in full swing, and we were pleased to see that this client had made his own spreadsheet to track important trends over time.

After a few days on the job, we made an astonishing discovery: Due to an unfortunate spreadsheet error (we're going to be charitable here and call it a typo), this company was working on the assumption that they were paying an average of $3.80 per click as opposed to the actual value of $0.26! Can you imagine how that affected their advertising budget, not to mention their opinion of the value of their paid search campaign? Can you imagine the smoke that rose up from our speedy phone-dialing fingers when we realized what they had been doing wrong?

Even if you're like one of us (hint: not the one of us with a degree in engineering) and gave up math class at an embarrassingly early age, you need to know this simple equation:

Cost per click = (cost) ÷ (# of clicks)

As we've mentioned, any paid search advertising service provides this kind of data for you. But if you ever decide to create your own reports, you can save yourself a big headache if you take some time at the start to double-check your own formulas against your paid search service's prefab reports.

Wednesday: Write Your Ad Text

Depending on your talent with words, today may be a fun little excursion into copywriting, or it may be a scary stretch outside of your comfort zone. If you have writers on your team, this is a great time to include them.

For each of your keyword categories, you're going to create a succinct, compelling ad that is substantially more interesting than your competitors'. You may want to write two or three ads for each ad group and let your paid search service rotate the ads for you.

Your HTML title and meta description tag for each landing page are a good starting point, but you'll probably need to edit them substantially for paid search use, in part due to editorial guidelines and character limits. You can read your paid search service's guidelines for lots of advice on writing ads (after all, they make money on your click-throughs, so they have every interest in your success!).

Here are some additional tips that we think will help you:

DO use keywords in the text. Studies show that people are more likely to click on your ad if the exact keyword they searched for is incorporated into your ad text.

DO be true to your landing page. Make sure that you write each ad with its intended landing page(s) in mind. Does the ad mention a specific product or solution? The landing page had better contain a clear path to it. Does the ad set up a need? The landing page should tell your visitor exactly how to fulfill it.

DO snoop on your competitors. If you're stumped, and even if you aren't, enter your keywords into the search engines and see what you're up against in the paid search venue. If everyone's ads are mentioning a certain topic, such as their low, low prices, you might not want to ignore it in your own ad. Then again, if you notice that you're competing against a clutch of nearly identical ads, as seen in Figure 8.7, you may want to describe yourself using language that will help you stand out.

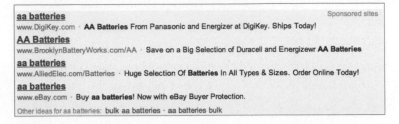

Figure 8.7 These sponsored ads for the term <aa batteries> look awfully homogeneous.

DO use dynamic keyword insertion if it's available... You researched on Monday whether your paid search service of choice allows you to automatically insert searched-for keywords into your title. If a searcher enters the term <halogen bulbs> or <chandeliers>, you may want to format your ad to say, "Halogen bulbs and other lighting products" or "Chandeliers and other lighting products" to match the search. This can be a powerful way to attract the attention of your targeted audience.

...but DON'T insert the wrong keywords. If you've ever seen what appear to be inappropriate paid search ads, you can probably blame careless dynamic keyword insertion. It can create almost comical messages like "Tonsillitis: Buy Now at Shop-n-Ship.com." Likewise, if you're sponsoring misspelled versions of your keywords, skip the dynamic insertion.

DO include a compelling message. What makes your audience tick? Is it price? Is it the hope of succeeding at something or the fear of failing at something? Is it convenience? A desire for quality? A need to fit in or to stand out? Use your ad text to speak to this need.

 Now: Following your paid search ad service's guidelines, write your ads.

Thursday: Turn On Your Campaign

Is your site ready for its big debut? Before you flip the switch, make sure your landing pages will be clearly relevant to your paid search ads and targeted users will be able to find what they need. If your site content doesn't match your advertising campaign, it will confuse or annoy your visitors, and it may be removed by the paid search service for noncompliance with editorial guidelines.

Assuming your site is ready for the trick-or-treaters to come ringing the bell, let's get started. It's best to start this task early in the day so you can check that all is well before you go home for the night.

Here are things to watch out for:

No Impressions Don't expect miracles, but do make sure you actually turned on the campaign.

Too Many Clicks If you're already close to blowing your budget after a few hours, something is out of whack. Either you underestimated the number of clicks your ad would receive (you could have worse problems!) or you entered your bid price incorrectly.

The Wrong Ad Showing Up for the Wrong Keyword It would be a fairly easy mistake to, say, place an ad meant for your Industrial Products category into your Home Products category. Enter some of your keywords into the search engine and view your ads to make sure you haven't made this kind of error. Google's ad diagnostic tool, available for logged-in advertisers at `https://adwords.google.com/select/DiagnosticTool`, will allow you to preview your ads more easily.

We do not recommend micromanaging your ads on a daily basis; the paid search services' bid management tools should make this unnecessary. Regardless, today is a good day to monitor them closely to make sure you haven't made any boneheaded mistakes. Also, seeing your paid search ads online is a moment for celebration in your SEO campaign!

> **Now:** Turn on your campaign. Check your account later today for errors and unexpected results.

Friday: Paid Search Quick Check

Many paid search advertisers adopt a "set it and forget it" approach, but we suggest you make a plan to review your paid search campaign at least once a week—and once a day for your brand-new campaign. This weekly Quick Check will ensure that your campaign doesn't go dramatically out of whack over the course of a month. We estimate that your Quick Check will take about 15 minutes.

Here are the steps to include in your paid search Quick Check:

1. Log into your account.

2. Check your total campaign spending so far for this month. Is your campaign on track to spend your monthly budget on schedule? If you've set your daily budget appropriately, it's difficult to spend too much—but bugs on paid search services are not unheard of. You should also keep in mind that spending too little can be just as bad as spending too much, especially if it means you're getting less traffic than you want. If your campaign is low, you may wish to add more keywords or increase some of your bids. If your campaign is high, reduce bids or remove or disable keywords.

3. For each keyword category, figure out how to sort the list of keywords by total amount spent. Some keywords are going to be naturally more popular and costly than others, so it's probably not realistic to expect that your spending will be distributed evenly among the keywords. If one or two keywords are using up too much of your budget and you don't think they're converting well enough, you may wish to temporarily disable them or lower their bids. Some keywords with extremely high click-through rates may need to be checked on a daily basis. If you've found a keyword that is gobbling up your entire budget, consider moving it into its own ad group so that you can watch and manage it more closely. If you are testing multiple ads for some keywords, review which are performing better.

 Now: Add a weekly Paid Search Quick Check to your calendar. If you think you have enough data to review, perform a Quick Check now.

Now, with your site structure improvements in place and your paid search campaign purring, you've never been more ready to get serious about selling through search!

Week 7: Selling Through Search

If we had a nickel for every good company that settles for bad search visibility for their online store, well, we'd have a big shiny pile of nickels. And we'd spend those nickels buying stuff from an easy-to-find online store. This week we're going to push you to move your store beyond good enough and into the realm of thoughtful SEO strategy and solid optimization. This week applies whether your online store is a stand-alone entity or a component of your brick-and-mortar business.

Monday: Shopping Search Opportunities
Tuesday: The Search That Sells
Wednesday: Basic Store Optimization

Thursday: Your Google Merchant Center Account
Friday: Seller Ratings

Monday: Shopping Search Opportunities

The search engines are constantly rearranging their interfaces, but they never fail to feature shopping options in the sweet spots. Shopping is thoroughly integrated into the standard search experience, as you can see from the following Bing and Google searches for <front loading washing machines> (Figure 8.8 and Figure 8.9).

If you sell online, here are some of the major opportunities for placing your site in front of potential buyers:

Organic Search Listings Because you've manually assessed your search engine ranks, you already know whether or not your business is showing up among the top results for your favorite keywords. If you skimmed over the rank checks before, look again with a shopping-centric point of view. Are you satisfied that any products and prices showing in your snippets are accurate and flattering? Is there a compelling call to action? And, forgive us for asking an obvious question, but *do your listings make it clear that you sell something?* You may find that simply adding the word "Buy" or "Store" somewhere in your HTML title is all you need to clarify your site's purpose.

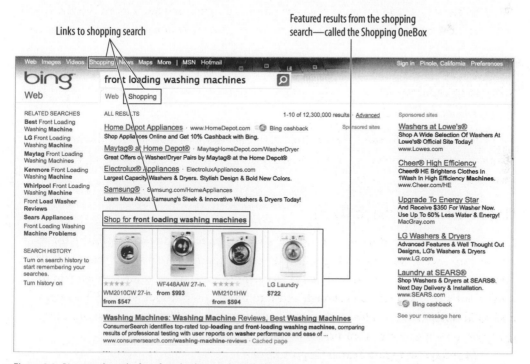

Figure 8.8 Bing search results for <front loading washing machines>

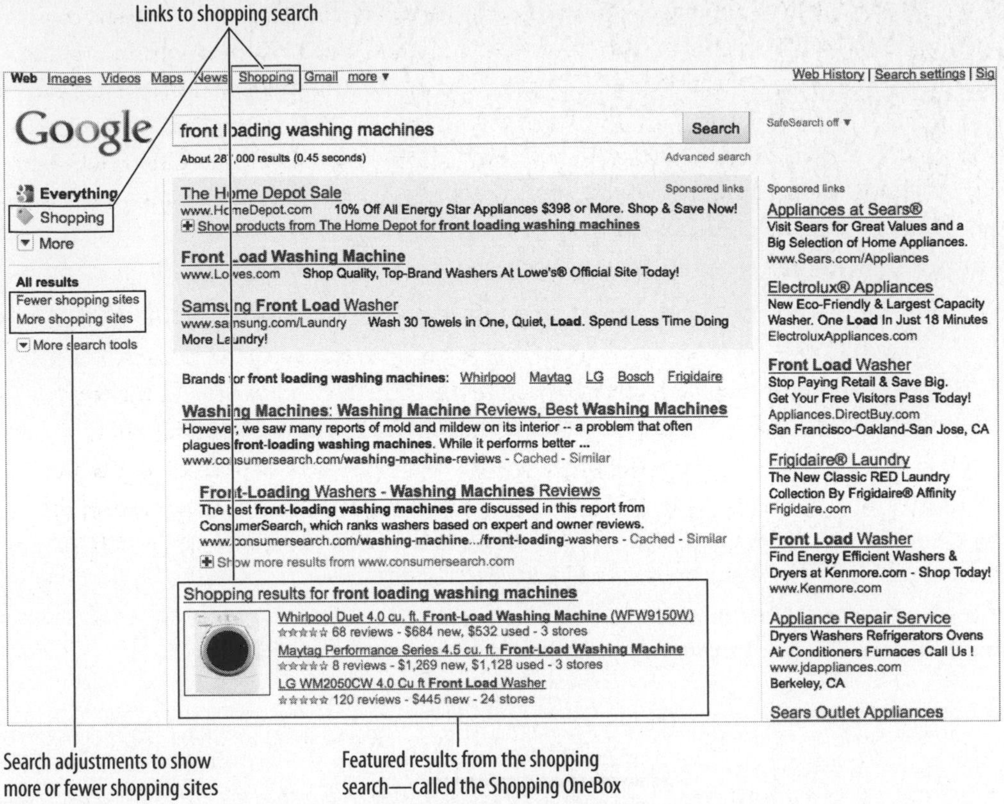

Figure 8.9 Google search results for <front loading washing machines>

Shopping Results Click on one of the many links labeled "shopping" that we highlighted in Figure 8.8 and Figure 8.9, and whoosh! You've been transported into what SEO pros call *shopping verticals*: page after page of shopping-only results that are derived using different methods from the ones that determine organic listings. For a chance at placement in these shopping results, your site will need to publish a *product feed*, a file that lists your products as well as related information such as price, description, and photo. Google and Bing offer this service for free. We'll walk you through setting up your product feed for Google Product Search (a.k.a. Google Shopping) on Thursday of this week.

Shopping OneBox The Shopping *OneBox* is a visually distinct area of the integrated search results that displays product photos, prices, and review stars. The OneBox is pulled from results in the shopping verticals; therefore listings within them can only be attained by sites that publish a product feed. This is an e-tailer's holy grail: to be one of the five or fewer shopping results that occupies this primo position for your top keywords.

Shopping Comparison Sites Sites such as `BizRate.com`, `Shopping.com`, and `PriceGrabber.com` are shopping search engines in their own right and also have a presence within organic search results for many keywords, especially product names. Selling via these sites can channel potential buyers to your site, but it comes at a cost: Typically, listing your products on these sites is a pay-per-click arrangement. Shopping comparison sites might be a good option for you if you frequently find these sites in the search results for your target keywords.

More Shopping and Fewer Shopping Options In Figure 8.9, you can see Google's More Shopping Sites/Fewer Shopping Sites options at the left of the page. Clicking on one of these links causes the search results to bias for or against e-commerce sites. For example, search for <tennis racquets> and note the difference between the sets of search results when you click on More Shopping Sites and Fewer Shopping Sites. Chances are, with More Shopping Sites selected, you'll see sites selling tennis racquets, and with Fewer Shopping Sites selected, you'll see sites giving advice on choosing the right racquet size. Your goal is for Google to display your site when people click on More Shopping, which means Google needs to be able to understand that your site is a store. Basic store optimization, which you'll work on tomorrow, will help your site show up where you want it.

> **Now:** Today is a study hall day. Review the search samples we just described and click on the search engines' shopping options to develop a familiarity with shopping search opportunities.

Tuesday: The Search That Sells

Here's one thing to love about having an online store: It's easy to measure success. You probably didn't have to do a lot of deep thinking in Chapter 1, "Clarify Your Goals." On your site, it's all about the sales!

When people search Google or Bing in a buying or pre-purchase-research state of mind, they often use certain keyword patterns. SEO pros call these keywords *transactional searches*, and they can include terms like <buy>, <reviews>, and product names. For example, a person in the process of purchasing a camera online might search for keywords like these:

- <best digital camera>
- <digital camera reviews>
- <canon t21 review>
- <buy canon t21 online>
- <canon t21 free shipping>

You want your business, or positive reviews of your business, to have the best possible presence on pages that Google and Bing create for transactional searches. Selling through search starts well before the sale: You want to capture visitors throughout the buying cycle, even in the early, lookie-loo stage.

 Now: Perform a search for each of your target keywords on Google and Bing. Make a note of the shopping listings in the top page of results.

If you don't see shopping search results for any of your target keywords, the keywords you chose aren't identified by the search engines as being shopping oriented. This does not necessarily indicate a problem with your keyword strategy; for example, there are some lovely B2B e-tail sites whose nicely targeted keywords are just a bit too niche to trigger shopping results in the search engines. Regardless, it's worth your time to revisit your keyword list and consider optimizing for some additional terms that shout "Sell to me!"

 Now: If needed, add transactional keywords to your target list.

xtra cred During your prep month in Chapter 6, you set up analytics for your site. If you sell products online, you can measure online revenue in your analytics program to identify which keywords are bringing in traffic that generates revenue.

Wednesday: Basic Store Optimization

Your online store is a website, so all of the general SEO recommendations in this book apply to it. But there are some pitfalls and opportunities that are specific to online stores. Today, you'll square away your basic store optimization with product and category page titles and search-friendly URLs, and you'll troubleshoot common obstacles to organic search success.

Product and Category Page Titles

In the Chapter 7 sidebar, "Product Page Optimization: Playing by the Rules at Dragonborn Games," you learned about choosing formulas for product and category page optimization. Your e-commerce platform might be doing a decent job of this, or it may default to less-than-desirable category and product page HTML titles. At a minimum, each product page title should be unique and should contain the name of the product.

A Sample Pack of Formulas for Product Page HTML Titles

To jumpstart your store optimization, here are some formulas for product pages and real-world examples:

{Brand}{Product Name}	Moen 85800 Aquasuite Single Handle Laundry Faucet Bar Faucets
{Product}{Store Name} - Free Shipping	Moen Kingley Faucet - FIND NOW at eFaucets.com - Free Shipping
{Store Name}: {Product Keywords}	Dirt Cheap Faucets: Cheap Kitchen Faucets, Pot Filler Faucets

And here are some category page formulas:

{Store Name}: {Category}	Amazon.com: Moen Bathroom Faucets
{Category} at {Store Name}	Moen Faucets at Faucet.com
{Brand} {Category} at {Store Name}	Moen Faucets & Sinks at FaucetLine.com
Shop {Category}:{Subcategory}:{Brand} at {Store Name}	Shop Plumbing: Faucets: Moen at Lowes.com

Use your keyword knowledge to create the right formulas for your store. If searchers often include brands in their search queries, then you should include brands in your formulas. If your product name is less well known than the generic description of the product, some additional descriptive keywords may be desirable. For example, suppose Cusheroo is the name of your fabulous car seat cushions. Your product page titles should say "Cusheroo car seat cushions" rather than just "Cusheroo." If free shipping or any other feature is a major selling point, consider adding it to your HTML title to increase click-through rate and differentiate your listings from those of your competitors. If subcategories include more relevant keywords than parent categories, you might leave parent category names out of the HTML titles.

It's often a good idea to include your store name in HTML titles as a differentiator, especially if you have a recognized or credible brand. Use your own judgment to determine whether your store name is helpful here.

Now: Take a look at the formula your store currently uses for product and category page HTML titles. Does it need improvement?

Search-Friendly Store URLs

You already know that human-readable URLs are preferable to the kind that look like they were spewed out by R2D2. In most cases, the formulas for category and product page URLs can be simple:

```
category-name-separated-by-dashes.html
```

And:

```
product-name-separated-by-dashes.html
```

For example:

- `http://www.efaucets.com/f/moen-one-handle-bathroom-faucets.shtm`
- `http://www.westsidewholesale.com/rothbury-single-handle-lavatory-faucet-with-drain-assembly-chrome.html`

We've used `.html` in the examples, but they can be whatever extension your site uses.

Changing the URLs of your live pages could introduce problems with your site's search engine presence, so don't change existing URLs without first planning carefully to preserve your pages' existing search power. (You can read up on the proper way to handle changes to URLs in the "What's Your Problem?" week in Chapter 9, "Month Three: It's a Way of Life.") Today, you can talk to your webmaster or review your e-commerce platform's documentation to determine how you can create search-friendly URLs for the future.

Now: If your e-commerce platform allows it, make a plan for setting up search-friendly default URLs.

Troubleshooting Store Optimization

If your store is underperforming despite having basic optimization in place, or you just want to make sure you've done everything you can, here are some rough spots that might need smoothing:

Remember: product pages = landing pages. Site visitors can arrive on any page of your site—that includes your product pages. Write your product pages for the prospective customer who entered directly from the search engines. This may mean describing your product and your business in more detail than you think you need.

Link to top-priority products. Let's say you're selling 1,000 products in a competitive market. You probably won't rank well for every one of those products, so why not concentrate your link authority on the products that have the best shot of breaking out of the pack? Five or so "top seller" links from your home page might give your most promising pages a juicy boost.

Categorize by audience. Maybe your store divides your products into logical categories like blenders, frying pans, toasters, and so on. But rather than an inventory list of your products, why not create categories around your audience segments? "For Newlyweds," "For Baby Girls," "Gifts for Foodie Friends," and so forth. Each of these segments represents keyword-rich categories, and some very targeted messaging, that you can use to your advantage.

Be normal. Sure, we encourage our kids to march to their own drummers, but we won't be saying that to *you*. Your online store should follow standard technical and design conventions wherever possible. Conventions such as including breadcrumb navigation at the top of category pages, listing products with prices on category pages, and linking to a featured selection of products from your home page can help the search engines interpret standard e-commerce conventions on your site and display them with proper formatting. For example, Google had an easy time interpreting and displaying product and pricing information for this site:

> **Gardening, weeding, and pruning tools and accessories - White ...**
> NEW! **Garden Trowel**   **$27.95**
> Bulb **Trowel**, 12in. Long   **$16.95**
> Bulb **Trowel**, 18in. Long   **$19.95**
> ⊞ 2 more items from $15 to $28
> www.whiteflowerfarm.com/**garden**-tools.html - Cached

...but not this one:

> **Fist Grip, Easi-Grip Ergonomic Garden Tools: Trowel, Fork and ...**
> Ergonomic **garden** tools: **trowel**, fork and cultivator that lesson **gardening** strain and injury.
> www.lifewithease.com/fistgrip1.html - Cached - Similar

Standard formatting can also improve the chances that Google will display your site when a searcher clicks More Shopping. Moreover, using standard conventions like having the shopping cart link in the upper right on a page will help your users navigate effortlessly to a sale.

Clean up pagination. Lots of stores have categories made up of multiple pages of products, connected by "next" or "page 3," "page 4," and so on. These pages are useful for visitors who are browsing your site, but they do not make good search engine landing pages. In addition to providing a poor entry experience, these pages can bog down the search engine robots and dilute your site's search engine power. If your site contains a large collection of pages that are nearly the same (don't worry about two or three pages—we're talking in the hundreds or thousands), take these steps to tidy up the excess pages:

1. Create a View All Results page that lists all of the products in a category.
2. Add a canonical tag, which you learned about in Chapter 7, to all of the other results pages (for example, page 1, page 2, page 3, and so on) specifying the "view all results" page as the primary page for the category.

If your categories are too large to fit all of your products onto a single View All page, just make sure that your paginated category pages contain unique (and preferably human-readable) URLs as well as unique page titles and meta description tags. For example, you might use titles such as "Women's Shoes – Page 1" and "Women's Shoes – Page 2." This will encourage the search engine robots to crawl additional category pages and to index product pages that are not linked from Page 1.

Deindex shopping cart pages. Pages on your site that are within the shopping experience, such as shopping cart and checkout pages, don't belong in search engine results. Deindex them either using the `robots.txt` file or the robots meta tag you learned about in Chapter 7.

 Now: Identify problems that may be holding back your online store. Think through priorities and identify who you'll need to speak with in your organization to address them.

Spread Too Thin at Butterknife, Inc.

Butterknife, Inc. (the company name and identifying details have been changed) is a labor of love for its longtime hobby chef owner. The site, built using out-of-the-box storefront software, offers about 1,800 varieties of artisan knives and kitchen utensils. Each utensil has something special to offer, and product descriptions are detailed and well written.

Despite all it had going for it, this site had almost no traffic coming from search engines, especially Google. Ranks weren't great, and upward of 80 percent of the site was in Google's holding pen for unloved web pages, the Supplemental Index. (This index no longer exists—Google combined its primary and supplemental indices in late 2007. We're almost sorry they did, because the pages that used to be in Supplemental were easy to identify as disadvantaged.)

We think that Butterknife, Inc., had such a large percentage of underachieving pages because the site's authority was spread too thin. With only a handful of inbound links, the amount of PageRank to go around simply couldn't support a site with many hundreds of pages. This, combined with the fact that many pages did not have unique HTML page titles, was enough to get the site snubbed by Google.

The best way to handle a spread-too-thin site is described by Google engineer Matt Cutts on his blog: "The approach I'd recommend in that case is to use solid white-hat SEO to get high-quality links (e.g., editorially given by other sites on the basis of merit)." We also recommend a sitewide cleanup of duplicate content and a little extra attention to internal link structure strategies described in Chapter 7.

Butterknife got serious about making positive changes, and after six months its numbers improved: About 40 percent of the supplemental pages were migrated into Google's standard index and ranks rose significantly. Now that the company has a handle on page authority, they'll soon be a cut above their competitors!

Thursday: Your Google Merchant Center Account

Earlier this week, you saw the importance of shopping search results in both Google and Bing. We're happy to share the good news that both Google and Bing offer free avenues into their shopping search results. On Google, your shopping search opportunity awaits you in the Google Merchant Center, and that's what you'll focus on today.

A product feed is a list of your products, along with important information such as price and description, formatted just the way Google likes, and uploaded to a place where Google can gobble it up. Google uses product feeds from merchants to create all of the listings it shows in its Google Product Search results.

If you haven't already set up a Google product feed, you'll do it today. Here are the steps to take:

Create your account. From the Google home page, click on Shopping, then Information for Merchants, as seen here:

On the next screen, click the "Start a data feed" button and follow Google's instructions to create an account. You'll need a Google account to manage the Merchant Center.

Here's a tricky thing about the Google account you use for your product feed: Only one account can be authorized to upload a product feed to Google Merchant Center for each website. Unless you're a one-person operation, you probably don't want to use a personal email address for this. Instead, why not create a separate Google account that can be used just for SEO?

Verify your website. Google will need you to prove that you're authorized to represent the website. The way Google does this is by checking that you're verified in Google Webmaster Tools. Remember how we said that Google Webmaster Tools verification was extra credit in Chapter 6? It's time for you to become teacher's pet. Visit Google Webmaster Tools at www.google.com/webmaster and follow the instructions to add and verify your website.

Create and upload your feed. Most e-commerce platforms allow you to generate a Google Product feed directly from the administration panel and upload to Google from there. Your system might refer to this feed as Froogle or Google Base, which were previous names for Google Products. See Figure 8.10 for an example of Google Base exporting from the e-commerce platform Volusion.

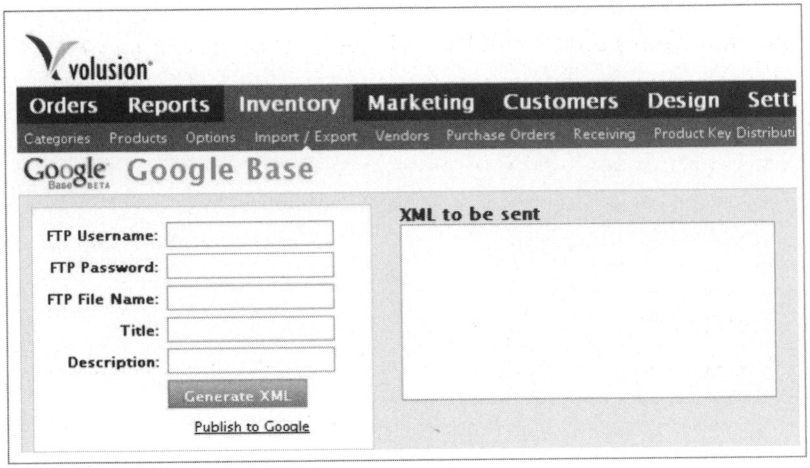

Figure 8.10 Exporting a Google Product feed from Volusion

If your e-commerce system doesn't generate a Google Product feed, you can also create one manually. It's easiest to create your product list in Excel and convert it over to the formats that Google accepts (TXT or XML).

At a minimum, U.S.-based product feeds must contain the following attributes for each product:

title The product name

link The product page URL

price The product price

condition The condition of the product—for example, new, used, refurbished

description An accurate text description of the product, up to 10,000 characters long

id A unique identifier

upc The UPC code, which is required for all products except books

Visit Google's Merchant Center support for details on each attribute: `www.google.com/support/merchants`.

With your feed created, you'll register and upload it within your Google Merchant Center.

Now: Set up your Google Merchant Account and create your first product feed.

Having a product feed in place is a crucial first step to getting placement in product search ranks, and maybe even a spot in the elusive Shopping OneBox. Now that you have a product feed, you can improve your position by paying attention to the following ranking factors:

Keywords in Title and Description Your product will have a better chance of ranking well for keywords that are in the title and description. Of course, you should never include terms that don't accurately describe your product.

Low Price A low price may or may not improve your ranks in shopping search, but it will certainly help your position when a searcher sorts products by price from low to high, as seen here:

Feed Freshness Some SEO pros believe that a fresher product feed will result in better ranks. An up-to-date feed will also ensure that your customers never have the annoying experience of clicking through a listing with one price or availability, only to see something different on your site. At a minimum, you must update your feed every 30 days or it will expire.

Additional Product Attributes You've probably got a lot to say about your products. Go beyond the bare minimum attributes we just described! Some of the most important attributes you can include are:

brand The brand name of your product.

image link The location of your product image. Make it high-quality!

product type The category of product being sold. Use Google's suggested categories, rather than making up your own.

mpn The manufacturer's product number.

You can also invent your own fields, called *custom attributes*. If there is another way that potential customers are likely to mentally organize your products (age range? size? karats? how gnarly?), make an attribute for it. But don't go overboard and use this as a place to stuff keywords; only add attributes if they genuinely improve the description of the product.

Now: Improve your Google Product feed with the optimization factors described here.

xtra cred You can take a peek into your competitors' feeds using the free tool at dev .tomthedeveloper.com/googlebase/ca/.

> ## Bing Shopping
>
> In August 2010, Bing announced that its shopping search engine, previously a pay-per-click service, now offers free listings. What great news! Bing accepts a feed very similar to the Google Product feed you've learned about today, so the work you did for Google will be a big help when you set up your Bing shopping feed. Here's where to get started: `http://advertising .microsoft.com/search-advertising/bing-shopping`.

A solidly optimized product feed is a fantastic accompaniment to any online store. Tomorrow, you'll find ways to enhance the merchant reviews that your potential customers may see alongside your product listings.

Friday: Seller Ratings

Google reps have publicly stated that reputation is a factor in product ranking. Many SEO pros interpret this to mean the quality and quantity of your seller ratings is important for product search rankings.

What Are Seller Ratings?

Seller ratings, also called merchant reviews, are online reviews about your e-tail business. Seller ratings typically live on third-party sites such as `Epinions.com` or `PriceGrabber.com`.

The search engines recognize several different kinds of reviews:

> **Pearl of Wisdom:** For SEO purposes, it's useful to classify reviews in three separate categories: *seller ratings* or *merchant reviews*, which rate businesses that sell online; *product reviews*, which a customer might leave on your site rating an individual product; and *local business reviews*, which rate a customer's experience in your brick-and-mortar shop.

Seller ratings display on Google as a row of stars (representing the average from multiple reviews) beneath your business name in shopping results, as seen here:

Seller ratings can also display beneath Google AdWords ads, as seen here:

Hair Shampoo
www.Walgreens.com Shop At Walgreens For Your Favorite Brands Of Hair Care Products.
Walgreens.com is rated ☆☆☆☆☆ on Google Products (86 reviews)

Click on the seller rating link, and you'll see Google Product Search's collection of ratings for your business:

ShampooLine.com

Seller rating: 3.3 / 5 - Based on 36 reviews

| 1 star | 3 stars | 4 | 5 stars |

"Easy to order, reliable,and fast shipping thanks"

"Great product and service"

"Loved the service and the product."

"Customer support is terrible."

"Shipping and handling too expensive."

"I feel as though the packaging was poorly put together."

Show reviews that mention
Price (7)
Customer Service (6)
Shipping (5)
Packaging (2)

Show reviews by source
BizRate.com (27)
Bizrate.com (9)

☆☆☆☆☆
5 / 5
Great product and service Read full review
By Online Shopper - Jul 1, 2010 - BizRate.com

☆☆☆☆☆
3 / 5
Shipping and handling too expensive. This does not turn out to be the bargain indicated, although the product is good. Read full review
By NIK - Jun 25, 2010 - BizRate.com

☆☆☆☆☆
5 / 5
Quality products- competitive pricing- timely delivery- FANTASTIC!
Read full review
By Gretch - Jun 20, 2010 - BizRate.com

☆☆☆☆☆
5 / 5
The tracking wasnt up to date so I was surprised when I received my package sooner than I expected Read full review
By Bcook - Jun 15, 2010 - BizRate.com

☆☆☆☆☆
1 / 5
They shipped to me EXPIRED product. They obviously knew it both products were expired, because they SCRATCHED OFF the expiration date and shipped it to me that... Read full review
By DZL - Jun 12, 2010 - BizRate.com

Google Product Search assembles seller ratings from various sources on the Web, including:

- Google Checkout Reviews
- PriceGrabber.com
- Epinions.com
- ResellerRatings.com
- BizRate.com

Of these, Google Checkout Reviews seems to deliver the biggest advantage in Google Product Search: Not only does it supply a large portion of the reviews there, but merchants who use Google Checkout get a nice-looking badge alongside their listings, which may encourage more click-throughs. Most of the other review sources are shopping comparison sites, which generally require a fee-based relationship. If you'd prefer to avoid any pay-per-click or commission arrangements, ResellerRatings.com, as well as the less-well-known RateItAll.com, offer free and inexpensive options for merchants that will allow you to begin gathering reviews on their sites.

 Now: Find the seller ratings, if any, that Google has assembled for your store. If you don't have a good number of ratings, consider setting up an account with one of the review aggregator websites we just listed.

How to Encourage Seller Ratings

One reason PriceGrabber, Epinions, BizRate, and Google Checkout are so prominent among seller ratings sources is that they doggedly follow up on purchases, seeking reviews from customers. If you're not selling with Google Checkout or via a well-known shopping comparison site, you'll need to take matters into your own hands! Use the following approaches to encourage ratings:

Reactive Request The simplest and perhaps least invasive way to encourage seller ratings is to request them from satisfied customers who contact you. You can use a standard email script, or a telephone script, requesting a review. Here's an example of a possible email communication:

"Dear HyperHammock, thanks for the great lawn chairs. I just wanted to let you know that they arrived safely. Thanks! - Sue S."

"Dear Sue S., Thank you for providing feedback to HyperHammock. We are so pleased to hear that your lawn chairs arrived safely! We would be very grateful if you could take a moment to tell others about your positive experience with HyperHammock. This will help other potential customers decide whether HyperHammock is the right choice for them. Here's a link: [link to HyperHammock ResellerRatings page]"

Proactive Request After every purchase, take the initiative and request a review from your customer. Including talking points such as "arriving on time" can help seed the reviews. Your request could look something like this:

"HyperHammock strives for perfection in our customer experience. Did your purchases arrive on time and in good condition? Was your customer service representative knowledgeable and helpful? Did we respond promptly to all questions?

Please help us improve by sharing your experience on [link to HyperHammock ResellerRatings page]"

Links on Your Site While it's not likely to have a major impact, you can add links throughout the site in key locations such as home, contact, or product pages. Text on the page can be short and sweet:

"Returning customers: Take a moment to review your last purchase!"

> **Now:** Determine which approaches to gaining more seller ratings will work for your business. Write your script or email template.

Your store is optimized, your product feed is speaking Google's language, and you've amped up its optimization. Not too shabby! Next week, you'll rock the local search results.

Week 8: Local Search

In Chapter 2, "Customize Your Approach," we talked a bit about the wonders of local search. Been waiting in line for coffee too long? Pull out your smartphone and search for another café in the vicinity. Sitting at home on a Saturday night? Order pizza and a video directly through the Web. What's good for the searcher is even better for the search-savvy local business owner. Even if your organization doesn't have a brick-and-mortar component, if there's any local component to your business, you want to tackle local search this week.

> **Monday:** Local Search 101
> **Tuesday:** Central Data Providers
> **Wednesday:** Google and Bing Local Listings
> **Thursday:** Onsite Edits for Local Optimization
> **Friday:** Consumer Reviews

Monday: Local Search 101

You'll focus this week on the major search engines: Google, Bing, and Yahoo! All show local search results within standard listings for location-oriented searches. For example, type <boston bakery> into Bing, and you'll see prominently featured local results at the top, plus a tab marked Local Listings (see Figure 8.11).

Click Local Listings and Bing displays more local details (Figure 8.12).

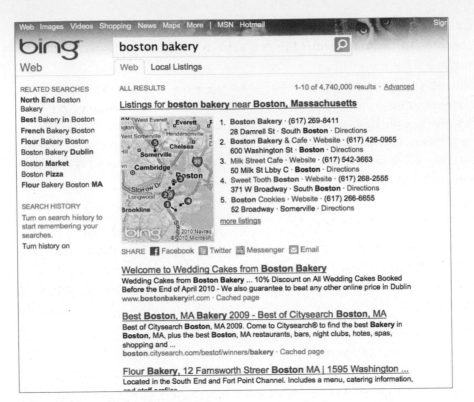

Figure 8.11 Bing search results for <boston bakery>

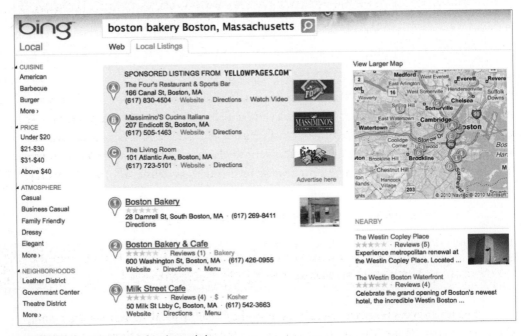

Figure 8.12 Bing Local Listings for <boston bakery>

Wouldn't it be nice to be listed there, maybe even with some sizzling five-star reviews next to your company name? Here's a summary of the major opportunities in local search:

Local Search OneBox As you learned last week, a OneBox is the name for the specialty search listings that are featured within standard web search results. (Jargon alert! These can also be called 3-pack, 7-pack, or 10-pack, depending on how many listings they show.) When the search engines decide that a search query is deserving of the local treatment, they will often display a local OneBox featuring between 3 and 10 local listings, along with important info such as phone number and address.

When Is a Search a Local Search?

The search engines are often smart enough to deliver relevant local search results, even when searchers don't give strong clues that they are looking for a local business. For example, type these search queries into Google or Bing and look for a local OneBox or featured local listings in the results:

<gift shop seward ak> Google and Bing interpret the city and state in the search as a location-based query and show you a OneBox containing gift shops in Alaska.

<once in a blue moose> Google recognizes this query as the name of an Alaskan gift shop chain and shows you featured local listings for Once in a Blue Moose locations. Bing does not identify this as a local search.

<gift shop> Google and Bing don't know which city, or which store, you're looking for but they know where *you* are based on your IP address and other information. So they show you a list of gift shops near you.

Local Listings Local listings on search engines are derived from a separate index than the main web search results. On Google, these are called Google Places. On Bing, they are called business listings. It's possible for your business to have a listing in local search without you taking any action, but you'll want to claim your listing in order to improve and control it. You'll learn how to manage your listings on Wednesday and Thursday of this week.

Don't let Google's own branding problems cause *you* problems:

Pearl of Wisdom: Google Places is the name for listings on Google Maps, which many people also call Google Local. Don't let the different names confuse you—they're all the same service!

Search engines regularly tweak the way they display local search results among standard results. Make it your goal to be among the featured local listings, however they are displayed.

Local Review Sites Review sites such as Yelp, InsiderPages, and CitySearch feature local business reviews and have a strong presence in organic search results. Figure 8.13 shows how prominent these sites can be in Google when a local business is searched. On Friday, we'll help you determine which of these local review sites deserve your attention.

Best Crab house in Miami, Ft Lauderdale even Palm Beach vicinity ... ☆
8 posts - 6 authors - Last post: Jul 7, 2008
Which places would you recommend for best **crab house**...we've seen some ads in ... **Joe's**
Stone Crab in **Miami**!!! http://www.joesstonecrab.com/ ...
chowhound.chow.com/topics/417023 - Cached - Similar

> Stone **Crabs** in **Miami** area - **Miami** - **Ft. Lauderdale** - Jan 4, 2010
> The **Crab House**, on 79th St Causeway, **Miami** - any good? - **Miami** ... - Nov 6, 2008
> **Crab** Shacks in Orlando - Florida - Apr 8, 2007
> where to go for stone **crab** in Ft. Lauderdale/**Miami** area? - Florida ... - Mar 27, 2003
> More results from chowhound.chow.com »

Joe's Stone **Crab** - **Miami** Beach, FL, 33139 - Citysearch® ☆
☆☆☆☆☆ 36 reviews
Jul 19, 2010 ... **Joe's** Stone **Crab** in **Miami** Beach. Come to Citysearch® to get information, directions, ... **Joe's** Stonecrab House - A Unique Experience ...
miami.citysearch.com › Miami Beach › Restaurants - Cached - Similar

Joes crab house Miami Beach ☆
Reviews on **Joes crab house** in **Miami** Beach - **Joe's** Take Away, **Joe's** Stone **Crab**, CJ's Crab Shack, The Crab House, Prime One Twelve, Smith & Wollensky, ...
www.yelp.com/search?find_desc=Joes+Crab+House&find_loc=Miami...

Joes crab house Miami ☆
Reviews on **Joes crab house** in **Miami** - **Joe's** Take Away, **Joe's** Stone **Crab**, Oceanaire Seafood Room, Garcia's Seafood Grille & Fish, The Fish House, ...
www.yelp.com/search?find_desc=joes+crab+house...Miami%2C... - Cached
⊞ Show more results from www.yelp.com

Joe's Stone **Crab**: Restaurants in **Miami** ☆
Miami Beach, FL 33139. Phone: 305-673-0365. Get Directions. 3 Reviews. **Joe's** Stone **Crab** Average Main Course Price 60 out of 100 based on 5 ratings. ...
www.10best.com/destinations/florida/miami/south.../joes-stone-crab/ - Cached

Figure 8.13 Local reviews in search results for <joe's crab house miami>

Standard Search Results for Local Keywords Although local listings are prominent in search results for location-oriented keywords, standard web search results also have a significant presence for these keywords. When searchers scroll beyond the featured local listings, you'll want your site to be right there in the standard results, too.

 Now: This is a study hall day! Perform some location-oriented searches and click around the results on Google and Bing.

With a good familiarity with the local search landscape, you're ready to start managing your own business's local presence.

Tuesday: Central Data Providers

Many sites, including Google, Bing, and tons of lower-end directories, use data from large central databases to populate their local listings. Although these databases strike us as dusty holdovers from the age of the printed phone book, they continue to be an important place for local businesses to be listed.

Today, we recommend some not-so-exciting footwork: making sure your business information is correct on the major central providers of local business data. Here's how:

infogroup/InfoUSA infogroup/InfoUSA has a database with millions of local businesses, which is used by the major search engines, CitySearch, and many other local directories. In 2010, InfoUSA launched a business-friendly site to help local businesses create and update listings at www.expressupdateusa.com. A screenshot is shown in Figure 8.14.

They'd like to separate you from some of your money with an enhanced business listing, but you can create or update a basic business listing for free. Start at the Check My Listing box shown in Figure 8.14.

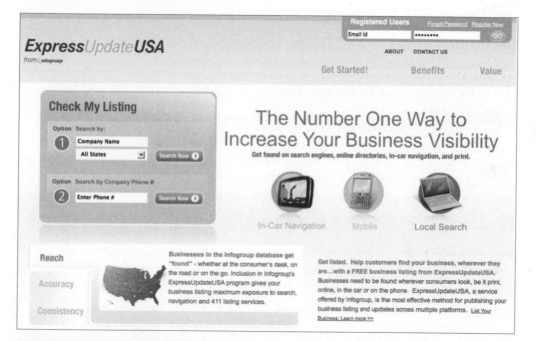

Figure 8.14 ExpressUpdateUSA home page

Chances are, your business is already listed in this database. If not, follow the links to add your business:

You will need to be verified in order to make changes to a listing—InfoUSA will call you at the business number to confirm. Once you have access to your business listing, you can make sure that your business name, phone numbers, website, category, and description are just the way you want them.

 Now: Add or update your listing on infogroup/infoUSA.

slacker If you've reviewed your listing and all of the information is correct, you can skip this and move on to the next site.

Localeze Much like InfoUSA, Localeze lists local businesses and offers a free, relatively easy way to update business listings. From the home page at www.localeze.com, click List Your Business Today (Figure 8.15).

Figure 8.15 Localeze home page

Localeze calls this their "Business Registration Manager." You will be required to create an account and verify that you are the actual business owner before you can make changes to the Localeze listing for your business.

Localeze is working hard to place its data at the crossroads of the social and local Web, and forged a deal with Twitter in 2010 to provide business information for Twitter Places. We think it's worth your time to claim your business listing here.

> **Now:** Add or update your listing on Localeze.

xtra
cred

The list goes on, but you only have an hour today, so we stopped at two. If you've got the time and inclination, two additional sites that deserve your attention are `Superpages.com`, which is free, and `UniversalBusinessListing.org`, which charges a modest yearly fee.

Wednesday: Google and Bing Local Listings

Both Google and Bing allow business owners to maintain and update their local listings for free. Today, you'll mark your territory in these important places.

Your Google Places Listing

In the words of a certain cybernetic collective, "Resistance is futile," so get yourself signed up on Google Places now.

Find your listing. Even if you have never created a Google Places listing, Google may have assembled information about your business from other sources. Your first assignment: See if your site already has a Google Places listing. To do this, search for your business name and the city it's in—for example, <buchwald seybold jewelers miami>. Look for the telltale signs of a local listing: a Places icon, your business name, and its address, as in this example:

```
Buchwald Jewelers, Fine Jewelry and Diamonds in the Seybold ...
Miami Jewelry, Miami Jeweler specializing in Engagement Rings, wedding bands, discount
jeweler, jewelry, diamonds, Anniversary rings in the Miami, ...
www.buchwaldjewelers.com/ - Cached - Similar
  Suite #123, 36 NE 1st Street, Miami        13 reviews
  (305) 373-5683                             Place page
  yahoo.com (6) - tripadvisor.com (3) - citysearch.com (2) -
  frommers.com (1)
```

If your initial search doesn't bear any fruit, try a few variations. Expand the locality to a state or zip code, experiment with alternate spellings of your business name, or try clicking on Maps and performing the same search there.

If, after performing these searches, you still haven't found a listing, then your business probably isn't in Google Places and you should make a new listing.

If your business doesn't have a Google Places listing... Go to `www.google.com/local` and click Put Your Business On Google Maps.

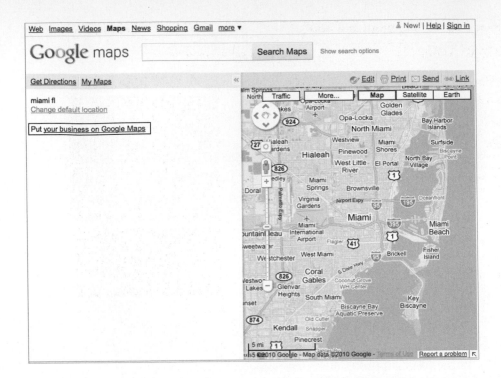

You'll need a Google account to begin adding your business listing, and Google will require verification that you are really the business owner, either via phone or postal mail, before the listing is published.

If your business already has a Google Places listing… Claim your listing by taking these steps. First, click on Place Page to see the page that's all about your business. See Figure 8.16 for an example of a Google Place page.

Next, click Business Owner? to claim your listing. You'll need a Google account, and Google will require verification that you are really the business owner, either via phone or postal mail.

Local Listings on Yahoo!

Bing began powering Yahoo!'s organic and paid web search results in 2010, but as of this writing, Yahoo! is still powering its own news and local search results. We don't know whether this will continue to be the case by the time you read this book, so here's our assignment for you: Run a search on Yahoo! for a local-themed query. (Can't think of one? Try <apartments chapel hill nc>.) Open a new browser window and run the same search on Bing. Next, compare the two results. Do they look different? If so, you'll want to set up an account on Yahoo! and manage your local listing there, in the same way we've instructed you for Bing and Google. Get started here: http://listings.local.yahoo.com/ (you'll need a Yahoo! account).

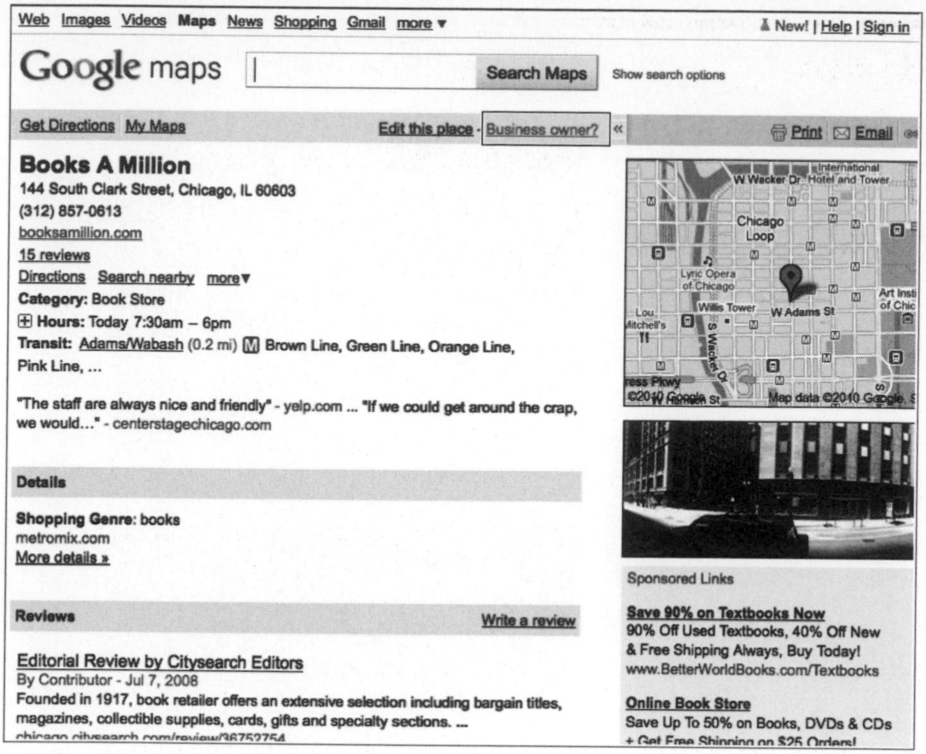

Figure 8.16 Google Places page for Books-A-Million in Chicago

Your Bing Local Listing

Here are the steps to adding or claiming your local business listing on Bing:

Find your listing. To see if your site already has a Bing Local listing, search for your business name and the city, state, or zip code it's in—for example, <buchwald seybold jewelers miami>. Here's an example of a local listing in Bing:

If, after trying your business name and location searches you still haven't found a listing, then your business probably isn't in the Bing local index and you should make a new listing.

If your business doesn't have a Bing local listing... Go to www.bing.com/local and search for your business. When no results come up, you'll have the opportunity to add your business by clicking "Add or edit your business listing in the Local Listing Center."

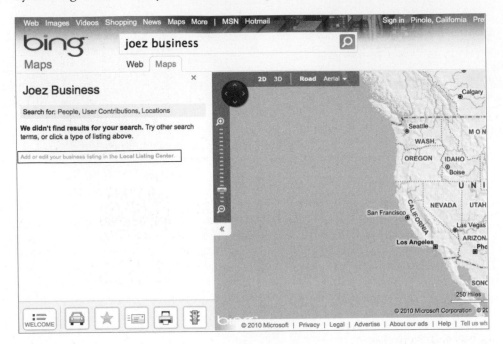

You'll need a free Windows Live ID to begin adding your business listing. Bing will verify that you are really the business owner by sending a postcard containing a PIN to the business address. You will need to enter the PIN before the listing is published.

If your business already has a Bing local listing... Claim your listing by taking these steps. First, click on your business name in the Bing listing to see the page that's all about your business. See Figure 8.17 for an example of a Bing local page.

Scroll down and click on Change Your Business Listing to claim your listing.

UPDATE THIS LISTING

Report incorrect information

Change your business listing

You'll need a free Windows Live ID to claim your business listing. Bing will verify that you are really the business owner by sending a postcard containing a PIN to the business address. You will need to enter the PIN before your edits are published.

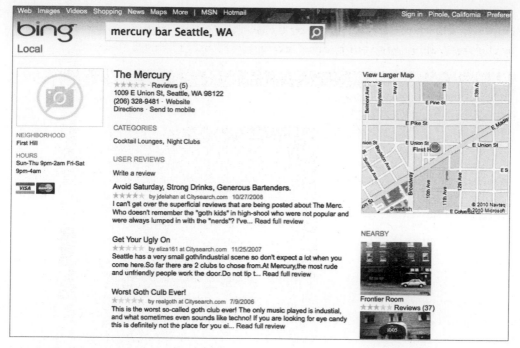

Figure 8.17 Bing local page for Mercury Bar in Seattle

Optimize Your Business Listings

You've taken control of your business's local listings on Google and Bing. What a great start! Here are some tips to be sure you make the most of these listings:

Add complete and accurate business info. Naturally, you should fill in your business's complete address, phone number, description, hours of operation, brands offered, and so on. Keywords in your business title are likely to influence rankings, so don't leave them out or abbreviate them. For example, this Google Place listing for "Hiura & Hiura & Han" is for an optometrist, but you'd never know it from the business title shown here:

Your company description, tagline or slogan, specialties, and professional affiliations provide additional opportunities to accurately describe your business using keyword-rich text.

Choose topical categories. Both Google and Bing allow you to choose several categories for your business, and these are likely to play a role in rankings. Take advantage of this opportunity to choose categories that contain your target keywords. For example, a store selling outdoor equipment might choose to be in these five categories:

- Sports & Recreation > Outdoor Recreation
- Sports & Recreation > Hunting & Fishing
- Hunting & Fishing > Hunting Equipment & Supplies
- Camping > Camping Equipment
- Sporting Goods > Sporting Goods Sales & Rental

Having trouble coming up with a list? Both Google and Bing will suggest categories based on keywords. Or, look up your competitors and see what categories they're in—then add your own business to the same ones.

Beautify your listing. Your listing needs some visual interest! It's easy to upload photos on both Google and Bing, so why not give your local search surfers one more reason to visit your business? Google will also allow you to add videos to your local listings. You will need to upload the videos to YouTube in order to use this feature.

Specify locations you serve. Your business address is an important part of the local ranking algorithm: A business located in the city of Chicago will have a much better chance of ranking well for searches containing <chicago> than a business located in a distant suburb. Businesses with a local area code as their primary business phone number may also have an advantage. Google also allows you to specify areas served, either as a radius around your central location or with a list of cities. Fill these in as accurately and completely as possible. And for the love of Pete, *don't* click the box that allows you to hide your business address.

Develop citations. Local listing *citations* are the web pages that Google and Bing will sometimes display on a business's local listing page, labeled "websites" or "web results," as seen in Figure 8.18.

These are web pages that are relevant to your geographic location and that mention your business by name, address, phone number, or with a link to your website. CitySearch is often featured among these links, as are the local review sites we'll be discussing on Friday, along with a large number of local directories, Yellow Pages, and business lists. Experts in local SEO believe that citations are an important signal to Google and Bing that your business is genuinely what and where you say it is. The work you did on Tuesday, adding your business to central databases, should help you build local citations. Look at the local business listings of your competitors for more ideas for places to get your business listed.

 Now: Search for local listings for your business on Google and Bing. Claim existing local listings for your business, or create new ones if none exists. Maximize your local business listing optimization by implementing the tips we described.

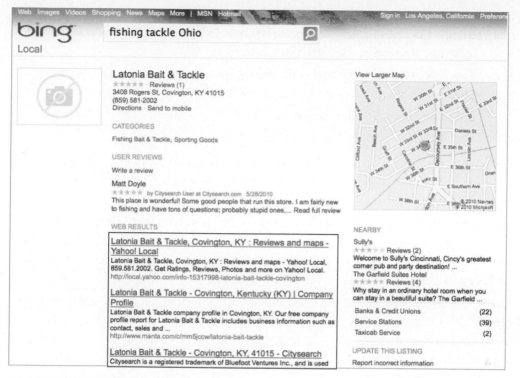

Figure 8.18 Local listing citations in Bing

Congratulations! Your local listings have been primped and preened, and they're ready to strut their stuff. Tomorrow, you'll direct your attention back to your business website to give your business an even stronger local search presence.

Thursday: Onsite Edits for Local Optimization

Most SEO pros believe that your business's ranks in local search, and its chances of making its way into the featured local listings, depend primarily on the local listing optimization you performed yesterday, and not on your website itself. But not every search causes local listings to display in the results, and not every searcher wants to click on featured local listings. Your website will rank better in standard web search results for location-oriented keywords if your website clearly reinforces your geographic location, in the following search-friendly ways:

Use traditional on-page optimization for location keywords Site optimization for location keywords means incorporating location names in crucial on-page spots: HTML titles, visible page text, linking text, and URLs. Include variations of your locality keywords (such as "WA" and "Washington"), and don't forget the importance of neighborhood or region names.

Integrate contact info throughout your site. Include your business address and local phone number on all pages of the site. This is easy to accomplish using a text footer or template, and it sends the search engines a strong message about your whereabouts.

There is a special address format called hCard that might help search engines recognize your contact info. See Chapter 10, "Extra Credit and Guilt-Free Slacking," for details.

Give a shout out to all the locations you serve. If your business operates out of several locations, create a separate landing page for each one. If some of your customers hail from a nearby city, talk about it on your site. You might integrate your service area into a tagline, such as, "...serving Milwaukee, Racine, Elmwood, and the entire South Wisconsin area." Or, you could add pertinent locations on your FAQ, answering real-world questions such as "Do you deliver to Jackson Hole, Wyoming?"

Explore localization in paid search. We're big fans of maximizing free opportunities to improve your site's local visibility; however, Google offers a couple of paid options that you may find mighty appealing as a local business.

The first option is called Location Extensions, and it's available for Google AdWords advertisers. All you have to do is hunt down the wily Ad Extensions tab that Google has carefully hidden from you in your AdWords interface. To do this, on the Campaigns tab in your AdWords management interface, find the More Tabs menu, which looks like a down arrow.

| Campaigns | Ad groups | Settings | Ads | Keywords | Networks | Audiences | **Ad extensions** | ▾ |

View: Location Extensions ▾   All but deleted ▾   Columns   ⬇

Review performance statistics for ads that have appeared with an ad extension. You'll only see statistics for the campaigns you are currently viewing, for eligible ad extensions that have been triggered. Learn more about ad extensions statistics

⊟ Addresses from Google Places

| ✚ **New extension** | Delete |

| **Google Places Account** | **Campaign** |

Automatically include address information in your ad.
Learn more.

⊞ Manually entered Addresses

Once you've found the tab, use the features on it to link your AdWords ad to your Google Places listing or enter an address manually. This will add local flavor to your AdWords ads by displaying your full address to local searchers, as in this example:

Sponsored links

Crate & Barrel
Shop **Crate & Barrel** Stores Near You
for Classic Designs for Your Home!
www.CrateandBarrel.com
75 W. Colorado Boulevard, Pasadena, CA

Enabling Ad Extensions in AdWords will also cause your paid search ads to display within Google Maps results, as in this example:

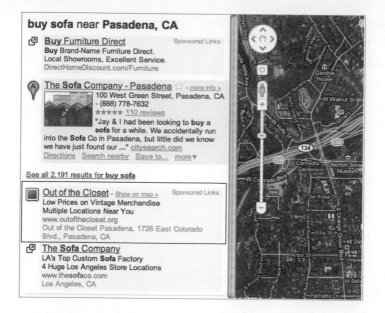

Feeling fancy? Go the extra mile and select or upload your own map icon to dress up your listing even more.

Another snazzy local option is a yellow pointer that can be added to Google Places listings. Google calls these *tags* and you can learn about them at www.google.com/help/tags. Not much more than eye candy, these little yellow icons draw a searcher's eye to your listing, as in this example:

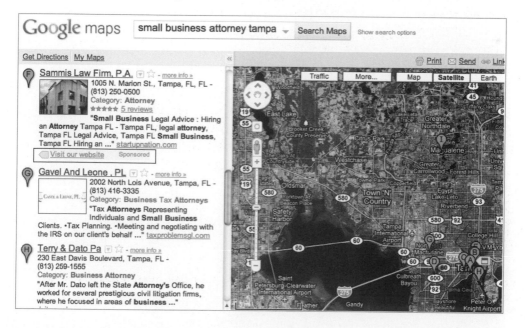

Paying for tags will not improve your rankings, but it may improve your click-through rate. Why not give tags a try before your competitors do?

 Now: Incorporate location information on your site.

With your business listings and your website well optimized for local search, you'll spend tomorrow looking outward to your customers, as they express their opinions about your business in the most public of venues: online reviews.

Friday: Customer Reviews

A local merchant shares this story: "Some customers came into my store and said, 'You know, you have terrible reviews on Yelp!' And I said, 'What's Yelp?'"

Don't let that happen to you! If there are conversations going on about your business online, you want to know about them and influence them in any way that is appropriate.

Google and Bing both display customer reviews as a part of your local business listings. Some reviews are created directly on Google and Bing, and lots of other reviews are sourced from third-party sites like Yelp, InsiderPages, and CitySearch.

The importance of customer reviews as a ranking factor in local search is disputed among SEO pros, but we can all agree that reviews can make or break your business listing's success—a frowny icon or a short stack of stars can be all it takes for a potential customer to pass you by. Research has confirmed what you already know intuitively: Consumers are using online reviews increasingly before making a purchasing decision. As of 2010, 64 percent of online shoppers spent 10 minutes or more researching online reviews before making a purchase (Source: PowerReviews, *2010 Social Shopping Study*).

Although consumer product reviews are important in their own right, today we're talking about reviews of your business, not the individual products you sell. Today, you'll put some real effort into getting your customers to do you the very big favor of spending their precious time writing nice things about you online.

What Venues Should You Care About?

Consumers have so many options for adding business reviews that you may not know where to find your own reviews, much less devise a realistic plan for monitoring them all or encouraging new ones. Here is partial list of sites in the online word-of-mouth landscape:

Social Media:	Facebook
	LinkedIn
	Foursquare
Merchant Reviews/	Google Checkout
Seller Ratings:	Epinions
	PriceGrabber
	Shopping.com
	ResellerRatings.com
Local Reviews:	Yelp CitySearch
	InsiderPages
	Google Places/Google Maps
	Metromix
Niche Reviews:	Chowhound
	Zagats
	ServiceMagic.com
	HealthGrades.com
	Tripadvisor.com
	Weddingwire.com
	Angie's List

You could devote untold hours to going through every online word-of-mouth venue looking for your business, but here are a few shortcuts to try instead:

- Look at your business's Google Places and Bing local listings and see what review sites are showing up there.

- Don't have a Google Places or Bing local listing yet? Try a search for your full business name and look for review sites in the standard search results.

- Ask your customers. Use Twitter, Facebook, a customer survey, or an honest-to-goodness in-person conversation to ask "Where do you go for online reviews?"

Now: Using the shortcut that applies to you, search for sites that are displaying reviews for your business.

We'll call these sites your top-priority online word-of-mouth venues. If you're still not finding any reviews, try searching for some of your competitors. Where are *they* being reviewed?

Add or Claim Your Business Listing

Review sites want their listings to be as accurate as possible, so they encourage businesses to claim their listings or add a listing if one doesn't already exist. By verifying that you are the business owner, you may have the opportunity to update your listings, receive notifications when you receive new reviews, and even get badges for your site that proudly proclaim the number of reviews you have on that service.

Claiming a business listing on a local review site generally starts by finding a link on the listing page containing text such as "Are You the Owner?," "Edit Business Info," or "Do You Own {Business Name}?" (see the following graphic for this link on Yelp). The verification process and cost varies from site to site.

Penny's Noodle Shop

122 reviews   Rating Details

Like

Category: Thai [Edit]
950 W Diversey Pkwy
(at Sheffield Ave)
Chicago, IL 60614
Neighborhood: Lakeview

(773) 281-8448
www.pennysnoodleshop.com

Add Photos

Nearest Transit: Diversey (Purple Express, Brown)	**Price Range:** $	**Wheelchair Accessible:** Yes
Good for Groups: Yes	**Good for Kids:** Yes	**Outdoor Seating:** No
Accepts Credit Cards: Yes	**Takes Reservations:** No	**Good For:** Lunch, Dinner
Parking: Street	**Delivery:** Yes	**Alcohol:** Beer & Wine Only
Attire: Casual	**Take-out:** Yes	
	Waiter Service: Yes	

Edit Business Info   Work Here? Unlock This Business Page   First to Review   Dee W.

Send to Friend   Bookmark   Send to Phone   Write a Review   Print

If your business doesn't already have a page on a local review venue that you care about, you may be able to add one. As with verification, costs and processes vary. Adding a business listing on CitySearch starts at around $20/month. There's no charge on Yelp.

Add or Claim Your Business Listing *(Continued)*

> demeanor. We started with naan and three dips: hummus, babaganoush, and one other dip...I think it was **yogurt** based. We also ordered the plum chutney and some rosemary naan. The hummus was perfectly
>
> **⬇5. Central Market**   ⭐⭐⭐⭐⭐ *123 reviews*
> Categories: Grocery, Cooking Schools   5750 E Lovers Ln
> Neighborhood: Upper Greenville   Dallas, TX 75206
>   (214) 234-7000
>
> baked baguette -prosciutto or capicola ham -poblano/corn chowder -marcona almonds (when available) -fig jam -fage **yogurt** -lucky layla farms guava **yogurt** -la tur cheese -dolmas -terra chips i still
>
> **⬇6. American Airlines Center**   ⭐⭐⭐⭐ *43 reviews*
> Category: Stadiums & Arenas   2500 Victory Avenue
> Neighborhood: Victory Park   Dallas, TX 75219
>   (214) 222-3687
>
> not the roll, but it was lean and the BBQ sauce was tasty. Also indulged in the **frozen yogurt**, it was delicious. Make sure to wear a coat, I was freezing! Also, I was disappointed that most
>
> 1 to 6 of 6
>
>   Got search feedback? Help us improve.
>
> **Not here? Tell us what we're missing.**   [Add A Business]
> If the business you're looking for isn't here, add it!

Remember, these business listing pages often show up in the search results, so it's smart strategy to claim yours and exert whatever control you have to make them look good!

Know Your Online Reviews

How is your business faring in the sharp-toothed world of online reviews? Visit each of the top-priority online word-of-mouth venues and locate your company's page to find out.

We don't *really* have to tell you the next step, because once you see a review of your business online, you'll have a hard time tearing yourself away.

Now: Open each of the review sites on your top-priority list, find your company, and read the reviews.

Now you know what's online today. But we want you to monitor your reviews in an ongoing way. Here are a couple ways to keep your ear to the ground:

Add feeds to your feed reader. Many review sites, such as Yelp, offer a feed for every business page. You can find the RSS feed icon in the browser address bar next to the address.

See Week Five in this chapter for a walkthrough of adding feeds to your iGoogle homepage.

Use MyReviewspage.com **to monitor reviews.** This service pulls together stats on the reviews your business has received on a handful of large review sites and will email you whenever you get a new review on one of these sites.

Get notifications directly from review sites. Some review sites provide you with email notifications when your business receives new reviews. Flip back a couple of pages to see the sidebar "Add or Claim Your Business Listing" to learn how to start this process by claiming your business on Yelp.

Accentuate the Positive

Last week, we shared approaches for online stores to pursue seller ratings from customers. Your local reviews may be sourced in a different group of review sites, but your assignment is the same: Pursue customer or client reviews with a passion. Here are some ideas for cultivating positive reviews:

Come right out and ask. If you have happy customers, a polite request for a positive review is not bad etiquette—it's good business sense. There are lots of ways to follow up directly with customers. Send a follow-up email after you've shipped your product. On your "thank you" page, mention how much you'd appreciate a review. Print a reminder on your packing slip. Throw a card into each shopping bag. Set up a computer kiosk in your store and ask for reviews at the point of purchase. Send a note via postal mail. If you don't have a way to contact individual customers, cast a wider net and ask for reviews in your email newsletters and on Twitter and Facebook. And while you're asking, make it easy to follow through! Provide your customers with a link to the reviewer page.

Give a little guidance. Not everybody feels confident about their writing skills. You can help by politely providing talking points to your potential reviewers. We're not suggesting that you write your own reviews, but you can say, "We'd be honored if you'd consider mentioning our quick service when you review us on Yelp." And it never hurts to provide simple instructions on exactly how to create a review.

Plant a seed. If you have friends who are also customers, reach out and ask for a quick review. This may spur additional reviews from friends of friends, and set a review trend in motion for your business. But keep your reputation clean: *Don't fake reviews or encourage friends to do so!* The Federal Trade Commission (FTC) would not be amused. Sites like Yelp have spam-catching techniques that suppress fake reviews, and over-the-top enthusiasm may be seen as less credible by your target audience.

Stomach the negative. As the Yelp website states, "Negative reviews can feel like a punch in the gut." When you run across a particularly spiteful one, here are a few steps you can take to mitigate the situation:

- Step up your efforts to crowd it out with positive reviews.

- Resist the urge to respond in your own defense—this only makes you look worse. If you must respond, stick to expressing your gratitude for the feedback.

- Check the review site's editorial guidelines to see if the review violates any. It probably won't (mean, nasty, and crazy talk is within bounds here), but if the review contains personal attacks, secondhand information, or bigotry, you have a chance of having the review removed.

Paying for Blog Reviews

Although it is clearly contemptible, no-good, sleazy, and slimy to pay for a positive review on a consumer-generated review site, there is some wiggle room in the area of paying for blogger reviews. Services such as PayPerPost and ReviewMe connect businesses with bloggers who are willing to write about their product—for a fee (ranging from roughly $50 to $200). All bloggers are required to disclose the paid relationship, which keeps it out of the ick zone and in compliance with the FTC's blogger guidelines. However, if you choose to go this route, be aware that the links in the reviewer post will probably be considered paid links in Google's ranking algorithm, so don't expect a ranking boost from them.

Whether you do all of the above or nothing at all, try not to dwell on the negative review or two you receive. There are always bound to be a few chuckleheads out there!

 Now: Determine who in your company has the opportunity to ask for positive reviews. Determine which venues you will pursue and help craft the requests.

You've socialized, shopified, and localized your way through another month of SEO awesomeness! Now, you're ready to move on to the third month of Your SEO Plan. Join us in the next chapter, when SEO becomes a way of life.

Month Three: It's a Way of Life

With so many SEO elements—organic, paid, onsite, offsite, social—in the works for your website now, you've built up a holistic approach to SEO that you can be proud of. But don't rest on your laurels yet. SEO is never done!

This month you'll find SEO-friendly solutions for expanding your site's presence in blended search results, and you'll smooth out any rough edges on your website's visibility. You'll take your SEO reporting a step further, and you'll find all the SEO news and info you need to stay current.

Chapter Contents

Week 9: Special Opportunities: Video, Mobile, and More

By now, you've got a good idea of how your target audience behaves in its natural habitat. This week we'll help you develop an optimization plan that expands and enhances your brand's footprint beyond the basic text links in search results. You'll target a presence in less well known search verticals such as video, image, and blog search, and you'll learn how to take every opportunity to enhance your site's search presence on mobile devices.

Monday: Image Search

Tuesday: Video Search

Wednesday: Blog Search

Thursday: Mobile Search

Friday: Improve Your Search Engine Snippets

Monday: Image Search

There are lots of separate specialty search engines, a.k.a. verticals, within Google and Bing. On Google, book search, blog search, image search, finance, patents, and so on can all be accessed and enjoyed on dedicated home pages, but it's much more common for people to find these results mixed into their standard search results. Mixing verticals into the main page of search results is called Universal Search on Google; most non-Googlers call it *blended search*. See Figure 9.1 for an example of images in Google search results.

You've already gotten a great start optimizing for local and shopping results in Chapter 8, "Month Two: Establish the Habit." Today you'll learn how to put your best pic forward in image search results. Here are a few indicators that your site is a good candidate for an image optimization push:

- One of your site's differentiating factors is its images. Are they especially interesting, unique, or numerous?

- Querying any of your target keywords brings up images at the top of the standard search results.

- Your business sells products that translate into compelling photographs.

- You have a strong interest in reputation management. Celebrities and politicos may fall into this category.

If any of these apply, don't overlook image optimization as a way to snag some targeted visitors and to mwnage your search engine branding.

Your site is not likely to rank well in image search if you are a reseller using the same catalog photos as several other sites. If this describes your site, concentrate on the text optimization ideas you are about to read, but it's probably not worth the effort to go out of your way to modify your site structure.

slacker

Figure 9.1 Images in Google search results for <dragon parade>

Image Search Optimization

As you've learned, search engines can't read or understand images. So to rank images, they scout around for clues: text in critical locations tied to the image file and surrounding the picture on the page. For the best chance of getting the image search rankings you desire, each image should be presented on its own page. Remember to think like an SEO when assigning images to pages:

 **Pearl of Wisdom:** An image has a better chance at top search rankings when you display it on a page that is optimized for the keywords you want it to rank for.

That means your pictures of red rutabagas will have a better chance of showing up in search results for the term <red rutabagas> if you put them on a dedicated "red rutabagas" page rather than mixing them with other images on a more general "veggie varieties" page. Creating a separate page for each image allows you to maximize your chance for image rankings by optimizing both the image and the page that it resides on.

For a chance at top ranks, you need to take image optimization further. Be sure to include keywords in these important spots:

Image File Name For example, if your image is a photo of a red rutabaga, the file name `red-rutabaga.jpg` says it all!

Captions Directly Beneath or Above Images For example, "Our red rutabagas are farm fresh and delicious mashed or roasted." makes a clear and keyword-rich caption.

ALT and TITLE Tags Use them both, and it's OK if you use an identical ALT and TITLE tag on the same image. Don't stuff them with keywords, though—stick to a simple and descriptive title.

Text Links Pointing to the Image For example, <u>click for larger picture</u> contains no keywords, but <u>Red Rutabaga – View Larger</u> Photo provides keyword-rich, and descriptive, clickable text.

Text on the Same Page as the Image When a caption isn't enough, you can always add a longer description of the photo in the body of the page.

Now: Look at the images on your top landing pages. Starting with the most promising ones, figure out where you can add keywords and then communicate your edits to the person who can make the changes.

Getting well-placed keywords around your images is a great start. Here are a few additional steps you can take to maximize your image search presence:

- Check and see how your images look when they're reduced to thumbnail size. Readable? If not, consider recropping or upping the contrast for a better presentation in image search results.

- Verify with your webmaster that he or she didn't do something that will hamper your image search efforts such as excluding the /images folder using the `robots.txt` file.

- Within the image search verticals, searchers can roll over images to read descriptive text from the page where the image resides. This text may include the file name, the HTML title, or text placed near the image. If you have images displaying in Google or Bing Image Search, review this text and make sure it provides more than just keywords. Does it give a compelling reason to click? Figure 9.2 shows the difference between compelling and not-so-compelling rollover text on Google Image Search.

Now: Perform a <site:> search for your site on images.google.com and www.bing.com/images. Review any image listings you find and determine whether they can be improved.

rutabaga.jpg
318 × 295 - Organic Food Nutrionally
Superior – Delicious **Rutabaga Recipe**
organictobe.org

master.k.m.us.Rutaba
200 × 200 - **Rutabagas**:
Main Image
evitamins.com

Figure 9.2 The descriptive text on the
left gives context and a reason to click.
The text on the right could be improved.

Your site has the primo images, and now you know how to flaunt them! Next stop: video search.

Tuesday: Video Search

If your website offers videos—whether they're local celebrity blooper reels or ultra-techie product demonstrations—you'll want to put some energy into video search optimization. The goal of your video optimization efforts today is to gain a video thumbnail listing for your business within the standard web search results on Google and Bing, as shown in Figure 9.3.

Figure 9.3 Video results in Bing for <hot rod>

If you think video doesn't matter in your niche, we hope you'll reconsider. From e-commerce (Home Shopping Network has over 50,000 videos uploaded to YouTube) to B2B (IBM has video case studies—why not you?), online video is becoming ubiquitous. And people aren't just watching movie trailers or adorable kittens: In 2009, 43 percent of US online adults reported watching news and 38 percent watched educational videos online (source: Pew Internet). And one of our favorite Google Trends charts is this one, showing the increase in searches containing the words "watch online":

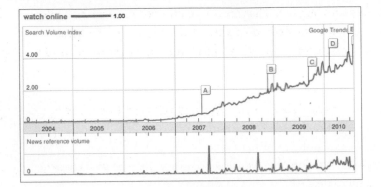

Video strategies can be boiled down to two approaches:

Sharing Your Videos for Webwide Distribution This usually involves uploading your video on video-sharing sites such as YouTube, which allows others to watch and share your videos off your site.

Making Your Videos Available Only on Your Site This usually involves hosting the videos on your site or a video-hosting and -delivery service, such as Brightcove or Bits on the Run, and publishing a video Sitemap to help the search engines find your videos and deliver searchers to your site.

Here's some help figuring out which approach is right for you and maximizing your presence either way.

To Upload or Not to Upload

Sometimes, we're amazed at all the original content people are just *giving* away to YouTube. Other times, we're shocked that a company *wouldn't* want to upload videos that could be useful in promoting their services. To decide whether video uploads are a good strategy for your organization, ask yourself these questions:

- Are these videos directly or indirectly promoting my business?
- Are these videos branded, and do they provide a clear identification of my organization and website?
- Would it be OK if these videos displayed on a total stranger's blog, with no link to my site or other identifying message?

- Am I completely comfortable with the terms of service of the upload site? (Yeah, we don't read those either. This time, you should.)

- Would I be happy if the video on the upload site started showing up among standard search results, possibly even higher than my own website?

If you answered no to any of these questions, then a video upload is probably not in your organization's best interest. If your videos exist primarily to engage, inform, or entertain your website visitors, and not as stand-alone marketing entities, then you may want viewers to see them only on your site. That means you'll need to forgo the upload option and stick to hosting the video on your own site. That way, any video listings you get in search results will bring people directly to your site, rather than the third-party video-sharing site.

Now: Decide whether your strategy will include uploading videos, showing videos on your site, or both.

There are four variations of the upload/not upload option for you to consider, each with its own special blend of ease, control, and search potential:

Upload only, and don't include the video on your site at all. This won't be a good strategy for most sites, but if you have technical or policy limitations that prevent the display of video on your site, you might consider it.

Upload video to a sharing site, and embed on your site using the video-sharing site as the host. This is a common approach because it's a piece of cake to set up, and it eliminates the cost and complication of hosting video yourself. The uploaded video may get a thumbnail in search engines, but the embedded one on your site probably won't. (In other words, YouTube will probably get the ranks and search traffic for your video.)

Upload video to a sharing site, and also host video on your own site or a streaming platform. We like the kitchen sink approach, because you may get a rank for the uploaded video, you may get a rank for the video on your site, or you may get both.

Don't upload—only host video on your own site or a streaming platform. With this highly controlled approach, you can be sure that any search listing for your video will link directly to your site, not the upload site page.

If your strategy is pointing you toward one of the first two options, some of the tips here will help you, but you should also read up on getting good ranks for your video-sharing pages in the book *YouTube and Video Marketing: An Hour a Day* (Sybex, 2009), or get helpful tips from ReelSEO at www.reelseo.com/video/marketing/youtube-marketing.

Your Site's Videos: Spidered

If you've decided to keep your videos exclusively on your site, read on to learn how to encourage the search engines to find, index, and prominently rank these videos.

Search engines can recognize and index videos on your site all by themselves, but they do a much better job if they get a little help from you, in the form of a video Sitemap or media RSS (mRSS) feed:

Google Video Sitemap A Google Video Sitemap is an XML file containing descriptive information about your videos, such as URL location, title, description, and duration. Here is the process:

1. Create your Sitemap (find quick instructions in the next sidebar, "Generating a Google Video Sitemap in Ridiculously Brief Detail") and upload it to your domain.

2. Log into Google Webmaster Tools and submit the Sitemap location.

   Creating a Google Video Sitemap is a simple and powerful way to improve your videos' chances at good indexing on Google and has been strongly recommended by Google reps. Here are some tips to maximize your Sitemap's effectiveness:

   - Although the Sitemap protocol allows multiple videos on a single URL, we recommend that each video be presented on a separate URL. That way, they may each get their own, individually optimized thumbnail listings.

   - Match the Sitemap <title> and <description> to the HTML title and meta description for the page on which the video is presented.

   - Include all the minimum required information, but also consider going beyond the minimum. Your Sitemap can include beyond-the-basics parameters such as tags, category, publication date, family-friendly status, and rating.

   - We've seen Google generate thumbnails for videos that don't have thumbnail images specified in the Sitemap. But why leave it up to the search engine to create your thumbnails? Make your own thumbnails if at all possible.

For full Google Video Sitemap instructions, visit Google Webmaster Center at www.google.com/support and search for <video sitemap>.

Media RSS (mRSS) Feed An mRSS feed accomplishes the same basic goal as a Google Video Sitemap: It provides descriptive information about your videos in a way that search engines can read. The mRSS feed format is accepted by both Google and Bing and is also a more generally accepted syndication format. In 2010, Bing introduced the Bing mRSS feed, which is like the standard mRSS feed with a few additional Bing-specific parameters.

What's not so great about the mRSS feed is that it's significantly more cumbersome to create than a Google Video Sitemap. Throw Bing a bone and read up on its mRSS recommendations here: www.bing.com/toolbox/media/p/9602766.aspx.

Like two schoolyard foes reluctantly shaking hands, Bing and Google will each accept the other's preferred type of Sitemap (with some caveats: Bing will accept a Google Video Sitemap as long as it contains Bing's minimum required information). Give it a try if you want to avoid learning two different specs.

Now: Create your Google Video Sitemap or mRSS feed or figure out who in your organization will do this, and get the ball rolling.

Generating a Google Video Sitemap in Ridiculously Brief Detail

For each video page, you'll need the following minimum information in your video sitemap:

- The title of the video (match the HTML title on the page), in the `<video:title>` tag
- A brief description of the video, in the `<video:description>` tag
- The location on your site where you've uploaded a thumbnail (recommended: 120 × 90 pixels in JPEG, PNG, or GIF formats), in the `<video:thumbnail_loc>` tag
- The URL of the page where visitors will view the video, in the `<loc>` tag
- The URL of the location where the video is hosted, in the `<video:content_loc>` tag and/or the SWF player URL, in the `<video:player_loc>` tag

Put this information into an XML file, as seen in the following sample text:

```
<urlset xmlns="http://www.sitemaps.org/schemas/sitemap/0.9" ➥
 xmlns:video="http://www.google.com/schemas/sitemap-video/1.1">
  <url>
    <loc>http://www.mysite.com/my-video-1.html</loc>
    <video:video>
      <video:title>My Awesome Video by Joe</video:title>
      <video:description>Here's a video of Joline</video:description>
      <video:thumbnail_loc>http://www.mysite.com/pic.jpg ➥
</video:thumbnail_loc>
      <video:content_loc>http://www.mysite.com/myvideo.flv ➥
</video:content_loc>
      <video:player_loc allow_embed="no"> ➥
http://www.mysite.com/videoplayer.swf</video:player_loc>
    </video:video>
  </url>
</urlset>
```

For more details, go to www.google.com/support/webmasters and search for <creating a video sitemap>.

Video Optimization

You've got a feed and your videos are rolling. Here are some places to include your nicely dressed, keyword-rich messaging (most of these tips apply both for videos on your site and for video uploads):

On-Page Text and Links to the Video Page As we mentioned previously, make sure all the videos on your site are presented on individual URLs. Text near the video, and links pointing to the video page, give contextual help to search engines, so include keywords there.

Video File Name Just like search-friendly URLs for HTML pages, video file names should contain descriptive terms, separated by hyphens.

Closed Captions and Transcripts If there's anyone who needs closed captions to understand a video, it's a search engine robot! Text in closed captions on YouTube is indexed in Google. It's only a matter of time before all closed captions are indexed, so take advantage of this opportunity to get that keyword-rich content into the search engines. If you can't include closed captions, consider adding a transcript of your video in HTML text on the same page as the video.

Video File Metadata Many video-production/encoding tools allow the input of metadata in the video file itself. This can include content-specific elements such as title, description, or even a text transcript, and can also include technical information such as format/encoding quality. If you have control over these elements, there's no reason not to include keywords.

Google Video Sitemap and Media RSS Tags Of particular usefulness in SEO are the `<title>`, `<description>`, `<keyword>`, and `<text>` tags in your Google Video Sitemap and mRSS feed. We've already given you guidelines for title, description, and keyword tags for your web pages—that advice applies to tags that are describing your video content, too! As for the mRSS `<text>` tag, that's a great opportunity to include a full-text transcript of your video, if you can.

 Now: Look at your onsite or uploaded videos and find opportunities for optimization improvement.

You've hatched a plan to get more eyes on your videos. Now, let's hop on over to another vertical: blog search.

Wednesday: Blog Search

You've got great ideas, your writing is top-notch, and it's all coming together in the form of an appealing blog. But if you're like many bloggers, you may have built your blog around content with no thought about text optimization or an SEO-friendly structure. We'll get started finding and fixing any problems today.

Your blog posts (and comment pages, and category pages, and anything else in your blog with a unique URL) can be displayed in the search results just like any other page. Or they can be displayed in a blog vertical such as Google's, which is accessed by clicking on the "Blogs" link, as shown here:

The optimization tips you work through today will help your blog positioning in both standard and vertical search results.

Basics of Blog Optimization

The on-page optimization you've already implemented provides a strong start to your search engine presence. But your blog optimization needs to go a few steps further to take advantage of the increased opportunities in search that blogs offer.

Since every one of your blog posts can be considered an equally important landing page, consider optimization rules as best practices that apply to every post. Here are a few touchpoints. Try to follow as many of them as you can, as often as you can:

- If you're creating a new blog, include keywords in your blog name. Many of your inbound links will use the name of your blog within the linking text, so this will provide a rankings boost.

- On your home page, include a tagline or other permanent text describing the blog. Since blog home page content is always changing, a basic description of your blog will provide consistent text, optimized for your top-priority keywords, for search engine robots to find.

- Write post titles that describe the content of the post and form a complete thought. Sometimes, these titles (rather than HTML titles) will be displayed on Bing's blog vertical results as the clickable text. See Figure 9.4 for an example.

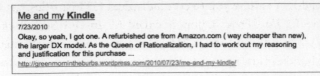

Me and my **Kindle**

7/23/2010

Okay, so yeah, I got one. A refurbished one from Amazon.com (way cheaper than new), the larger DX model. As the Queen of Rationalization, I had to work out my reasoning and justification for this purchase ...

http://greenmomintheburbs.wordpress.com/2010/07/23/me-and-my-kindle/

Figure 9.4 In this blog post, "Me and my Kindle" is the post title, not the HTML title for the page.

- Include keywords in your post title. Not only are post titles prominent in important on-page locations such as the URL, HTML title, and page heading, but they are likely to be the clickable text that others use when they link to your page.

- Use a search-friendly permalink URL for all posts. A simple formula is the-post-title-separated-by-hyphens. Popular blog authoring tools will allow you to make this the default setting. Here's how to do it in WordPress: click Settings > Permalink, select Custom Structure, and type in the following default file name: **/%postname%/**.

- Set your authoring tool to ping update services every time you write a new post. In Blogger, the answer to the settings question "Let search engines find your blog?" should be a resounding "Yes!" In WordPress, choose Settings > Writing, and enter the following URL under Update Services: **http://rpc.pingomatic.com/**.

- Tag your posts with descriptive, keyword-rich tags, as seen here:

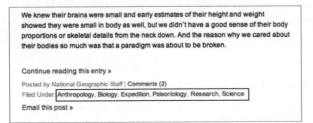

We knew their brains were small and early estimates of their height and weight showed they were small in body as well, but we didn't have a good sense of their body proportions or skeletal details from the neck down. And the reason why we cared about their bodies so much was that a paradigm was about to be broken.

Continue reading this entry »

Posted by National Geographic Staff | Comments (2)

Filed Under: Anthropology, Biology, Expedition, Paleontology, Research, Science

Email this post »

Not only will tags add keywords to your page in a useful and meaningful way, but the tag result pages that your users reach after clicking on these links are often inherently good SEO landing pages because they are so topic focused.

 Now: Take a look at your most recent blog post. How many of the best practices listed here did you cover?

If you've discovered that your posts aren't making the grade, today's the day to set up your new standards for the future.

Plug-in Power

Your blog post pages probably have a default HTML title and description built in. But you shouldn't settle for default optimization. We want you to dig deeper into SEO options.

If your authoring tool doesn't allow you to edit individual HTML titles, get a plug-in that makes it possible. In WordPress, a plug-in called All-In-One SEO Pack does the trick. Word on the street is that your HTML title should follow this pattern: {Post Title}:{Blog Title}, but customize yours to suit your individual needs. If your post titles tend to be long and your blog title is an important part of the branding, you may want to switch to {Blog Title}:{Post Title} or another variation. If you tend to give your postings titles that wouldn't have any meaning out of context, like "Today", take the time to write more descriptive HTML titles for these pages.

Now: If your blog authoring tool does not allow individual title tag edits, find a plug-in and set it up today.

With title tags squared away, explore more customization options. For example, if you use WordPress to write your blog, here is a sampling of what you can accomplish with free plug-ins:

- Automatically update an XML Sitemap and submit it to Google and Bing when you write a new post.
- Display a "tweet this" or Facebook Like button on each blog post.
- Add Google Analytics tracking capabilities to your blog.
- Control your canonical tags on each post.
- Display content related to the search queries that brought your audience to the blog (for example, "Searching for 'wholesale green clay'? You might like this related post...").

  Here are a few places to read up on available options for your blog:
- http://wordpress.org/extend/plugins/
- http://plugins.movabletype.org/
- www.sixapart.com/typepad/widgets/
- www.google.com/support/blogger/bin/topic.py?hl=en&topic=12453

Now: Explore plug-in or customization potential for your blog.

Blog Promotion

Your blog promotion efforts can range far beyond on-page optimization. If you're ready to get even more bloggerific, here are a few promotion directions you should explore:

Reach out. Like any site, your blog needs inbound links. *Unlike* other types of sites, blogs exist in the midst of a wildly link-happy environment.

Last month you learned about getting more connected in your online marketing efforts. For bloggers, this social element is mandatory.

Pearl of Wisdom: The best way to get your blog noticed is to actively participate in a community of bloggers.

Today, we want you to set a blog outreach goal that feels realistically within your capabilities. Can you join one conversation outside your own blog per week? How about writing one pithy comment a month? If even that sounds too hard, here's an easier assignment: Once a week, make a point of linking to another blog from one of your posts. Bloggers notice those links and are likely to reciprocate once in a while.

Claim your blog. Technorati allows you to officially "claim" your blog and take some control over how your blog listings look in search results on the site. For more information, read their FAQ, here: technorati.com/blog-claiming-faq/.

Tell your community. If you have a following on Facebook or Twitter, use those venues to spread the word every time you publish a new blog post. You can make these announcements manually, or you can use a blog plug-in such as MT-Twitter (for MovableType) or TweetMyBlog (for WordPress) for added convenience.

Feeding a Hungry Web

Most blogging tools will automatically create a feed, which is simply a file listing information (title, description, permalink, and so on) about each of your posts. Originally developed for syndicating content, feeds are now a major distribution venue for all web content, with many savvy consumers ditching the surfing part of their web experience altogether and opting to let content come directly to them via a feed.

There are zillions of ways to optimize and promote your feed, but you only have an hour a day. If you use one of the most popular blog authoring tools, such as WordPress or MovableType, the ping setting described under Blog Optimization should work nicely for you. If you're motivated to go the extra mile in promoting your feed, we suggest signing up for an account at Google-owned FeedBurner.com, which offers helpful optimization and monitoring tools for feeds.

Now: Set a blog promotion and connected marketing goal for your website. Can you write a comment on a related blog today?

With blog search optimization in your pocket, come along with us to one of the most exciting and rapidly evolving areas of SEO: mobile search.

Thursday: Mobile Search

As Google engineer Matt Cutts put it in a 2009 interview, mobile search "will be a big trend." Mobile searches made up nearly 10 percent of Google searches in June 2010, according to comScore, and the research firm Gartner forecasts that Mobile Web use will outpace desktop web use by the year 2013.

Today, we'll walk you through mobile search basics and point you toward a more mobile-friendly future. Most important, we hope to motivate you to take mobile search seriously, especially if your business is a brick-and-mortar with a walk-in customer base.

Mobile Search Basics

A person can search the Web with a mobile device using the apps offered by major search engines, or with mobile-only search apps such as Taptu, Siri, or find.mobi, or with a full Internet browser on their device. There are also myriad non-search-based ways to navigate the Web on a mobile device, such as through social networks, niche databases such as BigOven for recipes or Pandora for music, or location-aware applications such as Foursquare.

Google and Bing have special robots that surf the Web to build the mobile versions of their search engines. When one of these mobile robots arrives at your site, it identifies itself as a phone or other mobile device, and then it takes a look at what your site has to offer the mobile user. If your site shows a well-formatted, mobile-screen-sized functional mini-site, your site is likely to be indexed and favored by the mobile search engines. If your site shows the standard web page, then you can expect some disadvantages in mobile search.

Your first step to mobile search success is to see whether your website is indexed in mobile search engines. To check Google mobile search, visit google.com/m and search for your site using a <site:> search. See Figure 9.5 for an example. On Bing, visit m.bing.com and perform the same search.

> **Now:** Check to see if your site is indexed in Google and Bing mobile search.

Knowing your site is indexed is a great start. Next, we want you to check whether it renders successfully on mobile devices.

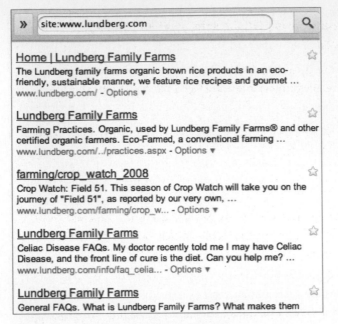

Figure 9.5 Checking for your site in Bing mobile search

Because so many websites don't display good mobile versions, mobile search engines sometimes employ a workaround. It's called *site transcoding,* and simply put, it means that the search engines generate their own, mobile-friendly version of your web page. What's not so pretty about this is that folks looking at the transcoded page aren't actually visiting your site's URLs. If they link to the page or bookmark it, they won't be linking to your domain; they'll be linking to the search engine's domain. What rot!

We haven't found a mobile device emulator for the desktop browser that we really trust. Until one is available, our best suggestion is to check out your site on a smartphone—yours or one you borrow for a few minutes. Open up your site and see what you find!

Now: View your site on a mobile device. Assess whether improvement is needed.

Playing for the Hometown Crowd with Gowalla, Facebook Places, and Foursquare

The details vary, but the general model is the same: Location-aware games and social networking services allow users to check in at physical locations such as bars, restaurants, parks, or museums, and broadcast their location to a select—or not-so-select—group of friends. Major location-aware tools include Foursquare, Facebook Places, Google Latitude, Yelp, and Gowalla.

Playing for the Hometown Crowd with Gowalla, Facebook Places, and Foursquare *(Continued)*

These services offer incentives to players who check in. For example, on Foursquare, players with the most check-ins at a location are declared the mayor of that location, which introduces a fun, competitive element.

Here are a few thoughts on how you can use location-aware services as marketing opportunities for your business:

Get Reviews

In addition to checking in, players can provide business feedback, making location-aware services a potentially important source of good (or bad!) word of mouth. Find out which services your clientele use, and encourage them to post reviews there.

Encourage Loyalty

Want repeat custies for your custard shop? Advertise special offers to people who check into your location. Services like Foursquare and Gowalla allow business owners to provide deals and giveaways to nearby players, which means people may be flocking to you for the perks.

Let Friends Advertise to Friends

Checking into a location is another way of saying "I endorse this business." Because location-aware services allow users to see where their friends are shopping, eating, getting haircuts, and so on, your local business may be able to indirectly reach out to friends of friends simply by being a check-in destination.

If you don't have big plans for your presence on location-aware services, at the very least you should create or claim a listing for your business. This will help you maintain control of your branding and prevent multiple variations of your business listings from popping up by well-meaning users who create listings for you.

Mobile Optimization

When someone opens up a search engine app on their device and speaks or types a query, the search engine does something similar to what it would do with a standard desktop-based query: It finds and returns a web page that it thinks matches the query best. All of the optimization you've been working on throughout Your SEO Plan will serve your website well in mobile search just as it does in desktop search. Here are some additional tips to keep in mind for mobile search optimization:

Pages that render nicely may rank better. Search engines on mobile devices want to provide a result that will be functional and readable on those devices. Your site may rank better and avoid site transcoding—and it will definitely provide a better user experience—if you create pages formatted for mobile devices. You might build separate pages, which are often given URLs such as `m.mysite.com` (the "m" represents "mobile"), or you could create a special style sheet suitable for mobile screens. Be sure to think about what mobile users might want to do on your site that is different than a person surfing from their desk. For more on running desktop and mobile versions of your website, visit `http://googlewebmastercentral.blogspot.com/2009/11/running-desktop-and-mobile-versions-of.html`.

Creating a mobile Sitemap is a best practice. Submitting a mobile Sitemap is likely to help mobile search engines discover and list your mobile pages correctly. To read up on the mobile Sitemap specs, visit `www.google.com/support/webmasters/` and search for <mobile sitemap>.

Local search ranks are extremely important in mobile search. Because it's possible for a mobile search engine to know exactly where a person is when they perform the search, it's likely that mobile search will incorporate location as a factor in results. Google's "Near me now," shown in Figure 9.6, is an example of a mobile search enhancement that incorporates the searcher's location into search results.

Figure 9.6 Google applies location information to mobile search.

Keyword searches are shorter. People just don't type long queries into mobile devices. That means keyword searches are shorter in length, and search engine suggestions (see Figure 9.7 for an example) gain in importance, because people are more likely to rely on the search engines to finish their thoughts for them. If you haven't looked at the search suggestions that come up when a person has typed the first one or two words of your top-priority keyword phrase, you should do that now.

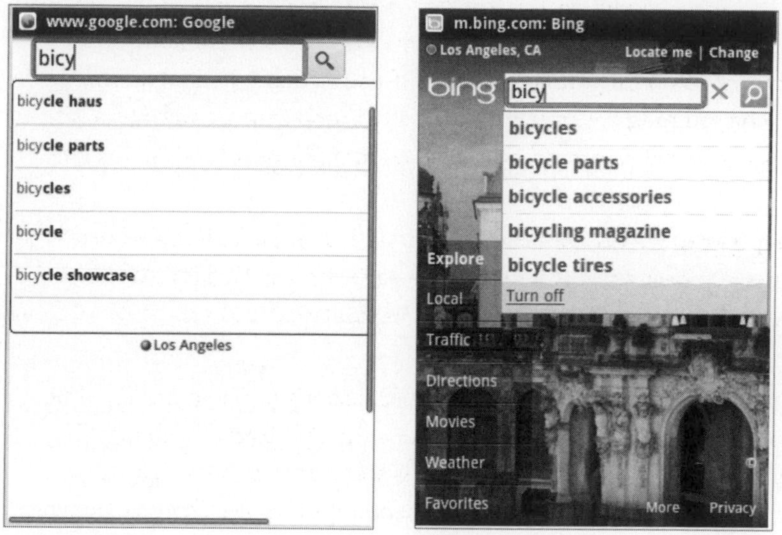

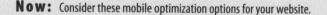

Figure 9.7 Google and Bing search suggestions on a mobile device

Now: Consider these mobile optimization options for your website.

The future of mobile navigation probably will not follow the traditional Person Enters Keyword > Person Gets Website procedure, so you need to be nimble in the mobile search space. Our advice: Gear yourself with whatever mobile technologies your potential customers are using. As an avid user yourself, you'll have a much easier time staying current with opportunities in mobile search marketing.

Friday: Improve Your Search Engine Snippets

You've already learned that searchers choose which result to click in a matter of seconds. Of course, you want your site to have the best possible representation in the search results—and that means you need a snippet that's on your side!

How Snippets Work

A snippet is text taken from a web page and shown when that page is listed in the search results. Google and Bing display snippets for many (but not all) search results. The most important thing to understand about search result snippets is that they are different depending on what keyword has been searched. For example, a Google search for the term <animal cloning> returns this snippet:

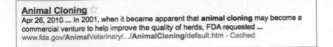

A search for the term <animal cloning risk> returns a different snippet for the same web page:

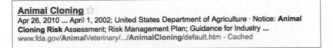

Notice how each snippet includes the keywords that were searched? That means a search for your company name will return a much different snippet than a search for another of your target keywords will, even if both results point to your home page!

Here are some basic rules for how snippets are generated:

- If the page contains the exact search phrase in the visible text on the page, it is displayed in the snippet along with roughly 50 to 150 characters of surrounding text.

- The snippet often excludes titles and navigational elements.

- If the landing page doesn't include the exact phrase searched, the snippet will show sentences that include the individual words in the phrase.

- Searched terms, along with stemmed and plural versions of the words (cloned, cloning, clones), are bolded in the snippet.

- Enhancements, such as breadcrumb navigation, review stars, and sitelinks, are added when the search engines have the information to do so.

Check Your Snippets

The first step to optimizing your snippets is reviewing them. To check your snippets, simply open the search engine of your choice and search for your target keywords. Scroll to your search result and see what you find.

Now: Search for your target keywords on Google and Bing. How do your listings look?

There may be other keywords you want to check as well. If you know phrases outside of your top-priority terms that are bringing traffic to your website, take a look and see if those snippets could use a makeover, too.

Snippet Makeover Basics

If you came across some snippets that you would like to improve, here are some possible approaches:

Add text. Sometimes, improving a snippet is as simple as adding one keyword-rich sentence to your page copy. Be sure that it is formatted the same as the rest of the page copy—titles and headers may not show up in snippets. And use your good copywriting skills so it doesn't seem jarring or tacked on.

Remove unnecessary ALT attributes. A graphic button displaying the words "Free Delivery in February!" should have an <img> ALT attribute containing matching text. But a tiny graphic that is used to create a corner on a button does not need an ALT attribute stating "white button corner." The page will be just fine without it.

Change your error messages. Search engine robots come calling at your website without any of the plug-ins, cookies, or JavaScript enabling that your site may require. If you're not careful, your search engine snippet might end up looking like this:

> this **site** requires **Flash Player** ☆
> this **site** requires **Flash** Player 8 or later. DOWNLOAD FLASH PLAYER · Mobile **Website** <<
> Click Here · Jobs Offered << Click Here ...
> www.mintny.com/ - Cached - Similar

We've already shown you the best ways to avoid this kind of listing: Be a stickler for good robot-readable content. But if you still have the odd error message making its way into the search results, remember that these messages are usually written by programmers without a marketing once-over. You might want to get in the loop!

> **Now:** Assemble your suggested edits for snippet improvement. Deliver them to whoever needs to make the changes, or complete the edits yourself.

If your search engine listings are haunted by an ugly description from an Open Directory or Yahoo! Directory listing, there are special meta tags that can help with your snippet makeover. Learn about them at www.yourseoplan.com/meta-tags.html.

The makeover doesn't have to stop here. Enhance your listings with goodies like extra links, breadcrumbs, and review stars. We'll show you how in Chapter 10, "Extra Credit and Guilt-Free Slacking."

We think you'll be glad you took this week's trek to the cutting edge of search. Now you'll get into an R&D groove as Your SEO Plan enters its next week!

xtra cred

xtra cred

Week 10: Research and Development

You're more than halfway through Your SEO Plan, which means it won't be long before you're out in the SEO wilderness on your own. We want the transition to be a pleasant one, so this week, we'll focus on showing you the best ways to research SEO and develop your ongoing plan. The goal is for you to come away with an approach to use whenever you need to learn something new about search.

If you aren't yet confident in your advanced searching skills, or if you generally don't trust an answer unless you get it in writing from a paid expert, this week will help you stretch your abilities and save your money in the long run!

Monday and Tuesday: SEO News and Trends

Wednesday: International Search

Thursday: Testing

Friday: Analytics Meditation

Monday and Tuesday: SEO News and Trends

SEO moves fast! In the weeks since you started doing SEO, there have probably been a few changes (significant or not so significant) introduced by the major search engines, big advances in mobile search technologies, and, oh, about 40 new SEO and social marketing tools that will do everything but wipe your nose, for a small fee. It might seem that every time you go out for a cup of coffee, you come back to a whole new set of important players, rumors, and must-haves that weren't there before.

You're busy, so nobody expects you to keep up with every little twist and turn along the SEO highway. In fact, staying a month or so behind the times can prevent you from crowding your brain with unnecessary SEO rumors and speculation:

Pearl of Wisdom: You can skip a heck of a lot of daily SEO minutiae and still get enough of the overall story line to know what's important, as long as you keep the Eternal Truths of SEO in mind and stay focused on your audience and your desired conversions.

But we recommend keeping up at least a passing knowledge of SEO current events and stashing some solid SEO researching skills in your tool belt. When it comes time to do SEO on your own, you'll need them! Coming up, we'll show you where to look.

SEO News and Advice

One day soon you're going to need to learn something about SEO, something specific to your own site that we didn't cover in this book. The Web is the only way to keep up with the latest SEO news and trends. Unfortunately, not every site is reputable, so you'll need to turn on your heavy-duty BS detector. You can't go wrong if you stick with articles on the following sites:

Search Engine Land (http://searchengineland.com) Danny Sullivan and a team of industry leaders offer a site bursting with updated search engine tips and insider information that nobody else comes close to. This well-organized and always up-to-the-minute site covers tips and news on a variety of topics, including organic SEO, paid search, and social media. The "How To: PPC" section is particularly helpful in breaking down paid search setup, management, and reporting tasks for newcomers.

Mashable (www.mashable.com) Pumping out smart and timely news on social media, the Mobile Web, and other tech topics, Mashable is a terrific resource for early adopters, curious consumers, and savvy marketers alike to stay up-to-date on the latest developments. Particularly useful are its reviews of new social tools and website features.

Sphinn (www.sphinn.com) Sphinn is a venue that takes over some of the information vetting for you, because the more trusted and more popular SEO articles rise to the top based on editorial review. A property of Third Door Media (which also runs www.searchengineland.com and the SMX conferences), Sphinn is a convenient place to see the advice of many well-respected SEO experts in a single eyespan.

SEOmoz (www.seomoz.org) Primarily a developer and provider of useful SEO tools (we recommend their Open Site Explorer tool at www.opensiteexplorer.org for link assessment), SEOmoz offers great guides and advice on tricky SEO topics. The person behind the site is Rand Fishkin, a well-known SEO consultant who has turned his focus to making the SEO process easier to quantify with the right tools.

HighRankings.com (www.highrankings.com) Jill Whalen offers cheerful, no-nonsense, often low-tech advice that's perfect for do-it-yourself SEO practitioners of all stripes.

ClickZ News (www.clickz.com) The ClickZ network as a whole offers an impressive gamut of expert advice, news, and commentary on all avenues of interactive marketing, not just SEO.

ReelSEO (www.reelseo.com) ReelSEO is the most in-depth resource for video SEO tips and best practices and video SEO news on the Web. The handy how-tos and timely analysis (much of it provided in the form of video) will help you keep your video SEO efforts one step ahead of your competitors.

Occam's Razor, by Avinash Kaushik (www.kaushik.net/avinash/) Author, speaker, and official analytics evangelist for Google, Avinash Kaushik combines unbridled enthusiasm and scientific methodology in this useful and engaging blog, which focuses on interpreting web analytics to improve your website and your business.

Information Overload

A thread on a search forum asked SEO professionals how they spend an average day on the job. Looking at the responses, you would think they are paid based on the number of search engine blogs they read, how many SEO podcasts are filling their libraries, and how many thousands of forum postings they've racked up. We won't bash this lifestyle, but we realized long ago that there's no need to live it.

Reading SEO info online can make even a seasoned Internet researcher hyperventilate. There are so many acronyms, rumors, and arguments (not to mention posturing), and so much conflicting advice that even if you understand what's being said, you probably shouldn't believe it at first blush. Follow these words of warning as you get your bearings in the overstimulating world of SEO news and advice:

- Always check an article or blog post's date before you read it. This way you'll know whether you're reading something brand-new or a two-year-old history lesson from the archives.

- Agencies offering SEO services publish a lot of great information on their sites—and a lot of questionable stuff, too. If you're inclined to follow the advice from an SEO firm's website, do a search for the author's name to help you determine if they are reputable in the larger SEO community. Here are some indicators that the advice you're reading is reliable: Multiple people on multiple sites seem to be giving the same advice, you can corroborate this advice via an article written by a recognized SEO expert, or you can find your own evidence (using the "I wonder why that's happening" method) to back it up.

- Pace yourself. Unless you've got a life-or-death situation (and these are very infrequent in SEO), take in a little information at a time. SEO resources on the Web are great for researching specific questions on a need-to-know basis. Just do your best to tune out arcane details, like which Google search tab moved where or how many pages Bing says it has in its index today.

In a short time, you'll have enough SEO expertise that you'll be able to choose a few sources that you trust and stick with them.

SEO Forums

In a conversation we had with Danny Sullivan, he cautioned, "Forums probably aren't the best place for beginners. They should do a lot of reading from more focused sites before diving in. As for advice, be wary of everything and always remember that nothing should be taken as fact." To begin your own SEO forum research, start with these tried-and-true conversation spots:

- `http://forums.searchenginewatch.com`

- `www.highrankings.com/forum/`

- www.webmasterworld.com
- www.searchengineforums.com
- www.webproworld.com
- Or search several SEO forums here: www.seroundtable.com/forums.html

Jump in on the forums whenever you have a burning question that needs answering, but don't count on them for your regular SEO news fix.

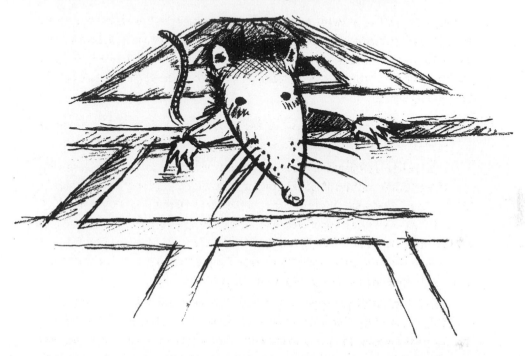

Search Engine Insiders

Perhaps as consolation for the hours SEO pros spend trying to divine the processes and preferences of the secret search algorithms, the search engines have offered up some genuinely nice and helpful people who give guidance to webmaster types on getting the most out of search for your site.

Matt Cutts (www.mattcutts.com/blog/) An honest-to-goodness SEO celebrity, the head of Google's Webspam team is a prolific writer and speaker on the topic of structuring websites in a way that benefits both visitors and search engines. Matt's clear language and tendency to provide helpful context and examples (plus his enviable intimacy with Google's algorithm) make his blog a terrific source of webmaster-friendly advice on staying on the good side of Google's quality guidelines.

Maile Ohye (http://maileohye.com/) Maile's blog, "Love and Technology," is a little of both, but we're adding her to this list because we recommend the technology part.

Maile coordinates Google Webmaster Central outreach efforts as a senior developer programs engineer and is a frequent conference speaker. Maile's advice is usually directed at webmasters, and her blog may not be the ideal spot for nontechie SEO newbies. For those well versed in tech vocabulary, however, she discusses many site, server, and search issues in a way that is refreshingly clear and straightforward.

Google Webmaster Central Blog (http://googlewebmastercentral.blogspot.com/) This is the spot to learn about official new algorithm changes and new tools for diagnosing problems with your site or promoting it on Google. Just for fun, watch the news get posted here first, then check out Twitter to watch the SEO pros' analysis start to fly. You may also find helpful specifics for shopping search and mobile search at http://googlemerchantblog.blogspot.com and http://googlemobile.blogspot.com.

Bing Webmaster Center Blog (www.bing.com/community/blogs/webmaster/) Keep your eyes on Bing's Webmaster Center Blog to learn about big changes at Bing and new features in Bing Webmaster Tools.

Yahoo! Search Blog (www.ysearchblog.com) This is a multipurpose blog pointing out topics of interest for searchers, developers, webmasters, and advertisers.

Almost every individual and site we've just recommended has one or more Twitter accounts. If you are inclined to use Twitter as a daily source of self-improvement, click "follow" when you visit the sites, and let Twitter bring the news and tips to you. You may also want to follow lists that SEO insiders have assembled; here are a couple of Twitter lists containing well-known SEO personalities:

- http://twitter.com/stonetemple/seo

- http://twitter.com/sengineland/team

- http://twitter.com/aaranged/inhouse-seo

Conferences

Although the fees can be steep, nothing else compares to the learning benefits of immersing yourself in the inspiration, ideas, and considerable jargon coming directly from SEO industry leaders live and in person. Here are a few popular conferences:

Search Marketing Expo (SMX) Danny Sullivan's Third Door Media is the organizational force behind Search Marketing Expo (SMX) conferences, which inspire SEO pros and beginners alike in North America, Europe, and Australia. Separate SMX Advanced conferences are also offered in select cities. Visit www.searchmarketingexpo.com for locations and registration.

Search Engine Strategies (SES) Search Engine Strategies (SES) conferences are held throughout the world, covering a broad range of search-related topics for participants of all levels. SES is owned by Incisive Media, publisher of ClickZ and the Search Engine Watch website. Learn more at www.searchenginestrategies.com.

PubCon PubCon, the conference arm of WebmasterWorld, takes place primarily in Las Vegas but sometimes extends to other big cities. This conference has a slightly more tech-centric reputation than the other conferences. Sign up at www.pubcon.com.

Training

Here are some of the better-known SEO training providers:

Bruce Clay "Bruce Clay" is synonymous with "SEO Training" in many minds. Offering comprehensive training sessions for marketing and design staff, and advanced certification for SEO professionals, Bruce Clay and his staff hold trainings at their California and New York facilities, or they can come to yours. Visit www.bruceclay.com/seo/training.htm to sign up.

SEOmoz Pro Training Series This Seattle-based training series (www.seomoz.org/seminar/series) is aimed at consultants and agencies who want to sharpen their SEO skills.

Conference Training Tracks

- As a nod to the newbies, the big search conferences offer specialized training opportunities and boot camps concurrently with their conference events. These include:

  - PubCon's one-day, two-track training program (www.pubcon.com/training.htm) brings in top SEO and online marketing pros to train those who have some catching up to do before the full conference begins.

  - SMX Boot Camp is "bringing search marketers up to speed" by offering intensive training sessions on the fundamentals of SEO and paid search. Visit www.searchmarketingexpo.com to see if SMX Boot Camp is coming to a city near you.

  - Visit www.searchenginestrategies.com and click on the city of your choice to see if SES training programs are offered in conjunction with an SES conference.

Webinars

Often cheap and sometimes free, webinars can be excellent learning tools for those without the budget for tuition or travel. Most webinars have a sponsor, and therefore a sales agenda, so while you're listening for helpful tips and tricks, try to remember that recommended tools or services are often advertisements.

- SEOmoz Pro webinars (www.seomoz.org/dp/pro-webinars) offer good ideas from SEO consultants, including strategy discussions and site reviews (you can even submit your own site for consideration). For a monthly fee, you can have access to all the SEOmoz tools, written guides, and webinars.

- Search Marketing Now (www.searchmarketingnow.com) offers a large array of free webinars on many topics that interest the online marketer.
- ClickZ offers online events and webinars featuring some of the industry's most established brands at www.clickz.com/webcasts.

Now: Go get schooled in SEO!

Bonus points if you can slip something interesting and *au courant* about SEO into your next conversation with your boss.

Wednesday: International Search

The Internet knows no borders, but unfortunately, your SEO campaign does. If your target audience includes an overseas component, you need to learn strategies for international SEO and put a focused effort into your international visibility. Ask yourself which country you are targeting. Is your international audience composed of English speakers? Which languages do you want to target? Answer these questions for your organization, and then start your research on international SEO with these general guidelines in mind:

International Paid Search Marketing Google AdWords and Microsoft adCenter make it easy to add new campaigns and set them up for different countries and languages. If you are planning to show your current ads to an international audience, it's very simple to edit the targeting preferences to include additional countries.

You should custom-write your ads for international site visitors, even if they speak the same language as your locally targeted ads, to address their different terminology or needs. Separate sites or landing pages will also improve localization.

International Organic Optimization Let's say you want your chic boutique website to rank well for searchers in France searching for the French words <parapluie jaune>. One approach would be to choose this term as one of your top target keywords and optimize your landing page accordingly. Good start, but there's more you can do to optimize for the geographic audience you desire. Here are a few tips to help you sell more of those yellow umbrellas:

> **DO make sure your landing page is written in the language of the country you want to target.** Your page titles and meta description tags should be in the target language, too. Even though there's an HTML meta tag that allows you to specify which language your web page is written in, the search engine robots will likely ignore it and look at the web page text to make their own determination of language. Don't confuse the search engines by sticking substantial portions of several different languages on the same page. From the Google Webmaster Central blog,

"You can help to make language recognition easier if you stick to only one language per page and avoid side-by-side translations."

DON'T use your home page for the sole purpose of selecting a language. If you are creating several subsites or site sections in different languages, don't waste precious home page real estate on choosing a language. Instead, include high-quality content in your most important language, with links to other language choices.

DO use a country-specific domain. Your site will get a lift if it has the appropriate country domain (also called a top-level domain, or TLD). This is a big clue to the search engines that the site should be shown to a searcher in your target country. The search engines look for multiple cues about whether your site is a good match for an international searcher, so in addition to having an appropriate TLD, it's advantageous to host your site in your target country, display local currency on the website, and even display a local address for your business.

DO consider building separate sites. Some sites redirect their international domains to their .com domain (for example, www.babyfuzzkin.co.uk and www.babyfuzzkin.de could both redirect to www.babyfuzzkin.com), and this is OK. Of course, it would be better—for your site and for your user—to create separate sites in separate languages (or in the various flavors of English), especially since key content like pricing and contact information may be different for each country. If you plan to display multiple languages within the same site, it's best to structure your site so that each language is in its own subdomain or subfolder. And don't fret:

Pearl of Wisdom: There's no duplicate content issue if your site displays the same information in multiple languages.

DON'T assume you know what language your target audience wants to read. Some sites automatically redirect visitors who are in a specific region to a particular language. This can be annoying for users and may confuse search engine robots. If you have similar content available in multiple languages, Google recommends linking translated versions of pages to each other to give the site visitor a choice and the search engine robot some context.

DO use Google Webmaster Tools to specify location. If you have separate sites targeting separate countries, you can specify your target country in Google Webmaster Tools (see Figure 9.8 for an example). If you have subdomains or subfolders targeting various countries, you will first need to set up individual Google Webmaster Tools profiles for each subdomain or subfolder, and then set your country targeting.

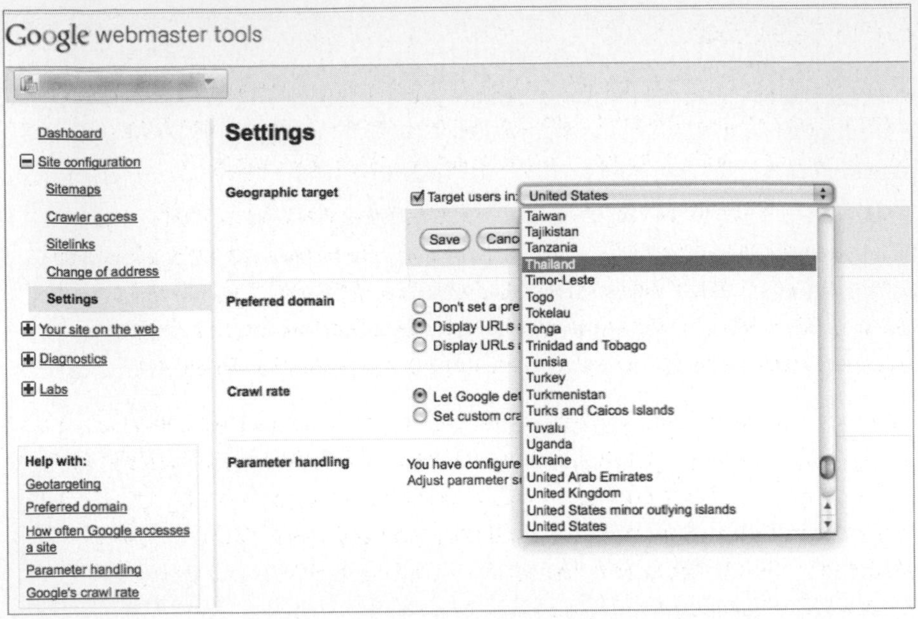

Figure 9.8 Setting geographic preferences in Google Webmaster Tools

DO seek inbound links from sites that are in your targeted countries. And be sure to request links in the appropriate language!

DO explore locally popular search sites. Find a list of worldwide search engines at www.searchenginecolossus.com, or follow the discussion about international search engines at www.webmasterworld.com/category93.htm.

You've probably figured out by now that a full-fledged international SEO campaign is outside the scope of your hour-a-day commitment. It may even involve a major web development effort, creating unique sites for each of your targeted countries. If international search is right for your site, here are the best places online to start reading up and developing your plan of attack:

- Search Engine Watch's International Search section at http://searchenginewatch.com/international-search.

- Search Engine Land's Multinational Search Column at http://searchengineland.com/library/multinational-search/.

- www.multilingual-search.com covers international SEO news and is owned by WebCertain Group, organizer of the International Search Summit (www.internationalsearchsummit.com).

- www.multilingual-seo.com is an international SEO forum, also run by WebCertain.

 Now: If international search is right for your site, start your research and determine your next steps.

Lost in Translation

So, you're planning to auto-translate your products page to another language. This low-budget approach is more than a little short-sighted, don't you think? (Or, to say the same thing using Google Translate, "Thrifty is the access to it, it is short, do not you think a little?")

If you're doing SEO right, you've spent hours researching keyword data for your website, pondered the importance of minor differences in phrases, and inserted your picks into your carefully crafted text. An auto-translation program won't come close to the quality of your original word-smithing. The resulting translation may confuse your international readers, or it may even be perceived as spam by the search engines, which may result in devaluation of your page.

If you use a firm that provides translation services, you may end up with a great translation…but it will probably be wholly unoptimized for search. Most translation firms do not have skilled SEO staff, nor are they paid to do keyword research or absorb your marketing message or your target audience's preferences and behavior. It's possible that you'll end up with similar shortcomings if you use an in-house staffer. After all, being fluent in two languages isn't the same thing as having strong SEO copywriting skills.

If you use a translation firm or a staffer to translate your site's text, it's often a good idea to overlap efforts by hiring a reputable local SEO firm in the country you are targeting to optimize the text and fine-tune the message. Targeting for multinational SEO goes far beyond language. To succeed, it requires research into culture and consumer behavior. A good local SEO firm may be able to provide additional value to your text by suggesting more culturally appropriate and effective messaging.

Thursday: Testing

In the first edition of this book, we wrote these fateful words: "You could easily gain some high ranks for, say, the term <hydroplaning monkey> because nobody else is optimizing for it…"

A few weeks later, mostly because of a hydroplaning-monkey sketch drawn in a Twizzler-induced haze, we posted a page at www.yourseoplan.com/hydroplaning-monkey .html, and in no time it was ranked #1 for the phrase on the major search engines. That's when the fun started! It wasn't long until someone else—an adoring fan, we hope—purchased the domain name hydroplaningmonkey.com and started to compete for the term. Over the intervening months, another domain, hydroplaning-monkey.com, appeared on the scene.

We love the fun and have continued to use the page to test various on-page optimization theories. In fact, we've found it so helpful that we're giving you a Hydroplaning Monkey day: a day to develop your own experiments. You don't have to create a new page or use nonsense phrases. Just try something new and keep track of the results.

Today, think of an SEO question or mystery, something that you've been wondering about, and an experimental approach to finding out what makes search engines tick. Here are a few ideas to get you started:

- Try updating the content on your top landing pages more frequently. Do your Google ranks improve? Do you see any difference in Google's crawl rate when you look at your site in Google Webmaster Tools?

- Change some of your Google AdWords ads from lowercase to title case, or vice versa. Do you notice a change in click-throughs?

- Find a page on your site that isn't indexed in the search engines and add a link to it from your home page. Did that do the trick?

- Add your full business address to every page on your site. Does this improve your visibility for local searches? How about on mobile devices?

- Convert your global navigation from images to text on just one page of your site. Did that page receive a rankings boost? What about the pages that this page links to?

- Change the color of your "Sign Up Now" button to bright orange, and increase the size by 50 percent. Did your conversions increase?

- Write a blog post that strays outside of your comfort zone, perhaps mimicking something that you like in someone else's blog but have never tried on your own. Now promote it on Facebook or Twitter (for example, "We tried something completely different on the blog today—what do you think?"). Do you have any new likes, retweets, mentions, or inlinks as a result?

Your experiments won't be truly scientific, of course, because you won't be working in a vacuum. Changes around the Web and on search engines will constantly interfere with what you learn. But we are quite certain that with a few of these tests under your belt, you'll have a whole new level of SEO confidence.

 Now: Think of an SEO experiment and get started!

Friday: Analytics Meditation

During your Prep Month, we pushed hard for you to set up an analytics program of some sort. We hope our message hit home and that you're sitting atop several weeks of data. If you still don't have any analytics capabilities, skip today's assignment and spend the hour in a serious effort to get some!

Today you're going to enter your analytics program and sift around the data, looking for jewels of insight. You are forbidden from focusing on the same metrics that you've been gathering forever, the key indicators that your boss asked for, or the measure that you read about in an article once. Instead, keep an open mind and look for information in unexpected places. We'll guide you with a few sample sessions:

- Are there any keywords that are bringing a large number of people to your site but for which you aren't providing a solution? For example, we once knew a site getting a lot of traffic for the term <buy wine> that didn't actually *sell* wine. Would there be any way to help those visitors or leverage that traffic?

- Which keywords are sending an unusually high percentage of people to undesirable pages? Which referring sites? Are you paying money for any of these clicks?

- Are you seeing anything in your analytics that seems too good (or bad) to be true? For example, reported bounce rates near 0 percent or 100 percent, or thousands of reported visits to your blog when you haven't seen a single comment from these supposed visitors? Could something be wrong with your analytics setup?

- Are there any entry pages on the site that surprise you? How many visitors are entering via the site map or Contact Us page? Are these pages designed appropriately for site entries?

- Look for patterns in navigation paths. For example, having a lot of people bouncing back and forth between two product pages may indicate that you need a comparison chart. Or are lots of visitors starting at a higher-priced product page and then clicking to a cheaper product? Maybe you need to work on explaining the benefits of the high-end product.

- Look for keyword trends. Are more people converting when they search for <hair loss treatment> or <hair loss prevention>? Rather than looking at the exact phrases, look for trends by filtering for *all* searches containing the words *treatment* or *prevention*.

- Review your site overlay if your analytics program offers this feature, which shows what links users are clicking on each page. Are a very large number of people going to just one place from your home page? Should you consider displaying that content directly on the home page? See Figure 9.9 for an example of a site overlay screen.

The purpose of today's exercise is to come away with an action, not just a finding.

Now: Look at your web analytics program and meditate on what you see, with an eye toward an action recommendation.

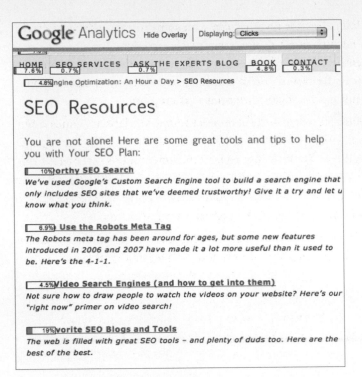

Figure 9.9 Google analytics site overlay feature

You've extended Your SEO Plan and expanded your mind this week. Now, get ready for a week of finding and fixing problems!

Week 11: What's Your Problem?

You're nearing the end of Your SEO Plan, so this week we'll give you a chance to tie up loose ends and chase down any remaining trouble spots in your search engine presence:

Monday: New Site, New Problems

Tuesday: Site Performance and Malware

Wednesday: Catch Up with Your Team

Thursday: Landing Page Optimization

Friday: Brand Busters

Monday: New Site, New Problems

It happens all the time, for big reasons or little ones, and it's one of the bigger challenges to an SEO campaign: a website redesign in which all or most of the URLs on the site change. Worst-case scenario: Every inbound link to your site is outdated. Bookmarks lead to broken links. Traffic plummets. Your search engine ranks drop off the map! And these problems can linger long after the revamp. But with some forethought, you can launch your redesign without suffering a dip in your search presence.

If your site was recently redesigned, or you're still working through repercussions from a long-ago revamp, or even if you're planning your site's next incarnation, here are some ideas for handling the sticky situations that crop up:

Page Redirects All of your outdated pages should redirect to appropriate new ones using a permanent redirect, called a *301 redirect*. Don't just redirect them to the home page. Ideally, each old page should redirect to a new page with similar subject matter. If this is not the case with your site, your task for today is to create a list of old URLs that are still getting visits and the new URLs that they should be redirecting to. Then send it to your IT team member, who can set up your 301 redirects on the server.

Google Webmaster Tools has a change of address capability if you're moving an entire site from an old domain name to a new one. In the tool, select Site Configuration > Change Of Address.

xtra cred

File Not Found Page Do you have a kinder, gentler File Not Found (*404 error*) page? The page should, first and foremost, apologize to your patient visitors for not being the page they're looking for. Next, it should *help them find the page they're looking for!* This could be by providing a site map, search box, or suggested links. And don't forget to include the global navigation on this page, just like on any other page of your site. If your File Not Found page is not helpful, your task is to propose new traffic-friendly content for the page and either implement it or deliver it to the person who can do so.

Inbound Links Do you still have a multitude of links pointing to your old URLs?

SEOmoz's free tool, Open Site Explorer, offers a handy way to see if broken pages are at the top of your list of pages that are receiving inbound links. (You'll have to pay to see the full list.) In Figure 9.10, Open Site Explorer shows that 18 different domains are linking to a broken URL, www.lundberg.com/recipes.html. It's likely to take much less effort to fix or redirect a broken URL and regain that lost link juice than it would take to gain 18 new inbound links.

If you have a verified account, Google Webmaster Tools is probably the best place to look for broken pages on your site that are still receiving inbound links. Under Diagnostics > Crawl Errors, the tool lists pages that were not found and even tells you from where those pages are linked.

xtra cred

Internal Links Did you clean up the links in your old navigation? You'll never know until you check. Run a *link validator*, a program that checks your website for broken links internally. Here's one to try: www.dead-links.com.

In case it's not obvious yet, Google Webmaster Tools is your best bet for free link diagnostics, so get verified and get started! Google Webmaster Tools can help you find broken internal links.

xtra cred

Page Title URL	HTTP Status	Linking Root Domains ▼	Page Authority
1 Home I Lundberg Family Farms www.lundberg.com/ 🔍 📄	200	460	43
2 Lundberg Family Farms www.lundberg.com/products/rice_nf_wildblend.aspx 🔍 📄	200	19	34
3 [No Data] www.lundberg.com/recipes.html 🔍 📄	404	18	33

Figure 9.10 Open Site Explorer results for Lundberg.com

Prevent Link Rot

Next time you redesign your site, use URLs that you won't need to change—ever. Put some serious thought into file-naming conventions that will grow and expand with your website. Here are some rules of thumb:

- Don't name files with words like new, old, draft, current, latest, or any other status markers in the file name. This status will surely change as "new" files become "old" and "draft" files become "final." (It's a common problem! Last we checked, there were 2,100 listings in Google containing the preposterous file name `final2.html`—for shame!—and 1,060 listings for `final3.html`.)

- Name nested folders by year, and possibly month, for press releases or other dated materials (for example, `www.zippyco.com/press/2011/august/newproduct.html`). Put files in their final location as soon as they are launched rather than starting them out in a folder called "current" and moving them later.

- Leave information that may change in the future out of file names. For example, you don't want to include the name of a current copywriter in the file name. This URL will feel outdated and awkward three years from now when that individual no longer works at the company. Names of servers, the city where you're headquartered, or any other contemporary information should also be left off file names.

Follow these guidelines, and your search engine presence may survive the next site redesign without a hitch!

Best Practices for the Big Day On the day of a new site launch, follow these tips to keep your search presence solid:

- Avoid server downtime. If your site is moving to a different server, be sure that the site stays live in both places until the change has fully propagated.

- Watch out for staging server robot settings. More than once, we've seen a robot setting for a staging server inadvertently get pushed live. You don't want to launch your site with a "noindex" or "Disallow" message going out to search engine robots, so double-check that what's intended for the staging server stays on the staging server.

- Manually spot-check your 301 redirects. Prior to launch, figure out your hot list of URLs that absolutely must be redirected properly. These will surely include your home page and top-priority landing pages, but may also include other pages with good search ranks or traffic. Immediately after launching your site, check that the redirects on your hot list are working as expected.

You can confirm that a redirect is a 301 redirect by looking at the HTTP header. The Firefox add-on Live HTTP Headers will show you this information, or you can enter the URL in Rex Swain's HTTP Viewer at `http://rexswain.com/httpview.html`.

Now: Choose from the "new site, new problems" tasks listed in this section, and get started on the one that most applies to you.

Tuesday: Site Performance and Malware

It's rare for search engines to publicly discuss the ranking algorithm, which is why the SEO industry pricked up its ears in 2010, when Google announced that site speed is a factor in Google ranks. Site performance and malware are two techie SEO factors that website owners should keep an eye on. Today, we'll show you how.

Site Performance

Your site's speed to load is an important factor in its usability: A 2009 Forrester study showed that 40 percent of consumers would abandon a page if it didn't load in 3 seconds. A speedy site can also help your search engine positioning. Site speed is a signal in Google's ranking algorithm, which means if all other things are equal, a faster site may outrank a slower one.

To get a handle on your own site performance, log into Google Webmaster Tools and select Labs > Site Performance. Here, you'll see a visual representation of your site's performance, as seen in Figure 9.11, along with suggestions for making your site load faster.

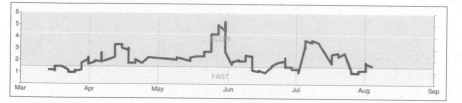

Figure 9.11 Visual representation of site speed in Google Webmaster Tools

If you don't have a verified Google Webmaster Tools login for your site, you can use YSlow, a Firefox add-on, to give you page speed information and suggestions for improvement.

Now: Review your site's performance.

As Google puts it, "Let's make the web faster." If Google Webmaster Tools or YSlow is reporting slow performance, or even if you just have a feeling that your site loads more slowly than you would like it to, you'll find many ways to speed it up described on this page: `http://code.google.com/speed/articles/`.

Malware

One of the most disturbing things you can see in your site's search listings looks like this:

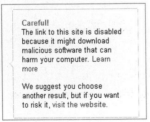

"This site may harm your computer" is a warning that Google adds to listings on websites that it believes contain *malware*, software that could invade your computer with hostile intent. Bing handles malware with a similar cautionary note, as seen here:

> Careful!
> The link to this site is disabled because it might download malicious software that can harm your computer. Learn more
>
> We suggest you choose another result, but if you want to risk it, visit the website.

If Google or Bing finds malware on your site, they will attempt to notify you via webmaster tools and—in Google's case—via email. Chances are, you'll be shocked to hear this news. You're reading this book, so we figure you're not a criminal spammer. More likely, your site was hacked and malware was added without your knowledge or approval. Figure 9.12 shows a peek at the Google Webmaster Tools screen we hope you'll never see.

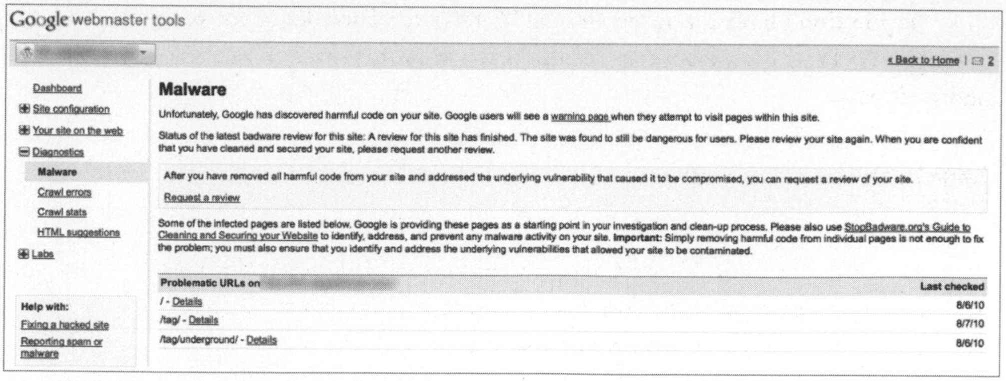

Figure 9.12 Malware notification in Google Webmaster Tools

If your site has been infected with malware, here are the steps you need to take:

- If you catch the malware problem before the search engines tell you about it, fix the problem right away. It's likely that you won't need to do anything further to preserve your search engine ranks.

- If the search engines have already noticed the malware and reported it to you, first take your site offline and scrub it squeaky clean. Then, request a reconsideration review from Google and Bing via their webmaster tools.

We've seen sites recover their rankings after a malware infection, but prevention is better than cure. At the risk of stating the obvious: Security against hackers must be a priority for your website.

You know what they say about an ounce of prevention:

Pearl of Wisdom: One of the simpler way to avoid malware is to make sure your site is always running the most recent version of its content management system (CMS) or blog authoring software.

If server configuration and security protocols make you want to hide behind a tall cup of hot cocoa, be sure there's someone in your organization who is responsible for this important task.

Now: Make a plan for ongoing malware checks and prevention in your organization.

Wednesday: Catch Up with Your Team

You're well into the third month of Your SEO Plan now—how is your team holding up? Are you all working together like a well-oiled machine? Or is your "team" more like a collection of squeaky wheels, revolving doors, and bottlenecks?

In Chapter 5, "Get Your Team on Board," we covered some strategies for encouraging members of your organization to join your SEO effort. Here are some good questions that may help you keep everyone on the same path:

Are my edits getting implemented? This is a biggie for many in-house SEOs: Just getting simple (or not-so-simple) edits made to the website may require jumping through design, IT, and even legal hoops. If your recommended edits aren't being taken care of, take time today and figure out why. Are you sending your requests to people who don't have authority or access to make the changes? Are your requests playing second fiddle to another department with more pull? Or did enthusiasm wane after the first round of edits didn't turn out the hoped-for quick results? Get an understanding of the holdup so you can take steps to flush it out!

Is SEO integrated into our processes? For Your SEO Plan to succeed, it needs to be part of the web development process. That means an SEO review before, during, or (worst case) after changes are made to the website. It also means integration of SEO considerations into the website style guide, if your organization has one. If you're feeling like an outsider, or if you think SEO is being given short shrift, you need to work on ways to integrate SEO into company processes. This means you may have to take on the role of SEO evangelist: Write up the first draft of an SEO style guide and deliver it to your developers. Ask to be included in copywriting or design meetings. You can even send articles or SEO tips to a team member who might benefit from this information.

Will the Real Home Page Please Stand Up?

You met search engine expert P.J. Fusco in Chapter 5, where she shared advice for getting your team on board. Here, P.J. tells a cautionary tale:

"We needed to optimize a handful of pages in a 4,000-page e-commerce site. One of the elements required was meta tags—unique title, description, and keyword attributes for eight different pages...."

"The project manager informed me this portion of the organic project was complete, so I audited the work. Everything looked good, except for one thing. Every single page of the site contained the meta tags for the home page. Can you imagine what a search engine spider thinks when it's trying to index 4,000 pages all proclaiming to be the official home page of the company?"

You've heard of Murphy's Law: If anything can possibly go wrong, it will. Nobody is going to look after SEO details the way you, the SEO team leader, will. So keep P.J.'s experience in mind, and be sure that you have a process in place to check your team's SEO-related edits, even when you're sure nothing can go wrong.

Are you getting what you need from your analytics? By now, we hope you have conversion tracking in place for your organization. If your analytics method requires participation by members of your team (for example, you need Sales to track calls from a special 800 number), revisit it today and see if it's working. Are you getting the information you need? If not, what needs to change?

Who's in it for the long term? Which members of your team have the energy, talent, and mindset for a sustained effort? By now, you have enough SEO experience that you can spot the personalities with a natural affinity for this work. Now it's your turn to be the squeaky wheel: Do what you can with your higher-ups to keep those people on your team for the long term.

> **Now:** Ask yourself the preceding questions and start sending emails or setting up the needed meetings for improvement.

Since your SEO team is made up of people who, like you, are busy doing other things, it's natural that your team's interest and ability to focus will wax and wane. So don't be surprised if you need to do checkups as you did today on a regular basis.

Thursday: Landing Page Optimization

Picture this: You're sitting in the conference room working out the last details of your landing page content. The web designer wants the call-to-action link to be "Get started now!" and the chief copywriter thinks it should be "Contact Sales." Everyone has an opinion, but nobody has any evidence to back it up. Landing page optimization can give you some real data on which to base these decisions.

The most common types of page optimization testing are *A/B testing* and *multivariate testing*. These are jargon for two very simple ideas: A/B testing (also called an A/B split) compares the performance of two page designs, and multivariate testing compares the performance of a larger number of page designs by swapping out content in several sections of the page at once.

Even if you have strong convictions about what you think your page content should be, we recommend letting a page optimization test provide more clues. Many website owners report being shocked by what their tests ultimately show to be the most effective content.

Both multivariate testing and A/B testing are available via a tool called Google Website Optimizer, at www.google.com/websiteoptimizer. You will need a Google account to access it. Other companies offering multivariate testing tools (for a fee) include SiteSpect and Optimost. You might as well start with the free Google option.

You can always move up to the paid services after you've fallen in love with page optimization testing.

Today, we're going to get you started on a page test of your own.

Your Multivariate Test

Ready to get started? We recommend performing multivariate testing rather than an A/B split for the simple reason that we think it's more fun. Here's how multivariate testing works:

- You designate a few sections of your web page that you would like to test. For example, you might specify the headline, the first paragraph of text, and an accompanying photograph as your three sections. Figure 9.13 shows a test in progress for www.workshare.com on Google Website Optimizer.

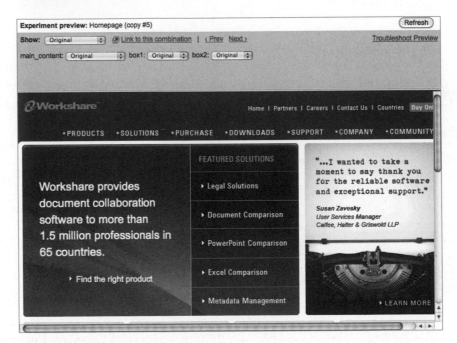

Figure 9.13 Google Website Optimizer

- For each section, you create two or more versions of its content.
- The multivariate testing system plays mix-and-match with your variations, showing a random combination to each of your website visitors.
- After the test has run for some time, the combination with the highest conversion rate wins! The most sophisticated testing systems can find the best combinations based on statistics, even when those exact combinations haven't been tested. Some test results are shown in Figure 9.14.

Combination	Status	Est. conv. rate		Chance to Beat Orig.	Observed Improvement	Conv./Visitors
Original	Enabled	6.45% ± 0.8%		—	—	218 / 3380
No high-confidence winner found. Learn more						
Combination 5	Enabled	7.36% ± 0.9%		85.8%	14.2%	246 / 3341
Combination 7	Enabled	7.29% ± 0.9%		83.8%	13.0%	241 / 3306
Combination 1	Enabled	6.98% ± 0.8%		73.9%	8.29%	239 / 3422
Combination 3	Enabled	6.82% ± 0.8%		67.2%	5.69%	236 / 3462
Combination 4	Enabled	6.49% ± 0.8%		51.8%	0.60%	218 / 3360
Combination 6	Enabled	6.48% ± 0.8%		51.3%	0.41%	222 / 3428
Combination 2	Enabled	6.46% ± 0.8%		50.6%	0.21%	214 / 3311

Figure 9.14 Google Website Optimizer test results

Blue Willow Dog Coats—Barking Up the Right Tree

Blue Willow Dog Coats sells custom-made dog coats through its website at www.bwdogcoats .com. Blue Willow's owner is Sharon Couzin—but one of us calls her Mom! Lucky for her, Sharon has access to some of the best SEO opinions a person could hope for. Nope, not ours—we're talking about the opinions of her own site users! When Sharon had some tough questions about content, she turned to Google Website Optimizer for answers.

Blue Willow specializes in coats for Sighthounds (those of us not in the dog show set know these dogs as Whippets, Greyhounds, and Italian Greyhounds). But they can be custom made for any breed. Sharon wondered: "What should I say on the home page headline? Should I focus on the fact that I make coats for those hard-to-fit Sighthound breeds? Or should I focus on the customization?" A further review showed that some great content was being pushed below the fold by a long introductory paragraph. A shorter intro would help, but "will people be interested in clicking to learn more?" asked Sharon. Sharon set up a Google Website Optimizer experiment to find the answers. She wrote two headlines: her original, "Extra Warm, Durable, Washable Winter Coats for Greyhounds, Iggys, Whippets and Dogs of all Shapes and Sizes," and a simplified revision, "Finally, a warm dog coat that really fits! Custom-made coats for dogs of all shapes."

Then, she wrote two versions of the intro paragraph: a long version that she liked, and one that felt painfully short. (In multivariate testing it's good to go outside your comfort zone.) Here are two examples of the resulting four versions of the page that Google Website Optimizer displayed for the test:

342

Blue Willow Dog Coats—Barking Up the Right Tree *(Continued)*

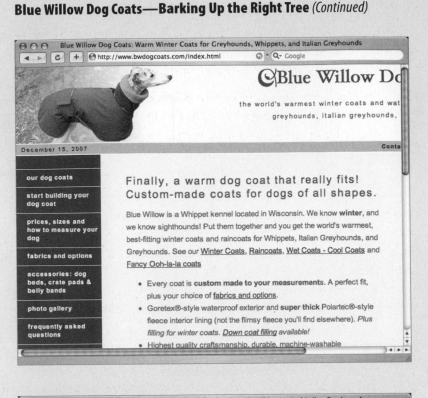

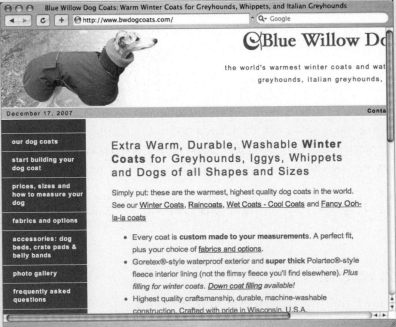

Website Optimizer will walk you through the steps for creating your own test. You will need the ability to add JavaScript to your HTML pages, so if you're not the person who edits the site, walk over to his or her cubicle and see if you can get a few minutes of assistance today. Here are a few tips to keep in mind, in addition to Google's instructions:

- If you have a low-traffic site (say, under 200 visitors per day), you can speed up your results by testing your most trafficked pages and using a high-volume conversion definition. For example, rather than defining a conversion as an actual online *purchase*, you can define it as a visit to a product page. With more conversions, you'll have more data to compare your different page designs.

- Keep in mind that all your page variations are going to be on display to your site audience—and your visitors have no idea that they're in the middle of a page optimization test. Use the preview feature to be sure that the content makes sense in all the assembled combinations.

- Landing page testing is not just for e-commerce sites. You can apply these tests to any of your pages and any type of online conversion goal.

- Take a chance and test some content that goes outside your comfort zone. We're not saying you should make statements that aren't accurate, but what about some zippier language or brighter colors? A true test needs to include some far-out options to be sure you're capturing the entire spectrum of possibilities.

Now: Go to Google Website Optimizer and set up your first test.

Alternatives to Landing Page Testing

Maybe there are forces beyond your control that make it impossible for you to pursue a landing page optimization test. We've seen it before: tech departments that won't abide new JavaScript tags or marketing teams that aren't open to wild text experiments. Here are some workarounds that you can use to incorporate at least a bit of content testing into Your SEO Plan:

- If you're using one of the major paid search providers, A/B testing for your ads is easy! Just write one or two additional ads for each of your ad groups and set your ad rotation preferences to show better performing ads more often. As clicks come in, your paid search service automatically judges which ad is more effective and will increase its prominence for you automatically. This information may even help you identify more effective text to include on the landing page.

- Run a time-based test, in which you display one page version for a week or month, and then switch to another page version. Though seriously unscientific (was it really the page design change that caused traffic to rise, or was it the holiday season?), this approach is still better than nothing.

- If your organization performs usability testing, ask to have content variations incorporated into the tests. You may also have fun with user testing and get some helpful feedback at a low-cost venue such as www.usertesting.com.

Does page optimization have its limitations? Of course it does. You may figure out that one page is doing better than another, but unless you interview your target audience, you'll never know exactly *why*. Plus, your tests are limited to your ideas for edits, so unless you're a master at thinking outside the box, there may be big improvements that you miss. Nevertheless, landing page testing is one of the few ways of getting real data on the persuasiveness of your site's message.

Accessibility Check

One of the fringe benefits of Your SEO Plan is that it will improve your website's accessibility for people with disabilities. By the same token, a more accessible website will tend to be more robot friendly as well. Jan Schmidt of Collaborint Web Management Services, a web design and development firm specializing in web accessibility, explains that many SEO practices "not only make it more efficient for search engines to crawl a website and index the content, but can also improve the disabled user's experience by providing easy-to-navigate links and machine-readable page text."

Tools are available to check your page with everything from voice browsers to color-blindness simulators. We recommend you start with Cynthia Says, a free web-based tool located at www.cynthiasays.com. Links and descriptions of many more accessibility tools can be found here: www.w3.org/WAI/ER/tools/complete.

Friday: Brand Busters

You might have a trademark on your product name, but that's no guarantee that your branding will hold up to your standards in the search engines. Today, you'll do something akin to looking at yourself in the dressing room mirror during swimsuit season—you'll scrutinize your search presence to find flaws in your branding. Squint if it makes you feel better—we're going in!

Other People's Sites

Brand-busting search listings can be sourced on your own website, or they can be under other organizations' control. Here are a few examples of other websites that may be negatively influencing your brand's presence on search engines:

Affiliates and Resellers If you're relying on other websites to help you sell your product, there's always the possibility that they can outrank you in the search engines. This is not necessarily a problem; however, you should check in periodically to make sure you're being represented in a good light. Take some time today to look through your affiliate listings, and make sure the wording in their listings matches your expectations (and any contractual agreement you might have in place). Another thing to look out for is algorithmically generated product matching features on your reseller sites. We once had a client whose high-end kitchen gadgets got mingled in an Amazon category with dog toys from another company with a similar name. This caused a lot of confusion with people who didn't know any better—even *we* thought they sold dog toys for a while!

> **Now:** Find search engine listings for your affiliates and resellers. Review the accuracy of the text. Click through to make sure the product page looks as it should.

Your Competitors There are a few ways your competitors might be trying to outrank you for your own brand name. One old trick is a product comparison page, in which your competitor creates a page chock-full of instances of your product name. The sneaky—but perfectly legitimate—goal is to rank well for your name, then draw people to their website and convince your potential customers to buy their product instead. See Figure 9.15 for an example. Another thing they might do is sponsor your product name in a paid search campaign. Editorial guidelines may prevent them from displaying your product name in their ad, but they can still display a targeted message to your audience.

> **Now:** Search <compare [your product name] and [your competitor's product name]>. See if you can find a competitor's page optimized for your own product. Next, search for your product name and scan the paid search listings. Did a competitor's ad show up? They're sponsoring your name in their paid search campaign!

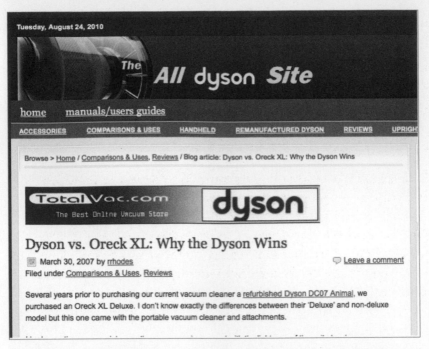

Figure 9.15   This site sells Dyson vacuum cleaners but has optimized a page for a competitor name, Oreck.

Your Exes   A web page can live well past its freshness date. This may be a problem if your product name or its features have changed over time but pages describing it on other sites such as vendors, affiliates, and partners have stayed the same. Chances are good that an old page like this isn't going to outrank your vibrant, well-optimized, and well-linked website, but you should scour the top 20 or so search engine listings for your product name just to make sure nothing noticeably bad is happening.

Now: Search for your product name along with some outdated keywords to try to trigger a listing for an outdated version of your product.

    What to do if you find something that made you wince? You have some options. Much of what you find will probably be unintentional, and probably nothing will be illegal, so you could try to approach the brand-busting sites and ask nicely for a deletion or a revision. For the intentional ones, you could try to beat them at their own game. Why not create a product comparison page or a pay-per-click ad, especially if you know your product will compare favorably to your competitor's? If neither of these options feels right to you, remember that living well is the best revenge. Create a well-optimized site, and make sure the listings you *do* control make you look good!

Spring Cleaning Your Website for Better Search

We usually advise our clients to add things to their website as part of their SEO strategies—keywords, landing pages, more content, more unique descriptions. But if spring fever has you wanting to toss more than just the moldy contents of your office fridge, we have some ideas for your website.

Here are a few things that you should consider pruning from your site in order to improve your presence in the search engines:

Non-HTML Documents That Make Poor Landing Pages Think of this scenario: Following a link from a search engine, a visitor enters your site by landing on your PDF product assembly instructions, or a blank financial spreadsheet template. Non-HTML documents are often poor entry pages to a website. Sometimes, spring cleaning involves hiding things away from public view, maybe stashing them in a closet or storage bin. In this case, the offending files could be listed in your `robots.txt` file so that they are hidden from search engine indexing. You might need these documents on your website, but you don't have to offer them as potential landing pages.

"Strategic" Outlinks Maybe you followed someone's outdated advice and took part in a reciprocal linking scheme, or joined an "undetectable" link exchange network. You were only trying to help your website, we know, but these links can be damaging to your site's ranks, especially if they are pointing to websites that have nothing to do with your own site's topical focus. Deep-six that "link partners" page! Instead, collect your inlinks in a way that's more beneficial to your site—by creating great content and making sure other sites know about it!

Outdated Content Almost every website has outdated content, ranging from little stuff (like old calendars) to big stuff (like obsolete product lines). The problem with outdated content is that it can make its way into your search engine listings—and that can cause confusion, frustration, or even a bad reputation for your company. Does your footer say, "ZippyCo: Copyright 2005?" You won't believe how many times copyright notices show up in search results. Are you displaying promotions that are no longer valid? Don't play bait-and-switch with your search traffic. Make it a priority, and take some time to update or redirect that dusty old content.

Whatever's Causing Your Slow Pages to Load So Slowly A slow-loading site is a double whammy, frustrating your site visitors and potentially hurting your search ranks. Toss out the heavy stuff and streamline your site's load time.

Remember, it's not just the sheer number of pages you have indexed in Google—it's the lusciousness of your listings! Any time of year is a good time to banish the parts of your website that are detracting from your search listings.

On Your Own Site

Could you have brand-busting factors on your own site? Here are a few likely suspects:

Broken Links The search engines don't want broken links in their results any more than you do. They will eventually figure out that a page doesn't exist and remove it from their indexes. But why let a perfectly good search engine ranking go to waste? Try one of the following approaches:

- Since the URL is already indexed and may already have some good rankings, inbound links, or bookmarked traffic, consider creating a new page and saving it at the missing URL. However, do this only if it makes sense to create a new page with similar content—it would be awkward if your cabinet hardware products were listed at a page called "floral-arrangements.html."

- Talk to your IT people about setting up a 301 redirect, which carries traffic on this page to another page of your choosing. But don't make the common mistake of pointing the redirect to your home page! Choose the page on your site that best matches the one that has gone missing.

- Sometimes, broken links linger in the search results because your server fails to mention that the page is missing. That's right; it's possible for a server to return a "Page Found" message even if a page is missing! It's a riddle wrapped in a conundrum, but luckily it's an easy fix for your IT folks. Google calls these *Soft 404* errors and reports them in Google Webmaster Tools.

Obsolete Offerings You don't want your potential customers seeing outdated product descriptions, promotions that are no longer active, or last year's price list in the search results. The best and fastest approach to this problem is to update your site's content while keeping the file in the same location so that it doesn't lose its search engine status.

In some cases, a simple update may not be so simple. For example, suppose you have found a well-ranked search engine listing for your web page featuring the Snackmaster 2010, but your company no longer sells this older model. Your website now has a new page featuring the Snackmaster 2011. If you rewrite your 2010 page to describe your new product, your site will contain two pages with identical content, which is a search engine no-no as well as an administrative headache. Instead, it's best to edit the 2010 page content to include a notice that a new model is available and link to the 2011 model page. A 301 redirect from the old page to the new one would be another option, especially if there are no customer support or archival reasons to keep the old page live.

Private or Inappropriate Material There it is, staring out at you from between listing #5 and listing #7: your company's holiday gift list, with addresses and phone numbers of all your best clients! You need to clean up your act—and fast. Here's how:

- Remove the page from your site. Or leave the offending file live, but immediately remove the offending content.
- Then request removal from Google and Bing using their respective webmaster tools.

By leaving the file live but changing the content, you may benefit from a quicker update than if you took down the page altogether. However, you should be aware that a search engine's cached pages may retain a snapshot of the content for longer than you're comfortable with, and there are historical web archive sites that may display the content forever. If you have serious legal concerns—for example, if you posted a disclaimer that said, "All information on this site is medical advice" rather than "...*not* medical advice"—you can use a copyright search method such as http://copyscape.com to search for instances of your content throughout the Web and seek removal.

> **Now:** Perform a <site:> search for your domain and scroll through the results looking for the potentially brand-damaging items described here.

Although these are all positive steps, in truth there's little you can do to prevent robots from indexing pages that are live and accessible. If you do not want pages to be found, secure them behind a password!

Week 12: SEO Status Report

Just like the talk you may be planning (or planning to avoid) with your significant other, the SEO Status Report is the time to turn your attention to the long-term view. SEO and your website have been in a relationship for three months now, four if you count the Prep Month. What's it all about? Where are you going? Are you committed to your keyword choices? Do the search engine robots still find your linking profile attractive? Do you have an itch to check out new competitors?

This week is not just about producing a report, although certainly that's important. It's really about the thinking, planning, reviewing, and analysis that you do while you are gathering the information for your report.

> **Pearl of Wisdom:** Without a period of time for review, reflection, and prioritization for the future, your SEO campaign can go off track, or just get lost in the busy day-to-day shuffle of your workplace.

We won't tell you exactly how to format your report, and we'll trust you to organize and present the information in a way that makes sense to you and your team. Some of you might like splashy colors or charts to compare the popularity of various keywords. Others might prefer a "just the facts, ma'am" approach. What's most important to us is that the information be documented.

Whether you ultimately choose to create an SEO Status Report on a weekly, monthly, or quarterly basis is a question of your organization's needs and your own tolerance for documentation workload. Regardless of how often you check in, a commitment to tracking and documentation will always separate the pack leaders from the also-rans. Open up the worksheets you started in Chapter 6, "Your One-Month Prep: Keywords, Priorities, and Goals," and fire up a new document to use as your written summary. We'll call the new doc your SEO Analysis document. Here are your tasks for this week:

Monday: Site Ranks and Indexing

Tuesday: Inbound Links and Social Status

Wednesday: Referring Keywords, Conversions, and Traffic

Thursday: Paid Search

Friday: Opportunities and Action Items

Monday: Site Ranks and Indexing

During your Prep Month, you established goals for your site's visibility on the major search engines. Today, you'll find out how your standings have changed. We'll ask you to check three values:

- Search engine ranks
- Indexed pages
- Listing quality

Search Engine Ranks

For this task, you will perform a rank check on the major search engines for all of your top target keywords. You learned how to do this back in Chapter 6.

 Now: Open your Rank and KPI Tracking Worksheet and update it with your current ranks.

With your before-and-after ranks side by side, it's easy to see what changes have occurred. If you were starting from zero or you had some easy fixes in your optimization, you may have some exciting improvement in ranks. If you aren't seeing the improvements you've been hoping for, take heart. As we often say, in SEO it's a marathon, not a sprint.

In this section of your SEO Analysis document, you'll summarize your current standings as compared to the Prep Month. Here are some examples:

- We gained top-20 ranks in Bing for three of our target keywords.

- We have a new #2 Google rank for the term "novelty napkin holders."

Next, put on your thinking cap and flesh out these bare-bones facts with some juicy analysis. How do these changes compare with the goals you established in the Prep Month? Are you noticing any trends in the keywords? Can you glean any insights based on which of your site's URLs are showing up in the ranks? Possible analysis might look like this:

- We gained top-20 ranks in Bing for three of our target keywords. They all contain the phrase "linen napkins."

- We have a new #2 Google rank for the term "novelty napkin holders." The page in the #2 position was recently added to our site as part of our SEO efforts.

Your ranks will almost certainly fluctuate from one rank check to the next. Depending on how competitive your industry is, your ranks may bounce around in ways that puzzle or alarm you. If you notice a serious drop in ranks, the best thing to do is to move forward and gather the remaining data in this SEO status report. The data you'll be gathering this week is exactly the kind of information an SEO pro would review when tasked with diagnosing a drop in ranks.

Now: Open a new document—we'll call it your SEO Analysis Document—and add your rankings summary and analysis.

Indexed Pages

In addition to monitoring search engine ranks for your top keywords, we recommend checking the total number of pages indexed. You learned how to do this in Chapter 6 using the site: search shortcut.

Now: Check the total number of pages indexed on your site in Google and Bing. Record the value on your Rank and KPI Tracking Worksheet.

The way this number changes from one reporting period to the next can alert you to structural problems or indicate structural improvements. Depending on your site's unique situation, you may be hoping for an increase or a decrease in indexed pages over time. If you have just removed barriers to search engine crawling, your measure of success may be an increase in indexed pages. If you have just cleaned up a messy duplicate content problem with your site, your measure of success will be a decrease in indexed pages.

If you're watching page indexing closely, you may have a special interest in robot activity. Google and Bing webmaster tools display crawling statistics, as well as XML Sitemap indexation info, for verified users. See Figure 9.16 for an example of crawl data in Bing Webmaster Tools.

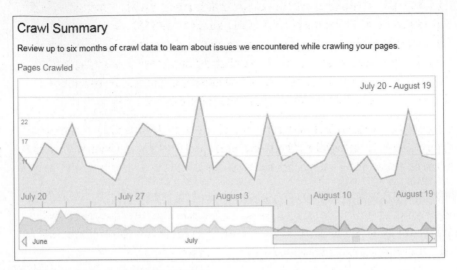

Figure 9.16 Crawl data in Bing Webmaster Tools

Listing Quality

Whenever we're called upon to get a very quick sense of a site's presence on search engines, we perform a site: search and assess the quality of the listings. You already know the total number of pages that are indexed on your site. Now, give them a once-over for quality. Are the listings compelling and clickable? Does each page have a unique listing? How is your branding? Your status report should call out any improvements or trouble spots.

> **Now:** Assess the listing quality for your site's search engine listings on Google, Yahoo!, and Bing and document it in your SEO Analysis document.

Slackers can choose to slice Yahoo! off their list, since most of Yahoo!'s and Bing's results will probably be identical.

I Hate Paperwork!

Do you hear that? Our eye-rolling detector is beeping! Someone out there is about to complain that all this documentation is useless!

In our opinion, the SEO Status Report is a cornerstone of a well-balanced plan. Why? Because we firmly believe that data is useless unless it's interpreted in a meaningful way.

A seasoned SEO professional confesses, "One of my first SEO projects was when I worked at a web development firm, and SEO was an add-on to building a website. With SEO being a new service, we had no established system for documenting or reporting on this work. I diligently performed all the tasks for the initial discovery phase of the project: choosing keywords, assessing the site and its competitors, and making recommendations for next steps. With each of these tasks, I worked closely with our client and emailed him all of the related data.

"At the end of the project, my boss (who didn't know SEO but certainly knew business best practices!) suggested that I put together a final report. What did I do? I printed out my previous documents and data, stapled them all together, and slapped on a title page.

"What a disaster! The client had nothing to show his boss, nobody wanted to wade through the data, and I wasted more time re-explaining everything I had done than I would have spent writing up a summary in the first place. Worse, all of the added value from my work—the thought, research, discussion, and analysis that had gone into our choices—was lost!

"Luckily, the client was forgiving. But I learned a hard lesson with that project: Document what you do and write it with a close eye on your intended audience!"

Have you guessed yet that the SEO pro quoted here is one of the authors? Lucky for you, you can learn from our mistakes! The point of this week is not just to document your work, but also to do the analysis and mental sifting that allows you to write about it intelligently. The way you tell your SEO story is what will ultimately separate you from the SEO hacks and newbies out there. Your SEO Status Report is a team-builder, a boss-pleaser, and a mental reinforcement for your SEO learning curve, all wrapped in a sensible white-inkjet-bond-paper bow.

Tuesday: Inbound Links and Social Status

These off-page factors—inbound links and social status—tend to make CEO types sit up and pay attention, so be ready to field questions about this section of your report.

Inbound Links

Perhaps more than any other number you pull into your report, you must provide context on the number of inbound links. There are several numbers you could choose to report, but we suggest reviewing Google Webmaster Tools or Open Site Explorer to gather the following:

- Total links to your home page, excluding links from within your own domain
- Total number of domains pointing to your home page

xtra cred

As long as you're gathering data, you may as well capture the same metrics for a few other top-priority pages in addition to your home page. You may also find that one number indicating how many domains are linking to your entire domain would be useful, too. Majestic SEO, at www.majesticseo.com, provides this in its free tool.

Remember, an increase in inbound links does not necessarily mean that you've achieved SEO success. Some questions you must investigate for every big change include:

- Did someone on your staff purchase ads or directory listings? This kind of purchase can make the total number of inlinks to your site increase dramatically, but paid ads carry no organic rankings benefits. Similarly, did some ads or listings expire? If this is the case, you may see a big drop in inlinks that would likely not affect organic ranks.
- What percentage of new links come from a single site? The total number of linking domains will give you an indication: If the number of linking domains goes up by just a few, but your total number of links goes up by hundreds or thousands, you can assume that only a small number of sites is responsible for the increase. If you see several new unpaid links from several different domains, congratulations! What on your site is responsible for this success?
- When was the link reporting database updated? If you aren't seeing the increase you were expecting, take heart! Your last big link building endeavor may not have been a bust; rather, your reporting tool of choice might not have been updated since you made those efforts.

Now: Record your inbound link data in your Rank and KPI Tracking Worksheet, then describe your findings in your SEO Analysis Document.

Social Status

Your documentation of social status will reflect any social marketing efforts you've undertaken recently. Some at-a-glance numbers to capture from social sites include:

- The number of your followers or fans on Facebook or Twitter
- The number of comments on your blog or on your Facebook page
- The number of retweets or mentions on Twitter
- Your blog authority, as reported by Technorati

From within your own analytics program, you can gauge social media success by recording the number of unique visitors referred from your targeted social sites, as well as their level of engagement on your site as measured by conversions, average number of pages viewed, or average time on site.

Spend a little time setting up an advanced segment in Google Analytics, and data for traffic coming from your targeted social sites will be a quick-and-easy grab for future reports. Learn more about setting up advanced segments by going to www .google.com/support and searching for <advanced segments>.

xtra cred

> **Now:** Record your social status data in your Rank and KPI Tracking Worksheet, then describe your findings in your SEO Analysis Document.

Google PageRank

Despite our misgivings about the usefulness of the Google PageRank value, we recommend that you track it for your landing pages. Why? It's an easy way to gather at-a-glance numbers that can help you see changes in your status over time.

You can see Google PageRank just by browsing to your landing pages and reviewing the Google Toolbar that you downloaded in Chapter 6.

> **Now:** Browse to each of your landing pages and record the Google PageRank on your Rank and KPI Tracking Worksheet. Document anything noteworthy in your SEO Analysis Document.

slacker

Google PageRank is good to know, but it's not essential. If you're short on time, you can skip this step.

Wednesday: Referring Keywords, Conversions, and Traffic

Have you fallen in love with your web analytics program yet? We sure hope so. Today, you'll look at some of the key measurements that can show the effects of Your SEO Plan and point you in the right direction for ongoing improvement.

Referring Keywords

Knowing your *referring keywords*, that is, the keywords that bring visitors to your site, is a must-have metric. And yet we often meet business owners who don't know the top referring keywords for their own site. Google Analytics provides a simple way to find referring keywords, as seen in Figure 9.17. Whatever analytics program you use, make sure you are viewing organic keywords only (we'll talk about paid keywords tomorrow).

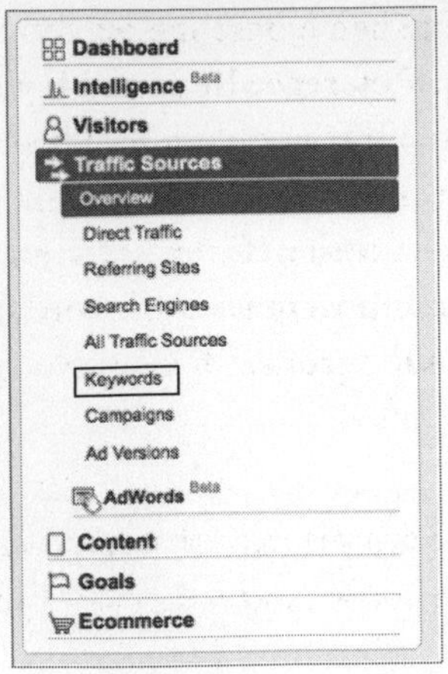

Figure 9.17 Finding referring keywords in Google Analytics

Here are ways to frame the analysis of your referring keywords:

- It's common for top referring keywords to be your company name and variations thereof. SEO pros call it "navigational search" when people type a company name into the search engines. Receiving a lot of traffic through navigational search is often a sign of basic health in your online marketing strategy, because it implies that not only do people know your company name well enough to search for it, but also that the search engines are giving your site the visibility it deserves for your name. However, if a high percentage of your search traffic is navigational, this may indicate there's room for improvement in your site's search presence for other terms.

- If you have strong ranks for a top-priority keyword yet this keyword is not referring traffic to your site, do some investigation. Is it possible that you chose the wrong keywords to target in the first place? Or is there something unappealing about your listing in the search engines that is discouraging people from clicking through to your site?

- Find a keyword for which your site has recently improved in the ranks, and compare recent traffic for this keyword to the traffic it brought in during a previous timeframe. Do you see more traffic correlating with higher ranks?

Now: Review your top referring organic keywords in your analytics program, then describe your findings in your SEO Analysis Document.

Conversions

Conversions, especially if you've defined them properly so that they match the overall goals of your organization, are truly the bottom line of Your SEO Plan.

During your Prep Month in Chapter 6, you established a baseline on conversions to the best of your ability and recorded it in your Quick Reference Report. Maybe you've got plenty of cold, hard facts and were able to document something like "One percent of site visitors, and 7 percent of search engine traffic, completed an online purchase transaction." Or perhaps you had to improvise a little: "Conversion tracking is not yet in place for our analytics program, however, there were no promotions or seasonal considerations to explain the increase in form submittals. I believe our new higher rank may be the cause."

Now: Open your analytics program and copy your recent conversion data into your Rank and KPI Tracking Worksheet. Or if you're using alternative methods of conversion tracking (such as a phone sales sheet), take whatever steps you need to gather that information.

Take a look at your current conversion data as compared to the data you compiled for your Quick Reference Report in Chapter 6. If there are differences, what caused them? Separating out all of the various factors that contribute to your bottom line—SEO efforts, seasonal effects, even regular month-to-month fluctuations—is almost impossible. Your mission in this report is to separate out the effects of your SEO campaign as well as you can. If there are any results that you *can* attribute directly to your SEO efforts today, make a note of them in your report. Here are some examples:

- Listing our site in the Home Décor Directory has resulted in a branding boost and 700 visits.
- Since we succeeded in getting the "Tea Time" page indexed in all of the major search engines, we have seen a 27 percent increase in lace doily sales.
- Three hundred visitors entered the coupon code that we promoted on Facebook.

Now: Document anything noteworthy about your conversions in your SEO Analysis Document.

Traffic

Your well-defined conversions are the most important measure of your SEO success, but they don't tell the full story on their own. After all, knowing that conversions went up is nice, but it doesn't give you insight into *why* they went up and what you can do to reinforce the trend. Here are some of the other measurements that we find useful:

Search Engine Traffic as a Percentage of Total Traffic and as a Percentage of Total New Traffic This is a good metric if you're dealing with skeptical higher-ups, because some nice increases may help justify your SEO campaign.

Overall Average Bounce Rate Compared to Bounce Rate by Referrer, Entry Page, or Referring Keywords
For example, "The overall average bounce rate was 56 percent. Bounce rate from search engine visitors was only 25 percent, while bounce rate from our top referrer, ExpensiveDirectory.com, was 87 percent. Of our top landing pages, our new Napkin Holders page had the lowest bounce rate at 22 percent." This information can tell you which audiences your website is serving best and which ones are disappointed by your offerings. It might provide ideas for new landing pages or keyword optimization choices.

Top Referring Sites This information helps you assess the value of your link building efforts.

Keyword-by-Keyword Conversions and Dollar Values This is a great way to assess your keyword choices and determine whether you need to adjust your focus. For example: "'Tea cozies' had 16 conversions with a total value of $345. 'Wholesale linens' had 4 conversions with a total value of $6,500."

Conversion Rate Broken Down by Audience For example, "Users who entered the site via pages in the Restaurant section had a 5 percent conversion rate, while users who entered via the Home section had only a 0.5 percent conversion rate." You can segment your audience in any way that you find meaningful, as long as your analytics program will support it.

Number of Page Views or Time Spent on Site by Keyword, Landing Page, Referrer, or Any Other Type of Audience Segmentation Although a larger number of page views is not necessarily a plus (it could signal that people are having trouble finding what they need on your site!), for many sites it is a good indicator of audience engagement.

Your goal in this section is not just to document traffic—it's to come up with ideas for site improvement. If you discover a trend that you can't explain, dig deeper until you have at least a hypothesis as to why it happened. Grab the most creative thinker on your team and brainstorm how you might test your guesses.

Now: Write your traffic data and commentary in your SEO Analysis Document. This may be the place to compare data with goals from your SEO Growth Worksheet.

Thursday: Paid Search

Your SEO Status Report should include important information about your spending and accomplishments with your paid search campaigns. Today, touch on these points:

- Paid search performance data
- Top-performing keywords
- Changes to campaigns

Here are some guidelines for making the most of the data you get from your paid search service.

Paid Search Performance Data

You have a lot of flexibility to create comprehensive, customized reports using your paid search service. Today, using your reporting interface, create a keyword report that includes the following data:

- Total number of click-throughs
- Click-through percentage
- Total cost
- Average total cost per click
- Total number of conversions
- Conversion percentage
- Conversion cost

> **Now:** Use your paid search service to create a keyword report for your campaign.

Top Performers

Identifying your top-performing paid keywords may be as simple as sorting your keyword list in descending order by the number of conversions and checking your conversion costs to make sure you aren't paying an unacceptably high price. It's often easiest to calculate your acceptable conversion cost if you are selling something at a fixed price. But if your type of conversion is less tangible—for example, completing a free registration or downloading a white paper—you'll probably be hard-pressed to place a numerical value on it.

For larger organizations, check in with your marketing department—they may already have a concept of the lifetime value of a new customer or client. For example, the paid search visitor who buys a free subscription today may sign up for a premium subscription in a month, and then recommend you to friends.

If you can't place an exact value on your conversion, the best approach is to manage your campaign diligently so that you stay within your paid search budget and strive for the lowest cost per conversion possible.

> **Now:** Use your paid search service to create a keyword report for your campaign. Document top keywords in your SEO Analysis Document.

Poor Performers

As you look through your paid search keyword performance data, you may find that there is a fairly even spread of clicks or conversions throughout your list of keywords. Or more likely, you may find a nice group of performers at the top and a steep dropoff thereafter. Perhaps you even have a disturbingly long list of zero-performers. Generating your paid search report is a perfect opportunity to identify red-flag keywords and determine a plan of action for fixing or eliminating them.

Here are the most common performance failures and possible ways to improve them:

- Keywords with low click-through rates
- Keywords with low conversion rates
- Keywords with high conversion costs

Keywords with Low Click-Through Rates As you learned in Chapter 4, "How the Search Engines Work Right Now," higher click-through rates can influence your rank on Google AdWords and Microsoft adCenter, so you may be tempted to start slicing and dicing keywords with low click-through rates. But while you may find these keywords bothersome, remember that as long as you're working in the standard search-targeted pay-per-click scenario that we advised you to set up, you're paying for clicks, not ad views, so they aren't costing you extra money. Ask yourself a few questions that may help you turn these low performers around:

Is my ad text doing its job? Take an honest look at your ad copy to make sure it addresses your low-performing keyword, and your audience, in a meaningful and compelling way. If the keyword doesn't have its own custom-written ad, perhaps it should. Consider inviting another writer on your team to give your ads a tune-up.

Does the keyword have enough impressions for me to make a judgment call? Make sure you're getting enough ad views to validate your doubts about the keyword. Sometimes, the number of impressions for an ad is so small that it's not getting a fair shot at success. This is especially true if the keyword is related to a seasonal or cyclical topic. Remember that keywords on the long tail of search are naturally only going to get a few impressions.

Did I start out with realistic expectations? This is a great time to reassess your trust in your PPC service's traffic-prediction tool.

Low Conversion Rate Keywords Much more worrisome than the keyword that isn't bringing in traffic is the one that actually *is* bringing in traffic but not resulting in conversions. You're going to hold these terms to a much higher standard than the low-click-through performers because every one of these clicks is costing you cash. But you may wish to give these underachievers a second chance before you dump them. Here are some questions you should ask:

Is the landing page a good match for the keyword? You may be about to drop a keyword when you should instead be planning to add a new page to your website to better accommodate it. At the very least, consider pointing a keyword to a more appropriate landing page that already exists. Exploring different landing page options with a multivariate test (described in Week 11) may also be in order.

Did I get caught in a word-matching snafu? If you are using a broad matching option, is it possible there's a broad match to your term that's drawing in the wrong audience? You can fix this with a *negative match*, a type of matching that excludes words you specify so that your ad doesn't show up for those terms. For example, you may want to sponsor the term "shredder" for your snowboarding site, but you probably don't want to pay for clicks from people who are looking for those paper-eating office supplies. In this case, you'd want to exclude the words "paper" and "document" for this keyword.

Am I inadvertently using bait-and-switch tactics? If you owned a bike shop in Santa Cruz, California, you might think it's perfectly reasonable to sponsor the search terms "santa cruz bikes." Unfortunately, this is also the name of a popular brand of mountain bikes! Many of those click-throughs are going to be disappointed by your site. If you're in a situation like this, you'll need to review your ad text to eliminate ambiguity. Make sure your ads clearly represent your offering.

Keywords with High Conversion Costs Don't overlook the simple but important step of sorting your keywords by conversion cost. Keywords with high conversion costs can be easy to miss: They're not in the zero conversion pile, and they might not be in the low click-through pile. But there's nothing more depressing than seeing a $90 conversion cost for a keyword that you're using to sell a $45 product.

High conversion costs can be caused by any combination of the factors we listed for low click-through rates and low conversion rates. Although our suggested efforts earlier today will also help bring down the high-cost conversions, lowering your bid is the most direct fix for this problem. If you discover that more than a few of your keywords are running at an unacceptable conversion cost, it's time to pause those keywords until you figure out what's going wrong.

> **Now:** List your low-performing keywords in your SEO Analysis Document, and note your ideas for addressing them.

Changes to Campaigns

Regular monitoring and constant tweaks are good for your paid search campaign, and it's important to connect those changes to any effects they had. Here is the place to record any changes that took place in your paid search campaigns this month—things like major bid changes, edits to ad copy, or landing page revisions.

Because even sharp minds like yours will eventually forget all the details of the changes you made, Google AdWords and Microsoft adCenter keep a change log for your reference. You don't need to export the whole report, but do make sure to jot down any big strategy or bidding changes in your SEO Analysis Document.

 Now: Document any noteworthy paid search campaign changes in your SEO Analysis Document.

With your paid search campaign monitoring complete, you're ready to finalize your SEO Status Report with some forward-thinking analysis and action items.

Friday: Opportunities and Action Items

Here is the section that everybody on your team will turn to when they get this report. And even if you're working alone, this to-do list will be an indispensable reference as you move forward into the next month.

One of the challenges that we've faced time and time again in our SEO efforts is writing reports that are complete and meaningful, readable, and most important, *actionable*.

 Pearl of Wisdom: The best reports are not just repositories of information; they are also tools to guide your team through the next steps.

To assemble your action items, review each of the previous sections of the report. Here are some likely candidates for your action items list:

- Ongoing tasks that need continued attention, like content development for link building
- Any unimplemented optimization recommendations that you have compiled and sent to your team
- Untapped potential: new opportunities you've discovered, either during this reporting week or during your analytics meditations earlier in this chapter
- Red flags: problems such as unindexed pages or bad-looking listings

Now: Write your action items in your SEO Analysis Document.

With your first SEO Status Report resting comfortably in your email outbox, your four-month journey is complete! But by now you know that SEO is never really done. Read on for the next steps.

Moving On: Forging Your Own SEO Path

Congratulations! Since you've opened this book, you've absorbed a tremendous amount of SEO knowledge, been promoted to SEO team leader, and become even more valuable to your organization. The scripted portion of Your SEO Plan is over, with the exception of some helpful ideas for extra credit and slacking in the next chapter.

You may have noticed that the further Your SEO Plan progressed, the less we held your hand and the more you had to create your own directions. That's because there really is no one-size-fits-all solution. You have to go where your organization needs to go, where your competition forces you to go, and where your market allows you to go. As you move forward on your own, you have endless options, but here are some possible ways to proceed:

- Start Your SEO Plan over again with a new audience or conversion goal in mind.
- Start Your SEO Plan over again with a new set of landing pages in mind.
- Start combing through your site, page by page or section by section, and optimize based on your current best practices.
- Ask your marketing team what short-term promotions are coming up. A contest? A seminar? A sale? Make sure you have a say in any promotional text that's going up on your site, and consider setting up your paid search campaign to promote it for the short term.
- Depending on what you've learned, you may want to drop paid search and go full bore on organic SEO. Or vice versa!

Intelligent Outsourcing

Maybe you've developed into a full-fledged SEO expert over the course of reading this book. But it's also possible that you've discovered that it's not your favorite pastime and you're ready to outsource. In the years that we've been in the SEO industry, we've seen growth in the number of high-quality SEO service providers. At the same time, we've seen at least 57 varieties of snake oil on the market! If you do choose to go the outsourcing route, keep the following caveats in mind:

- Watch out for any guarantee of a specific search engine rank. A legit search marketing service will not guarantee a rank that they don't have control over.

- Some companies direct your traffic through intermediate pages on their own hosted domains and then turn off your traffic when the contract is terminated. You need to have control over your own content and traffic, so don't agree to this type of business arrangement.

Intelligent Outsourcing (*Continued*)

Snake oil

- There are only a small number of important search engines to rank well on, so anyone who is talking about rankings on "hundreds of search engines" is probably best avoided.

- Good search marketing is time consuming, and there are no shortcuts. If a company is charging $79.99, you are not getting a legitimate full-service solution.

The best news is, now that you know so much about sensible, effective, and holistic SEO practices, you'll be able to make informed judgments about any SEO help for hire that crosses your path.

The world of search is ever changing, and Your SEO Plan will need to change with it. Technological advances in personalization, local search, demographic targeting, mobile devices, and so on will require constant adjustment on your part. Will reaching out through social marketing become more important than being found on the search engines? Will traditional SEO become obsolete as the online experience moves to mobile apps? Will contextual, location-aware, and personalized search require a dramatic evolution in SEO? Will visual and voice search replace keyword-based search? Whatever the future holds, we hope this book will help you enter it with great SEO habits in place and a strategy for continued learning. Continue to give SEO an hour a day, every day, and you'll be able to ride the waves of change with confidence.

Extra Credit and
Guilt-Free Slacking

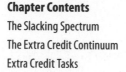

Since you're not a full-time SEO professional, sometimes other work obligations will get in the way, and you'll need to give your campaign a little less attention. Other times, your website's unique problems or your own curiosity will inspire you to dig deeper. In this chapter we'll help you sort it all out by defining a range of reasonable slacking and extra credit behavior.

Chapter Contents
The Slacking Spectrum
The Extra Credit Continuum
Extra Credit Tasks

The Slacking Spectrum

Be honest: Did you flip to this chapter before you even started your SEO campaign? Have you been planning to do the bare minimum from the get-go? If you expected us to disapprove, you're wrong. Let us reassure you:

 Pearl of Wisdom: Any amount of properly executed SEO that you can muster will bring about some positive effect.

And this is especially true if your competitors are doing absolutely nothing in the way of SEO.

Slacking, as we're using the word here, simply means taking an honest look at your time and abilities and determining whether you can put off, or even blow off, a task or a group of similar tasks. Slacking can be the result of a simple judgment call; for example, if a task we assigned in Your SEO Plan doesn't apply to your site, don't do it. Or slacking can be a path you're forced to take due to a lack of time, budget, or personnel.

Take heart: There's really nothing wrong with having a slacker mentality as long as you follow these important do's and don'ts about slacking and SEO:

DON'T beat yourself up. Periodic dips in SEO activity are to be expected for busy people in dynamic organizations. An occasional bout of inattentiveness to your campaign is common. Dropping the ball every once in a while is no reason to abandon your SEO efforts altogether.

DON'T slack if your competitors aren't. If you are in an extremely competitive market, there's probably no easy way to shirk. You will have to work harder on your SEO campaign to see changes for the better. Likewise, if one of your sleepy competitors wakes up to SEO, you'll need to step up your efforts accordingly or suffer the consequences.

DON'T blame it on the budget. Just as you don't need a big SEO budget to be an over-achiever, you don't need to slow down on SEO just because you're low on funds. Site edits, outreach on the Social Web, landing page A/B testing, and competitive analysis—to name just a few—are tasks that most organizations can do at no extra cost.

DO be realistic. If you anticipate that you *never* will be able to devote an hour a day to your SEO campaign, it's time to think about sharing the load with a coworker or hiring a consultant. (We gave some guidance on hiring SEO help in Chapter 9, "Month Three: It's a Way of Life.")

Ideas for Reducing Your SEO Workload

For many sites, an hour a day pretty much *is* the bare minimum you can get away with for an effective SEO campaign. If you're starting a new SEO campaign, following the plan as written from your Prep Month on through to the end of Week 12 will give your site the best shot at success.

Throughout the plan, we've pointed out tasks that we feel can be dropped without out a major impact on your SEO outcome. But if you think you need to trim down your SEO campaign even further, you may be looking for guidance on how to do it.

Some Slacking Is Not Guilt Free

Priorities will vary from organization to organization, but there are a few tasks you should never slack on because they form the foundation of your entire SEO campaign:

- Defining your conversion goals
- Identifying your audience
- Researching your keywords

And there are also certain red flags that you should not ignore because they can cause all your other efforts to be wasted:

- Malware reports from your site visitors or the search engines
- Problems, such as coding errors, that block the search engines from indexing your landing pages
- Problems, such as broken links, that dump your audience into dead ends instead of delivering them to your site

Here are some ideas for bringing Your SEO Plan in line with your own less-than-perfect reality, whether it's related to your time, your budget, or your team's willingness to help:

Cut out early. Consider going through the Prep Month and stopping after Month One of the plan. Choosing your keywords and getting them onto your site using sound SEO methods is a substantial step forward and may help you realize a positive change.

Cut out paid search activities. This is a no-brainer if you have no money to spend on it. Unlike paid search, organic SEO will continue to deliver improvements long after you've quit devoting time to it.

Cut out organic activities. Cutting organic SEO and focusing only on paid search may be a smart strategy if you are short on labor and have a healthy budget to work with. With a paid search campaign, you can expect quicker success than with organic SEO alone.

But proceed with extreme caution: If your site isn't optimized for your target audience, it may not be an effective destination for paid search visitors.

Be antisocial. Social media marketing is nothing if not time-consuming. Save it for later if you find it getting in the way of tending to your basic SEO activities.

Cut reporting loose. If you seriously don't have the time, consider delegating your SEO status data gathering to someone else in your organization. Yes, this will handicap your ability to analyze and improve your campaign. But asking an administrative assistant to gather numbers for you is better than not tracking at all. After all, if nobody's collecting information about your site's performance, how do you know whether you're wasting what little time you *do* have to spend on SEO?

Do it all, but with a smaller scope. If you're low on time, do your slicing the way the SEO consultants do: by limiting your campaign to fewer conversion goals, audiences, or landing pages. For example, focus on only one product line or one landing page, whittle down your top-priority keywords to just a couple, or focus on only one segment of your potential audience. In this way, you're still working toward increasing your targeted traffic using a holistic approach to SEO.

Be a dedicated dud-dropper. You'll save time if you drop activities that aren't delivering desired results. We'd love to be able to list SEO tasks in order from the best to worst effort-to-results ratios, but these factors vary widely from organization to organization. You will need to track your own results and figure out which SEO tactics are working for you and which are wasting your time. Once you have some data under your belt, feel free to slash and burn.

You may have the big idea to strip down Your SEO Plan to just focus on Google ranks and nothing else. Although this is a common sentiment expressed by clients we've come across, it really isn't a reasonable slacking mindset. There are a couple of reasons you shouldn't act on this kind of Google-centric instinct. For one, achieving good ranks in Google for any meaningful keyphrase requires the opposite of slacking; it's hard work! And second:

Pearl of Wisdom: Google does not exist in a vacuum.

In fact, a well-rounded approach to SEO is the *only* kind that will improve your website's ranks in Google. You can't really strip out all but the Google-related tasks and have less work to do.

Slacker Stories

Just like the rest of your campaign, your slacking plan will be customized. Here are a few fictional examples of well-constructed "slacker" efforts:

Focusing on Paid Search Jeanna works at a five-person B2B software development firm. As the only admin staffer, she is responsible for everything from payroll taxes to coffee filters. She had hoped to spend an hour a day on SEO, but other crises are always interfering with her plans. Still, her boss is looking for results. As she learned in Chapter 2, "Customize Your Approach," one of the advantages of a B2B business is a high conversion value. That means that even a small number of conversions can pay off big for her organization. Jeanna convinced her boss to invest in six months of highly targeted pay-per-click (PPC) advertising. She devoted about one hour per week to reviewing performance data and managing the campaign. Who knows? Maybe the new accounts that can be attributed to the PPC campaign can be used to hire Jeanna an assistant!

Focusing on a Single Goal or Audience Alonzo works on development at a mid-sized non-profit. The organization is optimistic about using search to improve volunteer awareness as well as to increase online donations. However, with limited time and almost no knowledge about the volunteer side of the organization, Alonzo chooses to focus his SEO efforts on online donations first and move on to volunteer awareness later.

Lengthening the Process Laura works in Marketing at a medium-sized B2C selling school supplies. She took advantage of the traditionally slow spring season to get started on her SEO campaign—the Prep Month and Month One only. She'll be able to see some advances from the basic optimization and continue with the remainder of the plan when time allows.

The Extra Credit Continuum

Extra credit in SEO doesn't require as much soul-searching and premeditation as slacking. Usually extra credit is just a natural extension of what you're already doing with your site. SEO encompasses a wide variety of disciplines and activities, from creative writing to coding. You may just discover one aspect of it that grips you and run with it.

But if you're extremely gung ho on SEO extra credit, we will wave this yellow flag:

Pearl of Wisdom: Don't go so deep in any one area of SEO that you ignore everything else.

If you're going full bore on the technology side of SEO, make sure it's balanced out with a fully developed approach to optimizing text and providing a strong conversion path, too. We've said it before: A holistic approach is best.

And one more thing: Keep your perspective. There is a difference between extra credit and wasting your time. Checking ranks every hour, stressing over daily ups and downs (unless you have a short-lived or time-sensitive campaign), and spending all your time trying to decipher tweaks in Google's algorithm are not worth the effort. Turn your attention instead to more reasonable tasks, like researching new keywords and gleaning new ideas from competitors, or legitimate never-ending tasks like content building or improving your relationships with your social media followers.

Extra Credit Tasks

As you went through your Prep Month and Your SEO Plan, we listed several options for extra credit for you to pursue if you've got the time and inclination. Each of these tasks is a spin-off of a task in Your SEO Plan, but even if you haven't completed the original task, you can benefit from the information that follows.

Internal Search Function

In Chapter 6, "Your One-Month Prep: Keywords, Priorities, and Goals," we mentioned that the internal search on your website can teach you about your site visitors, giving insight into who they are and what they need. If you already have an internal search engine on your website, don't let its data go to waste! Data from your internal search engine can help you determine the following:

What are your site visitors searching for? If you sell shrimp deveiners and your internal search function is logging a lot of searches for <shrimp deveiners>, that might be a good thing…or it may not. It's certainly nice that your visitors seem to want your product. But why do they need to search for it in the first place? Why can't they find it by navigating your site? Finding a large number of searches for your top-priority keywords in your internal search means that you may need to make this content easier to find.

What's the (key)word on the street? When you were choosing keywords in the Prep Month, we advised you to try to get into the minds of your potential customers. The in-site search engine is a great tool for doing just that. Are they searching for <shrimp de-veiners>, <shrimp deveiners>, or something unexpected, like <shrimp cleaners>? Keep in mind, though, that this audience, having already decided to visit your site, may not behave the same as the general search engine audience.

Who's coming to your site? If most of your site's internal searches are related to finding a job in your organization or some other activity that has nothing to do with your intended conversion, it may be an indication that a substantial portion of your site visitors are not your target audience.

Are they getting where they need to go? Find the top ten phrases entered by users of your internal search engine. Then, take each of them for a spin. What results came up? Were they your preferred landing pages or some crusty press releases? Depending on the technology behind your search function, you may be able to improve the results by taking advantage of the features provided by your internal search tool (you may be able to create specially formatted metadata or assign destination pages using an administrative interface).

For example, for your Clearance Products page, you can assign keywords like "discount" or "sale"—even if these words don't appear on the page—and your internal search will then be able to show your Clearance Products page to anyone searching for those terms. Of course, you should never manipulate your internal search results to be irrelevant; you don't want to display your Clearance page when someone is searching for <returns>, for example. But it's *your* site, and assigning reasonable synonyms and related concepts to your search function's metadata may be helpful to both your visitors and your conversion goals.

One of the easiest ways to find out all this data, and more, is by using the internal site search capabilities of Google Analytics. If you do this kind of extra-credit analysis, your internal search will be much more than a helpful feature for your visitors—it will also be a marketing tool for *you*!

Webmaster Tools

In Chapters 6–9, we talked extensively about helpful features in Google and Bing webmaster tools. These are the search engines' own services, designed to assist website owners and marketers—in other words, everyone reading this book—with getting your site indexed and listed properly. Find them at `http://google.com/webmasters` and `http://bing.com/toolbox/webmasters/`.

Webmaster tools won't directly improve your ranks (there's no "Rank me higher!" button). However, they are marvelous tools for troubleshooting indexing errors and communicating your preferences to the search engines. Here is some need-to-know info about these services:

Verification To sample the goodies inside Google's and Bing's webmaster tools, you must be a verified user. This process may require the help of your IT staff or hosting company.

- Both services require a login as a prerequisite. Create a Google account at `https://www.google.com/accounts/NewAccount` and a Windows Live ID account (for Bing) at `https://signup.live.com/signup.aspx`.
- Log into webmaster tools and retrieve the unique verification items that are tied to your account (see Figure 10.1.) Google and Bing both provide a meta tag or an HTML file for you to add to your site. Google also offers

the options of adding a DNS record or tying the webmaster tools account to an existing Google Analytics administrator account.

- Perform the required verification task, depending on the method you chose.

You're in!

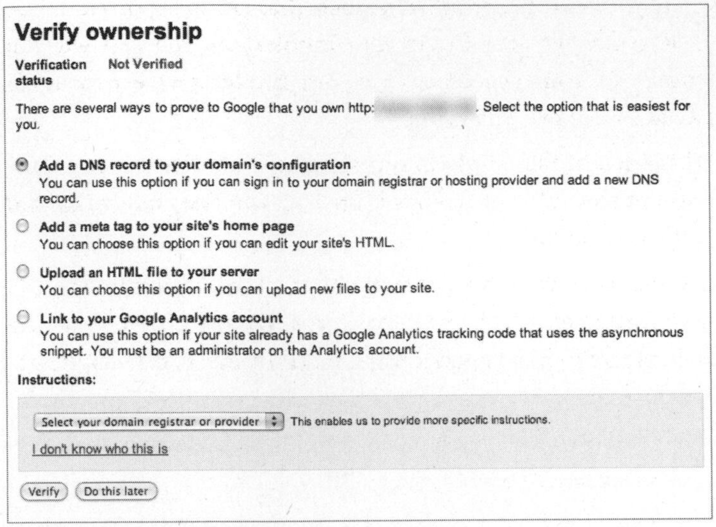

Verify ownership

Verification status   Not Verified

There are several ways to prove to Google that you own http:_________. Select the option that is easiest for you.

- ● **Add a DNS record to your domain's configuration**
  You can use this option if you can sign in to your domain registrar or hosting provider and add a new DNS record.

- ○ **Add a meta tag to your site's home page**
  You can choose this option if you can edit your site's HTML.

- ○ **Upload an HTML file to your server**
  You can choose this option if you can upload new files to your site.

- ○ **Link to your Google Analytics account**
  You can use this option if your site already has a Google Analytics tracking code that uses the asynchronous snippet. You must be an administrator on the Analytics account.

Instructions:

Select your domain registrar or provider ⬍   This enables us to provide more specific instructions.

I don't know who this is

(Verify) (Do this later)

Figure 10.1 Google Webmaster Tools verification options

Silverlight To see the full feature set of Bing Webmaster Tools, Bing requires an extra step: installation of the Silverlight plug-in. Follow the steps outlined in Bing's Webmaster Tools interface or at www.microsoft.com/silverlight/ to complete the installation.

Site Indexing and Crawler Stats A variety of factors indicate whether your site is crawler-friendly: Is your robots.txt file configured properly? Are there any internal broken links, or pages displaying error messages? Luckily, Google's and Bing's webmaster tools provide a shortcut for you by listing any red flags that they've found on your site.

Here are some helpful features:

- Google and Bing list crawl errors and graph their crawlers' recent visits to your site.

- Bing reports the number of indexed pages on your site.

- If you've submitted a sitemap (which is a practice that Google reps recommend), Google reports how many pages were submitted via the sitemap and how many pages are indexed in Google. Bing reports the submission date and status.

- Both services review your site's robots.txt file and let you know what files are blocked from crawler access.

- Both services alert you to malware problems on your site.

Inbound Links One common question people ask us is, "Why won't Google show all my inbound links when I perform a link: search?" We won't speculate about Google's motives, but we can tell you how to get a more comprehensive list of inbound links to your website. Log into webmaster tools, then click the Links tab. Voilà! Although this is about as good as inlink data gets, some folks find that the data can be a bit inconsistent and is perplexingly prone to sudden changes in reported inlinks. So if you encounter unexpected drops or spikes in your inlink data, you may want to double-check it against another source, such as Open Site Explorer at www.opensitexplorer.org or Majestic SEO at www.majesticseo.com.

Don't assume that each of these links is transferring authority to your site. Just because Google knows about the link and reports it back to you does not mean that the link has a positive effect on ranks.

Parameter Handling For various reasons, many sites tack parameters onto the ends of URLs. These parameters may be helpful for things like tracking visitor behavior or defining which elements to display on a page, but they can create duplicate content problems in search engines. For example, if the following two URLs display the same page content, you wouldn't want them to be indexed separately in search engines:

www.yoursite.com/shoes.html?referrer=buddy123

www.yoursite.com/shoes.html

Both Google and Bing webmaster tools offer a parameter handling tool to help you eliminate this pesky problem on your site. See Figure 10.2 for Bing's parameter handling screen.

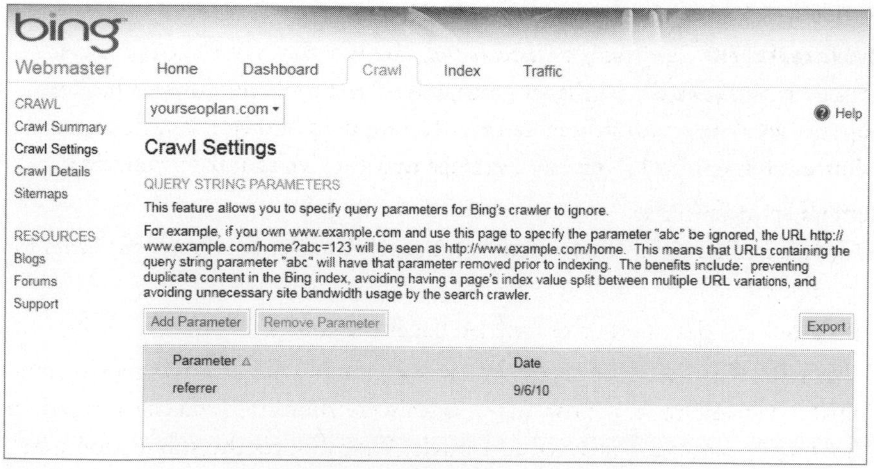

Figure 10.2 Parameter management in Bing Webmaster Tools

Sitemap Submittal Both Google and Bing webmaster tools allow XML Sitemap submittals, which are discussed in the section "XML Sitemaps," later in this chapter. This is also the place to submit your video Sitemaps, which you learned about in Chapter 9.

Webmaster tools are constantly advancing, so keep your eyes open for improvements.

Audience Segmentation

You started thinking about segmenting your target audience in Chapter 6, when you considered who you most want to visit and interact with your site. You've put effort into optimizing your site, and maybe you've even started a dialogue on the Social Web or published fresh, unique content to attract visits and links. After all your hard work, you need sophisticated tracking abilities to tell you which of your efforts are paying off and which may be falling short. Google Analytics provides just the advanced segmenting features you need.

Google Analytics offers default segments that you can access with a single click, including New Visitors (vs. Returning), Paid Search Traffic (vs. Non-Paid) and Visitors with Conversions. These default segments are a great start, but as Figure 10.3 shows, you can build custom segments, too. If you're willing to invest a few more clicks, here are a few examples of more audience segments you can set up:

Segment by Landing Page It can be helpful to know which pages are bringing in the audience you're looking for. For example, suppose you've spent long hours writing blog posts. Is the blog attracting and engaging new visitors? Use advanced segmenting to separately analyze visitors who land on the blog when they come to your site, and you'll know what your blog is delivering for you.

Segment by Referring Keyword Are visitors who already know your organization's name more likely to convert? Set up a segment for visitors whose referring keywords contain your company name. Are people who come to your site searching for your discontinued product line more or less likely than other site visitors to buy your new products? Set up a segment for visitors who came to your site by typing your old product name. For good segmentation by referring keyword, you'll need to try to capture all the possible variations. For example, if our fictitious nonprofit, Elderpets, was trying to segment visitors who came to the site by searching for the organization's name, this segment would need to contain the referring keywords <elderpets>, <elder pets>, <elderpet>, and <elder pet>.

Segment by Referring Site You were especially chatty on Facebook and Twitter this month. Did it inspire anyone to visit your site? Set up an advanced segment for those two sites, or, if you want a more general understanding of your site's appeal on the Social Web, pile all the social sites you can think of together and create a social segment. Same goes for partners, vendors, affiliates, or other referrers who deserve special attention.

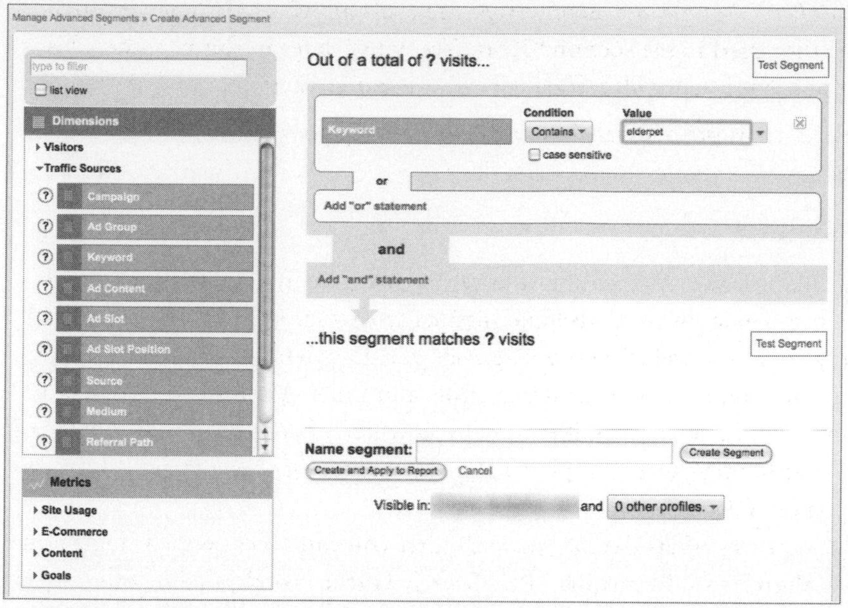

Figure 10.3 Setting up an advanced segment in Google Analytics

Segment by Engagement Web analytics guru and author Avinash Kaushik is a fan of creating a segment for visitors with three or more page views on your site—you might call these "Browsers." Who are the Browsers on your site? What about the Tire-kickers? When you identify a behavior that makes a person desirable, or different, create a segment to understand them better—and be sure to give it a name that your boss can instantly comprehend.

Segment by Mini-Conversions Of course you should look separately at the segment of your audience that makes a purchase, downloads a whitepaper, submits a form, or performs whatever conversion you want them to do. But for many businesses, especially B2Bs, the converters are a small percent of your site visitors. You can cast a wider net by redefining the concept of conversion to include smaller actions such as writing a comment on your blog, clicking through to your Facebook page, or viewing your "Contact" page. You'll have more information to work with, and you may figure out ways to engage this audience more deeply.

XML Sitemaps

An XML Sitemap is a specially formatted text file that lists your website's URLs for the search engines. A Sitemap might help a search engine find all of your pages if it would otherwise have a hard time indexing your site, for example, if your site has a very large number of pages, dynamically generated pages, Flash, or Ajax-based navigation. Here are the basics:

Deciding if You Need a Sitemap SEO industry opinions on Sitemaps range from "Every site needs a Sitemap" to "If you need a Sitemap, something's wrong with your site navigation." We tend to agree that a Sitemap shouldn't be necessary for a small or medium-sized website. The majority of these websites should be navigable by search engine spiders without any help.

Google interprets the URLs you include in a Sitemap as a signal for identifying your site's preferred URLs, so thoughtfully created Sitemaps can help ameliorate the effects of a canonical problem on your site. In addition to sites with canonical problems, Sitemaps can be beneficial for sites that uses in-site search as a primary mode of navigation, or sites that rely on Ajax or other less-than-robot-friendly technologies for linking to internal pages. And, of course, they're good for the head-of-the-class marketer who wants to be sure they've done absolutely *everything* possible to advance a website's search position.

Creating a Sitemap The simplest Sitemap consists of a text file listing all your site's URLs. You can supply more information if you wish, such as how often the page is updated and how important each page is to you. Everything you ever wanted to know about the *Sitemap protocol*—that's geek-speak for the rules and instructions for building a Sitemap—can be found at `http://sitemaps.org`.

Lucky for you, Google and Bing both abide by the same Sitemap format, so you can create one Sitemap file and use it for both search engines. There are numerous free or cheap *Sitemap generators* out there that will help you create your Sitemap file and keep it up-to-date. A hefty list of providers can be found at `http://code.google.com/p/sitemap-generators/wiki/SitemapGenerators`. You'll want to automate the process if you have a site that adds or changes URLs regularly. If you run a blog or an e-commerce site, there's a good chance that your site's authoring tool already generates a Sitemap.

Submitting Your Sitemap Next, you need the search engines to notice your Sitemap. Here are two good ways to do this:

- Our recommended approach: Sign up for a webmaster tools account at each search engine and then submit the Sitemap location from within the interface.

- Can't be bothered to sign up for webmaster tools? List the Sitemap inside your `robots.txt` file, using the following format: `Sitemap: http://www.example.com/sitemap-file.xml` (where *example.com* and *sitemap-file.xml* represent your domain and file name).

Using XML Sitemaps *won't* help you rank higher or increase your PageRank, and it doesn't guarantee that your pages will be indexed. But it can certainly give your deep or dynamic pages a fighting chance!

hCards

As you learned in Chapter 9, in the section "Friday: Improve Your Search Engine Snippets," microformats are ways to tag various types of content, such as resumés, events, or geographical coordinates so that they can be easily understood and classified by computer programs. The hCard microformat is designed for contact information, either individual or corporate.

Most likely you have some contact information on your website. Let's suppose it looks something like this:

```
Joe Strongly
Strongly Built Products
123 Mission Way
Dallas, TX 75287
(214) 555-2222
```

Certainly a search engine with some smarts will be able to look at this text and figure out that it's an address. But with an hCard microformat, you can eliminate guesswork for the robot. Here's how Mr. Strongly's hCard code might look:

```
<div class="vcard">
 <span class="fn">Joe Strongly</span>
 <div class="org">Strongly Built Products</div>
 <div class="adr">
  <div class="street-address">123 Mission Way</div>
  <span class="locality">Dallas</span>,
  <span class="region">TX</span>
  <span class="postal-code">75287</span>
 </div>
 <div class="tel">(214) 555-2222</div>
</div>
```

You might have noticed <div class="vcard"> in the example. hCard is the same thing as a vCard (an electronic business card format, typically exchanged via email), formatted for display on a web page. The hCard code will not change how your contact info displays on a web page, but it will give the search engines context and may improve the appearance or accuracy of your local listings, which can be especially useful in your efforts to target mobile users. The optional geo property allows you to assign latitude and longitude to your address, a process otherwise known as *geotagging*. Geotagging provides useful information to the search engines, and they may use it to place your location on a map with more accuracy. Geographical coordinates can also be helpful for your site visitors, who might want to enter them into their GPS.

Learn more about hCards at http://microformats.org/wiki/hCard, or build yourself an hCard listing with the user-friendly hCard creator at this URL: http://microformats.org/code/hcard/creator.

Listing Enhancements

In Chapter 9, you learned a few ways to improve your site's snippets in the search engine listings. But there are even more ways to dress up your listings. Have you seen them? Those extra-special search engine listings with eyeball-attracting features like review stars, breadcrumbs, and more? We're happy to tell you that, at least in some cases, getting these enhancements may require less effort than you think. Here are a few common listing enhancements, and how to get your own membership in this exclusive club:

- Sitelinks
- Breadcrumbs
- Rich snippets

Sitelinks

"Sitelinks" is Google's name for the secondary links you often see in top search results. Bing may call them sitelinks, deep links, or best match. See Figure 10.4 for an example.

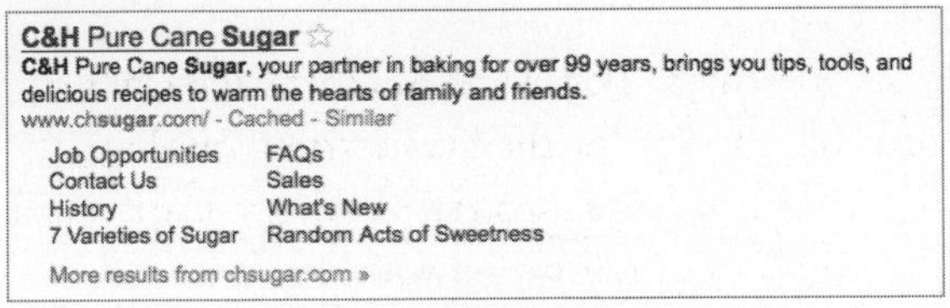

Figure 10.4 Google listing for C&H Sugar

Google and Bing can show as many as eight sitelinks on a single listing, which is sweet by any measure! Not only do these additional links greatly increase the prominence and appeal of a listing, but they may very well help your visitors get one step closer to their goal by clicking directly to an internal page.

So, you want sitelinks. We're glad to hear it! Unfortunately, sitelinks are algorithmically generated—no human intervention here—and there is quite a bit of speculation in SEO circles as to exactly how the search engines choose which sites qualify for sitelinks on their listings. We believe you can encourage the search engines to choose your preferred pages by showing them that you value these pages in the language they understand: link love! Link to them from top-priority pages on your site, using the linking text that you'd like to see in your sitelinks. You may want to link to these pages in your global navigation, but only if doing so makes sense within the context of good design and usability.

If you're fortunate enough to already have sitelinks on your listing, congratulations! You can maximize your benefits by doing the following:

- Keep an eye on your sitelinks pages: Any page that's listed in sitelinks should be considered a top landing page and designed accordingly.

- Use internal links to channel sitelink visitors from those landing pages to your favorite conversion pages.

- Google allows you to remove (but not add) pages from sitelinks using the sitelinks management tool in Google Webmaster Tools.

Breadcrumbs

Some Google listings show breadcrumbs in place of the page URL, as seen here:

What's nice about these links is that each page on the list is clickable. In this example, a person can choose to click on the home page, or `Clothing & Accessories` or `Women's Shoes`, depending on his or her preferences. That means more options for the searcher, and more exposure to your category pages. That's typically a good thing. However, not all website listings will be helped by the breadcrumbs—you might prefer your nicely written, human-readable semantic URLs.

To get breadcrumb links on your site's listings, include breadcrumb navigation consistently on your site. Follow standard conventions for the breadcrumb markup, location on the page, and the separator (usually ">"). Breadcrumbs that are page based and that do not change depending on the path a user follows on your site are more likely to translate into breadcrumb listings in Google.

Rich Snippets

Our favorite snippet improvement is the set of stars that shows the average reviews on a page, as seen here:

> **Metro Lighting - Berkeley, CA - Yelp** ☆
> ★★★★★ 11 reviews
> Aug 15, 2010 ... 11 Reviews of **Metro Lighting** "This is THE best lighting showroom in the
> East Bay, hands down. You think you may have seem similar fixtures ...
> www.yelp.com/biz/metro-lighting-berkeley - Cached

The secret to their success? Simple: The reviews on this page are tagged with annotations that search engines can understand. For example, Yelp shows the number of reviews using the following code: `<span class="count">11</span> reviews`. By naming the span class count, Yelp is speaking directly to the search engines, giving them information in a format they're looking for.

Google can recognize special formats for the following types of information:

- Reviews (individual or aggregate review data). Bing recognizes this format as well.

- People (name, nickname, image, and more).

- Businesses (name, address, URL, telephone number, location).

- Event (name, location, date, and more).

- Recipes (name, photo, type of dish, and so on).

If your site contains any of these features, you're past due for adding annotations in microformat or RDFa formats. Look them up today and have at it! Even if your site doesn't include any of these items, keep your eye on added rich snippet opportunities for the future by visiting www.google.com/support/webmasters and searching for <rich snippets> or <structured markup>.

You can check how your site's rich snippets appear right now with Google's nifty Rich Snippets testing tool, here: www.google.com/webmasters/tools/richsnippets.

Now: Pat yourself on the back! You've completed the last task in this book.

Whether you've followed Your SEO Plan to a T, had to make some tough choices to cut out some tasks, or have earned yourself an A for extra-credit effort, be proud of yourself! You're well on your way to becoming an SEO pro!

Appendix

In this appendix, you'll see screen shots of the worksheets that are referenced throughout the book. You can download these documents from the Search Engine Optimization: An Hour a Day *companion website,* www.yourseoplan.com/book.

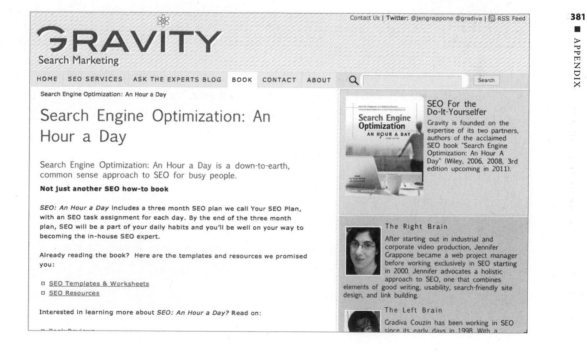

From Chapter 1, "Clarify Your Goals," you'll recall the Goals Worksheet, named GoalsWorksheet.doc, a Word document where you can record the specific goals of your organization. This worksheet will help you lay the foundation for your entire SEO campaign.

SEO: An Hour a Day

Goals Worksheet

Business Goals
(Fill in the blanks. Use as many or as few spaces as you need.)

Primary Goal	
Additional Goal	
Additional Goal	
Additional Goal	
Additional Goal	

Website Features
(Check all items below that exist on your website or are future goals for the site.)

This is included on my website now.	This is a goal for the site in the future.	Rating (Excellent/ Good/Fair/ Poor)	
☐	☐		Corporate history, news, and press releases
☐	☐		Executive biographies
☐	☐		Product and service information
☐	☐		Online purchasing/donation
☐	☐		Support for existing customers, clients, and students
☐	☐		News and current events
☐	☐		Articles, white papers

In Chapter 6, "Your One-Month Prep: Keywords, Priorities, and Goals," we introduced several worksheets to help you organize Your SEO Plan. First off, there's the Keywords Worksheet (KeywordsWorksheet.xls), an Excel spreadsheet where you can list possible target keywords for your website along with important measures that will help you finalize your top picks.

Next, the Site Assessment Worksheet (SiteAssessmentWorksheet.doc) provides a checklist of factors to quickly assess the current optimization level of your website's landing pages and a place to record any conversion data you've been collecting.

SEO: An Hour a Day
Site Assessment Worksheet

Home Page URL:	
Yes/No	
	This page has a unique HTML page title.
	The HTML page title contains my target keywords.
	This page contains at least a couple paragraphs of HTML text.
	HTML text on this page contains my exact target keywords.
	This page can be reached from the home page of the site in two clicks or fewer by following HTML text links or image links containing ALT attributes (not pull-downs, login screens, or pop-up windows).
	The HTML text links from other pages on my site to this page contain my target keywords.
Landing Page URL:	
Yes/No	
	This page has a unique HTML page title.
	The HTML page title contains my target keywords.
	This page contains at least a couple paragraphs of HTML text.
	HTML text on this page contains my exact target keywords.
	This page can be reached from the home page of the site by following HTML text links (not pull-downs, login screens, or pop-up windows) or image links containing ALT attributes.
	The HTML text links from other pages on my site to this page contain my target keywords.

The Rank and KPI Tracking Worksheet (Rank-KPI-Tracking-Worksheet.xls) is an Excel spreadsheet that you can use to document your website ranks, indexing status, inlinks and Google PageRank, social status, and conversions, as discussed in Chapter 6, "Your One-Month Prep: Keywords, Priorities, and Goals," and Chapter 9, "Month Three: It's a Way of Life."

SEO: An Hour a Day

Rank and KPI Tracking Worksheet

	A	B	C	D	E	F	G
		Baseline - (date)	Month 1 - (date)	Month 2 - (date)	Month 3 - (date)	Month 4 - (date)	
2				Search Engine Rank			Notes
3							
4				Search Engine: Google			
5	Keyword						
6	Keyword						
7	Keyword						
8	Keyword						
9	Keyword						
10	Keyword						
11	Keyword						
12	Keyword						
13	Keyword						
14	Keyword						
15				Search Engine: Bing			
16	Keyword						
17	Keyword						
18	Keyword						
19	Keyword						
20	Keyword						
21	Keyword						
22	Keyword						
23	Keyword						
24	Keyword						
25	Keyword						
26				Search Engine: Yahoo!			
27	Keyword						
28	Keyword						
29	Keyword						
30	Keyword						
31	Keyword						
32	Keyword						
33	Keyword						
34	Keyword						
35	Keyword						
36	Keyword						

Ranks | Pages Indexed | Links and PageRank | Social Status | Conversions | +

You can use the Competition Worksheet (CompetitionWorksheet.xls) to document the basic site optimization and search engine presence of your major competitors.

SEO: An Hour a Day

Competition Worksheet

Competitor 1: (Name)

	URL	Keywords of Note	Basic Optimization (yes/no)	Number of Inbound Links	Google PageRank
Home Page					
Interior Page 1					
Interior Page 2					
Interior Page 3					
Overall Site Ranks:					
PPC Sponsorship Assessment:					
Additional Notes About This Competitor:					

Competitor 2: (Name)

	URL	Keywords of Note	Basic Optimization (yes/no)	Number of Inbound Links	Google PageRank
Home Page					
Interior Page 1					
Interior Page 2					
Interior Page 3					
Overall Site Ranks:					

The SEO Growth Worksheet (SEOGrowth.doc) helps you assess your website's potential—an important step on the way to determining reasonable expectations for your SEO campaign.

SEO: An Hour a Day

SEO Growth Worksheet

SEO Room to Grow:	
Yes/No	
	Current search engine status is poor.
	Current optimization level is poor.
	I have compiled a list of well-matched, popular keywords.
	My SEO team is enthusiastic about making needed changes.
	I anticipate that it will be easy to make text changes to my website.
	I have the appropriate personnel available.
	I have the buy-in from the powers-that-be in my organization.
	I have a budget for paid search.
	My website faces a low level of competition.
	I have discovered untapped markets or SEO opportunities.
	My site is "buzzworthy" or my organization's activities are newsworthy.
Campaign Goals	

In Chapter 7, "Month One: Kick It into Gear," you started Your SEO Plan in earnest with basic site optimization and link building. The Site Optimization Worksheet (SiteOptimizationWorksheet.doc) provides a template for detailing the edits to be made on your website.

SEO: An Hour a Day
Site Optimization Worksheet

Landing Page 1 (Home Page)

Page URL:

HTML Title:

Meta Description:

Meta Keywords:

Text/Content Edits:

Internal Site Links:

Landing Page 2 (Page Name)

Page URL:

HTML Title:

Meta Description:

Meta Keywords:

Text/Content Edits:

Internal Site Links:

Landing Page 3 (Page Name)

Page URL:

HTML Title:

Meta Description:

Meta Keywords:

Finally, the Link Tracking Worksheet (LinkTrackingWorksheet.doc) gives you a convenient place to document links that point to your landing pages and to list sites that have the potential to link to yours.

SEO: An Hour a Day

Link Tracking Worksheet

Links to landing pages

	External Links to the Page	Number of Linking Domains	Notes
Landing Page URL			
Landing Page URL			
Landing Page URL			
Landing Page URL			
Landing Page URL			
Landing Page URL			
Landing Page URL			
Landing Page URL			
Landing Page URL			
Landing Page URL			

Summary: Quality of links to your site

Potential linking sites

URL of Linking Page	Requested Landing Page	Contact E-mail or URL	Date Requested	Link Received?	Notes

Glossary

301 redirect A server setting that redirects traffic from one URL to another while sending a 301, or "permanent," status code to the requesting client. Also called permanent redirect. *See also client.*

404 error The error returned by a web server when a requested file cannot be found. Also called File Not Found error.

A

A/B split A method of comparing the performance of two sponsored listings, landing pages, or other online content. Also called A/B testing.

A/B testing *See A/B split.*

acquisition source *See traffic source.*

Ajax Short for Asynchronous JavaScript and XML, a scripting technique that allows web applications to interact with the user and render changes to a web page without reloading the page. With Ajax, the user may have an experience that feels like visiting several different pages, while the page URL remains the same throughout.

algorithm Any step-by-step procedure for solving a problem. In SEO, a search engine algorithm is the formula that search engines use to determine the ranking of websites on their results pages.

ALT tag An attribute included in the source code of an image to define alternative text for site visitors who cannot or do not wish to view graphics. The ALT tag may also be displayed while an image is loading or when a user's cursor is rolled over the image. Also called ALT text, ALT attribute, or IMG ALT tag.

anchor text HTML text that links to another location on the Web. Also called linked text or linking text.

Atom A web feed format.

app Short for *application*, a piece of software that is designed to be used on a mobile device.

audience segmentation The practice of identifying and clustering together groups of website visitors in a web analytics tool. This allows each audience segment to be independently analyzed.

authority page A web page that search engines recognize as having an outstanding level of trust compared to other websites in a topical community. Inbound links are a significant contributor to a page's authority.

autodiscovery The process of a search engine or web browser software automatically finding an RSS or XML feed by following a link provided in a special tag on a web page.

B

bad neighborhood In SEO lingo, websites that have poor-quality or spammy content. Having excessive links to or from bad neighborhoods can be detrimental to a site's search engine ranks.

backlinks *See inbound links.*

banned Removed from a search engine's index.

bid In pay-per-click advertising, the amount that an advertiser offers to pay when a visitor clicks on an ad.

black hat An SEO methodology that includes techniques not in compliance with the search engines' guidelines for webmasters. Also used to describe a person who engages in black hat techniques.

blended search *See universal search.*

blogger A person who blogs.

blogosphere The entire community of blogs and bloggers.

blogroll A list of links from a blog to other blogs. Often, this list is displayed on every page of the blog.

bookmark search sites *See social bookmarking.*

bounce In web analytics, a site visitor who enters and exits on the same page, viewing a total of one page on the website. Depending on the analytics software, a bounce may also be defined as a visit lasting a very short amount of time, such as 10 seconds or less.

broad matching A paid search keyword matching option in which an advertisement is displayed for all search queries that include a given keyword or phrase—in any order, with or without additional words. Variants, synonyms, and plural forms are generally also included in broad matching. *See also exact matching* and *negative matching.*

C

canonical tag A meta tag that allows a website owner to specify the canonical (primary) URL for the web page on which the tag is placed.

canonical URL The preferred, or primary, form of a URL. Many websites are displayed using more than one URL format, for example, http://www.yoursite.com and http://yoursite.com, and it can be difficult for search engines to determine which is the canonical form.

Cascading Style Sheets (CSS) A website coding method that allows developers to control the style (font, color, background, and more) and placement of content, often in files that remain separate from the content itself.

checking in The act of entering one's own current location into a location-aware application such as Foursquare on a mobile device, typically to broadcast one's whereabouts to friends within a social network.

citation In local search, citations are websites that mention local businesses, typically listing the business name, address, and phone numbers.

client A program or computer that requests information from another computer over a network. For example, when a web browser such as Internet Explorer requests a web page from a web server, that browser is the client in the client-server relationship.

client-side tracking A web analytics technique that includes adding small scripts or images to web pages and monitoring user activity via a third-party server. Also called on-demand, tag-based, or hosted tracking.

cloaking A technique of showing different content to search engine robots than would be seen by visitors accessing a web page via a standard browser. Sometimes used as a spam tactic. Also called IP delivery.

comment spam *See spam comment.*

connected marketing Promoting oneself or one's organization through website participation, such as posting in forums or commenting on other people's blogs, and relationship building through social media or email.

content management system (CMS) Software that allows site owners to add content to a website without needing to use sophisticated code.

contextual advertising Paid search listings that appear on websites other than search engines. Contextual ads can be matched to the content of individual web pages through an automated matching algorithm, or the ad placement can be specified by the advertiser. Also called contextual placement.

contextual placement *See contextual advertising.*

conversion funnel A desired conversion path defined by a marketer or website owner. The conversion funnel is generally a linear, step-by-step process leading from site entry to conversion. It is conceptualized as a funnel shape because some users will depart from the path, leaving fewer users at the end than were at the beginning, while others will be "funneled" into completing a transaction. *See also conversion path.*

conversion (offline) An offline action taken by a website visitor that accomplishes the site owner's intended goal. Examples include telephone-based purchases and purchases made at brick-and-mortar locations.

conversion (online) An online action taken by a website visitor that accomplishes the site owner's goal. Examples include online purchases, downloads, and specific page views within a website.

conversion path The web pages that a site visitor passes through between entering a website and completing a conversion. *See also conversion funnel.*

conversion tracking The process of monitoring and measuring conversions.

cookie A piece of text placed on a user's hard drive by a website. The information it contains can be accessed by the site that originally placed the cookie but generally not by other sites.

crawl *See index.*

D

dayparting In online advertising, the distribution of an ad campaign so that it displays ads during specific segments of a day or week.

degraded In programmer lingo, simplified alternate content or code that is available to search engines or website visitors who cannot read the primary content or code on the page due to technical limitations.

digital native People who were born into a world in which digital technology was commonplace and who are familiar with and comfortable using these technologies.

directory A categorized, descriptive list of links to web pages, usually created and maintained by human editors.

direct traffic Website visitors who arrive at a site by typing the URL into a browser or clicking on a bookmarked link.

doorway page A web page, usually outside the parent website's navigational structure, designed to serve primarily as a destination for search engine traffic and immediately redirect that traffic to pages within the parent website. This term is generally applied to spammy pages that are used strictly for search engine traffic. *See also landing page.*

duplicate content A web page URL containing content that is identical or nearly identical to another page. Excessive duplicate content can be disadvantageous to a site's search engine visibility.

dynamic keyword insertion Automatic placement of keywords into pay-per-click ads to match the keywords entered by a search engine user. For example, the same ad may display the title "Save 30% on dog food" or the title "Save 30% on cat food," depending on whether the searcher entered the query <dog food> or <cat food>.

E

elevator speech Marketing slang for a brief but informative overview that one gives about oneself or one's business. So called because all of the important points should be delivered in approximately the duration of a 30-second elevator ride.

entry page *See landing page.*

exact matching A paid search keyword matching option in which an advertisement is displayed only for search queries that match the exact order and format of a sponsored keyword or phrase. *See also broad matching* and *negative matching.*

exit page The last page viewed by a website user during a visit.

F

feed *See web feed.*

flamed Treated with extreme derision in comments or forum postings.

followed link A link that is not tagged with the `nofollow` attribute. Sometimes called a dofollow link, although there is no such thing as a dofollow tag. *See also nofollow.*

G

geotagging Adding location-specific meta information to a video or image file, or to a business address on a web page.

geotargeting Specifying the geographic area that contains a website's desired audience, or specifying the region in which an advertising campaign will be displayed.

ghost bloggers Persons who are paid to write blog postings, typically without attribution, on behalf of another person or company.

global navigation A set of links that are displayed on every page of a website, typically linking to the top priority pages of the site.

graphical text Text that is shown in an image file such as JPEG or GIF. This text generally cannot be read by search engines.

H

hit A communication made from a web browser to a website server requesting an element of a web page. When a web page is viewed, each item (such as a graphics or media file) on the page will log one hit to the server.

hosted tracking *See client-side tracking.*

hot linking On a website, displaying media content, such as images or video, that is hosted on the content owner's server rather than one's own server. Typically this is done without permission of the content owner, and is considered bandwidth and copyright theft.

HTML page title Code contained in an HTML document that describes its contents. This text is usually displayed in a web browser's title window. In search engine results, the HTML page title is often displayed as the first line of a listing. Also called the HTML title tag.

hyperlocal search Search results that are tailored to individual neighborhoods or other tightly defined geographic regions, for example, ads that display only to Mobile Web users within 5 miles of the advertiser's store.

I

impression In online advertising, a single act of viewing a web page or advertisement.

inbound links Links pointing to a website from other sites. Also called backlinks and inlinks.

index A search engine's database of web page content. Also, the act by a search engine robot of following website links and gathering content. When a web page is included in a search engine's database, it is said to be indexed. Used as a synonym for *spider* and *crawl*.

informational search Queries performed by searchers that demonstrate an intent to find information, as opposed to an intent to find a specific website (*see navigational search*) or an intent to make a purchase (*see transactional search*).

invisible text Text on a website that is not visible to a site visitor using a standard browser.

K

key performance indicators (KPIs) A list of top-priority metrics that indicate the level of a website's success and that can be compared over time.

keyword A word or phrase describing an organization's product or service or other key content on its website. A word or phrase entered as a query in a search engine. Also called keyterm and search query.

keyword density The number of times a keyword or phrase appears on a web page divided by the total number of words on the page. Usually expressed as a percentage.

keyword exclusion *See negative matching.*

L

landing page A web page that is focused on a key audience or topic and that serves as a destination for search engine traffic. In this book, landing pages are the focus of optimization efforts. Also called entry page.

link equity A search engine's measure of the value of a web page based on the quality and quantity of inbound links to the page. Much like a currency, link equity is passed between web pages through links. Also called link juice.

link farm A website that contains links to other websites, created without an editorial review, often using an automated form. Links from these types of sites are low quality and not likely to contribute to search engine ranks.

link juice *See link equity.*

link rot The gradual increase over time in the number of broken links on the Web or on an individual website. Also called linkrot.

link validator Software that checks the working status of links within a website.

linkability A web page's perceived potential for receiving inbound links.

linkbait Web content that has high linkability or that is specifically created to draw inbound links.

localized search Search results that are personalized based on a searcher's geographic location. A type of *personalized search*.

location-aware application Software that incorporates the location of a mobile user directly into its functions. For example, a location-aware search tool may allow a smartphone user to search for businesses in his or her immediate vicinity.

long tail Search queries that are significantly longer, more focused, and less frequently used by searchers than average search terms. Short, more generalized, and more popular search queries are sometimes referred to as "short head" in comparison. *See also short head*.

lurk On the Social Web, to visit forums or other social sites without participating in the conversations taking place on them.

M

malware Short for malicious software, a program designed to run on a computer without the owner's consent, to perform unwanted tasks such as stealing data or using the computer to send spam advertisements.

masked domain A website that redirects site visitors but hides the fact that they have been redirected by keeping the original domain name in the browser address bar. Also called pointer domain.

media RSS (MRSS) An RSS feed that lists media files along with specially formatted information about those files, including title, description, thumbnail location, author, and text transcript.

merchant review For SEO purposes, a customer-submitted online review of a merchant. Merchant reviews typically reside off the seller's website and are treated differently by the search engines than product reviews. Also called seller rating. *See also product review*.

metadata Specially formatted information that describes characteristics of a document, such as its author, file structure, or keywords. Metadata can be used by search engines to help determine a web page's relevance and rank.

meta description tag Metadata contained in an HTML document that describes the content of a web page. Search engines may display the contents of this tag in their search results.

meta keywords tag Metadata contained in an HTML document that lists keywords related to the content of a web page. This tag is not influential in search engine ranking algorithms.

meta search engines Search sites that display combined results from several search engines.

meta tag Code contained in an HTML document that holds metadata. *See also meta description tag* and *meta keywords tag*.

metrics Measurements or methods of evaluation.

microblog A blog in which the posts are extremely short. Twitter is an example of a microblogging platform.

mobile search Web search tools designed to be accessed with mobile devices such as smartphones.

multivariate testing A process of displaying several different variations of content elements on a web page and testing—or predicting—the performance of the resulting combinations.

N

natural SEO *See organic SEO.*

navigational search Search query containing a brand or company name that indicates an intent to find a specific company online. *See also transactional search* and *informational search.*

negative matching A pay-per-click keyword matching option that prevents a sponsored ad from displaying if a particular keyword is used by a searcher. For example, a percussion website may want its ad to display for the term "drum" but not "ear drum." In this case, "ear" could be designated as a negative match. Also called keyword exclusion. *See also broad matching* and *exact matching.*

niche directories Directories that provide links to sites that focus on a similar theme or that relate to the same industry.

nofollow A tag that can be added to the linking code on a web page, indicating that search engines should not follow the link or pass link authority to the destination page.

O

offline marketing Methods of marketing that do not involve the Internet. Examples include direct mail, billboards, and print advertising. Also called traditional advertising.

offline sales Sales that occur in person or over the phone.

off-page factors Optimization factors that are not contained in an organization's own web pages. Off-page factors, such as the number and quality of inbound links, typically cannot be directly edited by website owners and must be influenced indirectly.

OneBox Featured vertical search results displayed at the top of the main search engine results page.

on-demand tracking *See client-side tracking.*

one-way link An inbound link to a site, where the receiving site does not link back to the linking site. *See also reciprocal link.*

on-page factors Optimization factors that are contained on an organization's own web pages. On-page factors, such as HTML page title, text content, and site speed, can be directly influenced by website owners.

online marketing Methods of marketing that utilize the Internet. Examples include search engine optimization, social media marketing, direct emails, and display advertising.

online reputation management (ORM) Monitoring, addressing and—where possible—influencing online communications that affect a brand.

orphaned page A web page that has no links pointing to it from the site on which it resides.

organic SEO Optimization efforts performed to influence search engine rankings that cannot be influenced by paying a search engine. Also called natural SEO. The opposite of *paid search*.

P

page authority *See link equity.*

PageRank Google's proprietary measurement of the importance of a web page. PageRank values vary from 0 to 10, with 10 being the highest level of importance. Often abbreviated as PR.

page view The group of hits that together make up a single viewing of a web page.

paid link Links that are created on a seller's site, pointing to the purchaser's site, in order to improve search engine ranks for the purchaser. Also called text-link advertisement.

paid listing An advertisement displayed on a search engine or directory in response to a search query entered by a user. Fees for advertisers are typically charged on a pay-per-click basis.

paid search Search marketing efforts, such as pay-per-click or contextual advertising, that are typically brokered through a search engine and require money in exchange for ad views or click-throughs. The opposite of *organic SEO.*

participation marketing *See connected marketing.*

path to conversion *See conversion path.*

pay-per-call Similar to pay-per-click, this is a form of advertisement in which the advertiser sponsors keywords and runs ads; however, the ad displays a toll-free phone number rather than a website link, and the advertiser pays a fee to the search engine each time a listing results in a phone call.

pay-per-click (PPC) A form of advertisement in which an advertiser designates the specific keywords for which its listings will appear in the search results. The advertiser pays a fee to the search engine each time the listing is clicked. A subset of *paid search*.

personalized search Search results that vary based on the searcher's profile, location, device, and past behavior.

ping In programmer's lingo, a way to check the validity of a link or connection between two computers by sending a small packet of data and waiting for a reply. In the blogosphere, a communication between a blog and a ping server indicating that the blog has been updated.

ping server A service that receives notification (a ping) from a blog every time the blog is updated. Usually the blog owner sets up this communication with a ping server as a means of gaining distribution.

pointer domain *See masked domain.*

product feed An XML file specially formatted with product information, (such as size and price) and submitted to search engines or other websites for the purpose of achieving accurate product listings on these sites.

product review For SEO purposes, a customer-submitted online review of a product. Product reviews typically reside on the seller's website and are treated differently by the search engines than merchant reviews. *See also merchant review.*

R

real-time results Search results that display current web content, such as news articles or tweets, and that are dynamically updated within the search results interface without the searcher needing to refresh the page.

reciprocal link An inbound link to a site, where the receiving site also links back to the linking site. Reciprocal links can occur naturally, but they are also often arranged based on mutual agreement. In the search engines' opinion, these links are likely to be less valuable than one-way links. *See also one-way links.*

referring keyword The keyword that a site visitor enters into a search engine, which then results in a click from the search results page to the destination website. Referring keywords are commonly tracked web analytics metrics.

rich Internet application (RIA) A web-based application with extensive interactivity that creates a user experience similar to a desktop-based application.

robot Software used by search engines to travel the Web and send content from web pages back to the search engine for indexing. Also called spider and crawler.

robots.txt A text file containing code that can exclude certain pages or folders from being indexed in the search engines. It can also be used to block access for a particular robot. The robots.txt file must be located in the root directory of the website or the root of a subdomain.

root directory The top directory within the file structure of a website; it contains all other

directories. Generally represented by a slash (/) after the domain name.

RSS Abbreviated form of Really Simple Syndication, a web feed format commonly used by blogs.

S

scraping An automated technique of copying content from one website to another. Often used as a method of stealing content.

search engine marketing (SEM) *See search marketing.* The term SEM may also refer only to paid search marketing efforts.

search engine optimization (SEO) *See search marketing.* The term SEO may also refer only to organic SEO.

search engine optimizer (SEO) A person who performs search engine optimization.

search marketing A wide variety of tasks intended to improve a website's ranking and listing quality among both paid and unpaid results on search engines, with the ultimate goal of increasing targeted traffic to the website and achieving more conversions. Also called search engine marketing (SEM), search engine optimization (SEO), and SEO/SEM.

search popularity The frequency with which a keyword is used as a query on search engines.

search query The keywords entered into a search engine by users who are performing a search.

seller ratings Google's name for consumer reviews of an online store. Seller ratings are influential components of Shopping search listings. *See also merchant review.*

SERP Abbreviation for search engine results page.

server-side tracking A web analytics technique that includes setting up software directly on the server that hosts the website being tracked.

sharebait Content intended to encourage site visitors to share the page on social networking sites.

short head Search queries that are short, generalized, and frequently used by searchers. Longer, more focused, and less frequently used terms are sometimes referred to as "long tail" in comparison. *See also long tail.*

site map generator Software that automatically crawls a website and creates an XML Sitemap.

Sitemap protocol Documentation that defines the format, content, and usage for XML Sitemaps.

site transcoding The process by which a search engine or mobile provider reconfigures a website and displays it in mobile devices without any development effort on the site owner's part.

snippet Strings of text taken from a web page and combined for use as a summary or description of the page's content, often as a part of search engine result listings.

social bookmarking The use of shared lists of Internet bookmarks. Social bookmarking sites allow users to save and share bookmarks and classify them with user-defined keywords, called tags.

social networking In Internet terminology, creating person-to-person connections through participation in a website that facilitates social connections.

social search Any system that uses information gathered from social networks to influence search results.

Social Web Broadly speaking, the various online spaces where people can interact with other people. Includes social networking sites such as Facebook and LinkedIn as well as blogs, forums, and Q & A websites.

soft 404 A page that displays content to the user indicating that the requested file was not found but that sends an incorrect server status message indicating that the file was delivered successfully.

source code In SEO, the HTML text and tags that define a web page.

spam Any of a wide variety of deceptive or abusive online practices, including sending unsolicited advertisements, misrepresenting a website to search engines, and posting nonsensical comments to blogs in an attempt to increase the visibility of a website. Can be a noun or verb (*to spam*).

spam comment A blog or forum comment that contains gibberish or irrelevant content and is intended only to promote the website of the person posting the comment.

spider *See robot.* May also be used as a verb, "to spider," in which case it is synonymous with "to index."

spider emulator Software that attempts to reproduce the way a search engine spider would see a web page. Also called spider simulator.

sponsored listing *See paid listing.*

sponsored search advertising *See paid search.*

stemming Combining variant forms of a word for one stem, or root, word. For example, *listen*, *listens*, and *listening* all share the same stem word.

stub pages A web page that contains only a page heading and little or no content. Often, stub pages are generated on dynamic sites. An example is a directory site with a category page containing no listings.

Supplemental Index In Google's terminology, a secondary database that was used to store less-desirable or unproven pages in Google's index. Google's Supplemental Index was eliminated in 2007.

T

tag A label or category that a user or website owner assigns to a web page, often as a category for organizing bookmarks or blog posts.

tag-based tracking *See client-side tracking.*

topical community A group of websites that share a common subject matter. Also called topical neighborhood.

traffic source In web analytics, the originator of a website visit. Often a search engine, referring website, or email link. Also called acquisition source.

transactional search Search query containing words like "buy" or "purchase" that indicates an intent to perform a transaction. *See also navigational search and informational search.*

tweet A short message (also called an update or status) posted by a Twitter user.

U

update On the Social Web, a short message (also called a status) posted by a user of a social site such as Facebook. On Twitter, updates are referred to as tweets.

unique visitors The number of individuals who visited a website one or more times during a given period. This measure is based on available—but often incomplete—information. For example, two visits by the same person using two different computers may be logged as two unique visitors, while two different people using the same computer may be logged as a single unique visitor.

universal search Integrated search results from vertical search indexes such as local, image, video, and shopping content within standard search results. Also called blended search.

usability The elements of a website's design and copywriting that affect a site visitor's ease of use and navigation.

user-generated content (UGC) Content on a website, such as blog comments, consumer product reviews, and forum postings, that is created by the website users.

URL shortener A service that redirects visitors from a short URL, located on the shortening service's domain, to a longer URL, which can be located on any domain. Commonly used on microblogging platforms such as Twitter in order to write a link with the fewest possible characters.

V

vanity alert Alerts received via email or RSS created for the purpose of monitoring web content and mentions on the Social Web about one's own name or company name.

vertical search The conceptual grouping of search engine results into separate categories based on type of result or subject matter. Shopping, video, image, news, and local are examples of vertical search categories.

visible text Text on a website that is visible to a site visitor using a standard browser.

W

web analytics The measurement and analysis of online activity, especially page visits, conversions, and search queries used to find individual pages. *See also metrics.*

web feed A file that is created by a website owner and is intended to be retrieved and displayed by other websites. Generally includes summary information and a link to the primary content page. Web feeds are most often used for blog and news content.

web log analyzer A software program that parses raw server log data and presents it in a more easy-to-read format along with filtering and sorting capabilities. Also called log file analysis software.

white hat An SEO methodology that includes only techniques that fall within the search engines' quality guidelines. Also used to describe a person who engages in white hat techniques.

widget Applications, such as news headlines or embedded media players, created for distribution across the Web and reuse on other websites.

X

XML Sitemap An XML file that lists URLs for a website along with additional information about each page (when it was last modified, how often it changes, and its relative importance on the site). An XML Sitemap can be submitted to search engines to help them crawl a website.

Index

Note to the Reader: Throughout this index **boldfaced** page numbers indicate primary discussions of a topic. *Italicized* page numbers indicate illustrations.